THE IMPACT OF THE CIVIL WAR

A SERIES PLANNED BY
THE CIVIL WAR CENTENNIAL COMMISSION

The Unwritten War

THE IMPACT OF THE CIVIL WAR

[THE CIVIL WAR CENTENNIAL COMMISSION SERIES]

Planned by Allan Nevins

Edited by Harold M. Hyman

THE UNWRITTEN WAR

American Writers
and the Civil War

by Daniel Aaron

New York: Alfred · A · Knopf
1 9 7 3

THIS IS A BORZOI BOOK
PUBLISHED BY ALFRED A. KNOPF, INC.

Copyright © 1973 by Daniel Aaron.
All rights reserved under International and Pan-American Copy-
right Conventions. Published in the United States by Alfred A.
Knopf, Inc., New York, and simultaneously in Canada by Ran-
dom House of Canada Limited, Toronto. Distributed by Random
House, Inc., New York.

Library of Congress Cataloging in Publication Data:

Aaron, Daniel, date.   The unwritten war.
  (The Impact of the Civil War)
  Includes bibliographical references.
    1.   American literature—History and criticism.
  2.   United States—History—Civil War—Literature and the war.
  I.   Title.   II.   Series.
  PS88.A18   810'.9'3   73–5982
  ISBN 0–394–46583–0

Manufactured in the United States of America
FIRST EDITION

For
JANET, JONATHAN, JAMES, & PAUL

Contents

Contents

Introduction

The American Civil War has probably inspired more miscellaneous commentary—histories, biographies, memoirs, fiction, poetry—than all of America's other wars put together. It is, indeed, *the* war whose course has been most minutely traced and whose causes and consequences most exhaustively debated. As Thomas Beer said, it "ceased physically in 1865 and its political end may be reasonably expected about the year 3000."

From its very beginning, the War seemed designed for literary treatment as if history itself had assiduously collaborated with the would-be writer. He had only to plagiarize from the plot of the Authorial Providence who first blocked out the acts and scenes of His cautionary epic, to draw upon the coincidences, portents, climaxes, tragic heroes, and villains of the heavenly scenario.

Milton had already written the first draft. If the cosmic war in *Paradise Lost* was not strictly analogous to America's "Great Rebellion," to the literary-minded Northerner it foreshadowed a conflict hardly less sublime. (See Supplement 1.) Consider the argument of such a Federal Epic:

In Heaven, a disgruntled Jehovah decides to rebuke the American people for whom He has hitherto felt (as Emerson put it) a "sneaking fondness." Repudiating the commandments of their fathers, they have become stiff-necked and luxury-loving. Northerners, besotted by materialism, forsake principles for profits and connive with Southern defenders of a cursed institution. After repeated warnings from above (financial panics, cholera epidemics, civil strife) God finally speaks through the pens and voices of His prophets. Harriet Beecher Stowe sermonizes under divine dictation; Garrison thunders; John Brown is martyred by the Harlot South. Around his gibbet gather principals of the cast—among them Lee, Jackson, Stuart, and Booth—who take major parts in the drama *to come. God blasts the nation with "fratricidal strife," but solicitous always, sends His servant Abraham to preside over its redemption. Lincoln frustrates the Satanic plotters of the South and preserves the Union just before God translates the Illinois Savior on that crucifixion day.* *

The Secessionist Epic, as we shall see, had a different plot, but probably few Americans in the 1860s, North or South, would have dismissed a providential interpretation of the War or seen it as inhibiting to the poetic imagination, or agreed with Walt Whitman's retrospective prophecy that "the real war will never get in the books." On the contrary, history demonstrated how great national crises taxed the sinews and souls of peoples and stimulated artistic expression, how noble thoughts inspired noble actions and noble actions noble thoughts.[1] Just as the scholar and poet, always the most susceptible to temporal influences, had been aroused by the annals of Greece and Rome, so would the "Great Rebellion" quicken the imagination of American bards.

No one enunciated this thought more eloquently than did the Boston Unitarian minister John Weiss—orator, scholar, and rhapsodist, friend and biographer of the abolitionist clergyman Theodore Parker. How does the War affect literature? he asked in 1862.[2] He offered no pat answer, for as the experiences of different countries showed, wars might depress or elevate a nation depending upon the condition of its intellectual life. But after reviewing a number of civil wars for national liberation, Weiss concluded: "A war must be the last resort of truly noble and popular ideas, if it would do more than stimulate the intelligence of a few men, who write best with draughts of glory and success." Wars fought for a noble purpose— to repel an invader, to strike at tyranny, "to oppose citizen-right to feudal right . . . to assert the industrial against the baronial interest"—strengthened the intellectual life of a nation. "The pen, thus tempered to a sword, becomes a pen again, but flows with more iron than before." Nothing intellectually fruitful emerged from wars prompted by dynastic or commercial motives.

For Weiss, as for many of his countrymen North and South, the Civil War was a holy war engendered by heavenly fiat. He called it "the first truly religious war ever waged," because it had nothing to do with rival theologies, because it was fought to "restore attributes and prerogatives of manhood," and because it signified a nation's attempt to uproot its own giant evils. The old "Union" had

* "If a dramatic poet had composed the war, could he have imagined a more effective close than history did, when she set the seal of death on the work of her protagonist in his hour of triumph, and consecrated him forever with the halo of martyrdom" (H. A. Beers, *Points at Issue* [New York and London, 1904], 71).

"transacted business for us, secured the payment of our debts, and made us appear formidable abroad while it corrupted and betrayed us at home." The new government demanded desperate sacrifices, but it also offered a chance to redeem dishonored ideals.

Although Weiss anticipated a thrilling aftermath, he did not minimize the vast demoralization produced by civil wars and their enduring taint. The end of this War, he warned, would find the United States "the most dangerous country on the face of the earth." Hence the religious purpose behind the suppression of the rebellion had to be kept uppermost in the minds of the federal leaders and all vindictiveness disavowed. The intellectual enlargement of the country was bound to follow "a war waged to secure the rights and citizenship to all souls," and a literature hitherto in the custody of cliques, alternately uncivilized and overrefined, and exhibiting at best a "maimed and grotesque vitality," would at last find a truly national expression.[3]

ii

John Weiss did not expect an American masterpiece to emerge from the War itself (it was time, he said, to stop sighing for *Iliads*), but almost immediately after Appomattox Northern commentators began to complain about the failure of American writers to do justice to the recent strife and to offer extenuating reasons why, as William Dean Howells wrote in 1867, "our war has not only left us a burden of a tremendous national debt, but has laid upon our literature a charge under which it has hitherto staggered very lamely."[4]

According to an anonymous reviewer in 1904, it was still staggering, still waiting until "some man of genius shall steep himself in it and assimilate it." Despite such popular successes as John Fox's *The Little Shepherd of Kingdom Come* or Winston Churchill's *The Crisis*, the "epic character" of the War (an "easy commonplace in talk") was not felt. It provided, he said, "a milieu full of color and possibilities," but it bored a generation who suspected its idealism and attributed its causes to a "variety of minor selfishnesses." The middle-aged writer of 1900, too young to have fought in the War and yet too close to see it as an epic, was incapable of reconstructing "the spirit of the last great struggle over an idea." In time, he thought, such treatment would be possible.[5]

But could a civil war "fought under modern conditions, and turning on such issues as negro slavery and the constitutional rights of secession" inspire an epic poem or a great novel? Was there "anything about the American conflict which would recommend it especially for poetic or literary handling?" Henry A. Beers, an English professor at Yale University who raised these questions in

1900, doubted whether any war later than the crusades would "lend itself to epic treatment." The epic required distance, remoteness, legend to give it the proper degree of enchantment. "A certain unfamiliarity," he declared, "is necessary for picturesque effect." Feeling his way through masses of statistics, bulletins, and dispatches, the would-be epic poet of the War was likely to lose himself in pedestrian details and fail to convert gun carriages and torpedoes into poetry. How could anyone evoke sublime thoughts about battles fought at such unromantic places as Bull Run, Pig's Point, and Ball's Bluff?

Beers refused to say categorically that the War would never respond to literary treatment. Unlike most wars, it *was* distinguished by "the grandeur of high convictions, and that emotional stress which finds its natural utterance in eloquence and song." In time, poets and romancers would fasten on the most dramatic episodes—Harper's Ferry, Gettysburg, the Andersonville prison, the death of "Stonewall" Jackson, the duel of the ironclads, the assassination of Lincoln—and the lesser events would fade into the background.*

He was right about the lesser events, but no Scott or Tolstoy appeared to illuminate the grander ones. Hundreds of writers came to regard the War as a field to be cultivated. It was "our" War, ripe for literary plucking, said Bret Harte, and he warned American writers who went to Europe in search of materials that "some Englishman or Frenchman will go to America and reap the field in romance which we should now, all local feeling having passed away, be utilizing to our own fame and profit."[6] But books written to "utilize" the War as a lucrative subject rarely penetrated its surface.

It seemed to the literary historian John Macy, writing in 1911, that the War so obsessively studied and dissected had yet to produce an unmistakable literary masterpiece. Out of "the most tremendous upheaval in the world after the Napoleonic period" came "some fine

* H. A. Beers, *Points at Issue*, 76, 59–61, 66, 83. Similar explanations had been offered shortly after the War. The "time has now come," announced one reviewer in 1866, "to write the history of the great rebellion. Prescott used to say that he wanted his heroes to have been at least two centuries underground before he undertook to reanimate them" (*Round Table*, III [July 7, 1866], 423). Horace Scudder wrote somewhat later: "We stand, perhaps, too near the scenes of the late war, and are too much a part of the conflict, to be able to bear the spectacle of that drama reenacted on the stage; but in due time the events not so much of the war as of the moral and political conflicts will find adequate presentation, when the best proportions of the theme will be reduced in epitome and made vivid in action, which concentrates the thought of the historic movement into a few characters and situations" (*Men and Letters. Essays in Characterization and Criticism* [Boston and New York, 1887], 131–32).

essays, Lincoln's addresses, Whitman's war poetry, one or two passionate hymns by Whittier, the second series of the 'Biglow Papers,' Hale's 'The Man Without a Country' "—but what else? Macy did not think the War was intrinsically unpoetic or insufficiently remote. He blamed the skimpy showing on the sterility of the American literary imagination. "If no books had been written," he reasoned, "the failure of that conflict to get itself embodied in some masterpieces would be less disconcerting. Yet thousands of books were written by people who knew the war at first hand and who had literary ambition and some skill, and from all of these books, none rises to distinction."[7]

Others before Macy had tried to explain why. Men of culture who fought in the War, it was said, considered it unsoldierly to write. When action was exalted, speech was despised. Moreover, the impossibility of reproducing authentic sensations of war discouraged "men of literary habits and antecedents" who had "passed through more battles than Herodotus relates" from saying a word about them. Hence the reliance on "professional correspondents for our histories of the war."[8] Thomas Beer offered a less involuted explanation. The "real" War was unwritten "because of that spiritual censorship which strictly forbids the telling of truth about any American record until the material of such an essay is scattered and gone." Too indelicate for female ears, it lingered in the memories of unpublished realists perched "on fences and the steps of stores in the sprawled depths of the nation"[9] and then faded away.

The "spiritual censorship" Beer spoke of was not imposed by women alone. Polite literature before and after the War excluded certain kinds of experience, and it is not surprising that the territory of the common soldier should have been placed "off bounds" by America's cultural guardians. Disease, drunkenness, obscenity, blasphemy, criminality could only be alluded to if mentioned at all; powder-blackened, lousy combatants daily exposed to bullets and shells, resenting their superiors, hating the "Nigs," were hardly presentable subjects to the predominantly feminine reading public. The few attempts even to approximate the seamy and unheroic side of the War met with small favor until the next century.

Hence many aspects of the "real" War can only be discovered in some of the published and unpublished memorabilia. A glance at this material shows how much of the War escaped even Whitman's searching and sympathetic eye. "The good Walt," as Henry James affectionately called him, had held up in "The Wound-Dresser" his "jagged morsel of spotted looking-glass to the innumerable nameless of the troublous years, the poor and obscure, the suffering and sacrifice of the American people,"[10] but his wails for "the mangled young" related only to part of the story. If the "marrow of tragedy" was concentrated, as Whitman thought, in army hospitals, the "many-threaded drama" also included "untold and unwritten history." Over the decades, buried details of that history have been uncovered, but as yet no novel or poem has disclosed the common soldier so vividly as the historian Bell Wiley does in his collective portraits of Johnny Reb and Billy Yank.

iii

One would expect writers, the "antennae of the race," to say something revealing about the meaning, if not the causes, of the War. This book argues implicitly throughout that, with a few notable exceptions, they did not. Some, like the majority of their fellow Americans (I paraphrase Oscar Handlin),[11] draped the War in myth, transmuted its actuality into symbol, and interpreted the Republic's greatest failure as a sinful interlude in a grand evolutionary process. Others, traumatized by the four-year nightmare, sought to distance themselves from it or suppress it or rationalize its terrors.* "The shrewdest people," Freud once observed, "will all of a sudden behave without insight, like imbeciles, as soon as the necessary insight is confronted by emotional resistance."

The "emotional resistance" blurring literary insight, I suspect, has been race. Without the long presence of chattel slavery, Americans would not have allowed the usual animosities springing from cultural differences to boil up into murderous hatreds. Without the Negro, there would have been no Civil War, yet he figured only peripherally in the War literature. Often presented sympathetically (which ordinarily meant sentimentally and patronizingly), he remained even in the midst of his literary well-wishers an object of contempt or dread, or an uncomfortable reminder of abandoned obligations, or a pestiferous shadow, emblematic of guilt and retribution.

But whether the literary dearth is to be accounted for by the blocking out of race, the reticence of veterans, the fastidiousness of lady readers, the alleged indifference of the most gifted writers to the War itself,[12] or simply by the general rule that national convulsions do not provide the best conditions for artistic creativeness, it

---

* (See Supplements 1 and 4.) "Thus wars, which become dramatic points on which to anchor a backward gaze, are themselves usually products of a refusal to face present issues, and the moral indignation required to prosecute them is a simplification of life into a morality play. It remains for the great writer—whether he be novelist, poet, or historian—to translate the play back into an imitation of life, converting the stage machinery of war into the experience of existence" (James Cox, "Walt Whitman, Mark Twain, and the Civil War," *The Sewanee Review*, LXIX [spring 1961], 185).

can still be argued (and I shall do so) that the paucity of "epics" and "masterpieces" is no index of the impact of the War on American writers. As I shall seek to show, the War more than casually touched and engaged a number of writers, and its literary reverberations are felt to this day.

"The war between the States," which a good many Southerners
prefer, is both bookish and inexact. "Civil War" is an utter misnomer.
It was used and is still used by courteous people, the same people
who are careful to say "Federal" and "Confederate." "War of the
Rebellion," which begs the very question at issue, has become the
official designation of the struggle, but has found no acceptance with
the vanquished. To this day no Southerner uses it except by way of
quotation, as in Rebellion Record, and even in the North it was only
by degrees that "reb" replaced "secesh." "Secession" was not a word
with which to charm the "old-line Whigs" of the South. They would
fight the battles of the secessionists, but they would not bear their
name. "The war of secession" is still used a good deal in foreign
books, but it has no popular hold. "The war," without any further
qualification, served the turn of Thucydides and Aristophanes for
the Peloponnesian war. It will serve ours, let it be hoped, for some
time to come.*

BASIL L. GILDERSLEEVE, 1897

* "A Southerner in the Peloponnesian War," *Atlantic Monthly*, LXXX
(Sept. 1897). Throughout this book, I follow the great classicist and ex-
Confederate soldier Gildersleeve's practice and refer to the Civil War as the
"War." By capitalizing the "W," I distinguish the Civil War from war in
general and from other wars in particular.

Part One

"THEY BREAK THE LINKS OF UNION"

BETWEEN 1850 AND 1859, AMERICAN WRITERS, LIKE MOST OF THEIR countrymen, were sucked into the political maelstrom preceding the armed conflict of the sixties.

It would be more accurate, perhaps, to call them "persons of letters" instead of "writers," because the number of men and women who lived by their pens during the first decades of the nineteenth century was still very small. Amateurs, whether scholars, preachers, lecturers, lawyers, journalists, housewives, or gentlemen of leisure, wrote most of what might be called "literature" and with few exceptions could not afford to devote their full time to literary work. Some lived in the West and South. The majority, and certainly the best known, were concentrated in New England and the Middle Atlantic states. Taken as a whole, they probably formed as nationalistic a group as could be found in the country in spite of their regional prejudices and parochialism. They shared a hope for a national culture, resented foreign slurs, complained of public indifference to intellectual and artistic pursuits.

As for their political and social views, writers occupied every

1

place in the spectrum, from the conservative to the radical extremes. Some had been "come-outers" in the reform movements of the 1830s and 1840s; others suspected "ultraism" of any sort or eschewed politics altogether. In the next decade, it became difficult for even the most apolitical to ignore the monstrous question, Slavery, that all but blotted the lesser ones.

For Southern writers, dependent upon Northern publishers and readers, the intensification of sectional strife was particularly ominous. The planters as a class spent little time reading books, and the cultivated minority among them showed little interest in native authors. Nor could Southern writers count upon the largely rural and illiterate underlying population to support their periodicals or read their books.* Between 1830 and 1860, new techniques in the advertising and marketing of books and a sharper appetite for popular literature in the North resulted in a growing literary professionalism. Not so in the South, where writing was confined pretty much to the gentleman amateur untempted by and contemptuous of the radical and humanitarian reform movements that provided material and audiences for many Northern writers. Increasingly their energies turned to a defense of Southern agrarian culture with its cornerstone of slavery.

In the North, which contained a much larger and more complex literary community than existed in the South, the sectional crises of the 1850s at first polarized and then inadvertently united hitherto antagonistic coteries.† A loosely linked radical wing harbored strong anti-institutional biases. Although it would not be strictly accurate to say that men like Emerson, Theodore Parker, Bronson Alcott, and Thoreau "had no fixed place in the community and no institutional loyalties" or to see them as secessionists from "organized society,"‡ they did espouse a species of individualism or anarchism. Ranged against them were the conservative-institu-

---

* White illiteracy was five times greater in the South Atlantic states than in New England, three times greater in the South Central states than in the Middle West (William Charvat, "The People's Patronage," in *Literary History of the United States* [New York, 1953], 517).

† The most comprehensive and astute treatment of the Northern intellectuals (New Englanders, most of them) before, during, and immediately after the Civil War is George M. Fredrickson's *The Inner Civil War* (New York, 1965), a work I have relied upon throughout. Although my own investigations, undertaken before his book appeared, have led me to make different emphases, in general, as will be seen, I subscribe to his thesis and am much indebted to him.

‡ Fredrickson, *The Inner Civil War*, 23.

tionalists who opted for all the social constraints—political, economic, religious—and repudiated with disgust the cult of the self.
These two antagonistic groups were sharply divided over the slavery
issue and other reform movements at first, until the convulsions of
the fifties touched off by the Fugitive Slave Act, the Kansas-
Nebraska Act, the Dred Scott decision, the attack on Charles
Sumner by Preston Brooks, and finally the escapades of John Brown
forced them into an anti-Southern coalition. But as we shall see, the
anti-Southern impulse of the Northern literary conservatives did
not spring from the humanitarian considerations of the reformers.
Local patriotisms, disdain for a "barbarian" culture, outrage at the
Slave Power's territorial ambitions, and dreams of a unified nation
managed by men of their class finally brought them into a not always easy alliance with radical abolitionists.*

* C. Vann Woodward, *American Counterpoint. Slavery and Racism in the
North-South Dialogue* (Boston, 1971), 140–62.

Chapter 1

Writers and Politics

The fact is that a crisis has been reached in the history of slavery which any one could have foreseen; the slave states are over-stocked, and space is needed to render the negro of any value as property. The Constitution must be bedeviled in order to do this. . . . The soi-disant patriots of that region are pulling down all these evils on their own heads. We are on the eve of great events. Every week knocks a link out of the chain of the Union—At the next Presidential election it will snap. Tinkering will do no good any longer. A principle must prevail, and that principle will be freedom.

JAMES FENIMORE COOPER, 1850

The slave interest is a spoiled child; the Federal Government is its foolishly indulgent nurse. Every thing it has asked for has been eagerly given it; more eagerly still if it cries after it; more eagerly still if it threatens to cut off its nurse's ears. The more we give it the louder its cries, and the more furious its threats; and now we have Northern men writing long letters to persuade their readers that it will actually cut off its nurse's ears if we exercise the right of suffrage, and elect a President of our own choice, instead of giving it one of its own favorites.

WILLIAM CULLEN BRYANT, 1859

Taking Sides

S TATE or regional affiliations alone did not determine a writer's political and social loyalties in the 1850s. Examples could be cited of Northerners with Southern sympathies and Southerners who considered their own section a benighted Sahara, but there was something that might be described as a regional outlook.

In New England, one strong contingent raged at what they took to be the government's immoral capitulation to the "Lords of

4

the Lash," whereas another, including a number of the eminent literary gentry, despised abolitionism and its reckless proponents. Yet, because of their common culture, they shared certain values and assumptions despite their differences.

Ralph Waldo Emerson, the priest of transcendentalism, was by definition antislavery and sympathetic to any doctrine that dissolved artificial distinctions. At the same time, a latent conservatism anchored him to the realities he could so easily dispose of in his rhapsodic moments. By 1850, however, events had turned him into a committed abolitionist; slavery and slaveholders released in him ancestral wrath.

Henry David Thoreau, carrying the individualism of his master, Emerson, to the extreme and distilling a purer strain of anarchism from the transcendental solution, had no taste for compromise. Of course he was an abolitionist but scornful of sentimental reformers and as hard on Northern condoners of slavery or the velleities of inactive humanitarians as he was on the slaveholders themselves.

James Russell Lowell, although ardently abolitionist in his youth and regarded, especially in the South, as an extremist, was already beginning to cool in the fifties. By 1860, he had moved closer to the position taken by Charles Eliot Norton, Richard Henry Dana, Jr., George Ticknor, Francis Parkman, and other conservative Brahmin and State Street–oriented Bostonians whose dislike of slavery in no way weakened their will to tolerate it.

Oliver Wendell Holmes was not much interested in social problems removed from the immediacies of his beloved Boston, the hub of the world. He was conservative on the slavery question and temperamentally opposed to "ultraism" of any sort.

Henry Wadsworth Longfellow announced his antislavery views as early as 1842 (*Poems on Slavery*), but gentle and forbearing, he refused to indict the slaveholder for the sin and shrank from active political agitation.* His lifelong friend, the hot abolitionist Charles Sumner, kept him in touch with public affairs.

---

* His *Poems on Slavery* (1842), composed during his return voyage from Europe, were written, he assured an English correspondent, in the spirit of kindness: "Denunciation of Slaveholders would do more harm than good; besides, that is not my vein. I leave that to more ferocious natures" (*The Letters of Henry Wadsworth Longfellow*, ed. Andrew Hilen [Cambridge, Mass., 1967], II, 481). To another friend he wrote in 1843 that his slavery poems, far from being "incendiary," were "so mild that even a Slaveholder might read them without losing his appetite for breakfast" (*Ibid.*, 538). By 1854, Longfellow's attitude hardened toward the South, especially after Preston Brooks struck down his dear friend, Charles Sumner—"this great feat of arms of the Southern Chivalry" (Longfellow to Sumner, May 24, 1856, Longfellow Papers, Houghton Lib.).

John Greenleaf Whittier was the earliest and most undeviatingly committed antislavery literary figure in New England. A sometimes splenetic Quaker, half volcano,[1] half iceberg, his abolitionism clashed with his pacifism. In the 1850s, he was less of a zealot than Garrison.

Nathaniel Hawthorne lived abroad throughout most of the 1850s and did not feel the political quakes of the decade. Although a Democrat and impatient with abolition and abolitionists, he was no apologist for slavery and held no brief for the South.

The principal writers of the Middle States, with some exceptions, tended to be less doctrinaire in their political views than the New England radicals, and closer to the Boston conservatives. The Yankeephobic South did not raise their hackles, and they were not given to antislavery crusades.

James Fenimore Cooper's death in 1851 removed from the scene one of the last of the Knickerbocker conservatives. Cooper was a strong Unionist and a stickler for constitutional niceties. He frowned on demagoguery and fanaticism from any quarter. Although he considered the possibility of civil war a remote one, he placed responsibility on Northern antislavery agitators should the split occur.[2]

Washington Irving lived on until 1859, but this gentle and politics-hating man (much admired in the South) belonged like Cooper to an earlier era. At the time of his death he was a beloved but anachronistic institution.

William Cullen Bryant was linked by age and association to Cooper and Irving. This tough, argumentative, and politically minded journalist-poet and New England transplant remained an influential figure before, during, and after the War. Although a Unionist and strongly antislavery, he spoke for the free-soil wing of the movement and kept his poetry and politics in separate compartments.

Herman Melville shared his friend Hawthorne's contempt for windy reformers and a measure of his conservatism. Melville's sense of evil as "the chronic malady of the universe" deepened as the War approached, but he was less parochial than Hawthorne and more concerned about the contradictions and paradoxes of American democracy.

Walt Whitman was the most nationalistic of all the Middle States group, the most enraptured by the vision of Union. Not an abolitionist, like Bryant he was a committed free-soiler.

* * *

Moving from New York to Pennsylvania and farther South, many writers suggest themselves, but few of much literary importance. By the 1850s, even the most Union-loving Southerners were under pressure to refute Northern aspersions against their section. Some, like William Gilmore Simms and a number of the minor fry of poets, fiction writers, and essayists, had already become partisans for the Southland and defended, with varying degrees of enthusiasm, the "peculiar institution." Others, like John Pendleton Kennedy of Maryland (whose Irvingesque celebration of the plantation, *Swallow Barn*, looked back nostalgically to a gentler South), remained faithful to the dream of Union.

The sectional war of words intensified as the decade lengthened, with radicals in both North and South making it hard for the moderates to keep to the middle way. Abolitionists of the Garrison–Phillips–Theodore Parker stamp objectified the great sin of the South in the slaveholder and pictured the Cotton Kingdom as one vast brothel ruled by brutal whip-swinging bashaws.* New York and Pennsylvania writers looked more benevolently upon the South than the New Englanders did,[3] perhaps because closer contact with Southerners made them readier to see slavery as a national or historical calamity—not a Southern crime. But even those like Bryant or Whitman who paid brief visits to the South or had Southern acquaintances possessed only the flimsiest knowledge of Southern life and institutions.[4] Southern writers displayed no greater understanding of the North notwithstanding their Northern publishers and friends. What they saw or read confirmed their distrust. Professional ties between Northern and Southern writers snapped easily in the months before secession.

* "I was informed that in every plantation there was a Harem and that every planter was a Sultan, that he flung his handkerchief to any black houri he chose, and woe be to her who declined his condescending patronage. I was told that the Amuraths of the South never experienced the slightest scruples in selling their cast-off mistresses or the base-born children; and that on the auction-blocks of Charleston and New Orleans beautiful young girls, as white as you or I may be, dear sir, were, as a common occurrence, exposed for sale, and that they were as commonly bought for the vilest of purposes by the proprietors of dens of profligacy. I was told that in every town in the South, there was a public calaboose or whipping-house, whither masters and mistresses who had no regular apparatus for torture on their own premises—who were too lazy to become themselves the executioners, or too sensitive to have execution done under their own eyes—were accustomed to send their slaves to be punished, and that women and young girls were, as a matter of course, dragged to these places, stripped, and lashed by the hands of men" (G. A. Sala, *My Diary in America in the Midst of War* [London, 1865], I, 35).

The irrevocable break caught the Northern men of letters unprepared. For all their dislike of slavery, the majority would have blanched at the thought of its being extinguished by American blood. Charles Eliot Norton of Boston, later a key figure in the federal ideological battalion during the War, spoke for a number of the conservative intelligentsia when he conceded in 1853 that slavery "has often associated with itself many of the finest exercises of human virtues; it has given opportunity for the display of many of the noblest and most precious qualities of character; it has inter-woven itself with the interests, the affections, and the religion of men."[5] Not only proslavery apologists took this line. Harriet Beecher Stowe said as much in *Uncle Tom's Cabin,* published a year before. Yet the widely held opinion that distinguished slavery, the "historical evil," from the personally blameless slaveholder and reproached both abolitionist and "Fire-Eater" soon became unten-able.

Compromise, momentarily successful in 1850, failed to settle bitter sectional controversies and left ideologues on both sides dis-satisfied. Webster and Clay merely swept the telltale dirt under the national carpet. Moderates might hail Frederick Law Olmsted's massive report on the seaboard slave states in 1857 as an undoc-trinaire picture of the slave system, but the time had long passed when Americans could weigh the pros and cons of slavery. A sizable minority denounced it (along with the coercive government that abetted it) as unjust and iniquitous. The majority of Northern people, writers and intellectuals among them, went along with the moderate-gradualist-ameliorative stand on slavery so long as it stayed within its prescribed boundaries. By 1859 not even the most cautious standpatters among them were sure it would or could.

The Fallen Angel and the Risen Saint

Two events in the 1850s deeply engaged a number of American writers. One was Daniel Webster's defense of the Fugitive Slave Act on March 7, 1850, the other the trial and execution of John Brown nine years later.

The first, of special import for the antislavery literati in and out of New England, dramatized (in the eyes of the radicals, at least, and even some moderates) the moral fall of the great legalist and compromiser, the eloquent defender of the Constitution. A Yankee Milton might have treated it as the prologue of an epic tragedy, replete with a lofty hero, fervid soliloquies, and climactic scenes. The episode took place at a time when the nation resounded with oratory, and the protagonist, a colossus of the forum, was the grandest orator of all. The plot of the transcendentalist drama, "The Seventh of March, or the Fall of a Titan," might be summarized as follows:

A New Hampshire man of yeoman stock (an "oak tree," a "man-o-war," a "loaded cannon," a "steam engine in breeches") comes to Boston and quickly establishes himself as a lawyer and statesman. In Congress he defends the principles as well as the interests of New England. His Plymouth Speech, his thrilling reply to the South Carolinian Hayne, and his appearances before the Supreme Court enchant the nation. He has faults, but they are the masculine and venial failings of a vascular man. Gradually his constant association with power and place begins to work upon him. The marvelously endowed man who might have gained eternal fame as leader of the antislavery cause falls from grace through ambition. The temporizer is rejected by both North and South.

Contemporary versions of this story can be found in the selected prose of Whitman, the political sermons of Theodore Parker, the lectures and journals of Thoreau, in Whittier's polemical poem "Ichabod," and in the asides of Alcott, Longfellow, Lowell, Horace Mann, Bryant, and others. But the most anguished comment on the Websterian tragedy and the most dramatic account of Webster's rise and fall is Emerson's.

The Webster first mentioned in young Emerson's journals of the 1820s was a national phenomenon like Niagara Falls, a composite of Napoleon, Prometheus, and Thor.

His voice is sepulchral—there is not the least variety or the least harmony of tone—it commands, it fills, it echoes, but is harsh and discordant.—He possesses an admirable readiness, a fine memory and a faculty of perfect abstraction, and unparalleled impudence and a tremendous power of concentration—he brings all that he has ever heard, read or seen to bear on the case in question. He growls along the bar to see who will run, and if nobody runs he *will* fight.

Emerson plainly adored the bruiser for the right, God-inspired "to say gigantic things," but it was "the majesty of his moral nature," not his rude strength, that drew Emerson to him, the beauty and dignity of his principles. As a good transcendentalist, Emerson identified intellectual power with goodness. He was ready to place Webster in the company of Milton and Burke.[6]

But by the late 1830s and early 1840s, Emerson's adulation waned. He still admired his hero's "great cinderous eyes" and the

"rich and well-modulated thunder of his voice," still condoned his
venalities as the Greeks excused those of Themistocles, but he
began to sense in Webster a disposition to truckle. Might this latent
weakness prove to be the cankerworm that could rot the glorious
oak?[7]

Webster's defense of the Fugitive Slave Law on March 7, 1850,
confirmed Emerson's apprehensions; Webster's greatness, he reluctantly concluded, lay behind him. The "Titanic Earth-Son" was not
guided by principle. He had deserted Milton, Burke, and Luther for
Castlereagh, Polignac, and Metternich and merely blustered when
he talked of Union. "The worst mischiefs that could follow from
Secession," he charged, "and new combination of the smallest fragments of the wreck were slight and medicable to the calamity your
Union has brought." So Emerson's pride, Webster, became his
mortification. "The fame of Webster ends in the nasty law."

He knew the great man and his friends dismissed such re-
criminations as the "trashy sentimentalism" of "transcendentalists
and abstractionists and people of no weight." Such men usually
resorted to "the cheap cant of lawyers"[8] in defending immorality;
but the poet's duty was to preserve reverence in the hearts of the
people:

> It must always happen that the guiding counsels of ages and
> ages should come not from statesmen or political leaders, al-
> ways men of seared consciences, "half villains," who, it has
> been said, are the more dangerous than whole ones (Mr.
> Webster would be very sorry if this country should take his
> present counsel for any but this particular emergency), but
> from contemplative men aloof by tastes and necessity from
> these doubtful activities, and really aware of the truth long
> before the contemporary statesmen, because more impres-
> sionable.[9]

This proud assertion of the artist's primacy against the Websterian
council of expediency defined the conflict between what Emerson
called "the laws of the world" (Fate, Memory, "the must") and "the
laws of the heart" (Right, Duty, Hope, "the may").

To Emerson, the very notion of a broker-politician reconciling
Right and Wrong was a profanation. To Webster and his friends,
who took disunion sentiment seriously and struggled to shore up a
collapsing Union, the Emersonians threatened the Founders' dream
by their egotistic fantasies. Webster may have palliated the horror
of slavery, but in 1850 when the average antislavery Northerner
(poets, clergymen, and senators included) misread the Southern
temper, Webster and the Southern Unionists did not exaggerate the

secession threat.* Webster's logic made no sense to an abolitionist who believed the Union was already rotten with the slavery cancer and thought it prudent, as well as moral, to lop off the most diseased portion and establish a slaveless republic. In the fifties, a handful of New England intellectuals willingly accepted this possibility and discounted presaged calamities.

That is why the response of some writers in and out of New England to John Brown's raid was one of exhilaration even when mixed with disapproval,† and why they relished his martyrdom and saw him both as a portent and a messenger of good tidings. To the dedicated antislavery man, any compromise with a filthy institution was an immoral expediency at best. John Brown, as primordial and as epic-making a figure as the godlike Daniel and ripe for legend even while alive, symbolized the moral man's reply to slavery.

Antislavery writers condoned his bloody acts and mourned his "crucifixion." Even the unwarlike Longfellow felt moved to write in his journal the day Brown was hanged: "This will be a great day in our history; the date of a new Revolution,—quite as much needed as the old one. Even as I write, they are leading old John Brown to execution in Virginia for attempting to rescue slaves! This is sowing the wind to reap the whirlwind which will soon come."10

By this time, the man whom the South reviled as a murderer and incendiary had become for many a redemptive figure whose

---

* In his introduction to E. P. Whipple's *Recollections of Eminent Men* (Boston, 1887), Cyrus A. Bartol defended Emerson's contemporaries who kept faith in Webster. In their eyes, Webster "foiled fresh plots of secession, pushing with his giant shoulders to postpone the Civil War for ten years,— from the time when we should have been beaten, until we might husband our resources and father strength to prevail. . . . Whipple's judgment of Webster was generous; Emerson's ideal, natural, inadequate, though loftily severe. Frederick Douglass tells me that a lady at the North having heard him score Webster as cruel, made answer thus: 'Mr. Douglass, in many things I agree with you, but in that verdict not. I knew Webster well. Depend upon it, he is a tender-hearted man.' " Bartol adds that Webster was no "Ichabod" or "lost leader" to him (xvi–xvii).

† Lydia Maria Child coupled her solicitude for Brown (that "brave and generous" old man "though sadly mistaken in his mode of operation") with a suggestion that the statue of Daniel Webster be continuously placarded with messages "calculated to rouse the moral sense of the people" until the "abomination" was taken down. The following stanza from her own versified polemic was the kind of "caustic" rebuke she recommended to be placed every week on Webster's "hollow heart": "Sold—bargained off for Southern votes—/ A passive herd of Northern mules,/ Just braying through their purchased throats,/ Whate'er their *owner* rules./ And he, the basest of the base—/ The vilest of the vile—whose name/ Embalmed in infinite disgrace,/ Is deathless in its shame" (L. M. Child to W. L. Garrison, Oct. 28, 1859, Garrison Papers, Smith).

lawless acts could be forgiven because he himself was right.[11] He had struck a blow at what he called in his last letter to his family "that sum of all villainies" and made authority tremble.

If he was mad—a fanatic in the style of Peter the Hermit or Ignatius Loyola (types to whom he was likened by his contemporaries)—he was no criminal. The times had conditioned his spirit and goaded him into ferocious action:

> He was born of rapine and cruelty and murder. Revenge rocked his cradle, disciplined his arm, and nerved his soul. We do not mean to say that revenge alone was the motive power that actuated him. His moral nature was roused, and its instincts and logic backed his determination with a profound power. But Kansas deeds, Kansas experiences, Kansas discipline created John Brown as entirely and completely as the French Revolution created Napoleon Bonaparte. He is as much the fruit of Kansas as Washington was the fruit of our own Revolution.[12]

Such were the views of those who were shocked, or professed to be shocked, but who at the same time inwardly rejoiced that at last someone with nerve and dagger had struck a blow against Southern bullies. Peaceful men vicariously relished the violence. Law-abiding men who reassured themselves that Brown was justly tried and justly hanged still sensed something superhuman in his bearing. He incurred the kind of fear or hatred or reverence so often extended to great activists.

The incident at Harper's Ferry electrified the apprehensions of one section and the religiosity of the other in spite of efforts by a few to make light of it. A contributor in New York's *Vanity Fair*, a magazine of humor and satire, ridiculed the message sent from Rome by the dying Theodore Parker ("a moral Etna in a chronic state of eruptions"): "We have all given up J. Brown in these parts. He is not mentioned unless it is absolutely necessary. The national air is clearer for that great thunder-bolt propelled into it by a strange destiny. The people everywhere are restored to their temper, and their business, and can afford to laugh at the frights and follies they were betrayed into by one old Round head, born in a wrong age."[13] And out of the frightened South came a song, "The Happy Land of Canaan":

> In Harper's Ferry section, there was an insurrection,
> John Brown thought the niggers would sustain him,
> But old master Governor Wise
> Put his specs upon his eyes,
> And he landed in the happy land of Canaan.

Refrain
Oh me! Oh my! The Southern boys are a-trainin',
We'll take a piece of rope
And march 'em to a slope,
And land 'em in the happy land of Canaan.[14]

But although the raid had proved a fiasco, amateurishly conducted
and failing utterly to win support from either free Negroes or
slaves, few Americans found much to laugh about. Southern Unionists who did not accept the view, widely held in the South, of John
Brown as a tool of a vast Abolitionist conspiracy nevertheless feared
his insurrection would touch off civil war. The majority in the North
did not confuse John Brown with Christ, but to many he was a
"portent," as Herman Melville would shortly call him. By 1859
exponents of conflicting views on the Great Question found it
almost impossible to communicate with each other or to understand what the other side was about.

Chapter 2

The "Wholesome Calamity"

A Word for the Hour

The firmament breaks up. In black eclipse
Light after light goes out. One evil star,
Luridly glaring through the smoke of war,
As in the dream of the Apocalypse,
Drags others down. Let us not weakly weep
Nor rashly threaten. Give us grace to keep
Our faith and patience; wherefore should we leap
On one hand into fratricidal fight,
Or, on the other, yield eternal right,
Frame lies of law, and good and ill confound?
What fear we? Safe on freedom's vantage-ground
Our feet are planted: let us there remain
In unrevengeful calm, no means untried
Which truth can sanction, no just claim denied,
The sad spectators of a suicide!
They break the links of Union: shall we light
The fires of hell to weld anew the chain
On that red anvil where each blow is pain?
Draw we not even now a freer breath,
As from our shoulders falls a load of death
Loathsome as that the Tuscan's victim bore
When keen with life to a dead horror bound?
Why take we up the accursed thing again?
Pity, forgive, but urge them back no more
Who, drunk with passion, flaunt disunion's rag
With its vile reptile-blazon. Let us press
The golden cluster on our brave old flag
In closer union, and, if numbering less,
Brighter shall shine the stars which still remain.

JOHN GREENLEAF WHITTIER, 1861

14

I N the last days of December 1860 and the first weeks of the new year, the nation waited apprehensively for the tremors sure to follow South Carolina's declaration of secession. Like his neighbors, Bronson Alcott rushed every morning for the newspapers. "None can foresee the issues or how the coil of compromises is to be unravelled," he wrote in his journal. Would spiteful South Carolina persuade her sister states to secede? "Here at the North, we are impatient with Buchanan's vacillations, and do not hesitate accusing him of complicity with the designs of the South, thinking he has sold us to the Slave Power. The South is insanely in earnest, and intent on . . . her interests at any cost: even to civil war and its frightful evils. I suppose the day must come, and the deadly conflict, to adjust the scales of justice, and give freedom to the Slaves, at the nation's cost."[1]

Implicit in these hasty remarks was a whole set of "truths" widely held in the North before the bombardment of Fort Sumter. First, the conviction, often repeated by abolitionists but shared by an increasing number of their critics after Lincoln's election, that "Old Buck" was a do-nothing President if not an out-and-out traitor and criminally negligent in his toleration of disloyalty. Second, the belief that South Carolina's secession was part of a larger conspiracy, long plotted and relentlessly executed, to smash the Union. Third, the belated realization that a "perfidious" South, maddened by fancied wrongs, seriously intended to carry out its threats. Fourth, a feeling that secession with or without war would settle the Negro question once and for all.[2]

Until Fort Sumter was actually fired upon and the shock of the Federal defeat at Bull Run fully registered, most Northern writers gave little thought to the prospects and consequences of civil war. Some engaged in the sectional slanging matches conducted during the half-dozen years before armed conflict, but few if any expected harsh words might end in killing. The South had been crying wolf for at least a decade, and Southerners, as everyone knew, were masters of brag and bombast, strong on talk but weak in action. Then, too, Southern moderates could always be counted on to cool the hotheads. A region inferior to the North by every measurable test would never dare to challenge its power.

Yet any systematic reading in Southern pamphlet and periodical literature between 1850 and 1860 would have disclosed a change in the Southern literary temper from mere dislike of Northern attitudes and pretensions to positive hatred. Southern magazines had long and angrily denied Northern claims of cultural superiority and had blamed Northern editors and publishers for undervaluing Southern genius. As sectional political tensions began to aggravate sectional mistrust, Southern writers enlarged their assault.* Not only the literature and scholarship of the North came under savage scrutiny but also the culture and institutions that produced it. Even the *Southern Literary Messenger*, which had tried, according to its editor, "to cultivate kindly feelings between the two divisions of the country, believing that in the Republic of Letters at least there should be no strifes and bickerings, and that the domain of the Beautiful was a sacred realm into which all might enter without bringing with them the prejudices of party,"[3] finally succumbed to the virus of Southern nationalism. In the deepening crisis, Southern writers turned their talents to a kind of agitprop defense of their society and reserved their fiercest animus for New England—and Massachusetts in particular. Here in the seedbed of fanaticism, Yankee abolitionists cultivated and propagated their destructive notions. Not every Yankee writer came under the Southern ban. Longfellow, Prescott, and Holmes, for example, received respectful treatment in the Southern press, but they belonged to an honorable minority. A truer gauge of the Massachusetts mind was the *Atlantic Monthly*, with its bad reviews and its "violent political articles," its "insidious skepticism" and atrocious political principles. Should its opinions infect the rest of the Northern States, the *Messenger* declared in 1858, "the sooner the Union is dissolved the better."[4] The same magazine noted two years later how intervening events had widened the gulf between New England and the South. "The lamentable fact must be admitted, the people of the two sections instinctively hate each other, and had slavery never existed,

---

* Southern critics, at least up to 1860, attempted to separate the gold from the dross in Northern literature to distinguish between the "literary" virtues of a given writer or periodical and the bad politics or bad morals that infected them. Thus, Lowell might be censured for his ultra-abolitionism and his failure "to exclude his *political* principles from the region of his *art*," and at the same time praised for talents that "give him a high position among the more imaginative of American writers." Irving met with almost universal approval, Hawthorne with a mixed reception, and Whitman—pictured in the Southern as well as Northern press as an atrocious blackguard drowning "in an immense black pool of filth and blasphemy"—with complete disapprobation. J. R. Thompson, among the ablest of the Southern literary editors, found Margaret Fuller "courageous, pious, liberal, poetical, and yet uncritical, vague and grandiloquent." Whittier, "some of whose lyrics are not to be surpassed by any similar compositions of the present day," was nonetheless "inflamed with so intense a hatred of the South that we can regard him as anything but a *friend*, and can only pity his malignity and hurl back his scorn, while we admire his genius." See *Southern Literary Messenger*, XXVI (Feb. 1858), 155–57; *Southern Field and Fireside*, I (1860), 34, 267.

this hatred would have exhibited itself just as fiercely and unmistakeably upon other grounds—the tariff, public lands, what not."[5]

William Gilmore Simms and Southern Wrongs

A classical articulator of Southern antipathy for universal freedom was the South Carolinian William Gilmore Simms. Like other Southern writers of note, his outpouring of historic romances, poetry, and criticism (some eighty-two works in all) found more Northern readers than Southern, and in the 1830s and 1840s, he was as much a nationalist as Cooper, a literary patriot who urged his fellow writers to use American themes and idioms. Some of his books, in fact, might have been cited to corroborate Northern assertions of Southern barbarity. Nonetheless, Simms was first and last a South Carolinian and a defender of slavery. He held most of the prejudices of his testy state even though the class he celebrated paid scant attention to his work, and when Lincoln's election convinced him of the futility of further compromise, he enthusiastically plumped for secession. The withdrawal of the Cotton States, he was certain, would spell the collapse of New England's economy. Secession involved no risk because should war occur, the outcome (Northern defeat and the breakup of the Northern confederacy) was so clearly predetermined.

All of Simms's confidence and truculence, all of his hatred for Black Republicans and Yankee abolitionists, and all of his rage against Northern injustice to the South he poured into a letter to a "Northern friend," an expanded and public version of which appeared in the Charleston *Mercury* in January 1861. It is a long and sarcastic tirade or rather a fire-eating editorial in epistolary form. Simms scornfully rejects his friend's hope that the South will return to the Union. The cant of Union is only a disguise for federal usurpation under which the South will further suffer outrageous treatment:

> I look in vain, my excellent friend, among all your excellent letters to me, to find one single expression of your horror at the John Brown raid in Virginia! Your indignation, I suppose, was so intense as to keep you dumb! I cannot, of course, suppose that you were indifferent! Oh! no; your expressions of love forbid that idea! So, too, I see not a word of your wrath and indignation, in any of these letters, at the burnings of our towns, and the poisoning of our fountains, in Texas, by creatures of the same kidney with the vulture Brown! And when Brown is made a martyr of in the North, and his day made a

sacred record in the Northern calendar, I do not perceive that you covered your head with sackcloth and ashes, and wrote to me lamenting!

And, when your people *did* rise, after a fashion, and at a very late hour—you among them—to oppose Abolitionism, you had neither the virtue, nor the wisdom, to take issue with the enemy by a manly justification of the South! You only moved *to save the Union*—in other words, *not to lose the keeping of that excellent milch cow,* whose dugs have yielded, for sixty years, so large a proportion of the milk and butter which have fattened your hungry people. You claimed nothing for the South—asserted nothing; asked nothing; had no purpose beyond the preservation of the Confederacy, *as it was;* the South being the victim still—the North the wolf.

Both as a Christian and a spokesman for his people, Simms refused to support a Union devised by the Devil, "a union with hell, and crime, and lust, and vice." A section, in disdain of the South, had elected a President, "a creature wholly unknown before, save, as it appears, a rail-splitter, in which few well-trained Southern negroes cannot excell him," and a Vice-President "who, according to report, possesses no single quality in mind or manhood, so well marked as a streak of the negro in his blood."[6]

Not all Southern intellectuals by any means accepted Simms's radical views on the Union and the future of the South. Even the antisecessionists, however, agreed with his summation of Northern injustice and Southern wrongs. As an old and honored celebrator of his state and section, he appealed to many Southerners who shared his disunionist opinions even though unwilling to act upon them.

Northern writers, Simms noted bitterly, habitually referred to the South as "worthless, wanting in moral and energy; unprosperous, grossly ignorant, brutal; uneducated, wanting literature, art, statesmanship, wisdom—every element of intellect and manners."[7] He exaggerated a little, but many Northerners did not disown such opinions, especially after the *mystique* of the "Southern Gentleman" (hitherto as pervasive in the North as in the South)[8] came increasingly under attack. Once the fighting started, bloody-minded civilians on each side dropped with relief the few inhibitions that previously restrained them. Patriotism sanctioned vilification. "The Southern man is quick to murder," *Vanity Fair* editorialized. "So is the Italian peasant." Now no fear of "irreparably widening the breach" prevented it from speaking honestly about the South:[9]

We rejoice and are exceeding glad that the drawling, ignorant, arrogant, and dissipated Southron will no longer parade

in our Society his snobbish provincialism and ostentatious
Gentility, his habitual and characteristic disregard of the feelings of Northerners, his bowie-knife braggadocio and those
innumerable impertinences which an enormous stretch of
our affability has suffered to pass as "ease of manner." We
are glad that the loafing, idle, whiskey-julep sucking "cavalier" is to lose caste and make way by universal consent in
American society for a far higher type of Gentleman—for the
brave-hearted, truly educated, practical, and sensible cos-
mopolite man of the world. . . . We see the full development of such character among our Northmen in this splendid
war—so hurrah again for that![10]

Southern jingoists more than held their own in the sectional
mudslinging contest. "Yankee scum," "impious Puritans of the
North," "infernal fanatics of Yankeedom," "an infernal race that
even our Negroes despise and hate," "canting hypocrites of New
England" do not begin to exhaust the arsenal of abuse.[11] The
North, to continue the Southern arraignment, had been corrupted
by its prostituted priesthood:

Her women abjuring the delicate offices of their sex, and
deserting their nurseries, stroll over the country as politico-
moral reformers, delivering lewd lectures upon the beauties
of free-love and spiritualism, and writing yellow back literature, so degraded in taste, so prurient in passion, so false in
fact, so wretched in execution, and so vitiating to the morals
of the mothers in the land, as almost to force them to bring
daughters without virtue and sons without bravery.

Northern politicians tried to justify their wickedness by appeals to
"the *higher law* standard,—and their unsexed wives, mothers,
daughters, scream in acclamations of pious delight." This licentious
spirit had been fed by vast numbers of European immigrants "ignorant of the nature of government of any sort, and imbued with the
wildest visions of absolute and unrestricted liberty."[12]

As in the North, Southern nationalists welcomed war, the
cleansing if fearful wind; to oppose it would be to "retard the operations of Providence."[13] Only a series of hard-fought battles, George
W. Bagby declared, would "ever get rid of the black, bad blood in the
veins of both sections. The North contemns us, and we hate the
North. A fair fight will give us a better opinion of each other."[14] His
prophecy turned out to be true, but at the War's outset, Southern
champions dismissed Yankee armies as a bobtail mob of bumpkins
and foreign riffraff for whom Southern yeomen were preparing
"hospitable graves":

> Well, we've hills, plains and plantations; and we're waiting
>   with impatience
> To have them well manured and enriched with Nantuck oil.
> But send your *greasiest* forces, and we'll *use* their rotting
>   corses,
> And plough them in, and sow the earth, and teeming crops
>   shall wave
> Above their sleeping squadrons—these praetorians of the
>   moderns—
> These hordes of Northern vandals who desire a Southern
>   grave—
> Aye, these hordes of Northern vandals, with Natick shoes for
>   sandals,
> Shall help to make our fields grow white with harvests they'll
>   not reap.[15]

Infused with the spirit of their "fair ones," Southern cavaliers would display superhuman courage. Disdaining to fight behind ramparts in cowardly Yankee fashion, they would "charge the foe and vanquish him. At close quarters, with the bayonet or the Bowie-knife, the men, whose arms are nerved by the spirit of the finer and more sublimated matter in human nature, will always vanquish those who have no other strength or courage than that . . . derived from the spirit of the flesh."[16] In the long run, both sections would benefit from war; chastisements would teach a mercenary and cunning foe that even military despotism was better "than mob-rule and lucre-worship," and soldierly "pride and manliness" superior to "the trader's mean 'cuteness.' " War also had its lessons for "the brave but indolent, improvident, forethoughtless, political hair-splitting Southerner."[17]

Following Sumter, all inhibitions about defending slavery as a positive good disappeared from the Southern press, and the pro-slavery propaganda of the past two decades became Confederate gospel. Jefferson and his generation had been misled by false doctrines of the French Revolution; their enlightened descendants knew better. The best and happiest society was not one "in which all are free and equal, but in which equal races are free, and the inferior race is wisely and humanely subordinated to the superior, whilst both are controlled by the sacred bonds of reciprocal duty." African slavery was not unnatural, barbaric, and unchristian as the abolitionists alleged—"but an integral link in the grand progressive evolution of human society as an indissoluble whole."[18] No longer would the South be grateful to those Northerners who merely denounced abolitionists:

> An Abolitionist is any man who does not love slavery for its
> own sake, as a divine institution; who does not worship it as

the corner stone of civil liberty; who does not adore it as the only possible social condition on which a permanent Republican government can be erected; and who does not, in his inmost soul, desire to see it extended and perpetuated over the whole earth, as a means of human reformation second in dignity, importance, and sacredness, alone to the Christian religion.[19]

By this criterion, every Northerner, no matter how moderate or conservative on the slavery issue, was an "Abolitionist."

George Templeton Strong—Reluctant Abolitionist

One Northerner, a conservative New Yorker of New England antecedents, had by 1860 built up a tremendous rage against the Southern nationalists and particularly against Simms's state—that "damnable little hornets' nest of treason."[20] His name was George Templeton Strong.

This opinionated lawyer is remembered today, if at all, for a diary he kept between the years 1835 and 1875. A civic leader and much esteemed man of affairs, he never occupied top positions, never coveted the limelight, influenced no one of any importance. He lived a decorous and respectable life. He participated actively in the educational, religious, and cultural life of his turbulent city. He served with distinction as Treasurer of the United States Sanitary Commission during the War. He died without national lamentation in his fifty-fifth year.

What his contemporaries never knew, and what is still unrecognized (despite its publication in 1952) is that Strong's diary is a literary achievement as well as a treasure-trove for pillaging historians. To see him merely as a colorful eyewitness of his times, a source for pungent quotations, is grossly to undervalue him. He also happens to be the most readable and brilliant of the nineteenth-century American diarists (the "diary" as distinguished from the less topical "commonplace book" or "journal" kept by men of letters like Emerson or Hawthorne), a kind of novelist manqué, a satirist and humorist of high order, and an alert reporter in the tradition of Pepys, his self-acknowledged prototype. His unmatchable forty-year commentary on wars, scandals, books, concerts, fires, fads, riots, social events, politics, and personalities reveals the "minor but unmistakable share of genius" that marks the work of the authentic diarist.

Strong's diary is not only the richest and most informative day-to-day account of his times; it is also the candid autobiography of a representative type—the New Yorker as gentleman, the Federalist-

Whig conservative tinctured with the prejudices of a class Edith
Wharton later anatomized. We watch him emerge from a priggish
and precocious adolescence (the diary begins in his fifteenth year)
into a troubled maturity. He holds himself up to self-examination,
revises or abandons some of his firmly held opinions, and stubbornly clings to cherished biases. His diary is at once the story of a
man's education and an illustration of how public events can temper
or dissolve convictions. The great event of Strong's lifetime, of
course, was the Civil War. During the years immediately preceding
it, and the War years themselves, he came to terms with himself
and his country, and it is a piece of luck that such a complex and
reflective man was on hand to observe them.

Thanks to geography, social position, and talents, Strong found
himself close to the centers of power (he came to know Lincoln,
Seward, Stanton, and Grant, among other notables), and yet he
remained just detached enough, in spite of his sometimes ferocious
partisanship, to report these years with surprising perspective. The
entries between the Compromise of 1850 and Lincoln's assassination make up the most absorbing section of the diary. Alternating
between despair and exultation and punctuated by crises and explo-
sive episodes, Strong's narrative unfolds like a historical novel.

How deliberately he composed his War story it is hard to say.
Certainly his manifold duties left him little time for literary polish-
ing. But his long apprenticeship in diary-keeping had perfected his
technique of swift and personal reporting, and his occasional nods
to the as yet unborn suggest an eye cocked toward posterity. As
early as 1843, he speculated on the value of chronicling small beer
for the twenty-third century: "What with novels and newspapers
and magazines, the future investigators of the antiquities, manners
and customs of the nineteenth century won't want my help. In all
probability they'll be blinded with excess of light—and die off
ingloriously from plethora and over-feeding on the abundant feast
that we shall certainly bequeath them and so the race will become
extinct." He was wrong. Diaries like his own and Mrs. Chesnut's
(the only other journal of comparable literary quality) enable us, as
Strong put it, "in some degree to realize and understand past times
and the great men of those times—when the times are worth
understanding and the men truly great."[21]

By nature and training, Strong despised tender-minded humanitarians and referred to abolitionists in terms scarcely less
rancorous than Simms's. He applauded Webster's March 7 speech,
detested Garrison and Phillips, and thought John Brown well
hanged. But he was also a high-minded and reflective person who
detected saving virtues in the men and causes he opposed.

Strong considered "the possible rupture between North and

South on the slavery question" as early as 1848, and so the triumph of extremism after Sumter did not catch him unprepared. Like most conservatives, he deplored the entrance of abolition into politics. And although he saw slavery as a vestige of barbarism, he refused to stigmatize it as a sin. Could the rights of "Cuff and Dinah," he wondered, be obtained without destroying the rest of society? His doubts hung on through the mid-fifties, but he found it increasingly hard to maintain his legalistic stance. Slavery was not a wrong per se, he told himself; its iniquities were "probably curable by legislation."[22] Yet it degraded and demoralized the South and impeded its material development. If Congress had no business trying to interfere with slavery where it existed already, it did possess the power to ban it in the territories.

Gradually the humanitarian superseded the lawyer. The slavery system, he charged in 1856, told three million people they had no legal rights, no right to improve themselves morally or intellectually, that they were and would remain "three millions of *brutes.*" Strong still regarded slaveholders as "infinitely better than their system," but, he added:

> It strikes me that this institution—slavery as it *exists* at the South with all its "safe-guards" and "necessary legislation"— is the greatest crime on the largest scale known in modern history; taking into account the time it has occupied, the territory it covers, the number of its subjects, and the civilization of the criminals. It is deliberate legislation intended to extinguish and annihilate the moral being of men for profit; systematic murder, not of the physical, but of the moral and intellectual being; blasphemy, not in word, but in systematic action against the Spirit of God which dwells in the souls of men to elevate, purify, and ennoble them.[23]

At this juncture, Strong's irritation with the South, steadily mounting since the Mexican War, hardened into hatred. For him the South had always been the nursery of violence and lawlessness, if not the "great Brothel" of the Garrisonians, but he looked upon Southerners as more comical than sinister, especially the gasconading "great nation of South Carolina," always "restless and vituperative." After Preston Brooks caned Charles Sumner, Strong denounced the so-called chivalry of that "retrograde" civilization as a "race of lazy, ignorant, coarse, sensual, swaggering, sordid beggarly barbarians" and henceforth reserved his choicest epithets for the "nigger-breeders" and "woman floggers."

> A few fine specimens have given them a prestige the class don't deserve. We at the North are a busy money-making

democracy, comparatively law-abiding and peace-loving, with the faults (among others) appropriate to traders and workers. A rich Southern aristocrat who happens to be of fine nature, with the self-reliance and high tone that life among an aristocracy favors, and culture and polish from books and travel, strikes us (not as Brooks struck Sumner but) as something different from ourselves, more ornamental and in some respects better. He has the polish of a highly civilized society, with the qualities that belong to a ruler of serfs. Thus a notion has got footing here that "Southern gentlemen" are a high-bred chivalric aristocracy, something like Louis XIV's noblesse, with grave faults, to be sure, but on the whole, very gallant and generous, regulating themselves by "codes of honor" (that are *wrong*, of course, but very grand); not rich, but surrounded by all the elements of real refinement.[24]

Harper's Ferry shocked Strong the lawyer, but Brown's behavior at the trial and his demeanor on the gallows forced him to rethink his position:

Many heroes of the Newgate Calendar have died game, as he did; but his simplicity and consistency, the absence of fuss, parade and bravado, the strength and clearness of his letters, all indicate a depth of conviction that one does not expect in an Abolitionist (who is apt to be a mere talker and sophist), and that tends to dignify and to ennoble in popular repute the very questionable church of which he is a protomartyr. Slavery has received no such blow in my time as his strangulation. There must be a revolution in feeling even in the terrified State of Virginia, unless fresh fuel be added to the flame, as it well may be, within the month. The supporters of any institution are apt to be staggered and startled when they find any one man, wise or foolish, is so convicted of its wrong and injustices as to acquiesce in being hanged by way of protest against it. So did the first Christian martyrs wake up senators and landed gentlemen and patrician ladies, *tempore* Nero and Diocletian, and so on. One's faith in anything is terribly shaken by anybody who is ready to go to the gallows condemning and denouncing it.

He had predicted that the "grisly antics of insane Southern mobs and the idiotic sanguinary babblings of Southern editors and orators" would drive him to abolitionism, make him a disunionist. In 1861, the New York gentleman who ten years earlier defended the Fugitive Slave Act, who declared John Brown justly hanged, who once doubted that Negroes were worth saving, found himself on the fringes of the abolitionist camp.[25]

Yankee Literati and the "Holy War"—Dr. Holmes

Strong was not the only conservative antiabolitionist who revised his opinions of John Brown as the sectional split widened. The spirit of Unionism together with anger and impatience with the South began to spread among other Northern men of letters irrespective of party or social background. Simms only exaggerated a little when in 1860 he accused all Northern writers of being, in effect, abolitionists.

And nowhere was this truer than in New England, the section in which ultraist ideas, "isms," and reforms of every kind had flourished for the past twenty-five years. "There is about the New Englander," an English observer wrote in 1862, "a strong marked individuality, a religious zeal bordering on intolerance, a sturdy attachment to his own state, a passion for land, and a love of labour—qualities which have been handed down with little change, from the Pilgrim Fathers. Amongst a people, with such characteristics, it is not strange that there should be an earnestness, possibly a ferocity, about the war one hardly comes across in the more modern States."[26] Even among the New England literati—pacifists, conservative academics, transcendentalists, humanitarians—this ferocity began to show. The shift in sentiment could be traced in the changing attitude toward abolitionists (especially in Boston) from fear and hatred, to grudging toleration, to tacit agreement.

On July 4, 1858, Rufus Choate—friend and supporter of Webster, upholder of compromise, and blunt adversary of abolitionist "fanaticism"—declared: "There is a distempered and ambitious morality which says civil prudence is no virtue. There is a philanthropy,—so it calls itself—pedantry, arrogance, folly, cruelty, impiousness, I call it, fit enough for a pulpit, totally unfit for a people; fit enough for a preacher, totally unfit for a statesman."[27] Such sentiments, common in 1848, had been challenged by antislavery writers. By 1858 they found little favor even with conservatives like Richard Henry Dana, Jr., Charles Eliot Norton, Oliver Wendell Holmes, James Russell Lowell, Francis Parkman, and John Lothrop Motley. Three years later, men of this stamp and others more conservative than they proclaimed their support for a war which promised to be "a kind of religious crowning of our nationality."[28]

Richard Henry Dana, Jr., author of *Two Years Before the Mast* (1840), rooted in the old Federalist aristocracy, was a perfect exemplar of the New England Whig Establishment. Until 1850, Dana hardly deviated from his attachment to the conservative gentry, North and South, sharing their respect for breeding, education, property. Especially congenial to him were his Southern equivalents, the Lee and Randolph families. When Whiggery split after 1850 into its "Conscience" and "Cotton" factions, political differences broke up old friendships. Dana's involvement in free soil politics and particularly the free legal aid he provided for fugitive slaves alienated Boston's cotton-mill magnates and their lawyers. Events had transformed Dana into a militant free-soiler, as they had other conservative Bostonians whose social prejudices and concern for tradition and form were not intense enough to vitiate their ethical and moral convictions. Perhaps a lingering Puritan heritage prevented them from sacrificing conscience to property rights. Certainly Dana never thought the money he earned from his law practice required him to accept all opinions of the class he served. Years before the Compromise of 1850 he had disparaged Boston and the Bostonians—their coldness, stiffness, unpleasant voices*—and yet he believed (as did most literary Bostonians) in the superiority of New England and New England ways. Few of these men were any more national-minded than their South Carolinian opposites. But after the Kansas-Nebraska Act of 1854, they began to close ranks. When Dana defended Anthony Burns, a pathetic refugee from slavery, he received support and sympathy from businessmen and lawyers previously hostile to him—including Rufus Choate.[29]

Another Brahmin of Brahmins, Charles Eliot Norton, tempered his socially conservative and elitist views with an impulsive heterodoxy. In 1855 he wrote one of the few sympathetic notices of *Leaves of Grass* and voted for the Know-Nothings. Ten years later, the photographs of John Brown and Abraham Lincoln stood on his mantelpiece.

Like George Templeton Strong, Norton in the fifties did not strenuously object to slavery as an institution and took for granted the "facts" of Negro racial inferiority; at the same time, he found slavery, Southern style, distasteful. It was not unusual in those days for well-meaning men at once to fear the consequences of emanci-

---

* "I fancied I could already distinguish the manners of Southern & Western men from those of the N. England race & from other free states. There is an independence, a self reliance, a self-sufficiency (in opposition, I mean, to the circumspection, fear of others, & the imitativeness, too characteristic of the Northern character) in the air & manner of these men which you can hardly be deceived in. They think for themselves, they speak for themselves, they dress to suit themselves, & not because such & such is the way of such & such people & in this & that circle. They have pleasant voices, too, & an agreeable enunciation & address. They are not aiming after a precocious & half attainable gentility" (*The Journal of Richard Henry Dana, Jr.*, ed. R. F. Lucid [Cambridge, Mass., 1968], I, 238).

pating what they took to be a horde of debased blacks and to declare Southern slavery immoral. Others of his persuasion shared Norton's mixed response to Harper's Ferry. Brown acted rashly. He made a "criminal attempt to right a great wrong by violent measures," and yet his magnanimity, if not his course, did "something to raise the tone of national character and feeling."[30]

The outbreak of the War found Norton, in contrast to many of his jittery friends, calm and assured. He professed astonishment and disappointment "to find the South should prefer to take all the risks of ruin to holding fast to the securities afforded to its institutions and to all the prosperity established by the Union."* Any prudent man would feel the same. Obviously the South was mad and obviously it was "bringing awful calamities upon itself." The North, too, would reap the whirlwind, "but when reaped, the air will be clearer and more healthy." Now the North needed the "discipline of steel" to recover its moral tone.[31] Had Norton's circle, as well as the more ardent abolitionists, been able to calculate the human and material costs of this whirlwind, they might have been less jaunty, perhaps, but they would not have haggled over the price.

Not Dr. Oliver Wendell Holmes, whose political and social conservatism, still firm in the mid-fifties, had all but dissolved by the time the first Charleston cannon "spat its iron insult at Fort Sumter" and "smote every loyal American full in the face."[32] Contrary to most of his Boston friends, Holmes did have Southern connections. During a long sojourn in Georgia, his father encountered a mild form of slavery, and Holmes, who as a child read about Negro insurrections and who scorned cranky abolitionists, was not susceptible to Garrison's appeal. Only when Southern politicians turned into secessionists did his latent Unionism assert itself; the War completed the transformation from skeptical onlooker to patriot to

---

* As late as December 1860, it is worth noting, Norton wrote a most equivocal letter to a South Carolina acquaintance, William Porcher Miles (a close associate of Simms and an ardent secessionist) congratulating him "on the accomplishment of the first step in work of disunion." He assured Miles that he wished his plans would prosper, that he supported the interests of the Cotton States if only "their interests and those of the other States could be preserved unimpaired by the separation." "I have no jealousy," he assured Miles, "of the prophecied increase of Southern prosperity and power. . . . I have no lamentations to utter over the destruction of the nominal Union." Still, he remained skeptical "as to the success of your experiment." The North had nothing to offer the South, but, he added ambiguously, "there are higher laws than the Constitution and higher ordinances than those of Conventions, the inevitable operations of which will in my opinion save the country from destruction and preserve all that is worth preserving in our Republic" (C. E. Norton to W. P. Miles, Dec. 22, 1860, William Porcher Miles Papers, Southern Historical Collection, University of North Carolina).

antislavery advocate. Now he likened the slaveholders to Pharaohs who blasted "with hereditary curses throughout all time, the bronzed foundling of the New World" and the Southern people to "proud and arrogant Asiatics"[33] bent on predatory conquest. In the next four years, he took on the self-appointed role of exhorter and comforter, closely following the vicissitudes of battle and dashing off poems, articles, and orations to prop up sagging morale.

These might be compared to doses of medicine, judiciously spooned to the sick body politic. The Doctor adopted a cool and cheerful public tone. Although suffering from a grievous disease which required bloodletting, the patient would be all the stronger after its bout of illness. War burned away national poisons and released untested potentialities; it congealed disparities and unified internal divisions by its "rough chirurgery." Fanatics did not ignite the conflagration or provoke sectional antagonism. That was "the consequence of a movement in mass of two different forms of civilization in different directions, and the men to whom it was attributed were only those who represented it most completely, or who talked longest and loudest about it." Slavery lay at the heart of the matter, and it was useless to seek any other divisive agency:

> Match the two broken pieces of the Union, and you will find the fissure that separates them zigzagging itself half across the continent like an isothermal line, shooting its splintery projections, and opening its re-entering angles, not merely according to the limitations of particular States, but as a county or other limited section of ground belongs to freedom or to slavery.[34]

For Holmes, then, "our Holy War" offered no ambiguities: it was irrepressible, honorable, and heroic, a fight against "that great General who will bring to it all the powers with which he fought against the Almighty before he was cast down from heaven." The outcome was certain, but the prolonging of "its dull, dead ghastliness" would bring out "the true meaning of the conflict" and expose "the mother cause of all the progeny of lesser antagonisms." Such were the truths Holmes divulged to his "patients"—his diagnosis of collective illness delivered in his best bedside manner. Even his son's involvement hardly upset his aplomb.[35]

Holmes, Jr., had been among the first to enlist, not waiting to graduate with his class. Notified by telegram that Captain Holmes was shot through the neck at the battle of Antietam, Dr. Holmes traveled to Maryland to recover him. Three months later he described the experience to his *Atlantic* readers. Perhaps he intended to stir up support for the War, perhaps to pay tribute to young soldiers less fortunate than the wounded captain.

This piece, at moments irritatingly breezy and occasionally smug, perfectly expresses Holmes's response to the War. He is committed to the Union cause, of course, but the War acquires a special character now that a member of his own family has been grazed by it. The article is filled with personal asides about "the little matters that interested or amused me" and written in the facetious, bookish style of the witty Autocrat of the Breakfast Table. The un-Boston-like country he enters and the gory scenes enveloping him as he reaches the battlefields are duly noted but at the same time refracted through his inveterately "literary" consciousness:

> At intervals, a dead horse lay by the roadside, or in the fields, unburied, not grateful to gods or men. I saw no bird of prey, no ill-omened fowl, on my way to the carnival of death, or at the place where it had been held. The vulture of story, the crow of Talavera, the "twa corbies" of the ghastly ballad, are all from Nature, doubtless; but no black wing was spread over these animal ruins, and no call to the banquet pierced through the heavy-laden and sickening air.[36]

Adorning the narration are graceful eulogies of dead Bostonians, philosophical asides on human behavior. The instructive doctor can draw sensible or edifying maxims from any situation.

Although calling himself "as venomous a hater of the Rebellion as one is likely to find under the stars and stripes," Holmes could not expunge all his sympathy from the untidy South and the slovenly Confederate prisoners he interrogated. "They looked slouchy, listless, torpid,—an ill-conditioned crew, at first sight, made up of such fellows as an old woman would drive away from her hen-roost with a broomstick." But not all the Southerners he talked to lived up to the "poor-white" stereotype. One young Mississippi officer, set apart from the yeomanry by his civility, feminine mouth, and "pleasant, dangerous smile," was lettered enough to have heard of his questioner. Holmes, always on the lookout for "Brahmins" (those "pallid, undervitalized, shy, sensitive creatures, whose only birthright is an aptitude for learning"), discovered another Southern equivalent in a wounded North Carolina youth of "good family":

> One moment's intercourse with such an enemy, lying helpless and wounded among strangers, takes away all personal bitterness towards those with whom we or our children have been but a few hours before in deadly strife. The basest lie which the murderous contrivers of this Rebellion have told is that which tries to make out a difference of race in the men of the North and South. It would be worth a year of battles to abolish this delusion, though the great sponge of war that

wiped it out were moistened with the best blood of the land. My Rebel was of slight, scholastic habit, and spoke as one accustomed to tread carefully among the parts of speech. It made my heart ache to see him, a man finished in the humanities and Christian culture, whom the sin of his forefathers and the crime of his rulers had set in barbarous conflict against others of like training with his own,—a man who, but for the curse which our generation is called on to expiate, would have taken his part in the beneficent task of shaping the intelligence and lifting the moral standard of a peaceful and united people.[37]

He appeared almost indifferent at times to the signs of suffering (a toughness—callousness would be too strong—that his son was later to exhibit). The aftermath of Antietam evoked in him more disgust than compassion ("I picked up a Rebel canteen, and one of our own,—but there was something repulsive about the trodden and stained relics of the stale battle-field. It was like the table of some hideous orgy left uncleared"), but the sight of a wounded gentleman moved him to tears. Very likely his own son came to mind when he saw some wounded or captured counterpart, yet Holmes seldom rose high enough to see beyond the Boston horizon or ventured very far beyond the precincts of his class. If the War widened his sympathies and shook his complacence, he interpreted "these toiling, agonizing years" allegorically—God's punishment for a sinful people—and never sounded its tragedy.[38]

James Russell Lowell—Agitator-Conservator

When the Republicans took control of the government in 1860, James Russell Lowell, veteran of the antislavery wars, was still loyal to the Great Cause of his youth but no longer the "ultra-democratic" philanthropist who ripped up the "thousand masks" of respectability. He had chided Holmes in 1846 for not arraying himself against war, slavery, and intemperance, a charge Holmes coolly deflected. He believed in the irresistible power of ideals and judged the soundness of a moral stand by the degree of opposition it provoked. He wittily scarified old-fogyism ("Undoubtedly the zoöphyte taxes the barnacle with a rash activity, and considers the framework of society endangered by the unsettled notions of the periwinkle"); defended abolitionists ("a little knot of fanatics is a great force. Indeed the men who *do* anything great must be fanatics. Poets prophesy what is right, philosophers see it, fanatics accomplish it"); and challenged the clergy to preach true Christianity lest the more truly Christian lay preachers supersede them.[39]

The most attractive aspect of his romantic radicalism at this time was his one-man campaign against race snobbery and bogus ethnology. Americans, he noted, happily restricted their benevolence to remote areas. They opened their pockets "to rescue the souls of Hindoos from Satan, and the soles of Nestorian Christians from the Mahometan bastinado," but excused the iniquity of their own "social system by tracing it up to some inscrutable divine arrangement. Whatever revolts from the natural religion of the human heart they shore up with the props of their artificial and traditional religion." Here was a paradox and a danger as well, for if they encouraged treason abroad, could they logically discourage it at home? The exploitation of a minority, be it Jew, Pole, Negro, or Irish, only induced the oppressed group to harbor the fictions of race as an escape from its degradation.[40]

Antislavery advocates concentrated their offensive against the Southern racists. Lowell undertook the harder task of showing how folklore about the black man beguiled the super-refined as well as ruffian element in the North. It was widely believed, for example, that Negroes smelled bad, although Portuguese voyagers exploded this fiction as early as the fifteenth century, and Sir Thomas Browne listed the same charge brought against the Jews among his vulgar errors. A case might be made, Lowell allowed, for an aristocracy of intellect, even of birth, "but a patent of nobility founded on no better distinction than an accidental difference in the secreting vessels of the skin would seem ridiculous even to a German Count who had earned his title by the more valid consideration of thirty-six dollars." As for the Negro's alleged racial inferiority, which in the eyes of many, including abolitionists, made him a superior species of ape, Lowell offered some withering comment. How ironic that Christians should despise the Negro for his patience, fortitude, and gentleness and contrast him invidiously with the warlike Indian. What a paltry defense of slavery to maintain Southern bondmen were better off than factory operatives in the North, or in Europe, as if a people "are necessarily elevated to a state of perfect bliss by a bellyful of hominy." And how disingenuous to judge and condemn Negroes, free or slave, by statistics, as if they had ever been given the chance to exercise their talents: "While our moral atmosphere is so dense and heavy with prejudice, it will be impossible for the colored man to stand erect or to breathe freely. Even if he make the attempt, he can never attain that quiet unconsciousness so necessary to a full and harmonious development." All oppressors, Lowell decided, justified their sins by impugning "the moral and intellectual qualities" of their victims or fell back on the claptrap of racial superiority. Abolitionists had an obligation to dispel such prejudice by setting a good example in their treatment of the Northern blacks.[41]

Lowell spoke in this vein until the late forties, after which his latent conservatism began to assert itself.[42] Now a little uneasy in his role of poet-pamphleteer and unable to swallow the disunionism of the Garrisonians, he gradually discarded many of his former assumptions about the state, war, and human nature and inclined to the faith of his fathers. This new phase was less of a turnabout than some of his radical friends believed it to be. He had always espoused what he called the "true" conservatism: a knowledge of the past that would help to cushion the shock of the future. In the mounting anarchy of the fifties, the Union became for him a symbol of stabilizing authority, of law, and he discerned a new beauty in slow evolutionary process. The times made him prudent, and the man who "swore fealty" to abolitionism in 1839 was "editorially" twenty years later "a little afraid of John Brown."[43]

Although no longer "tainted with Abolitionism," Lowell had not lost his antipathy for the Southern principle "that hangs the franchise of human nature on the kink of a hair" or his detestation of slaveowners on moral and pragmatic grounds. What he preached in the first set of *Biglow Papers* (1846) he repeated less artfully in the sequel published between 1861 and 1866. Collectively his political poetry and prose constituted a massive assault against a "thievish chivalry" adept at flogging, swearing, and fighting and addicted to "orgies of loquacity" but scarcely above the "average darky" in intelligence.[44]

Until April 1861 Lowell refused to take Southern threats very seriously. The acrimonious presidential campaign of the previous year, an outlet for the "ill humors" of the nation, did not dismay him, and he predicted a weakening of the secession menace after Lincoln's election. When the slave states withdrew, thereby committing "one of the greatest crimes in history," he denounced their action as an unprovoked rebellion and took it almost as a personal affront. His outpouring of essays, poems, and letters about the dominating events of the next four years comprise a clear if unsystematic interpretation of the War.[45]

It did not spring from sectional alienation, he thought, nor did the tariff provoke rebellion. The causes lay deeper than social prejudice or political theory: "in the recklessness, the conceit, the sophistry, the selfishness, which are necessarily engendered by Slavery itself."[46] Men long accustomed to violent crimes against humanity for the sake of profit would not be deterred by political obligation, and their sham grievances were not worth consideration. Northern weakness induced Southern conspiracy and tempted "Secessia's" leaders to try for a *coup d'état*. They correctly diagnosed Northern legislators, a timid and mercenary breed, but they misjudged the Northern people and failed in their scheme to enshrine slavery with the aid of "Doughface" allies. Balked in what it hoped would be a peaceful capture of the nation, the South miscalculated. The Northern "rabble" did not capitulate nor did Europe intervene. Military prowess was not enough to offset its fatal internal weaknesses.

Federal setbacks in the early stages of the War partially explain Lowell's advocacy of a ruthless policy toward "Copperheads" rather than a conciliatory one and his defense of "coercion," a term he defined as "legitimate and responsible force prudently exerted."[47] Despite his claim to have early discerned Lincoln's greatness, he first sized him up as a weak and undaring leader, at best "an honest Chief magistrate of average capacity" who encouraged a "little Bopeep" policy toward prodigal Confederate sheep. Lowell had no faith in conciliation. Already he envisaged an organic nation, forged in iron and blood, in place of a shabby league of states. If it took "the rough kingship of a Jackson" to win the War and create that nation, then Lowell was prepared to cut constitutional corners. Slavery, the relic of barbarism, had to go, of course, but not at the expense of unsettling a nation and turning a whole generation "adrift in the formless void of anarchy." When it became clear emancipation would strengthen the Union cause, he supported Lincoln's policy as both prudent and righteous.[48]

"A single empire," Lowell wrote in 1861, "embracing the whole world, and controlling, without extinguishing, local organizations and nationalities, had been not only the dream of conquerors, but the ideal of speculative philanthropists."[49] The American dominion he had in mind at least approximated this ideal, and Lowell's War was being fought primarily to attain it—not to free slaves. His dream of one people, preferably of the same race, speaking the same language, and responsibly ruled was an up-to-date version of the Puritan Holy Commonwealth, a kind of industrialized theocracy managed by God's "Stewards." In such a system, the Old South, inefficient as well as indecent, was an anachronism.[50]

There is something parochial about Lowell's vision of Union in which a Yankeeized South, cleansed of its sins, harmoniously reposed, and something revealing in his comparison of America to "the princess of the fairy tale, enchanted by prosperity" who awakens "at the first fiery kiss of war . . . conscious of her beauty and her sovereignty."[51] This is the same Lowell who felt, upon hearing the victory tidings, "a strange and tender exaltation" and a love "almost like one feels for a woman."[52] The purification of polluted Columbia left Lowell free to woo her.

Three of his favorite nephews and the sons of friends and

kinsmen died to bring about this happy state, but only occasionally could he memorialize his grief in public utterance. All his War poems were "improvisations"⁵³ hastily dashed off, and the second *Biglow Papers* (written during the War) were less the public talk of plain men "vivified and heated by conscience"⁵⁴ than the political and ethical reflections of a gentleman scholar. Invariably the occasional poet, Lowell never forgot his audience, never lost himself in himself, notwithstanding his claim to have written the Harvard Commemoration Ode when it was still in his blood and not his memory. Here, too, the War looms like a splendid abstraction. The fallen soldiers appear dimly through the fog of sentiment. The poet's anguish is diluted in rhetoric.

Emerson Goes to War

Ralph Waldo Emerson suffered fewer qualms than Lowell about the future of the republic and rarely permitted the War to disturb his excruciating serenity. The doctrine of Compensation, functioning within him like a moral gyroscope, kept him steady. Confident that every evil produced a countervailing good, it took him little time to search out and to discover the benefit of battles.

Why did these monstrous events occur? And what would be the outcome? To a skillful translator of Nature's hieroglyphics, the text was plain enough. Every stable civilization rested upon a rock of morality. Every healthy society yoked will with principle and ran "in the grooves of the celestial wheels."⁵⁵ When the machinery broke down and society slipped its cogs, the dark powers took command.

For many years, Emerson reasoned, America had been trying with decreasing success to fuse two incompatible civilizations, one moral and cultured, the other immoral and barbarian. The test of a civilized state was the kind of men it produced and its attitude toward law, labor, and learning:

> But if there be a country which cannot stand any one of these tests,—a country where knowledge cannot be diffused without peril of mob-law and statute-law,—where speech is not free,—where the post-office is violated, mail-bags opened, and letters tampered with,—where public debts and private debts outside of the State are repudiated,—where liberty is attacked in the primary institution of their social life,—where the position of the white woman is injuriously affected by the outlawry of black women,—where the arts, such as they have, are all imported, having no indigenous life,—where the laborer is not secured in the earnings of his own hands,—

where suffrage is not free or equal, that country is, in all these respects, not civil but barbarous, and no advantages of soil, climate, or coast can resist these suicidal mischiefs.

The War was a contest to decide which civilization would envelop the other. Nature and Providence working "through the brains and arms of good and brave men,"[56] declared for the flawed but salvageable North. Southern perversity had driven a people drugged by prosperity reluctantly to duty. That is why Emerson felt spiritually refreshed even amid the defeats of 1861. At least the North no longer truckled to the South, no longer clung to a morally untenable position. Guided by conscience, a militant North would "redeem America for all its sinful years since the century began"[57] and divert the nation from its mean pursuits. Henceforth, any man would have a fair chance; no crime would be "tucked in under another name, like 'persons held to labour,' meaning persons stolen, and 'held,' meaning held by handcuffs, when they are not under whips."[58]

It cheered him to find the country intact while "we are undergoing a huge Revolution,"[59] although only a few years before, in his dread of centralism, he had called upon states to resist the government, cities to resist states, and villages to resist cities.[60] Now he welcomed the pervasive nationalism which operated as inevitably as natural law. Antebellum patriotism had been a mere "fire-work, a salute, a serenade, for holidays and summer evenings," inspired by "cotton thread and complaisance"[61]; the sacrifices and determination of millions gave it substance. The War welded what had once been a casual conglomeration of states into a nation. Abandoning his fear of federal encroachment, he called upon government to stop acting the parish clerk and justice of peace and to assume "in any crisis of the State, the absolute powers of a Dictator."[62] He accepted and relished his assignment as visitor to West Point and wanted this "Ship of Power," if anything, to be more technical and professional.[63] The man who in 1860 asked his countrymen to foil the attempt to make Washington "the center" of the nation, four years later endorsed Charles Sumner's scheme to establish a national academy of letters with its center in the capital.*

* Emerson, Lowell, and Holmes, meeting December 12, 1864, to discuss the proposal, agreed (Emerson reported to Sumner) "that the existence of such a society was inevitable; . . . We agreed on the general objects of such a society; as, for the conservation of the English language; a constituted jury to which questions of taste & fitness in literature might be carried: a jury to sit upon abnormal anomalous pretentions to genius, such as puzzle the public mind now & then. Custodians of sense & elegance—these colleagues are to be, —in literature. They would be the college of experts, to which the Government might sometimes wish to refer questions touching Education, or historic forms

All of Emerson's political comments hinge on a single theme—the winning of the War no matter what the cost. Rough Democrats who hated Garrison only less than Southern traitors appealed to him more than liberal gentlemen who simply out of habit gave money and lip service to the national effort. He supported emancipation on moral grounds, but so long as Lincoln hesitated to recommend it, Emerson offered cogent practical reasons why the abolition of slavery would bolster the Union cause in America and abroad and weaken the Southern foe.

War aroused a Puritan harshness in the transcendentalist-scholar. Now he declared "the peace of the man who has forsworn the use of the bullet seems to me not quite peace" and urged young men to fight, while conceding the whole State of South Carolina was not worth the death of one Harvardian. He sternly ruled out the possibility of any peace or treaty papering over "the lips of that red crater" until justice and humanity prevailed, and he preached total war: "To bargain or treat at all with rebels, to make arrangements with them about exchange of prisoners, or hospitals, or truces to bury the dead, all unconstitutional and enough to drive a strict constructionist out of his wits. Much more in our future action touching peace, any and every arrangement short of forcible subjugation of the rebel country, will be flat disloyalty, on our part." Against a foe who treated war as a "chivalrous sport" and whose victories he attributed to a Mussulman-like fanaticism, Emerson urged the fiercest retaliation. Better the rebels be "pounded instead of negociated [sic] into a peace," he wrote as the War drew to a close, and he feared General Grant's lenient terms might prevent "the high tragic historic justice which the nation, with severest consideration, should execute."[64]

These and similar pronouncements did not constitute a dramatic reversal of his war views. He had never been an unqualified man of peace nor did the War suddenly transform him into a bloody jingoist. According to a friend and biographer, Emerson never recovered from the ordeal of the War,[65] and any close reader

---

or facts. They would suggest to the Government the establishment of prizes for literary competition. Certain aesthetic & moral advantages did not fail to appear, as the matter was more considered. What recommended to us a cordial sympathy with the proposition, was, the belief shared by us & we believe by the community, that, we are at an important point of national history, & one from which very great expansion of thought & moral & practical activity in all kinds is likely to follow; &, that organizations hitherto sterile may easily hereafter come to be of great scope & utility" (*The Letters of Ralph Waldo Emerson,* ed. R. L. Rusk [New York, 1939], V, 395–6). Sumner introduced his bill for a national academy of literature and art on July 2, 1864. The bill failed (*The Works of Charles Sumner* [Boston, 1875–83], XI, 402–4).

knows at what personal cost he maintained his transcendent optimism. War and peace, like all phenomena, wore for him a double face; each had its glories and corruptions. Strong arguments against war can easily be found in his early writings: he never denied its wastefulness, stupidity, and cruelty and always held up peace as the ideal state of affairs. Wars occurred when people, living in isolation from one another, were seized by irrational impulses. They provided crudely simplistic solutions to complicated questions, suppressed right reason, dehumanized the participants, hurled men back from refinement to savagery, and defied "the blazing truth that he who kills his brother commits suicide."[66]

War had its uses, too, "educating us to a trust in the simplicities" and demonstrating "the bankruptcy of narrow views."[67] It inculcated self-reliance, silenced brag, deflated reputation shortened speeches, tested character. It reinforced "manly power a hundred and a thousand times" and restored "intellectual and moral power" to "languid and dissipated populations." It taught resolute men to seize the bayonet and apply themselves to the business of fighting if they wished to conquer. In short, war, the ultimate realist, shattered "everything flimsy and shifty," exposed and cauterized rottenness. "We watched its course," Emerson wrote in his journals, "as we did the cholera, which goes where predisposition already existed, took only the susceptible, set its seal on every putrid spot . . . and left the granite. So the war."[68]

Long before Federal and Confederate soldiers began to slaughter each other, then, Emerson worked out his dialectic of war and peace, and he had no difficulty accommodating it to American facts. A great evil poisoned America politically, religiously, and culturally; it threatened to invalidate the truths he had been confidently announcing for thirty years. The War (the "human means through which nature crushed the effort to nullify its decree")[69] was a private signal from the Over-Soul that its Concord transmitter had not erred. The degradation of the black man did not cause him sleepless nights (although he came to think better of the Negro's prospects, he apparently never lost a slight colorophobia), but the transformation of a man whatever his color into a "thing" struck him as a profanation and a monstrous wrong. The moral dirt produced by slavery had to be cleaned up in order to make the United States inhabitable for the white man.

His eyes fixed on the future, Emerson accepted the War that devastated the families of his friends. Like other sedentary and bookish types, he preferred natural savagery to overcivilized softness. He found power invigorating, wherever manifested, and his disgust for mass-men made him seem heartlessly indifferent to those "rueful abortions that squeak and gibber in the streets." Far from injuring them, war tamed, drilled, and broke them up—drew individuals from them. The seer who once announced that men of self-possession regarded "battle very little more dangerous to life than a match at foils or at football" but who came no closer to gunpowder than sniffing it in the Charleston Navy Yard, maintained his view of war (and the American War in particular) as both brutal and purgative.[70]

Men of Emerson's generation, South as well as North, habitually read their personal aspirations, needs, and antipathies into historical tendency and found a remarkable unanimity in their own judgments and God's. When Jehovah spoke with a Southern accent, He promised to chastise the despotic and mercenary Lincolnists. Yankee Jehovah launched thunderbolts against monstrous conspirators and honored His covenant with His chosen people. Both sides agreed the War would settle the question of slavery—an abomination, an embarrassment, a blessing, a necessity, depending upon the point of view of the observer—but only a few writers peered beyond the rosy visions of victory or expressed misgivings about the outcome.

Part Two

A PHILOSOPHICAL VIEW
OF THE
WHOLE AFFAIR

MOST OF THE NORTHERN INTELLIGENTSIA, LITERARY OR OTHER-
wise, came to regard the War as a celestial railway to authentic
nationhood, or as a testing ground for the martial spirit. Three
writers, however, who had done their best work before the fighting
began and who clung, not without misgivings, to what Herman
Melville called the "Founders' dream," pondered its darker meaning.

Each in his own way was an outsider—but patriotic and ambitious for his country. Each distrusted faddists and blatherskite reformers. Of the three, only Walt Whitman managed to fit the War
into an evolutionary and visionary prospectus of America, but if he
could suppress his anxieties about his sacred Union more easily
than Nathaniel Hawthorne and Herman Melville, he was hard put
at times to maintain his feverish and aggressive optimism. None of
the three hankered for the smart, efficient, consolidationist state
projected by the Northern elitists or disavowed his affection for the
old preindustrial republic. As young authors, they had identified
themselves (or were claimed by) the literary nationalists, Demo-

crats in politics and adherents of "a specifically American and Democratic culture."

The War tumbled Hawthorne's America into ruins and turned Melville into a brooding Marius. Whitman professed to find grandeur and sublimity if not wholesomeness in the calamity, but the War quieted his bluster, weakened his confidence for all his protestations to the contrary, and darkened the democratic vista that had once seemed so blue and cloudless.

Chapter 3

Hawthorne: Lonely Dissenter

I heard Mr. Emerson lecture on war. Furious wind.
DIARY OF MRS. NATHANIEL HAWTHORNE, JULY 1, 1862

How glad I am that Sumner is at last elected! Not that I ever did, nor ever shall, feel any pre-eminent ardor for the cause which he advocates, nor could ever have been moved, as you were, to dedicate poetry—or prose either—to its advancement. There are a hundred modes of philanthropy in which I could blaze with intenser zeal. This Fugitive Law is the only thing that could have blown me into any respectable degree of warmth on this great subject of the day—if it really be the great subject—a point which another age can determine better than ours.

NATHANIEL HAWTHORNE TO HENRY WADSWORTH LONGFELLOW,
MAY 8, 1851

We were in the little parlor of the Wayside, Mr. Hawthorne's house in Concord. Mr. Alcott stood in front of the fireplace, his long gray hair streaming over his collar, his pale eyes turning quickly from one listener to another to hold them quiet, his hands waving to keep time with the orotund sentences which had a stale, familiar ring as if often repeated before. Mr. Emerson stood listening, his head sunk on his breast, with profound submissive attention, but Hawthorne sat astride of a chair, his arms folded on the back, his chin dropped on them, and his laughing, sagacious eyes watching us, full of mockery.

I had just come up from the border where I had seen the actual war; the filthy spewings of it; the political jobbery in Union and Confederate camps; the malignant personal hatreds wearing patriotic masks, and glutted by burning homes and outraged women; the chances in it, well improved on both sides, for brutish men to grow more brutish, and for honorable gentlemen to degenerate into thieves and sots. War may be an armed angel with a mission, but she has the personal habits of the slums. This would-be seer, who was talking of

41

it, and the real seer who listened, knew no more of war as it was,
than I had done in my cherry-tree when I dreamed of bannered
legions of crusaders debouching in the misty fields.

Mr. Hawthorne at last gathered himself up lazily to his feet, and
said quietly: "We cannot see that thing at so long a range. Let us go
to dinner," and Mr. Alcott suddenly checked the droning flow of his
prophecy and quickly led the way to the dining-room.

REBECCA HARDING DAVIS, 1904

Neutralist

IN 1863, John Pendleton Kennedy, the Maryland Unionist and
man of letters, wrote to a number of American writers requesting from each a holograph to be sold at the Baltimore Fair, the
proceeds of which were to help finance the work of the United
States Sanitary Commission.[1] Nathaniel Hawthorne obliged by
copying out a passage from "Earth's Holocaust," a curious choice
when compared to the nationalistic or inspirational selections sent
by his fellow authors.

In this grim little sketch, composed fifteen years before the
Fort Sumter bombardment, "all weapons and munitions of war" are
thrown into a great bonfire along with the rest of the world's "worn-
out trumpery."

> And now the drums were beaten and trumpets brayed all to-
> gether, as a prelude to the proclamation of universal peace
> and the announcement that glory was no longer to be won by
> blood, but that it would be henceforth the contention of the
> human race to work out the great mutual good. . . . The
> blessed tidings were accordingly promulgated, and caused
> infinite rejoicings among those who stood aghast at the
> horror and absurdity of war.
>
> But I saw a grim smile pass over the seared visage of a
> stately old commander.

Hawthorne sent the above to Kennedy. He omitted the next words
of the old veteran predicting that this philanthropic foolery would
only make more work for the cannon founders; and he omitted, too,
the sardonic comment from "one who neither felt benevolence nor
had faith in it [presumably Hawthorne's ubiquitous Devil]. 'When
Cain wished to slay his brother, he was at no loss for a weapon.' "

Hawthorne's holograph for the Sanitary Commission may also
have been a commentary on his blasted utopian hopes. Although as

patriotic as Kennedy (whose dislike of Southern and Northern extremism resembled his own), he had not welcomed the sectional contest with the confidence of those "best minds and natures," as Howells judiciously puts it, who were "stirred to the noble abhorrence of slavery." Howells continues:

> he not ignobly held aloof from the strain and stress of that period of impassioned politics, and kept pure the artistic soul from those public ethics which penetrated even the aesthetic privacy where Longfellow dwelt apart if not alone. When the great war came, he indeed found himself in enmity to secession, but as much critically amused as impassioned in his patriotism.[2]

Very likely Hawthorne knew by 1863 that Brook Farm, the setting for *The Blithedale Romance*, had been converted into an army training post and renamed Camp Andrew in honor of Massachusetts' militant governor.*

Bull Run and subsequent Union defeats enhanced the "war gloom and general despondency," Hawthorne's editor, James T. Fields, later recalled. "The North was naturally suspicious of all public men, who did not bear a conspicuous part in helping to put down the Rebellion."[3] In such a perfervid atmosphere when New England poets hailed war as the drastic corrector and references to it were couched in the language of exaltation or despair, Hawthorne was an anomaly.† His old friends tried to extenuate his skepticism

---

* "My first object was to visit Camp Andrew. This is the old Brook Farm, the scene of Hawthorne's 'Blithedale Romance,' and his original and subtle genius might, I think, devise a new romance out of the wonderful transformation effected" (*The Works of John Lothrop Motley* [Netherlands edn.; New York, 1900], XVI, 134). Motley did not know his man, but an ironical sequel to Hawthorne's ironical story of the communitarians might not have pleased him. Hawthorne's decision not to attend a Saturday Club dinner in honor of the Governor had as much to do with his distaste for Andrew's politics as with his dislike of public dinners (Hawthorne to Horatio Woodman, Nov. 5, 1860, Huntington Lib.).

† How far he deviated from the Boston consensus can be seen by contrasting him with his antitype, Francis Parkman, whose War-mystique is exemplified in the series of emotional and hortatory letters he dispatched to the *Boston Daily Advertiser* between August 1861 and September 1862. Disqualified by chronic illness from enlisting, Parkman grieved over his deprivation ("It was the lamentation of the moth, in despair, because, being burned already, he cannot fly into the candle") and at the same time hailed the War that "like a keen fresh breeze . . . has stirred our clogged and humid atmosphere." His antipathies throughout the War were pacifists, Copperheads, stay-at-homes, and politicians. He argued strenuously for a responsible military and political elite and recommended that the North emulate the spirit and dedication of the "valiant traitors" who despite their "passion, ignorance,

toward their Holy War as the aberration of a dreamy, unworldly man. "This strange being from fairyland," as Moncure Daniel Conway wrote, "was not to be judged by common standards."[4] Others were less indulgent. Antiadministration Democrats, according to Conway, blamed him for being lukewarm in his opposition to the War. Passionate Unionists became irritated by what they took to be his treasonable whimsy—so much so that by the time of his death in May 1864 his affronts to their feelings had placed him in a moral if not social Coventry. His refusal to align himself clearly with either the pro- or antiwar factions practically made him another Philip Nolan, for during the War years (to paraphrase Conway), a man without a party was a man without a country.

Even an admirer like George William Curtis regretted that one so adept at disclosing the protean guises of the devil in his New England haunts should fail to detect his presence in the slave-pens of Carolina. "What other man of equal powers," Curtis asked a few months after Hawthorne's death, "who was not intellectually constituted precisely as Hawthorne was, could have stood merely perplexed and bewildered, harassed by the inability of positive sympathy, in the vast conflict which tosses us all in its terrible vortex?" To Curtis as well as to Lowell, Holmes, Emerson, Norton, and Motley, Hawthorne's alleged neutrality was incomprehensible. While civilization hung in the balance and the blood of New England youth was "flowing not merely to maintain a certain form of government, but to vindicate the rights of human nature," Hawthorne seemed "to insinuate that it would have been better if the war had been avoided, even at that countless cost to human welfare by which the avoidance was possible."[5]

The older view of Hawthorne as a stranger from fairyland, the cold "disembodied intelligence,"[6] has been supplanted by the torn and anguished patriot who saw, as did few of his contemporaries, the "ethical and political complexity"[7] of the War. If Hawthorne himself is to be believed, the War destroyed his will to write. "It takes away," he wrote in his introduction to *Our Old Home*, "not only my scanty faculty, but even my desire for imaginative composition, and leaves me sadly content to scatter a thousand peaceful fantasies upon the hurricane that is sweeping us all along with it, possibly, into a limbo which our nation and its polity may be as

---

and blindness" did not confound commercial with universal morality or subject themselves to a "many-headed despotism." Hawthorne deplored the coming of the War. Parkman welcomed "the day when from spires and domes, windows and house tops, the stars and stripes were flung to the wind, in token that the land was roused at last from deathly torpor" (*Letters of Francis Parkman*, ed. W. R. Jacobs [Norman, Okla., 1960], I, 153, 143, 160–62, 157).

literally the fragments of a shattered dream as my unwritten romance."[8] Whether or not it shortened his life, as Lowell believed,[9] can be neither proved nor disproved, since financial worries, apprehensions about his daughter's health, and his own wasting illness sapped his energies after 1860. More troubling questions hinge upon Hawthorne's lonely role as a dissenter against an orthodoxy of former dissenters.* Was he the tragic Isolato and prophet?[10] Did he possess a deeper awareness of the War's darker implications than his critics?[11] Did his opinions spring from a superior understanding? Or did they merely signify his inveterate provinciality?

Chiefly About War Matters

Nothing Hawthorne ever wrote or said betrayed any evidence of political adroitness, and he never spoke more truly than when he described himself in his preface to the campaign biography of his college mate Franklin Pierce as "being so little of a politician that he scarcely feels entitled to call himself a member of any party."[12] Such self-deprecation did not prevent him from puffing his mediocre friend beyond recognition and interpolating his eulogy with bland asides on slavery and abolition.† Like almost all of his literary confreres of the North, his ignorance of the South was colossal (he never really considered Southerners Americans), and his letters breathe sectional prejudice—notwithstanding his association with the truculent and chauvinistic "Young America" movement.

Hawthorne lived abroad during most of the tumultuous fifties, too long, perhaps, for him to have appreciated how profoundly the slavery issue affected national politics. He returned in 1859 to find old friends fired by what seemed to him the fanaticism of anti-slavery. Two years before, he had sent back unread an abolition

---

* So the emancipationist Conway saw him in retrospect: "Being a Virginian who had known the loneliness of social exile on account of my anti-slavery views, I felt some nearness to this Northern man, whose opposite views had suddenly isolated him" (M. D. Conway, *Life of Nathaniel Hawthorne* [New York, 1890], 205).

† To wit: "But there is still another view, and probably as wise a one. It looks upon slavery as one of those evils which divine Providence does not leave to be remedied by human contrivances, but which, in its own good time, by some means impossible to be anticipated, but of the simplest and easiest operation, when all its uses shall have been fulfilled, it causes to vanish like a dream. There is no instance, in all history, of the human will and intellect having perfected any great moral reform by methods which it adapted to that end" (*The Complete Writings of Nathaniel Hawthorne* [Boston and New York, 1900], XVII, 166).

pamphlet written by his sister-in-law, Elizabeth Peabody. "No doubt," he told her, "it seems the truest of truth to you; but I do assure you that, like every other Abolitionist, you look at matters with an awful squint, which distorts everything within your line of vision; and it is queer, though natural, that you think everybody squints except yourselves. Perhaps they do; but certainly *you* do."[13] A few months later he lectured her:

> Vengeance and beneficence are things that God claims for Himself. His instruments have no consciousness of His purpose; if they imagine they have, it is a pretty sure token they are *not* His instruments. The good of others, like our own happiness, is not to be attained by direct effort, but incidentally. All history and observation confirm this. I am really too humble to think of doing good![14]

Repeatedly in his tales and novels he came down hard on those who presumed to speak and act for the Almighty. The War seemed to be the outgrowth of mad enthusiasms.

Always a nationalist[15] and defender of his country against foreign slurs, he had been comfortable in a republican America which presented a common front against European privilege while peaceably maintaining sectional distinctions at home. Men of his "simple generation," as Henry James said, "who had no place in their scheme" for civil war, were given the alternatives of fighting the South or fraternizing with it. Hawthorne preferred to do neither and mockingly speculated on the possibility of detaching the New England States from the Union, that manmade unnatural contrivance. He raised the question in a letter to an English friend:

> Don't you think England (if we petition her humbly enough) might be induced to receive the New England States back again, in our old Provincial capacity? What a triumph that would be! Or perhaps it would be a better scheme to arrange a kingdom for Prince Alfred [sic] by lumping together Canada, New England, and Nova Scotia. Those regions are almost homogeneous as regards manners and character, and cannot long be kept apart, after we lose the counterbalance of our Southern States. For my part, I should be very glad to exchange the South for Canada, though I have not quite made up my mind as to the expediency of coming either under the Queen's sceptre or Prince Alfred's. But if any such arrangement takes place, I shall claim to be made a peer for having been the first to suggest it.[16]

The same facetious note sounds in other letters Hawthorne wrote in the first years of the War, perhaps in unconscious response to the mounting fervor of correspondents like Charles Sumner and John Lothrop Motley and the exhilaration of the War party.* But a grimness soon tinged the humor. "I wish they would push on the war a little more briskly," he writes to Ticknor. "The excitement had an invigorating effect on me for a time, but it begins to lose its influence. But it is rather unreasonable to wish my countrymen to kill one another for the sake of refreshing my pallid spirits; so I shall pray for peace."[17]

By 1862, Hawthorne's stand on the War was still confused and paradoxical. He seemed to support it in principle and deem it inevitable; yet he deplored it, thought "it should have been avoided," and feared its consequences.[18] The Union, he decided, was cracking up. It could not and ought not to be restored. For having started the War, the Confederates should be soundly thrashed and then, excepting the Border States, given a "parting kick" and allowed "to go to perdition in their own way."[19] "All we ought to fight for," he wrote to Horatio Bridge, "is the liberty of selecting the point where our diseased members shall be lopt off. I would fight to the death for the Northern slave states, and let the rest go."[20]

Even granting the North had to fight, he could not conceive of the War as a purifying fire or a clear confrontation between Right and Wrong. Sometimes, it is true, an almost Emersonian note crept into letters to English friends whose unsympathetic attitude toward America's plight aroused in him an unconvincing bullishness.† But these moods, inspired by the resolute temper of the people and the

---

* "What are we coming to?" reads Hawthorne's postcript in a letter to Charles Sumner, April 11, 1861. To which Sumner replied (April 11, 1861): "At least Freedom & Slavery are to stand face to face in battle; a United North against a United South. Alas! that it should be so. But I am always for Freedom." Motley advised Hawthorne (July 14, 1861) that he was wrong about the War, although he agreed with him that the nation would be changed and predicted an end "to Southern dominion, Southern chivalry, Southern dash & all that rubbish that we have been brought up on." Massachusetts' response had been magnificent: "In brief, where is the government in the world that can stamp its foot & cause 250,000 armed men to come out of the earth, in ten weeks, when no army existed before."

† "I never imagined what a happy state of mind a civil war produces," he writes, "and how it invigorates every man's whole being. You will live to see the Americans another people than they have hitherto been; and I truly regret that my youth was not in these days, instead of in a quiet time." Or again: "It is really wonderful how all sorts of theoretical nonsense, to which we New Englanders are addicted in peaceful times, vanish in the strong atmosphere which we now inhale. . . . The whole world, on this side of the Atlantic, appears to have grown more natural and sensible, and walks more erect, and cares less about childish things. If the war only lasts long enough (and not too long) it will have done us infinite good" (Hawthorne to Henry Bright, Nov. 14).

stirrings of Northern power,[21] were fleeting. The prevailing tone of his letters was pessimistic, and increasingly he saw the War more as a curse than a blessing. "Not being a very sanguine man," he wrote in 1862, "my fears are greater than my hopes."[22]

The reasons a man gave for fighting, he noticed, depended upon "the section of the country in which his sympathies are enlisted." Southern men said: "We fight for State rights, liberty, and independence." Middle Westerners avowed they fought for Union, while Northern and Eastern men swore their impelling motivation was "liberty to the Blacks and the annihilation of slavery." How could Heaven answer the conflicting prayers offered by these earnest petitioners? "The appeals are so numerous, fervent, and yet so contradictory, that the Great Arbiter to whom they so piously and solemnly appeal must be sorely puzzled how to decide."[23] According to the English jurist Edward Dicey, who met him in 1862, Hawthorne "envied keenly the undoubting faith in the justice of their cause, which was possessed by the brother men-of-letters among whom he lived."[24] If so, the "envy" was ironically conveyed.

Emerson, transformed by the War from anarchist to a celebrator of West Point, was "breathing slaughter,"[25] and other members of Boston's Saturday Club (among them Hawthorne's solicitous friends) were no less bellicose. "I went to the Club, last Saturday," he writes in 1863, "and met all the usual set, besides some generals and colonels, fresh from the battle-field, war-worn and wounded. The tone of feeling was very patriotic, the mildest men and most abstract philosophers being, as it seemed to me, the most truculent. Emerson is as merciless as a steel bayonet; and I would not give much for a rebel's life if he came within a sword's length of your friend Charles Norton."[26]

Old men remained at home and beat the drums of war, while "our young men, in the bloom and heyday of their youth" fought and died. If he had his way, only those over fifty—men who "already had their natural share of worldly pleasures" would "fight our battles." What better or "more honourable exit from the world's stage than by becoming food for powder and gloriously dying in defence of their home and country."[27] Hawthorne, customarily reserved in his social dealings, usually confined such ironies to his personal correspondence, but he was never able entirely to suppress them. Hence strong partisans were disturbed by his dour jocosity and doubted his patriotism; "in fact," he confided to the Englishman Henry Bright, "I have been publicly accused of treasonable sympathies;—whereas, I sympathize with nobody and approve of nothing; and if I have any wishes on the subject, it is that New England might be a nation by itself."[28]

Shortly after Hawthorne's death, Emerson sadly referred to his "perverse politics and unfortunate friendship for that paltry Franklin Pierce."[29] To appreciate this comment, it is necessary to consider two pieces of Hawthorne's that shocked and puzzled his friends, one an article published in the July 1862 issue of the *Atlantic Monthly,* "Chiefly About War Matters," and the other Hawthorne's dedication of his book on England, *Our Old Home,* in 1863.

The first, an account of a month's trip to Washington undertaken for reasons of health in March 1862, is surely one of the most curious War documents written by an American man of letters.[30] "Sparkling, graphic, cynical" (so Moncure Conway accurately described it)[31] and steeped in irony, it was calculated to irritate the True Believers as much by its manner as by its content. Throughout Hawthorne is playfully self-deprecatory. Under the pseudonym of "A Peaceable Man," he presents himself as one without "pretensions to statecraft or soldiership" entering a scene "full of vague disturbance."[32] The genial tone of the sketch persists, even in the ominous forebodings that counterpoint the breezy commentary; and the footnotes or annotations (ostensibly the comments of a polite but highly critical editor chiding the writer for his irreverence and even treasonable wrong-headedness but written by Hawthorne himself)[33] are in reality less the author's own half-serious second thoughts than satirical thrusts at those who consider the substance and tone of his remarks "reprehensible" and "impolitic."

Hawthorne's device of putting the sentiments of those who deplored his War views in the mouth of a self-righteous and somewhat obtuse "Editor" is wickedly effective. The "Editor," a Massachusetts man and "sound" on the Union, has no doubts about the justice of the Northern cause nor any qualms about the means employed to bring about "the complete triumph of Northern principles." Rebellion is to him "an intolerable crime," and like some of Hawthorne's acquaintances, he considers the author (as he politely phrases it) "premature in his kindly feelings toward traitors and sympathisers with treason." The "Peaceable Man" admits, the Editor notes, that he is a novice when it comes to war and politics, and yet he indulges in licentious descriptions (which the Editor has, of course, excised) of Congressional and Administration leaders. It is painful "to see a gentleman of ripe age, and who has spent years under the corrective influence of foreign institutions, falling into the characteristic and most ominous fault of 'Young America.'" Sometimes the Editor does not "thoroughly comprehend the author's drift." More often he takes exception to the "Peaceable Man's" skepticism. For example, Hawthorne remarks: "No human effort, on a grand scale, has ever resulted according to the purpose of its projectors. The advantages are always incidental. Man's accidents are God's purposes. We miss the good we sought, and do the good

we little cared for." To which the Editor replies in his notes: "The
author seems to imagine he has compressed a great deal of meaning
into these little hard pellets of aphoristic wisdom. We disagree with
him. The counsels of wise and good men are often coincident with
the purposes of Providence; and the present war promises to illus-
trate our remark."[34]

Throughout the article, Hawthorne treats sacred themes with a
dangerous lightness. He speculates on the likely postwar political
scene: a "preponderance . . . of military titles and pretensions"
with the prospect of "one bullet-headed general" succeeding another
in "the Presidential chair" and veterans holding offices "at home and
abroad" and filling "all the avenues of Public life."[35] He flippantly
dwells on the ridiculous aspects of McClellan's belated discovery of
the Rebel's "Quaker guns" while defending the General's character
if not his competence.* He draws devastatingly acute portraits—
half cartoons, half psychological studies—of public dignitaries, not
sparing the President himself although his account of "Uncle Abe"
is decidedly good-natured. He turns his descriptions of forts and
army camps into a bitter homily on the stupid ravages of war. He
displays an almost treasonable or at least "premature" sympathy for
the Southerners adhering to a bad cause out of understandable
motives; warns of the sufferings Negroes are sure to experience
once their freedom has been won;† and philosophizes sardonically
on murderous human nature.

The subtlety of his satire sometimes postpones its impact. For
example, what begins as an apparently admiring vignette of a
young staff officer, "a gallant cavalier, high-booted, with a revolver
in his belt, and mounted on a noble horse," blurs into an ironic
celebration of the camp and battlefield where recent civilians can
blamelessly kill and gloriously die "in the spirit of Homer's heroes":

> Set men face to face, with weapons in their hands, and they
> are as ready to slaughter one another now, after playing at
> peace and good will for so many years, as in the rudest ages,
> that never heard of peace societies, and thought no wine so

---

* "It was as if General McClellan had thrust his sword into a gigantic
enemy, and beholding him suddenly collapse, had discovered to himself and
the world that he had merely punctured an enormously swollen bladder"
(*The Complete Writings of Nathaniel Hawthorne* [Boston and New York,
1900], XVII, 367).

† "I am given to understand that for the whole of this bloody business—
for this Slaughterhouse and Shoddy Crusade, to emancipate the nigger, but
to kill him off in a war-Christian manner,—Nathaniel Hawthorne professed,
to his few intimates, his profound distaste and abhorrence" (G. A. Sala, *My
Diary in America in the Midst of War* [London, 1865], II, 24). Sala, it should
be noted, was a highly biased reporter.

delicious as what they quaffed from an enemy's skull. Indeed, if the report of a Congressional committee may be trusted [here he offers a dig at alleged Confederate atrocities] that old-fashioned kind of goblet has again come into use, at the expense of our Northern head-pieces,—a costly drinking cup to him that furnishes it! Heaven forgive me for seeming to jest upon such a subject!—only, it is so odd, when we measure our advances from barbarism and find ourselves just here.[36]

Very likely such jests prompted George W. Curtis's comment to Charles Eliot Norton: "What an extraordinary paper by Hawthorne in the Atlantic! It is pure intellect, without emotion, without sympathy, without principle. I was fascinated, laughed, and wondered. It is as unhuman and passionless as a disembodied intelligence."[37]

Curtis missed both the anger and despair in Hawthorne's cryptic essay. Edward Dicey came closer to the mark: it was not the Northern cause Hawthorne hated "but its inevitable accessories— the bloodshed, the bustle, and, above all, perhaps, the bunkum that accompanied it."[38] The *Atlantic* article, Hawthorne's covert response to the evangelicalism of the noncombatants, also memorialized the courage and self-sacrifice of civilians and soldiers both North and South. His humane skepticism prevented him from considering any question from a single point of view.

James T. Fields, the prudent editor of the *Atlantic,* fearing Hawthorne's kindly references to the South might "outrage the feelings of many *Atlantic* readers," asked Hawthorne's permission to strike them out. He also asked him to cut his comical description of the President lest the country's enemies "gloat over the monkey figure of 'Uncle Abe.' "[39] Hawthorne amiably agreed, but not without protest. His "interview with Uncle Abe," he answered, had a "historical value" and was the only part of the article "really worth publishing." Rather than tamper with it, he preferred to omit the entire passage about Lincoln. He had "already half-spoilt" his piece, he wrote to William D. Ticknor, "by leaving out a great deal of spicy description and remark, and whole pages of freely expressed opinion, which seemed to me as good as anything I ever wrote, but which I doubted whether the public would bear. The remainder is tame enough in all conscience, and I don't think it will bear any more castration; but still I don't wish to foist an article upon you that might in anywise damage the Magazine."[40]

Hawthorne's Daumier-like sketch of Lincoln, excised from the original *Atlantic* article, was restored in 1871 when Fields reprinted "Chiefly About War Matters" in his *Yesterdays with Authors.* The Lincoln portrait is perceptive and prophetic. Hawthorne was among the first to see in him the transmutation of American rawness and crudity into a type of popular genius hitherto decried by the gentility—or condescended to.* His Lincoln resembles an Illinois Ichabod Crane; he is awkward, exhibits an "aptness and not-to-be-caughtness," jerks and wriggles himself out of dilemmas "with an uncouth dexterity," reveals "no bookish cultivation, no refinement"; he is also "sagacious" and "kindly," betrays the "rich results of village experience," is "honest at heart, and thoroughly so, and yet, in some sort, sly,—at least, endowed with a sort of tact and wisdom that are akin to craft, and would impel him, I think, to take an antagonist in flank, rather than to make a bull-run at him right in front."[41] This slanted yet benign appraisal is far more prescient than, for example, the decorous and misleading estimates J. L. Motley and other gentlemen observers made at the same time.

A greater indiscretion by far than the *Atlantic* piece in the eyes of the public and most of his friends was Hawthorne's stubborn decision (despite the warning of his literary advisers) to dedicate *Our Old Home,* his brickbat bouquet to England, to Franklin Pierce. Hawthorne's refusal to suppress his dedication to an old friend and to the man, as he wrote to Fields, who "put me into the position where I made all these profound observations of English scenery, life, and character,"[42] was a gesture of personal loyalty and a rebuke to those who switched their opinions for policy's sake. Some newspapers attacked him for honoring a "traitor" and mistakenly inferred that he and Pierce held the same views on the War. Unlike Pierce, he believed the War was irrepressible (although he thought it would "only effect by horrible convulsion the self-same end that might and would have been brought about by a gradual and peaceful change").[43] Pierce, in Hawthorne's words, was "bigoted to the Union" and saw "nothing but ruin without it."[44] Hawthorne neither expected nor wanted to see the Union restored. He had no hunger for martyrdom but made no effort publicly to point out these dis-

---

* The early view of Lincoln as the commonplace, sincere, and unsophisticated Western clown gradually changed in New England as the "honest railsplitter" became "the President" and finally "our martyred Chief"—"A nature modelled on a higher plan,/ Lord of himself, an inborn gentleman" (George H. Boker, *Our Heroic Themes* [Boston, 1865], 16–17). Had Hawthorne lived through 1865, it is unlikely he would have approved of the prose and verse in which Lincoln figured as one of Tennyson's knights or Socrates or Christ. Though never a "gentleman" to Hawthorne, he was pleased enough to have him occupy the presidency and remarked to Dicey "that the popular instinct chooses the right man at the right time" (Edward Dicey, "Nathaniel Hawthorne," *Macmillan's Magazine,* X [July 1864], 244). A year later he wrote to an English friend: "Meanwhile I enclose a card of Old Abe—an honest man, I do believe, but with extra folly enough to make up for his singular lack of knavery" (Hawthorne to Henry Bright, March 8, 1863). (See Supplement 2.)

agreements and willingly risked social ostracism rather than play the poltroon.

The Terrible Allegory

One is tempted to see in Hawthorne's lonely dissent something prophetic as well as tragic, to endow him with an insight into the meaning of the War denied to all but a few of his contemporaries. Yet his sectional bias and provincial outlook, his resentment against the national clamor that disrupted his privacy,* prevented him from taking in the immensity of the drama as Melville and Whitman did. Everything beyond New England was alien to him—England, Italy, the South. He created a fictive world environed by his section's moral if not always geographical boundaries and peopled by characters who with few exceptions bore little resemblance to the busy materialistic Americans of his own times. If he felt, as he sometimes hinted, any impulse to submerge himself in this life, he controlled it pretty well.

Conservative by nature, he distrusted enthusiasm and innovation, whether home grown or foreign inspired. He was as suspicious of naturalized Americans as he was of orthographic reforms and new words. Such a man could hardly examine the antislavery movement dispassionately—much less sympathize with it—or consider John Brown any more objectively than did Emerson or Thoreau. He shrank "unutterably," he said, from Emerson's alleged remark "that the death of this blood-stained fanatic has 'made the Gallows as venerable as the Cross!' "[45] and when he heard a different version of Emerson's pronouncement, he professed to be pleased that the sage allowed "the reader or auditor . . . to put John Brown at a lower level than Jesus Christ."[46] It did not occur to Hawthorne, as it did to Melville, to see in Brown a weird portent of a national catastrophe. The incident at Harper's Ferry hardly touched his imagination; it only made him indignant. He dismissed John Brown as a maniac justly hanged for his stupidity if not for his wickedness.

Having no personal stake in the War (he was too old, and his son too young, to fight),[47] Hawthorne did not, openly at least, grieve at the carnage. "People must die," he wrote, "whether a bullet

* "On the whole, I enjoy this respite from the daily repetition and contradictions of telegraphs about skirmishes, victories, and defeats, and could almost be content to remain in the same ignorance till the war is over" (Hawthorne to Rose Hawthorne, Aug. 5, 1861).

kills them or no; and money must be spent, if not for gunpowder, then for worse luxuries."[48] Nor did he change his opinion that it was "sentimental nonsense" to risk American lives in order to liberate slaves.[49] He seems to have been genuinely opposed to slavery and sympathetic toward Negroes but, characteristically, doubted if freedom would improve their lot.* Doubting everything, in fact, but human fallibility and self-deception, he could not give himself wholeheartedly to either side in the "Conflict of Convictions." The spectator-moralist watched it as a terrible allegory on the contaminated heart. If the actors who came into his limited focus were real enough (he retained his "hawk-eye"), the issues which engaged them remained abstract to him. Given his temperament, his prejudices, his voyeuristic view of life, Hawthorne's recognized "spiritual insight into evil" did not itself qualify him either to re-create or to interpret the Great War.†

Nor did it encourage him, as it did many of his industrial-minded contemporaries, to see anything "progressive" in its ultimate consequences. Undoubtedly the War accelerated certain tendencies already operating in American life, but the swiftness with which it seemed to devalue cherished antebellum attitudes and values, to make them appear outmoded, did not constitute in his eyes any proof of the superiority of the new over the old. A passage in "Chiefly About War Matters" contrasts the splendid wooden vessels in the Union navy with the ironclads that have made them obsolete, "being as much a thing of the past as any of the ships of Queen Elizabeth's time which grappled with the galleons of the Spanish Armada." The elderly flag officers who stiffly and pompously pace the wooden decks are the last vestiges of romantic warfare: "Henceforth there must come up a race of enginemen and smoke-blackened cannoneers" to replace them. The iron machines they

---

* Conway writes: "For I remember his asking me questions about the ghost-beliefs of the negroes, among whom my early life was passed. One of these was a negro who saw an enormous conflagration near by, but on reaching the spot found only one firecoal and heard a dog bark. Hawthorne was interested in this, and spoke in a sympathetic way about the negroes that I did not expect. But he evidently suspected that the war conflagration would end in a small ember for the negroes, and I suspect did not believe that race would be made happier than he had been by freedom and culture" (M. D. Conway, *Emerson at Home and Abroad* [Boston, 1882], 276).

† H. F. Floan, *The South in Northern Eyes, 1831–1861* (Austin, Tex., 1958), 87. Floan regards Hawthorne as the one "writer of his generation most capable of re-creating for all time the American tragedy of his time" but thinks that by 1861, he was too remote from the center of the tragedy to deal with it emotionally. That task he left to Whitman, whose view of the War was less complex and regional, more spontaneously sympathetic. In my view, Hawthorne lacked the temperament to deal with the War positively at any time.

inhabit, looking like gigantic rattraps, can "annihilate whole navies and batter down old supremacies."[50] Here is a premonition of the new mechanic power that haunted Melville and Mark Twain.

Hawthorne identified himself with the age of wood. He, too, felt obsolescent, unable to believe in "the most miserable war"[51] smashing the old Union "into the fragments of a shattered dream."[52] Nor could he any longer compose romances, because

> it is impossible to possess one's mind in the midst of a civil war to such a degree as to make thoughts assume life. I hear the cannon and smell the gunpowder through everything. Besides, I feel as if this great convulsion were going to make an epoch in our literature as in everything else (if it does not annihilate all), and that when we emerge from the war-cloud, there will be another and better (at least, a more natural and seasonable) class of writers than the one I belong to. So be it. I do not reckon literary reputation as a heavy item on the debtor side of my account with Providence;—indeed, I never realized that I had any at all, and am in doubt about it now.[53]

A new kind of writer and a new kind of style did emerge—in the North, at least, when Howells and Mark Twain turned the guns of realism against Sir Walter Scott (a writer Hawthorne held in much affection) if not against Hawthorne himself. The cult of Scott lasted longer in the South, and so it was fitting, perhaps, that *The Southern Review* should single out Hawthorne in 1870 as a writer born and raised in New England "as ambergris is engendered in the spleen of a dyspeptic whale" and miraculously free of the dogmatism and intolerance "which has made New England a hot-bed for every ism that the diseased imagination of man ever spawned."[54] We can imagine with what mixed feelings Hawthorne, had he been alive, would have received this accolade.

Chapter 4

Whitman: The "Parturition Years"

Then the camp of the wounded
O heavens, what scene is this?
Is this indeed humanity? these butchers' shambles? . . .
There they lie, in the largest, in an open space in the woods,
From 500 to 600 poor fellows—the groans and screams—
The odor of blood, mixed with the fresh scent of the night,
    the grass, the trees—that Slaughter-house!
O well it is their mothers, their sisters cannot see them—
    cannot conceive . . . these things. . . .
While over all the clear, large moon
Comes out at times softly, quietly shining. . . .
What history, again I say, can ever give—for who can know?

WALT WHITMAN, 1863

I do not ask the wounded person how he feels, I myself become the
wounded person.

WHITMAN, 1855

As I have look'd over the proof-sheets of my preceding pages, I have
once or twice fear'd that my diary would prove, at best, but a batch
of convulsively written reminiscences. Well, be it so. They are but
parts of the actual distraction, heat, smoke and excitement of those
times. The war itself, with the temper of society preceding it, can
best be described by that very word convulsiveness.

WALT WHITMAN, 1882

Sounding the Tocsin

IF the War killed Hawthorne, it completed Walt Whitman. Without the "Secession War," he declared in 1888, "the strong flare
and provocation of that war's sights and scenes," his *Leaves of
Grass* "would not now be existing."

I went down to the war fields in Virginia (end of 1862), lived thenceforward in camp—saw great battles and in the days and nights afterward—partook of all the fluctuations, gloom, despair, hopes again arous'd, courage evoked—death readily risk'd—*the cause*, too—along and filling those agonistic and lurid following years, 1863—'64—'65—the parturition years (more than 1776—'83) of this henceforth homogeneous Union.[1]

Like many other of Whitman's self-revelations, this one is untrustworthy. He wrote the best sections of *Leaves* before the War began. He saw no battles of any kind, and he had only the briefest firsthand acquaintance with army camps. All the same he did not exaggerate its "direct and indirect stimulus" upon him. He "partook" of it, was glutted by it, and although the ardors of hospital work may have wrecked him, the insights gained from tending the wounded confirmed his mystic Unionism.

The first two editions of *Leaves of Grass* subordinated politics to personality. Whitman sought to put himself "fully and truly on record"[2] and referred only indirectly or not at all to controversial social issues of the day. By 1857, however, the political rumbling dimly heard in *Leaves* disturbed him to the point where he felt obliged to announce his disgust with the American party system and to outline in "The Eighteenth Presidency"[3] a preposterous solution for his country's redemption.

The Voice of Walt Whitman to the mechanics and farmers of These States, and to each American young man, north, south, east and west, an oratorical daydream, might better have been condensed into a leaf for his poetical garden. In this address, he urges American farmers and mechanics to eschew political partisanship and to snatch away the government from the "office vermin" who have befouled the national nest. Three hundred and fifty thousand slaveholders, supported by Northern lickspits, declare the superiority of slavery. President Pierce "eats dirt and excrement for his daily meals, likes it, and tries to force it on The States." And who will elect his successor? Scythe-swingers, corn-hoers, shipbuilders, the rank and file from "that great strong stock of Southerners," inhabitants of Western clearings and prairies, the "untainted unpolitical citizens of the cities"? Alas, no. Once again the nominating delegates will pour out "from un-named by-places where devilish disunion is hatched at midnight," from jails, gambling halls, customhouses.

Walt Whitman's pamphlet sounds the tocsin and warns "butchers, sailors, stevedores, and drivers of horses" that the "north-

ern liars" and their diseased minions* are stifling the growth of
lusty America, turning workers into serfs, and abetting slavery's
spread into free territory. It calls for the abandonment of parties
and platforms which no longer reflect the whole America. It re-
asserts the principles of the Constitution ("I believe its architects
were some mighty prophets and gods"),[4] the Declaration of Independence, and the reserved rights of the states. And it exhorts
"American young men" to resist "the espionage and terrorism" of the
slaveowners and to deny them one more square foot of free soil.
The learned and the benevolent already subscribe to his message,
the pamphleteer says, but the mass of mechanics and farmers are
bewildered. He, Walt Whitman, will make himself known to them,
articulate their "best thoughts," and help them to disclose to the
world their as yet unacknowledged virtues. "No man knows what
will happen next, but all know that some such things are to happen
as mark the greatest moral convulsions of the earth. Who shall play
the hand for America in these tremendous games?"[5]

It would have been astonishing indeed had any "rich person"
accepted his invitation to reprint this manifesto and to "deluge the
cities of The States with it." Not until *Democratic Vistas* (1871)[6]
did Whitman harangue his countrymen in a similar vein. But "The
Eighteenth Presidency," set up in galley proofs and unpublished
until after his death, reveals a good deal about Whitman's political
thoughts just prior to the War and prefigures his response to the
War itself.

Since his newspaper days in the 1840s, Whitman equated
"Union" with "Democracy" and with "Americanism," that "solemn
and great word"[7] profaned like the word "Religion" by demagogues.
"Democracy" in his salad days signified pretty much the Jacksonian
party, whose platform he enthusiastically and uncritically supported. Yet even then his chauvinism (he was a great twister of the
English Lion's tail and a fervent annexationist) was qualified by his
faith in popular democracy and his hope that the United States

---

* "Who are they personally? Office-holders, office-seekers, robbers, pimps,
exclusives, malignants, conspirators, murderers, fancy-men, port-masters,
custom-house clerks, contractors, kept-editors, Spaniels well-trained to carry
and fetch, jobbers, infidels, disunionists, terrorists, mail-riflers, slave-catchers,
pushers of Slavery, creatures of the President, creatures of would-be Presidents, spies, blowers, electioneers, body-snatchers, bawlers, bribers, com-
promisers, runaways, lobbyers, sponges, ruined sports, expelled gamblers,
policy backers, monte-dealers, duelists, carriers of concealed weapons, blind
men, deaf men, pimpled men, scarred inside with the vile disorder, gaudy
outside with gold chains made from the people's money and harlot's money
twisted together; crawling serpentine men, the lousy combings and born
freedom sellers of the earth" (Whitman, *The Voice of Walt Whitman to the
mechanics and farmers* . . . , 100).

would become a haven for freedom. When he split in 1847 with the wing of the Democratic party opposed to the Wilmot Proviso, which banned slavery in the territory acquired from Mexico, he did so in the name of Union—the "political blessing . . . vouchsafed us by God." *Union* was the keel that kept his religion, philosophy, and aesthetic from foundering, and it was his need to believe in its almost mystical implications that separated him from Hawthorne and Melville. Having started as literary nationalists, both of these writers had become less worshipful of the "great Democratic God" and by the late fifties were pursuing their private quests; the War merely quickened their pessimisms. Not so Whitman. His psychic safety depended upon the Union's preservation. Given his personal expectations and his prophecies of American promise, he had to insist on the providentiality of the War and to wring optimistic conclusions from its horrors.*

He did not choose the slack and sleazy way of so many public poets whose patriotic verse filled the newspapers. Instead, he watched the War from the vantage point of Washington, where he could personalize it through his five senses and "tally" its ugliness and grandeur. So the partisan of the farmer and mechanic spent almost three years ministering to his beloved "athletes" who languished in Washington hospitals. From their words and wounds, Whitman absorbed the "real" War. The soldiers, North and South, provided him with irrefutable answers to the arguments of the doubters and scoffers he had been challenging for the past twenty years. They proved his old contentions: Americans were the toughest and noblest of people, democracy the grandest of systems and societies.

Blacks and Abolitionists

As for the origins and causes of the War, Whitman kept his own council. He refused to absolve either section from complicity and disavowed the apologists and propagandists of each camp. All sections were equally precious to the bard. Rather than add his voice to those who reviled Southern barbarism, he conducted a love affair with the Secessionist states, if not their misleaders, and his occasional outbursts against alleged Southern atrocities never soured his

---

* Whitman's poems before 1861 had affirmed the religion of the affections. His War poetry reasserted "the old urge toward union, adhesiveness, coherence, love, striving to preserve the Union in his name." He succeeded in confronting and incorporating the pain and grief of the War years "because he had anticipated them in language" (James M. Cox, "Walt Whitman, Mark Twain, and the Civil War," *The Sewanee Review*, LXIX [spring 1961], 191).

attitude toward the South as a whole. Evil men wore the blue as
well as the gray, and the madness of war tinged all.

No doubt Whitman's coolness on the slavery question helps to
explain his reluctance to place the entire blame for the War on the
Confederates. The rights of black men was an issue, but a secondary one so far as he was concerned—one which the "ultraists"
made too much of. In fact the Negro did not figure significantly in
his calculations for America's future, the Grand Plan of History;
and it is just as mistaken to confuse Whitman's prose opinion of the
Negro and the poetic *use* he made of him in *Leaves of Grass* as it is
to identify his antislavery position with abolitionism.

The speaker in *Leaves of Grass* rejects no one. The Negro is
magnificently memorialized in the "proud and commanding" dray-
man and in the runaway slave, "limpsy and weak," whom the Poet
hides and succors. "You dim-descended, black, divine soul'd African," he chants, "large, fine-headed, nobly-formed, superbly
destin'd, on equal terms with me!" But the invitation is postdated:
"You will come forward in due time to my side." During his lifetime,
Whitman usually referred to the Negro in his correspondence as
"nigger" or "darky" and never thought of including him in the restricted company of white America:

> Of the Negro race [a friend reported] he had a poor opinion.
> He said that there was in the constitution of the negro's mind
> an irredeemable trifling or volatile element, and that he
> would never amount to much in the scale of civilization. I
> never knew him to have a friend among the negroes while he
> was in Washington, and he never seemed to care for them, or
> they for him, although he never manifested any particular
> aversion to them. In defence of the negro's capabilities I once
> cited to him Wendell Phillips' eloquent portrait of Toussaint
> L'Ouverture, the pure black Haytian warrior and statesman.
> . . . He thought it a fancy picture much overdrawn, and
> added humorously, paraphrasing Betsy Prig in "Martin Chuz-
> zlewit," "I don't believe there was no such nigger."[8]

Neither before nor after the War did Whitman approve of
racial amalgamation. "Nature has set an impassible seal against it,"
he wrote in 1858. "Besides, is not America for the Whites? And is it
not better so? As long as the Blacks remain here how can they
become anything like an independent or heroic race? There is no
chance for it."* Nothing Whitman observed during the War or later

---

* Walt Whitman, *I Sit and Look Out. Editorials from the Brooklyn Daily
Times*, ed. Emory Holloway and Vernalian Schwarz (New York, 1932), 90.
"Yet we believe there is enough material in the colored race, if they were in
some secure and ample part of the earth, where they would have a chance to

changed his views. Whenever he met "black men or boys," he wrote
to his mother, he used them kindly, but after visiting a Negro hospital several times (they were notorious for their squalor), he could
not bring himself to go again. There was "a limit to one's sinews &
endurance & sympathies."[9] The plight of captured black soldiers
hardly concerned him, although the fate of the white victims of
Southern military prisons (his brother George was one of them)
aroused his ire and concern. After the War he would make allow-
ances for Southern repression of ex-slaves without condoning it and
refer in 1874 to "a powerful percentage of blacks, with about as
much intellect and calibre (in the mass) as so many baboons."[10]

Yet Whitman's want of sympathy for the Negro—even his
concession that slavery had "its redeeming points"—in no way
vitiated his hatred for the institution itself. The atrocities connected
with the slave trade revolted him, and he abominated the very
presence of slavery in an ostensibly democratic society. In his eyes,
the slavery apologist was "himself the worst slave," too benighted to
see "that the fatness of the earth" might be "bitter to a bondaged
neck."[11] Why then, to the dismay of his friends, was he so impatient with the abolitionists?

One reason he offered in later years: "Abolitionists were making quite noise enough . . . there were other things just as important which had to be attended to."[12] Among them were the Union
itself and the white mechanics and farmers who sustained it.
During the ebullient 1840s, editor Walter Whitman devoted many
columns to reminding abolitionists one could be against slavery
without defying "the settled laws of the land."[13] Editor Whitman
never advocated violent change. Any reform "must work its way
through individual minds. It must spread from its own beauty, and
melt into the hearts of men—not be forced upon them at the point
of a sword."[14] He would not, of course, abridge the abolitionists'
right to think and say what they pleased. Better excess than "that
morbid and sickly fear of disunion which sometimes robs our
private citizens and public officers of their manhood." But he deprecated the "hey-presto-change!" philosophy and the perversion of
benevolence into fanaticism.[15]

As the controversy over the extension of slavery into the
territories became more acrimonious, Whitman berated both "the
unquestionable folly and wicked wrong, of 'abolitionist' interference

---

develop themselves, to gradually form a race, a nation that would take no
mean rank among the peoples of the world. They would have the good will of
all the civilized powers, and they would be compelled to look upon themselves
as freemen, capable, self-reliant—mighty. Of course, all this or anything
toward it, can never be attained by the Blacks here in America" (*ibid*).

with slavery in the Southern States" and the slavery expansionists
who sought to transplant slavery in the territories. Both threatened
the integrity of the Union. No greater evil, he told his readers in
1847, could be inflicted on America and the cause of freedom
everywhere than the parting of the States "in bitterness and ill-
blood." It mattered little "what the ostensible cause may be—of
what fanatics (of which there are various kinds, in wide removes),
may state it to be. Any man with ordinary judgment must know,
that the disjunction of the Union would sow a prolific crop of
horrors and evils, like dreary night, compared to which the others
are but as a daylight cloud."[16]

He was ready to go more than halfway to allay Southern
fears—to leave slavery intact where it already existed, return fugitive slaves, pay tribute to Southern pluck, denigrate John Brown*—
if by so doing he might prevent a rupture. Only on one issue he
refused to compromise: he would not consent to the pollution of
free land by slavery. Almost up to the War's beginning, he hoped
the antagonists might strike a mean between rashness and cowardice and agree to differ on "points of doctrine or abstract right" as if
they were arguing an abstract question. Belatedly he learned men
could kill each other "for a bare idea and abstraction—a mere, at
bottom, heroic dream and reminiscence."[17] He came to see the War
not as a struggle fought by rival civilizations over cultural and
material differences "but a conflict . . . between the passions and
paradoxes of one and the same identity."[18] In 1861, however, he
had no such comforting assurances. The long-feared War shocked
and threatened him. He had to understand it, to interpret it, to
master it imaginatively.

"Deaths, Operations, Sickening Wounds"

When the War started, Whitman was forty-two, too old for what
was largely a boys' fight, although men his age and older could be
found in both armies. "I had my temptations," he told Horace

---

* According to Traubel, Whitman could never detect in Brown "the evidence of great human quality." Brown's execution aroused his emotions, he
told Traubel, but "not enough to take away my appetite—to spoil my supper.
. . . I am never convinced by the formal martyrdoms alone; I see martyrdoms
wherever I go: it is an average factor in life: why should I go off emotionally
half-cocked only about the ostentatious cases?" But while he " 'never enthused
greatly over John Brown,' " he did not deny that he was " 'a great and precious
memory . . . such devotion, such superb courage, men will not forget—
cannot be forgotten' " (Horace Traubel, "Whitman on His Contemporaries,"
American Mercury, II [July 1924], 329; *With Walt Whitman in Camden*
[New York, 1915], II, 486).

Traubel, "but they were not strong enough to tempt. I could never think of myself as firing a gun or drawing a sword on another man."[19] Disqualified by temperament from killing, he took readily to the tasks of comforter and healer. Even before taking up his hospital work in Washington in the spring of 1863, he visited wounded soldiers in a New York hospital. No sudden whim moved him to resume his self-appointed office of "wound-dresser" after a hurried trip to Fredericksburg in December 1862, to check on the condition of his brother George. He found Lieutenant Whitman already recovered from a slight cheek wound, but for nine days, hanging around the camp, he saw something of the muck and stench of real war as well as of its comradeship. He talked to the soldiers, helped tend the casualties in the field hospital, and returned with a train full of wounded to Washington. There in the hospitals for the next two years, Whitman found his war.

From some fragmentary notes written a decade after Appomattox, he appears to have "entertained a brief ambition" of writing "the History of the war, in a great volume, or several volumes," but on reflection he wisely abandoned the idea. He was not the man to sort out its complications—military, diplomatic, political, and social —but he was not being overambitious in thinking that "a sort of Itinerary of my Hospital experience, might be worth while from a Democratic point of view & even be specially serviceable."[20] This notion seems to have occurred to him as early as 1863 when he broached it to Emerson: "I desire and intend to write a little book out of this phase of America, her masculine young manhood, its conduct under most trying of and highest of all exigency, which she, as by lifting a corner in a curtain, has vouchsafed me to see America, already brought to Hospital in her fair youth—brought and deposited here in this great, whited sepulchre of Washington itself."[21]

The letter to Emerson foreshadows some of Whitman's War themes mentioned elsewhere in his notes and publications and spells out his conception of himself as the historian of the common soldier. He will contrast the politician, "well-drest, rotten, meagre, nimble and impotent, full of gab," skipping into the seats of power, to the "helpless worn and wounded youth" who justified his prophecies of an unrivaled race. He will chronicle the history of "these ranks of sick and dying young men," Southern and Northern, and demonstrate that "nearly all the entire capacity, keenness & courage of our army are in the ranks," not in the feudal-ridden officer class. Out of his hospital sketches and jottings he will compose a work which ventilates "my general democracy" and in which he will "not hesitate to diffuse *myself*." Such a work may "please women" and "be popular with the trade."[22]

Whitman partially realized this projected but never completed volume in *Specimen Days*, but his hospital impressions, movingly conveyed in letters to his mother, are the most undisguised record of the War's impact on his sensitive nature. They explain how he felt when the ambulances deposited the fearfully suffering casualties into overcrowded hospitals. ("Mother, it is the most pitiful sight I think when first the men are brought in—I have to bustle round to keep from crying.") One of his first sights during the visit to George Whitman's camp is a heap of amputated limbs; and the succession of horrors that meets his eyes in the months ahead evokes the spectacle of an entire nation "bandaged and bloody *in hospital.*" Gradually he becomes innured to gangrene, diarrhea, and fevers and fears he is growing callous, but even Washington's diversions cannot blot out the anguish of the wards: "It is curious—when I am present at the most appaling [sic] things, deaths, operations, sickening wounds (perhaps full of maggots), I do not fail, although my sympathies are very much excited, but keep singularly cool— but often, hours afterward, perhaps when I am home, or out walking alone, I feel sick & actually tremble, when I recal [sic] the thing & have it in my mind again before me." In fancy he would put himself in the cots and on the operating tables and vicariously suffer with his "soldier boys."[23]

Besides registering the shocks of war, Whitman's letters dramatized his role of hospital visitor and revealed the impression he made, or wished to make, on his correspondents. Reports of his life in the wards might induce outsiders to send gifts of money to help pay for the books, envelopes, fruit, candy, and paper he distributed to the soldiers; quite possibly they might also disabuse readers —especially women*—who had been taught to think of Walt Whitman as a lawless roughneck and celebrator of illicit passions. For all of his independence and his refusal to placate the prudish, Whitman craved recognition. He no longer wished to pose as the poet of "the madness *amorous*"; better the manly and tender wound- dresser, the surrogate father and mother of children subjected to "premature experiences."[24] Hence he welcomed and assiduously cultivated the *persona* of the "good grey poet" fashioned by his champion, William D. O'Connor.

---

* "There is a prejudice against you here among the 'fine' ladies & gentlemen of the transcendental School. It is believed that you are not ashamed of your reproductive organs, and, somehow, wd. seem to be the result of their logic—that eunuchs only are fit for nurses. If you are ready to qualify yourself for their sympathy & support,—that you may not unnecessarily suffer therefrom, is the sincere wish of your friend Jas. Redpath" (James Redpath to Whitman, Boston, May 5, 1863, in *The Emerson Society Quarterly*, No. 29, 1962, p. 25).

Not that he entirely extinguished the old swashbuckling image of himself. Even while his heart bled for the shattered boys, he remained curiously attentive to his appearance. He knew he looked like a character and enjoyed the attention he aroused by his uncommon appearance. Did his brother Jeff wonder if Walt's experiences with the dead and dying had changed his looks? "I weigh about 200," he answers, "and as to my face (so scarlet), and my beard and neck, they are terrible to behold—I fancy the reason I am able to do some good in the hospitals, among the poor languishing & wounded boys, is that I am so large and well—indeed like a great wild buffalo, with much hair—many soldiers are from the west, and far north—and they take to a man that has not the bleached, shiny & shaved cut of the cities and the east." He is pleased with his big, morocco-topped army boots that reach his knees, with "my well-brimmed felt hat—a black & gold cord with acorns." He still retains his "usual perfect shape," he jokingly confides. "My beard, neck, &c. are woolier, fleecier, whiteyer than ever."[25]

He felt almost ashamed of being so fit, he told his mother, and yet he sensed his air of radiating health acted as a balm for the patients. By the time he quit his hospital duties he had undermined it, but he never regretted the sacrificial experience—"the very centre, circumference, umbilicus, of my whole career,"[26] and did not exaggerate when he said the wounded boys did more for him than he did for them. Through them he sublimated and legitimized his homosexual impulses. Because of them he could transform himself into the Mother Nurse who petted and kissed her charges. Thousands of young men, the farmers and mechanics he had vainly appealed to in "The Eighteenth Presidency," now depended upon him. "It is delicious to be the object of so much love & reliance," he writes to a friend, and again to his mother: "You can have no idea how these sick & dying youngsters cling to a fellow, & how fascinating it is, with all its hospital surroundings of sadness & scenes of repulsion & death." Here in this microcosm of pain, the loving society of comrades Whitman conjured in *Leaves of Grass* really existed. "I pet them, some of them it does so much good, they are so faint & lonesome—at parting at night sometimes I kiss them right and left." No need to sound his barbaric yawp. He could be what he was, the matronly father weeping for his dead and mangled children.[27]

War—"The Real Article"

From the soldiers, too, he appropriated data on camp and battlefield which he interpolated into his own alleged firsthand experiences.

Perhaps the thought that his hospital sketches were not sufficient to establish his credentials as the soldiers' spokesman tempted him into making false inferences about his military career and exaggerating his involvement in the War. For a few days Whitman may have wrapped himself in a blanket and slept "in the mud with composure"; he may have "relished salt pork & hard tack." But references to the War in his letters and retrospective accounts convey the impression that he had spent months at the front and "seen *war-life*, the real article."[28]

He had—in his imagination. Whitman's powerful sense of identification compensated for his want of immediate experience. Although he caught only a glimpse of soldiering and witnessed no fighting, his portraits, camp scenes, and battle panoramas have the fidelity of eye-witness reports and show how attentively he listened to his informants. From them he learned about the movements of skirmishers and scouts, "the fights, the marches . . . glimpses of many things untold in any official reports or books or journals,"[29] the look of an army after a day's advance ("you wouldn't know your nearest oldest comrade—every face covered thick with dust—beard & skin all dirt, well set in—eyes red from the day's heat"), the corpse-strewn battlefields ("heaven looking, they lie in all attitudes—some shot through the heart—the dead lie mostly on their backs—they swell & bloat—they turn black & discolored").[30] To add texture and body to these derived facts, he introduced what he had seen with his own eyes: the soldiers *en masse*, hard-riding cavalrymen, foot soldiers awesome in columns or lounging in camp. He had come to know many of these men as persons, absorbing into himself their histories as well as their anxieties and wounds.

So Whitman, who closely observed and pondered the massive suffering and grasped to his satisfaction its tragic yet hopeful meaning, with reason considered himself better qualified to transmute the War into poetry than most of the so-called poets. They had not probed, as he had, "the living soul's, the body's tragedies, bursting the petty bonds of art,"[31] nor had they, with their "silly little tinkling and tepid sentimental warm water" verse sounded its sordidness and grandeur.[32] The real War would never get into books, but he thought his own poetic version, *Drum-Taps*, passionate yet controlled, a valid approximation of it. It satisfied him, he wrote in 1865:

> because it delivers my ambition of the task that has haunted me, namely, to express in a poem (& in the way I like, which is not at all by directly stating it) the pending action of this *Time & Land we swim in*, with all their large conflicting

fluctuations of despair & hope, the shiftings, masses, & the whirl & deafening din, (yet over all, as by invisible hand, a definite purport & idea)—with the unprecedented anguish of wounded & suffering, the beautiful young men, in wholesale death & agony, everything sometimes as if in blood color, & dripping blood. The book is therefore unprecedently sad, (as these days are, are they not?)—but it also has the blast of the trumpet, & the drum pounds & whirrs in it, & then an undertone of sweetest comradeship & human love, threading its steady thread inside the chaos, & heard at every lull & interstice thereof—truly also it has clear notes of faith & triumph.[33]

Drum-Taps, published in 1865 at Whitman's own expense (a sequel to it, containing his quintessential poem of the war, "When Lilacs Last in the Dooryard Bloom'd," quickly followed) is substantively all he said it was. The introductory poems express the militant exultation of the poet after the first mobilization, a counterpart of the popular mood. The verses grow somber after military setbacks and as the wounded flow into hospitals. As might be expected, the longest section consists of poems growing out of Whitman's hospital days, the poems of suffering, and these are usually the most authentic and touching. He had written the kind of letter to woeful parents he dramatizes in "Come Up from the Fields Father," kept night vigils by the bedsides of dying men, stared into the faces of corpses, performed disgusting chores ("The Wound-Dresser"), attended burials, loved his luckless charges, and watched the moonlight fall on carnage. Scarcely less believable are his improvised vignettes of army life. The painterly sketches of cavalry crossing a ford, of armies in bivouac and on the march, remind us of Winslow Homer's drawings of Civil War scenes, and one of his accounts of a battle, an artilleryman's reminiscence of a war he loathed and loved, already foreshadows the visions of De Forest and Crane.

Yet for all its descriptive and psychological accuracy (like Melville, Whitman marked the change between the flushed and reckless regiments heading southward in 1861 and those "returning with thinn'd ranks, young yet very old, worn, marching, noticing nothing"), *Drum-Taps* is not, as Whitman claimed, "superior to *Leaves of Grass*."* It is more calculating and concessive than the

---

* "[*Drum-Taps*] is in my opinion superior to *Leaves of Grass*—certainly more perfect as a work of art, being adjusted in all its proportions, & its passion having the indispensable merit that though to the ordinary reader let loose with wildest abandon, the true artist can see it is yet under control. . . . I probably mean [superior] as a piece of wit, & from the more simple & winning nature of the subject, & also because I have in it only succeeded to my satisfaction in removing all superfluity from it, verbal superfluity, I mean. I

early *Leaves,* not so verbally daring or radical or spontaneous. He is
working the emotions of his readers, who are also involved with the
Great War, as well as his own, and presenting himself in an acceptable guise: patriot, mourner, healer, sympathizer, reassurer. To do
so convincingly he has to eliminate what he called "the perturbations" of the early poems.

Whitman paid a poetic price for a gamble that he lost, but
Drum-Taps is nonetheless a personal if not necessarily a powerful
expression of the War's impact upon him. Interspersed between the
"public" poems are the covertly confessional ones that betray his
shifting moods during the War years. They show the poet meditating
rather than exulting, doubtful rather than sure ("One doubt nau-
seous, undulating like a snake, crawl'd on the ground before me/
Continually preceding my steps, turning upon me oft, ironically
hissing low"). They hint of an inner division: the hunger for clean
and uncluttered nature, and the pull of teeming cities and promis-
cuous comradeship. He defends his activities apologetically. Don't
put me down, he says in effect, as a parlor-room "delicatesse," a
dancer, a popinjay, or a possessor of beauty or knowledge, but as
one who has "nourish'd the wounded and smooth'd many a dying
soldier,/ And at intervals waiting or in the midst of camp;/ Composed these songs." He knows he is deemed lawless and dangerous,
yet the abuse he has suffered only makes him more resolute. And in
a goodbye message to a fellow veteran, he contrasts the return of
the old campaigner to peaceful pursuits to his own dangerous and
never-ending private war:

> Your mission is fulfill'd—but I, more warlike
> Myself and this contentious soul of mine,
> Still on our own campaigning bound,
> Through untried roads with ambushes opponents lin'd,
> Through many a sharp defeat and many a crisis, often
>   baffled,
> Here marching, ever marching on, a war fight out—aye here,
> To fiercer, weightier battles give expression.

"The fiercer, weightier battles" came sooner than he expected.
Drum-Taps, roughly handled by most of the reviewers, did not
constitute a re-entry permit into respectability. To be sure the poet
had "cleansed the old channels of their filth," young William Dean

---

delight to make a poem where I feel clear that not a word but is [an] indispensable part thereof & of my meaning" (Whitman to William O'Connor,
Jan. 6, 1865, *The Collected Writings of Walt Whitman,* gen. eds. G. W. Allen
and Sculley Bradley [New York, 1963–64], I, 246–47).

Howells observed, and poured through them "a stream of blameless purity,"[34] but Whitman remained in the eyes of his genteel critics the same dumb brute of old. It took more than hospital service and "violent sympathy" to woo the public, young Henry James, Jr., lectured the poet in a review both sharp and condescending.[35] Thomas Wentworth Higginson—abolitionist, war veteran, and literary watchdog—denounced Whitman as a counterfeit and dandy, an author who for "all his physique and his freedom from home-ties, never personally followed the drum, but only heard it from the comparatively remote distance of the hospital."[36] Accustomed to slurs, Whitman made no attempt to reply, but his friends were furious. John Burroughs wrote in his diary:

> Think of belittling him because he did not enlist as a soldier and carry a musket in the ranks! Could there by anything more shocking and incongruous than Whitman killing people? One would as soon expect Jesus Christ to go to war. Whitman was the lover, the healer, the reconciler, and the only thing in character for him to do in the War was what he did do—nurse the wounded and sick soldiers—Union men and Rebels alike, showing no preference. He was not an athlete, or a rough, but a great tender mother-man, to whom the martial spirit was utterly foreign.[37]

"Lincoln's Man"

Whitman may have not shouldered a musket or led black troops into battle, but unlike Higginson—the parochial Yankee who never overcame his reservations about the President—Whitman from the start suspected the greatness of Lincoln. He might even be said to have raised him out of the American soil when he described the ideal presidential candidate in his 1858 address to "the mechanics and farmers of these United States."

> I would be much pleased [he wrote then] to see some heroic, shrewd, full-informed, healthy-bodied, middle-aged, beard-faced American blacksmith or boatman come down from the West across the Alleghanies, and walk into the Presidency, dressed in a clean suit of working attire, and with the tan all over his face, breast, and arms; I would certainly vote for that sort of man, possessing the due requirements, before any other candidate.[38]

In later years, he recognized the difficulty of separating the real from the legendary Lincoln and blamed the myth-makers for translating the man Whitman had seen and heard into an idealized historical worthy. "This sort of thing," he told Traubel, "does throw a doubt upon all history—eats away at its foundations. . . . My experience with life makes me afraid of the historians: the historian, if not a liar himself, is largely at the mercy of liars."[39]

Inadvertently he contributed to the legend, but if he gradually transferred his attention from man to symbol, he was the only major writer to make much literary capital of Lincoln. The episode at Ford's Theater, according to one contemporary, seemed to have unmanned the poets of America, good and bad alike: "They were too astounded to sing and should not have attempted to do so. . . . The thought that any man of eminence in this country may be *celebrated* as Mr. Lincoln was, lends additional terrors to death."[40] Whitman, whose lament for "the sweetest, wisest soul of all my days and lands" is surely the most lovely of all the Lincoln elegies, was one of the few who rose to the occasion, partly because his poem was not an exercise for an occasion but the outcropping of a powerful emotion.

Whitman's Lincoln bore some resemblance to the national stereotype. He also figured as the tragic protagonist in a providential drama. Yet his "hoosier Michael Angelo" with "his idiomatic western genius"[41] and disregard for the decorums was neither a conventional Christ symbol nor an imperfect instrument of a vengeful God. Whitman conceived of him rather as the blessed offering for some kind of national fertility rite. His blood cemented a people and enriched the soil of art.

After the War, Whitman intimated he and the President had some undeclared relationship and treasured a story of dubious validity about Lincoln once having noticed him with admiration. He, in turn, took a proprietary interest in his alleged admirer. "Lincoln is particularly my man," he remarked to Traubel, "particularly belongs to me; yes, and by the same token, I am Lincoln's man; I guess I particularly belong to him; we are afloat in the same stream,—we are rooted in the same ground." A diary entry in 1863 reads: "I love the President personally."[42]

The "strange and awkward figure" shuffling onto the stage of history grew more towering in retrospect. Whitman did not mark him at first as the superior of Moses, Joshua, and Cromwell. "I did not enthuse at the beginning," he acknowledged, "but I made up what I may call a prophetic judgment from things I heard of him: facts, stories, lights, that came in my way."[43] The notes he kept during the War years show him attracted by the President's "gawky western manner" and by his courage in overcoming obstacles "unprecedented in the history of statesmanship." How could anyone look at that man's seamed and careworn face "without losing all wish to be sharp upon him personally?" he blurted out one evening in 1863. "Who can say he has not a good soul?"⁴⁴

As yet, Whitman's Lincoln was still the patient and tenacious Captain of the Ship of State; after the "fearful trip" was done came the canonization. The incident at Ford's Theater struck him as one of those "climax-moments on the stage of universal Time, where the historic Muse at one entrance, and the tragic Muse at the other, suddenly ringing down the curtain, close an immense act in the long drama of creative thought, and give it radiation, tableau, stranger than fiction."⁴⁵ Death enshrined the Commoner among the immortals, and in a curious and probably unconscious way, Whitman placed himself and his work in the reflected limelight.

He had long harbored the fancy of an "ancient soldier" or seer being questioned by awe-stricken lads and maidens: "What! have you seen Abraham Lincoln—and heard him speak—and touched his hand?"⁴⁶ And he had imagined such a role for himself, the beloved relic of a heroic past. There seemed to be little prospect, however, that he would be so regarded by a society uninterested in raking up embers of the War and hostile or indifferent to the poet himself. So celebrating Abraham Lincoln as the first great autochthonous American, "quite thoroughly Western, original, essentially non-conventional" and bearing "a certain outdoor or prairie stamp," amounted to a kind of self-celebration. Lowell and others had called attention to Lincoln's Western flavor, but who besides Whitman made so much of his centrality for a new American literature? Possibly he read a parallel fable in the People's Poet, persistently snubbed by the cultivated classes and excluded from their anthologies, and the "Rail-Splitter" barely tolerated by the "classical hairsplitters"* when they first confronted him in his uncombed state. Eventually they came around to Whitman's view and vied with each other in praising the "martyr." But with few exceptions, that was only after Lincoln had become an American avatar, fashioned, in Lowell's words, "as God made Adam, out of the very earth, unancestried, unprivileged, unknown."⁴⁷ To quarrel with this Lincoln was to quarrel with America. By accepting him, American writers could accept themselves and their country without apology or boastfulness. (See Supplement 2.)

---

* The American Scholar, Gurowski wrote in 1863, "is a product of that scholastic and verbal education which prefers words to things, and ancient to modern thought. . . . I rejoice that Lincoln's mind is not befogged by that limited scholarship; and if it comes to the worst, I prefer the railsplitter to any narrow, classical hairsplitter" (*Diary* [Boston, 1862–66], III, 548–50).

Since 1855 Whitman had been proposing himself as a comparable type and hinting that attacks against him were somehow unpatriotic if not blasphemous. In effect he had been saying, "I am the archetypal American articulating your inward thoughts, the 'I' who personifies the 'All' and incarnates the nation." But no kings or queens, much less his countrymen, recognized him as the President's surrogate, and the "fastidious critics" who praised Lincoln for wringing "his expression out of the very substance of his nature and the inmost life of the matter he had in hand,"[48] had little good to say of the poet who professed to be doing the same thing.

The Convulsive Years

"Do you ever go back to those days?" Traubel once asked Whitman. "I do not need to," Whitman replied. "I have never left them. They are here now, while we are talking together—real, terrible, beautiful days."[49]

The War book Whitman planned to write emerged in pieces, clear in its outline and meaning yet somehow mysterious. He called the War "a strange, deadly interrogation point, hard to define—Can we now safely confess it?—with magnificent rays, streaks of noblest heroism, fortitude, perseverance, and even conscientiousness, through its pervading malignant darkness."[50]

Whitman's war story and his views on its import and significance could be boiled down to the following:

Reassured by hordes of allies in the free states, a secessionist faction insolently tried to break up the Union. Thanks to the "American-born populace" the slaveholders and their Copperhead supporters were discomfited. The "People," good-natured and peaceable, impatient of discipline, submitted with docility to their often inept commanders and to a government honeycombed with treason and radiating "Confederatism." They did so "not for gain, nor even glory, nor to repel invasion—but for an emblem, a mere abstraction—for the life, the safety of the flag."[51] The Secession War, "the last material and military outcropping of the Feudal spirit, in our New World history," ended with the extirpation of an oppressive class.[52] With this impediment removed, "Radical Democracy" advanced throughout the world. By virtue of this war, "a great homogenous Nation" preserved itself, the South awoke from its nightmare, and the future development of America was assured.[53]

Whitman had to believe that his country's salvation could not have been won by any less rigorous means, but he could not extinguish the baleful afterglow of the War or rid his mind of its "malig-

nant darkness." Just as the tormented faces of the wounded
haunted the intervals when he was not tending the wounded, so the
atrocious cruelties performed by both sides stuck in his memory
long after the armies had disbanded. Multiply the atrocities, he said,

> by scores, aye hundreds—verify it in all the forms that dif-
> ferent circumstances, individuals, places, could afford—light
> it with every lurid passion, the wolf's, the lion's lapping thirst
> for blood—the passionate, boiling volcanoes of human re-
> venge for comrades, brothers slain—with the light of burning
> farms, and heaps of smutting, smouldering black embers—
> and in the human heart everywhere black, worse embers—
> and you have an inkling of this war.[54]

He remembered the thousands who died needlessly because of
mismanagement, the released prisoners from Southern camps;
"Can those be *men*—those little livid brown, ash-streak'd, monkey-
looking dwarfs?—are they really not mummied, dwindled corpses?"
He wailed for "the dead, the dead, the dead, *our* dead—or South or
North, ours all, (all, all, all, finally dear to me)."[55]

No other War poet could claim with better right, "I comprehended all, whoever came my way, northern or southern, and
slighted none." The "all," to be sure, "comprehended" Negroes only
in the most literal sense of that word, for Whitman incorporated
black men into his universal brotherhood schematically, not practically. But the white soldier, Blue or Gray, he absorbed into himself,
relishing his courage, language, strength, animality, his "fierce
friendship" and "lawless gait."[56] Watching a crowd of Confederate
prisoners, "wretchedly drest, very dirty & worthless in rig," his heart
filled with "compassion & brotherhood," and "the irrepressible absurd tears started in my eyes,—these too are my brothers." To
Whitman, suffering ennobled; the honors of "ribbon'd & starr'd
ambassadors" did not.[57]

More than any of his contemporaries, he had mentally and
emotionally prepared himself for the War. He had announced his
kinship with all classes and creeds, become the persecuted, the
injured, and the despised, and had not flinched at the ingredients of
earth's compost. The War tested his poetic credo. It validated the
message of *Leaves of Grass*. It justified his faith in "the average
impalpable quality" as personified by "the bulk, the people." It provided Americans with a literary subject, something for a national
literature, "a great mirror or reflector," to reflect.[58]

The War also made him a casualty, for by fusing himself with
those "poor boys, faint & sick in hospitals," he sacrificed, as he told

Traubel, "the vitality of my physical self."* The "ravages of that experience" reduced him to powder. "Still," he concluded, "I only gave myself: I got the boys, I got the Leaves. My body? Yes—it had to be given—it had to be sacrificed: who knows better than I what that means?"[59] Knowing how much importance he placed on health, we can calculate the cost of his illumination. The War did not make Whitman a better poet, but it taught him as no previous experience had done the "tragedies of soul and body" after which "all the usual little worldly prides & vanities" seemed contemptible.[60]

---

* Elsewhere Whitman wrote: "but the old machine the body & brain well shatter'd & gone (that secession war experience was a *whack* or series of whacks irrecoverable)" (Clarence Gohdes and R. G. Silver, *Faint Clews & Indirections*, Manuscripts of Walt Whitman and His Family [Durham, N.C., 1949], 135).

Chapter 5

Melville:
The Conflict of Convictions

"Wo unto them that call evil good, and good evil; that put darkness for light, and light for darkness; that put bitter for sweet and sweet for bitter!" Isaiah, 5:20 (*Underscored in Melville's Bible*)

QUOTED IN JAY LEYDA, The Melville Log, 1951

In *The Tempest*, V: 1, M scores & boxes:
    Mira[nda].   *O! wonder!*
  How many goodly creatures are there here!
  How beauteous mankind is! O brave new world,
  That has such people in't!
    Pro [spero].   *'Tis new to thee.*
M's comment: X *Consider the character of the persons concerning whom Miranda says this—then Prospero's quiet words in comment—how terrible! In "Timon" itself there is nothing like it.*

QUOTED IN JAY LEYDA, The Melville Log, 1951

Noble was the gesture into which patriotic passion surprised the people in a utilitarian time and country; yet the glory of the war falls short of its pathos—a pathos which now at last ought to disarm all animosity.

HERMAN MELVILLE, 1866

Melville and Whitman

W AS there ever a great popular movement, or revolt, or revolution, or attempt at revolution, without some solid basis interwoven with it, and supporting it?" Whitman asked in 1876, "at least something that could be said in behalf of it? . . . We are apt to confine our view to the few more glaring and more atrocious Southern features—the arrogance of most of the leading men and politicians—the fearful crime of Slavery itself—But the time will come—perhaps has come—to begin to take a philosophical view of the whole affair."[1] Whitman now tarred the North as well as the South with responsibility for the War ("in its precedents, foundations, instigations") and congratulated the nation for getting rid of its "bladder humanity"[2]—Fire-Eaters and abolitionists alike—who ignited it.* Unbeknownst to him, Herman Melville had taken a "philosophical view of the whole affair" a decade before.

The two presumably never met, although they knew of each other's work. Whitman, associated like Melville and Hawthorne with "Young America,"[3] had favorably reviewed Typee and Omoo. Neither writer referred to the other during the War years, but late in their lives English admirers linked them as the two great unappreciated American titans.[4] It is not known whether either relished the connection. An extant letter of Melville's alludes noncommittally to Whitman, and he appears to have discussed him at length with Edmund Clarence Stedman on at least one occasion, but the two had little in common socially or temperamentally. It comes as no surprise that they experienced and judged the War so differently.

This is not to say they were antipodal. Each was denounced or ignored by critics who misread him. Neither, though staunchly Unionist, was meanly partisan. Both were drawn to Southerners while reprehending secession, abominated slavery without examining its grim particulars or allowing black slaves to bulk very large in their considerations, and speculated even after 1865 whether free-

---

* "Already points of good unerringly begin, and will in due time overbalance the losses. Among the rest, two cases of relief are even now particularly welcome. In the Southern States, riddance of that special class forever blowing about 'the South.' The North and West have had, and still have, their full share of bladder humanity, but in the old Slave States there seemed to exist no end of blusterers, braggarts, windy, melodramatic, continually screaming in falsetto, a nuisance to the States, their own just as much as any; altogether, the most impudent persons that have yet appeared in the history of lands, and, up to 1860, with the most incredible successes have pistol'd, bludgeoned, yelled and threatened America into one long train of cowardly concessions.

"The North, too, has now eliminated, or is fast eliminating from itself, a fierce, unreasoning squad of men and women, quite insane, concentrating their thoughts upon a single fact and idea—(in the land, of all the world the land of all facts, all ideas)—full as welcome a release here as the riddance there. By that war, *exit* Fire Eaters—*exit* Abolitionists" (*The Collected Writings of Walt Whitman,* ed. G. W. Allen and Sculley Bradley [New York, 1963–64], VII, 311–12).

dom for the African was worth the bloody sacrifice.* Good Lincolnians, they urged an unvindictive policy toward the beaten foe. Both considered the War the most stupendous and consequential event in American history and sought, each in his own way, to capture (as Whitman put it) "the living heat and excitement" of the time before the hot facts were "marshalled for casting . . . into the cold and bloodless electrotype plates of History."[5]

Where, then, did they differ? Melville read no happy auguries in the War's outcome, nationalist though he was. Whitman detected a providential Hand behind the "Secession War," as if the United States advanced according to some kind of heavenly timetable. For him, the War tested American manhood and tempered a nation; for Melville, the massive bloodletting may have taught Americans something but in the process mocked the democratic dream. Both men viewed the War as concerned civilians, but Whitman breathed its fumes and mingled intimately with the combatants. Melville, more aloof, surveyed the conflict from his own lofty crow's-nest. The same age as Whitman and susceptible to rheumatism and neuralgia, it probably never occurred to him to fight. His antislavery opinions notwithstanding, he bore no special animus toward the South and distrusted doctrinaire abolitionism. Shortly before Sumter, he solicited a consulship from the new administration (possibly on the urgings of his relatives and friends) but did not seem perturbed when the State Department, despite Charles Sumner's backing, passed him over. Throughout the War years, he exhibited a steady if not passionate concern about the Union's military fortunes, but there is little to go on in trying to reconstruct his thoughts on the War during this period: a visit to the Brooklyn Navy Yard with Evert Duyckinck in July 1861—a rather unusual experience to

---

* "Can Africa pay back this blood/ Spilt on Potomac's shore?" Melville asked in "A Meditation" (*The Battle-Pieces of Herman Melville,* ed. Hennig Cohen [New York, 1963], 193). Whitman is more explicit: "The present condition of things [1875] in South Carolina, Mississippi, Louisiana, and other parts of the former Slave States—the utter change and overthrow of their whole social, and the greatest coloring feature of their political institutions—a horror and dismay, as of limitless sea and fire, sweeping over them, and substituting the confusion, chaos, and measureless degradation and insult of the present—the black domination, but little above the beasts—viewed as a temporary, deserv'd punishment for their Slavery and Secession sins, may perhaps be admissible; but as a permanency of course is not to be consider'd for a moment. (Did the vast mass of blacks, in Slavery in the United States, present a terrible and deeply complicated problem through the just ending century? But how if the mass of the blacks in freedom in the U.S. all through the ensuing century, should present a yet more terrible and more deeply complicated problem?)" (Whitman, *Collected Writings,* VII, 326).

which he never alluded,* references to the War in family letters,† a few acknowledgments to the Sanitary Commission, and one important excursion to Vienna, Virginia to see his cousin, Lieutenant-Colonel Henry Sanford Gansevoort. The last, which required a supporting letter from Charles Sumner to the War Department, brought Melville and his brother, Allan, close to the War zone. Melville went on a "scout" on that occasion (April 1864) and used it as background for "The Scout Toward Aldie."

Such passing brushes with the "real War" did not necessarily signify detachment or indifference. The episodes of the War itself, however, engaged his imagination less than their latent meaning for America's past and future, and he relied, as he had in many of his other books, upon published sources to provide the stuff for his poetic designs: newspaper and magazine reports, paintings and sketches, and especially the "comprehensive history of this struggle" as presented in *The Rebellion Record*, which sifted "fact from fiction and rumor" and separated the "poetical and picturesque aspects, the noble and characteristic incidents . . . from the graver and more important documents."[6]

Since he wrote few of the poems in *Battle-Pieces* before the fall of Richmond in 1865, his "Aspects of the War" and his "Verses Inscriptive and Memorial" were necessarily retrospective. In them he attempted to recapture the "variable moods" of the "coming storm" and to synchronize his personal and public misgivings as he distantly observed the ebb and flow of the battle tide. If his poems lack the vividness and excitement of a felt occasion struck off at the

---

* "To the Navy Yard with Hermann (sic) Melville. Visited the Savannah, the Iroquois, fresh from the Mediterranean and Garibaldi. Lt. Buckner of the former delivered a brief lecture on his Dahlgren gun. On the quarter deck of the (receiving?) ship the North Carolina, the body of Capt [James H.] Ward was lying, with lighted candles at the feet and head, brought from his vessel the Freeborn in the Potomac where he was slain at his gun by a *secessionist's* shot from Matthias Point. Who shall fathom the iniquity of this rebellion?" (entry in Evert Duyckinck's diary, July 1, 1861), quoted in Jay Leyda, *The Melville Log. A Documentary Life of Herman Melville, 1819–1891* [New York, 1951], II, 641).

† "—Do you want to hear about the war?—The war goes bravely on. McClellan is now within fifteen miles of the rebel capital, Richmond. New Orleans is taken &c &c &c. You will see all no doubt in the papers at your Agents. But when the *end*—'the wind up'—the grand pacification is coming, who knows. We beat the rascals in almost every field, & take all their ports (posts?) &c, but they don't cry 'Enough!'—It looks like a long lane, with the turning quite out of sight" (*The Letters of Herman Melville*, ed. M. R. Davis and W. H. Gilman [New Haven, 1960], 215).

moment of its occurrence,* the best of them are happily free of the attitudinizing and self-consciousness often afflicting occasional verse. What he loses in immediacy, he gains in penetration. Melville's War unfolds under the aspect of eternity.

Battle-Pieces *as a War Narrative*

Although Melville composed *Battle-Pieces* "without reference to collective arrangement" ("I seem, in most of these verses, to have but placed a harp in a window, and noted the contrasted airs which wayward winds have played upon the strings")[7] the shape of the contents is not without design. Chronology itself, as in Whitman's *Drum-Taps,* provided a frame and the fluctuating fortunes of the republic a dramatic structure. Echoes of the Bible, Shakespeare, Milton, and classical authors resound through the volume (Melville's civil war mimics real and imagined wars of the past), and a number of motifs weave through his poetic score: variations on the theme of Order against Anarchy, illumination through pain and terror, the triumph of mechanic power and its psychic and social costs, Nature's indifference to humanity's travail, manhood and heroism, pessimistic meditations on the future of democracy after fratricidal war.

 Battle-Pieces opens with foreboding lines on the hanged John Brown, "meteor of the war" and a portent of green Shenandoah's destruction ("gaunt the shadow on your green"). What Brown thinks and knows and suffers lies hidden under the black cap (he is veiled like the future), and Melville never discloses whether he regards him as a satanic or heavenly emissary. The inspired maniac ("Weird John Brown"), employer of bad means for noble ends, is the architect of disorder and one of the many who will give the lie to the "Founders' dream." He is also the hanged god as well as harbinger of doom ("But the streaming beard is shown") sacrificed to the Law he seeks to undermine. The duality pervading *Battle-Pieces* is set implicitly in this introductory poem. Order preserves Social Wrong or waits too patiently for Time to obliterate it; Anarchy con-

---

* "Is it possible—you ask yourself, after running over all these celebrative, inscriptive and memorial verses—that there has really been a great war, with battles fought by men and bewailed by women? Or is it only that Mr. Melville's inner consciousness has been perturbed, and filled with the phantasms of enlistments, marches, fights in the air, parenthetic bulletin-boards, and tortured humanity shedding, not words and blood, but words alone?" So commented one reviewer who admired Melville's skill but found his verses as insubstantial as dreams (*Atlantic Monthly,* XIX, Feb. 1867, 252).

vulses society by its lawless and brutal operations. Melville's John Brown is neither Emerson's Christ nor Hawthorne's "well-hung" scoundrel. He is the dark Anarch branded with a literal and emblematic "cut" who is at once a symbol and creature of Fate.

One year before John Brown swayed beneath the beam ("such the law"), Donati's comet streaked through the skies amid predictions of disaster. "It was impossible to tell what a day might bring forth," Francis Grierson remembered. "The morning usually began with new hope and courage; but the evening brought back the old silences, with the old unsolved questionings, strange presentiments, sudden alarms."[8] Something of this strange unrest, "the strangeness and solitude, to which the first sense of the great danger reduced all souls," is caught in "Misgivings (1860)." Melville recalls the fierce autumnal storms, the first of a series that will periodically harass soldier and civilian alike. He broods over his "country's ills—/ The tempest bursting from the waste of Time/ On the world's fairest hope linked with man's foulest crime." "Optimistic cheer" has "disheartened flown," and even a child can read the black face of Nature.

Yea and Nay sayers engage in "The Conflict of Convictions" as the War approaches. Satan, "strong and hale" like the old commander in Hawthorne's "Holocaust," speaks for the latter. Against the "disciplined captain, gray in skill," stands "Raphael a white enthusiast," leader of those who believe America's sectional War constitutes "one of the great hopes of mankind." The poet, aloof as God, impartially ranges the arguments of "Senior wisdom" against the grandiloquent expostulations of youth, but the direction of his thought is indicated when Satan's derisiveness is met with ominous silence in Heaven. In time, Michael and his angelic battalions will suppress the hellish subverters of Law, yet not before the idealists have learned that evil, if not omnipotent, is ineradicable and that America cannot escape history. The War may leave the "Iron Dome" (symbol of the Capitol and the nation) "stronger for stress and strain," but the prophecy of an imperial United States flinging its "huge shadow athwart the main" and establishing an iron dominion clashes with the Edenic hopes of the early Republic.

These truths of the "Middle Way" are as yet unknown to the enthusiasts, North and South, when "Sumter's cannon roar" in the springtime of sixty-one announces the start of a holiday war. Supplanting apathetic Age, elated Youth reduces the "Arch-fiend" to a dwarf while their elders, not without reason, shake with apprehension. Northern euphoria lasts until "The March into Virginia" where the innocents are savagely "educated" at Manassas. Having filed toward their fate in "Bacchic glee," the uninitiated victims of Moloch "Perish, enlightened by the vollied glare." What started out like a "berrying party, pleasure-wooed" culminates in a gigantic burial party. Others, less guileless but no less courageous, fly toward a death they sadly anticipate; they at least do not have to be "undeceived" by bullets.

Until February 1862, the Federals celebrate few victories. Northern hopes rise with the capture of Fort Donelson, a pivotal triumph and the subject of one of Melville's longest and most revealing poems. Here he illustrates a favorite axiom, "Nature is nobody's ally," in describing the storms erupting over both military and civilian fronts during the last four days of the assault. Icy winds, rain, and snow beat impartially upon the fighters and upon the civilians apprehensively scanning the bulletins streaked by beads of rain. Falling rain, the "death-list" flowing like a river, and the tears of thousands commingle in a mighty wave of anguish before the Mississippi opens itself to Federal gunboats. Weather controls the fight and enhances suspense, for the storms have cut telegraphic communication; but reports soon travel over the wires and "The habit of victory" begins. Donelson's fall is recounted without animus. If the rebels' course is wrong, they bravely resist the Union thrusts from "a perverted Bunker Hill" until overawed by the power of Law's lieutenant, General Grant.

As Melville ponders the supplanting of wooden vessels (anachronisms in a utilitarian age) by the ironclads, the War on the sea becomes if anything more portentous than the land War. Like Hawthorne, he interprets emblematically the displacement of wood (identified with the Past, preindustrial Man, Romance) by metal (the Present, Machinery, Utility). The "emblazonment" and "heraldry" of old sea fights "all decay." Mechanized sailors work in a "welded tomb," riveted to their places, for war has become a business cogently plied by warrior-operatives in their death-factories. It is properly placed "Where War belongs—/ Among the trades and artisans."*

Melville nowhere hints of any diminution in the manhood of American sailors. The men who fight inside the ironclads, "Sealed

---

* Melville elaborates this theme some years later in "Bridegroom Dick," included in *John Marr and Other Sailors* (1888). Here a garrulous monologuist reminisces to his wife about the days when he served in the old oaken navy and about his experiences after the wooden ships have been supplanted by "brute mechanic power." The foundering of the *Cumberland*, "stilettoed by the *Merrimac*'s tusk," ushers in a new and repellent era. Melville likens the sinking of the illustrious *Cumberland* to "leviathan" waylaid by a swordfish— a dumb show, perhaps, for the end of the old Republic. "Brave boys" drown. The "shoddyites" in the bazaars coin dollars "in the bloody mint of war" (*Collected Poems of Herman Melville*, ed. Howard P. Vincent [Chicago, 1947], 167–82).

as in a diving bell," are the same heroic breed who flourished in the age of sail—but they are less free. Did he intend an ironic echo of Emerson and Longfellow in the lines, "The ringing of those plates on plates/ Still ringeth round the world—/ The clangor of that blacksmith's fray,/ The anvil-din/ Resounds this message from the Fates"? Whether he did or not, they read like a composite parody of Emerson's "And fired the shot heard round the world" from "Concord Hymn" and Longfellow's invocation to the Union in "The Building of the Ship." ("We know what Master laid thy keel,/ What workmen wrought thy ribs of steel,/ Who made each mast, and sail, and rope,/ What anvils rang, what hammers beat,/ In what a forge and what a heat/ Were shaped the anchors of thy hope!") Emerson's hymn and Longfellow's patriotic prophecy expressed the afflatus of "Young America" still wrapped in the "Founders' dream." Melville's "Fates" held less auspicious prospects for a reeling and rusty republic.

Malvern Hill, Antietam, Stone River, all bloodily inconclusive, induce a moody meditation. Nature's cycle of birth, flowering, and death serenely operates amid "wilds of woe"; McClellan, "unprosperously heroical!" props up the national "Dome"; Rosecrans's victory over Bragg recalls the battle of Tewksbury in which both sides claim Heaven's support and slaughter each other with the blessings of the church and the encouragement of their women. Time may reconcile the antagonists, "But where the sword has plunged so deep,/ And then been turned within the wound/ By deadly Hate;/ where Climes contend/ On vasty ground—/ No warning Alps or Seas between,/ And small the curb of creed or law,/ And blood is quick, and quick the brain;/ Shall North and South their rage deplore,/ And reunited thrive amain/ Like Yorkist and Lancastrian?" Right and wrong blur in "the fair, false, Circe light of cruel War" so that even the thorn in the Union's flesh, Stonewall Jackson—"earnest in error" and "true as John Brown or steel"—puzzles opinion and sanctifies "the South's vain war."*

As the North grinds laboriously toward success, Melville's spirit alternates between exultation and doubt, with the latter mood deepening and darkening after Gettysburg. Even victories of that magnitude are balanced by setbacks. In Pennsylvania, Rebel "Pride" is "repelled by a sterner pride" and Dagon is smashed by the Lord of Hosts; in New York City "red Arson" is unleashed by the draft-rioters, an episode that inspires one of Melville's most powerful poems. "The House-Top" sardonically hails the redemption of the ravaged city by "black artillery." When man reverts to savagery

---

* Melville revised the line in his own copy to read, "And he fell in the South's great war" (*Battle-Pieces*, 239).

("Rebounds whole aeons back in nature,") the creed of Calvin is corroborated and punitive Draco's wisdom is confirmed. All the same, the spectacle of troops shooting down rioting civilians is a "grimy slur" on the republican dream.

Order triumphs once more when "Anarch" is dislodged from his "Torrent-torn" fastness on Lookout Mountain, and again when the Federals plunge forward from captured rifle pits and seize the heights of Missionary Ridge as Grant, calmly smoking his cigar—a picture of mastered nervousness—looks on. But then comes a vision of the terrible Wilderness campaigns together with glimpses of past disasters, the subject of a searching and troubled poem, "The Armies of the Wilderness." The story of bootless killing in a maze of second-growth Virginia forest is the War in microcosm, a riddle never answered. Rival armies view each other across blackened grounds or "Deep through the dim suspected wood/ Where the Rapidan rolls amain." Lolling "in their veteran rags," the "zealots of the Wrong," brave men *"foully snared/ By Belial's wily plea,"* display a "Feudal fidelity." The poem unfolds scenically and dramatically: a captured "gray-back" is interrogated to no avail; Federal scouts peer out at Confederate mounted pickets "Dotting the lowland plane"; "A hand reaches out of the thin-laid mould/ As begging help which none can bestow"; bluecoats light their camp-fires with parchment deeds, stable their horses in courthouses, and scatter the libraries of Virginia gentlemen; General Grant, meek and grim, scans the enemy positions, "Then drops his gray eye on the ground/ Like a loaded mortar." Soon his plans, having smoldered through the winter, will burst "into act—into war." Pushing through the glades, the Federals "meet skull after skull? Where pine-cones lay—the rusted gun,/ Green shoes full of bones, the mouldering coat/ And cuddled-up skeleton." After blind wild fighting (there is no longer place for chivalry and romance) the survivors emerge from the Wilderness behind a *"Pillar of Smoke"* fueled by the ghosts of the dead. No one knows what lies in the obscure forest and in the maze of creeping fire: "A riddle of death, of which the slain/ Sole solvers are."

Paeans of joy are modulated by the music of regret as Melville totals up the escalating price of victory. Farragut palsies Rebel power, "Strong as Evil, and bold as Wrong" in Mobile Bay, "but pale on the scarred fleet's decks there lay/ A silent man for every silenced gun." Sheridan rides fourteen miles and turns a rout into a triumph at Cedar Creek, but there is no knowledge of his glory "in the grave/ Where the nameless followers sleep." The listless prisoner in the Rebel pen droops and dies among a swarm of "plaining ghosts." At the head of his regiment, the "College Colonel" responds to the flags and "welcoming shouts" with an "Indian aloofness." He has lived a thousand years since he and his friends went blithely off to war. It is not his amputated leg, his maimed arm or racking fever that blanches his soul ("Self he has long disclaimed") but the "truth" distilled from the desperate Virginia campaigns, the Petersburg crater, and "dim/ Lean brooding in Libby."

This acid "truth" erodes the poet's confidence and satisfaction as the Confederacy begins to collapse under Sherman's blows. Even his often protested belief that Northern arms are carrying out Necessity's "stern decree" cannot still a growing skepticism toward his own affirmations.

Were the terror, the burned houses and wasted fields really "Treason's retribution"? In the spring of 1865, Melville began to question openly the military justification of Sherman's "scorched earth" policy and contrasted his systematic devastations in Georgia, the Carolinas, and the Shenandoah Valley with Pompey's policy during the Roman civil war of not sacking any city subject to the Roman people. Admittedly the "war of Pompey and Caesar divided the Roman people promiscuously; that of the North and South ran a frontier line between what for the time were distinct communities or nations," but the tactics of desolation, however expedient, would leave an unrescindable hate.[9]

By the time Melville records the fall of Richmond and Lee's surrender, the somberness of the dirge prevails over the exultation of the canticle. Now his eyes are on the "helmed dilated Lucifer" of the South, and although he still celebrates Hell's frustration and the toppling of the Giant Rebellion by the irresistible tidal power of the North, black clouds threaten to obliterate the rainbow's promise. Melville's feelings, always in contention, are more so after Lincoln's assassination. An advocate of clemency for the defeated South, he registers with mixed feelings the shock of popular rage while he cautions in a footnote not to condemn an entire section for one parricidal act. No one who has plumbed Shakespeare's "core" (avatar of all men seek or shun) could be utterly surprised by Lincoln's murder.*

* The theme of a key poem in Battle-Pieces, " 'The Coming Storm': A Picture by S. R. Gifford, and owned by E.B. Included in the N.A. Exhibition, April, 1865." Gifford's landscape depicting black thunderheads menacing the tranquility of a forest-girded lake was owned by the tragedian Edwin Booth, brother of Lincoln's assassin. The "demon cloud" of Melville's poem is reminiscent of "the black murk that hides the star" in Whitman's "When Lilacs Last in the Dooryard Bloom'd." Mystery and coincidence pervade each poem. A profound interpreter of Shakespeare who has caught something of his master's insight, Booth naturally responds to the symbolism of the painting. The idyllic lake threatened by elemental blackness is an allegory of the descent of the War into Edenic America, of the vulnerableness and culpability of untested innocence. See Battle-Pieces, 267–69.

Because the angelic and satanic squadrons are tainted with a shared complicity, Melville deplores the cry for vengeance raised by Northern civilians after Appomattox and argues for a distinction between the perished cause and the humbled foe lest a sleeping volcano erupt again. Credulity, passion, ignorance, courage, temerity are not confined to either side. Brave and generous lads "Went from the North and came from the South,/ With golden mottoes in their mouth/ To lie down midway on a bloody bed." What else could be expected from boys egged on by "priests and mothers in the name of Heaven"? It makes no difference now that one side warred "for Right, and one for Wrong." Confederate and Federal "striplings" acted out "their fated parts" and died "unabated" boys, never dreaming "what death was—thought it mere/ Sliding into some vernal sphere."

The "Collegians" are slain "in their flush of bloom," and the misgivings the old men voiced in sixty-one are confirmed. Youth and age disagree throughout *Battle-Pieces*, but the most sustained treatment of this theme is "The Scout Toward Aldie," a long narrative poem in part suggested by Melville's "scout" through Mosby country in April 1864.

The venture against Mosby and his men opens hopefully. The troopers are gay and confident, the young Colonel commanding the expedition assured to the point of arrogance. ("He is young, and command is a boyish thing.") Led by their green and cocksure leader, the "brave array" moves into the protean forest where it will flounder in mysterious greenery. The Colonel is no Mosby who rides through the dark green words "as glides in seas the shark." He and his boy-soldiers have no respect for the forest or its inhabitants and are blind to signs and omens. They ride by a hospital tent heedless of the bandaged cripples who "palely eye" them; the derisive cawing of crows carries no message. Nothing can dim the good spirits of the troop though all signs signal danger as it moves deeper into Mosby country: the dark chapel green with decay and covered with moss and lichens, the green hand of a corpse pointing out of the dry leaves and all but saying Mosby, moss, death.

"Experience" is incarnated in the green Colonel's seasoned subordinate, a "grizzled Major," the "contrast here like sire and son." Both men are brave, but the elder, tempered by war's vicissitudes, is unsusceptible to expectation. Having survived the "Seven Days," known what it means to fall back, and been wounded by Mosby's men, he is wary and recommends withdrawal after the Federals have captured ten partisans. "Bad plan to make a scout too long," he says. To which the cocky Colonel replies, "Peril, old lad, is what I seek." Soon after he has pooh-poohed the threat of "Mosby's rifle-crack," the Colonel is shot through the heart. Looking at his dead commander, the Major in "a hollow revery" observes: "The weakest thing is lustihood."

"Through Terror and Pity"

The Colonel's comeuppance can be read as a fable or cautionary tale: if men or nations are to survive their seasoning, then they must learn to include chance and mischance as a part of the normal course of things and recognize in themselves and others a common humanity and a common fragility. These and related ideas are tacitly or openly conveyed in the two poems and supplement that form a coda to *Battle-Pieces*. Robert E. Lee speaks in the first, a conciliatory "Northerner" in the second, but Melville speaks through both.

In "Lee at the Capitol," the Confederate leader talks more freely and fully than his historical counterpart did when he was queried by a Congressional Committee in February 1866. Melville's Lee is really addressing himself to the War as a whole. How sad and how paradoxical, the poet observes, that one allied to Washington by marriage should have led the invasion to destroy the Father's arch. Now sad and stoical, Lee is content to accept "asserted laws." He has pledged his honor not to fight again, but he is deeply concerned with the War's results, the "brood of ills that press so sore." "Does the South still cherish hate?" Would it join with a foreign foe to betray the government? his interrogators ask him. The South has yielded, he replies, not recanted. Be content with this, he tells the Committee, and bewail with her the men dead in the forests. They call, "Died all in vain? both sides undone?" It might prove so if the victors push their advantage too far.

In the remainder of Lee's exhortation and in the following and last poem, "A Meditation,"* Melville pushes the argument for magnaminity as the only way to buttress "re-established law." No matter whether the South was more to blame or whether malign meddlers in both camps kindled the war: "Common's the crime in every civil strife." What of the thousands in the South who tried to stem "Secession's pride, but at last were swept by the urgent tide/ Unto the chasm"? Was it so unforgivable that they "cast their lot with kith and kin"? Northerners, as "Bridegroom Dick" later pointed out, faced no such dilemma; their nation and their hearth and kin were

---

* "Attributed to a Northerner after attending the last of two funerals from the same homestead—Those of a national and confederate officer (brothers), his kinsmen, who had died from the effects of wounds received in the closing battles" (Melville's note, *Battle-Pieces*, 293).

one, whereas Southerners were cruelly torn. "Duty? It pulled with more than one string./ This way and that, and anyhow a sting./ The flag and your kin, how to be true unto both?/ If one plight ye keep, then ye break the other troth." Will the North, Lee asks, "infix the hate" and in the name of Union "forever alienate" the South? The "Northerner" in "A Meditation" seconds Lee's plea for generosity lest the winners incur the sin of Phariseeism. All through the War, "something of a strange remorse/ Rebelled against the sanctioned sin of blood," and left to themselves the soldiers would have fraternized. With the fighting ended former foes yearn to stop the "old upbraiding."

The prose "Supplement" to *Battle-Pieces*[10] spelled out more explicitly and at greater length than any single poem Melville's counsel of moderation. Speaking as one "who never was a blind adherent," he asked his countrymen to act with "common sense and Christian charity" toward a people "cajoled into revolution" by their misleaders and "entrapped into the support of a war whose implied end was the erecting in our advanced century of an Anglo-American empire based upon the systematic degradation of man." The South had been taught through "the terrors of civil war to feel that Secession, like Slavery, is against Destiny." It should not have to suffer the indignity of humiliating itself or of repudiating the grandeur of its heroes. "Patriotism is not baseness, neither is it inhumanity."

Lest his poems reawaken old animosities and encourage "an exultation misapplied," Melville sought to put the War into a larger perspective than zealous partisans customarily saw it. Perhaps it was irrepressible. Even so sectional hostility had been exacerbated by years of "unfraternal denunciations" which "at last inflamed to deeds that ended in bloodshed." The losers were "for years politically misled by designing men, and also by some honestly-erring men." They fought to preserve and extend slavery, but they were its "fated inheritors," not its "author." If Northern courage and skill undid them, so did "superior resources and crushing numbers."

To solve the problems of reconstruction, Melville believed, required the wisdom of Christ and Machiavelli, and he advocated a strategy of "effective benignity" to reclaim Southern loyalty. This did not mean abandoning responsibility for the Negro. "Those of us who always abhorred slavery as an atheistical iniquity, gladly we join in the exulting chorus of humanity over its downfall." He would not, however, gloss over the dangers of hasty policy. Negro emancipation had been "accomplished not by deliberate legislation" but "only through agonized violence." Unreflective humanitarian impulses together with laws "of dubious constitutional rightfulness" might "provoke, among other of the last evils, exterminating hatred of race toward race." Hence Melville, the conservative, cautioned reformers not to try to end racial antagonism by fiat: "Let us be Christian toward our fellow-whites, as well as philanthropists toward the blacks, our fellow-men." Being "Christian" meant showing forbearance to future Southern Congressmen. Granted "true reconciliation" seldom followed "a violent quarrel," a gentlemanly punctiliousness was a necessary preliminary to eventual friendship once the former abettors of "Insurrection" would again be permitted to hold national office. "Let us pray," Melville concluded, "that the terrible historic tragedy of our time may not have been enacted without instructing our whole beloved country through terror and pity; and may fulfillment verify in the end those expectations which kindle the bards of Progress and Humanity."

The note of dubiety or of qualified hope in Melville's prayer is a fitting finale to a volume which is in effect a sustained debate between belief and disbelief, which abounds in paradoxes, ironies, and conflicts, and which keeps denying what it affirms. No wonder most readers of *Battle-Pieces* were baffled by its point of view as well as ruffled by its harsh meters and prosaic vocabulary.

Prophecies and Misgivings

How deeply the War had bitten into Melville's soul and how *personally* he had taken it can be detected in his philosophical verse-novel, *Clarel,* probably begun in 1866, a year following *Battle-Pieces,* and published in 1876.[11] The interest of this long narrative poem does not lie in its skimpy plot but in the conversations and debates between the pilgrims whom Clarel, the questing hero, meets in the Holy Land. One of them named Ungar, an ex-Confederate officer self-exiled from a country and society he no longer can identify with, brings Melville back to some of the themes he touched upon in his War verses—but with a difference. "The years of the War," Melville had written in his "Supplement," "tried our devotion to the Union; the time of peace may test the sincerity of our faith in democracy." By the time he completed *Clarel,* his own faith in democracy showed signs of rust.

Melville's plea for the South in *Battle-Pieces* sprang from his sympathy with a "manful" enemy. ("By how much more they boldly warred,/ By so much more is mercy due.")[12] The strain of self-righteousness in the Northern attacks against the Confederacy had never been congenial to him, nor had he ever confused Southern foemen with their wretched cause. To act as avenging gods or worse, to act the part "of the live dog to the dead lion," seemed odiously ignoble.

During the War, Melville's compassion for the South deepened as its fortunes declined; in *Clarel* the "South" became a symbol for his own moral landscape. Defeated and misunderstood himself, Melville must have found in the mixture of rage, hurt, and despair that marked the unforgiving and unyielding ex-Confederates (reflected in the controlled resentment of his hypothetical Lee) an analogue to his private wounds and disappointments. He neither could nor would condone openly pessimistic judgments on America's prospects, but he could not deny them either. The still recalcitrant South became an outlet for his own rebellious notions. Like Ungar, the unreconstructed exile, he was also a spiritual refugee, too tough and too balanced to kill himself but honest enough to see that his monomaniacal Isolatoes had glimpsed Incurable Evil. And like Hawthorne, he saw the War as the "sad arch between contrasted eras;/ The span of fate." He could not secede from his gilded nation, but he refused to cheer with the optimists when all omens seemed to presage approaching disorders. In *Battle-Pieces* he looked behind the War, into it, beyond it; in *Clarel* he read and interpreted the handwriting on the democratic wall.

Ungar's bitterness and despair are not merely responses to Federal victories and Reconstruction "misrule," nor has he fled America to escape "the immense charred solitudes" of the wasted South. The War has instructed him in "Hadean lore" and subsequent "reading and revery" confirm his belief that not only the South but America as well has been defeated. He will not make his peace and prosper, nor will he pander to Democracy, "Archstrumpet of an impious age." To Ungar the legacy of the War is civic barbarism, a population "brutalized/ By popular science," and a "Thirty Years (of) War" which will surely "yield to one and all/ New confirmation of the fall/ Of Adam." Even America's enormous resources cannot long delay "The class-war, rich-and-poor-man fray/ Of history."[13]

Ungar's listeners know the source of his gloom and are not prepared to accept his reading of the future. (Melville in the "Supplement" had declared it a "foolish hope" to conciliate those Southerners "who have resolved never to be reconciled to the Union. On such hearts everything is thrown away except it be religious commiseration.") But Ungar's prophecy uncomfortably strengthens their misgivings. For Melville as well as his pilgrims, the War arrested "hope's advance."[14]

It also provided him with a subject around which he could coalesce his private woes and public concerns. If it temporarily routed him out of his mood of apathy and disbelief and restored to him "his sense of human largeness," it also solidified his pessimism. Even in the heady 1840s when he was writing briefs for "Young America," his historical piety qualified his ardent nationalism. It emerged sharply in the Vivenza (America) chapters of *Mardi* when Melville's mouthpiece warns the "sovereign-kings" of the brash republic that "though all evils may be assuaged; all evils can not be done away. For evil is the chronic malady of the universe; and checked in one place, breaks forth in another." Between *Battle-Pieces* and *Clarel*, Melville's message to an audience who ignored him became stark and clear. Disorder, it said, is abhorrent to Nature and society. Out of righteous motive can come horrid excess. All men are children of Adam—and none more so than the rash John Browns who fancy they have God's ear. Evil is not averted by averting the eyes. The wise man is the stoic.

In turning the War into a parable of human blindness, Melville lost sight of its cause; he had a profounder insight into the blight of Negro slavery before 1861 than after. *Moby Dick* can be read as a "portent" of the War just as readily as his poem of John Brown. But in the novel, the fate of the *Pequod* (an emblem of the United States) "freighted with savages, and laden with fire, and burning a corpse, and plunging into the blackness of darkness" is clearly linked with the national crime. Whale blubber is associated with black human flesh; the white man is nothing more than "a whitewashed negro." The corposants glowing on the *Pequod*'s yardarms symbolize God's judgment ("numbered, numbered, weighed, divided"), and it is "the gigantic jet negro Daggoo" who in the "ghostly light" resembles the "black cloud from which the thunder had come."

Negroes are virtually absent in *Battle-Pieces*, and the black storm clouds scudding through the poems do not refer specifically to slavery. The War is a white man's tragedy. While Melville's War poems express anguish and pity, they are also grim asides on a fatuous optimism that disowns "each darkening prophecy." They tell of a dearly bought national "enlightenment" acquired in the glare of bursting bombs—and not retained; of a foolish people, still young and inexperienced, still deluded into believing themselves immune from the leprosies infecting other nations, who sent their children to die. By portraying the War as historical tragedy, Melville defied consensus and took one further step toward popular oblivion.

Part Three

THE "MALINGERERS"

BERNARD DEVOTO ONCE REMARKED THAT AMERICAN LITERATURE was dominated for three decades after 1865 by men "who, of military age in war time, found matters of greater moment than campaigning under arms." The Civil War, he added, "did not greatly disquiet most of our authors."* This was not an ill-considered statement. The four most talented writers in post-War America did indeed shun the battlefields.

Henry Adams anxiously watched the grand spectacle from London. Henry James, Jr., heard the War's reverberations in Newport, Cambridge, and Boston. William Dean Howells, his literary plans momentarily "deranged" by Fort Sumter, sailed for Venice in November 1861 and served there as United States consul until his return in 1865. And Mark Twain, after a brief and not entirely creditable or credible few weeks as a lieutenant in a Rebel company of Home Guards, defected and accompanied his abolitionist brother

* Bernard DeVoto, *Mark Twain's America* (New York, 1933), 112.

to Nevada. In sum, the men probably best endowed, if not the most temperamentally suited, to record the War in history or fiction never got close enough to the fighting to write about it.

But to say the War did not "disquiet" them is another matter. No one who reads their letters or memoirs or fiction for explicit or implicit references to the War can doubt that each in very different ways had been shaken by it. They knew what sacrifices their kinsmen, friends, and contemporaries were making—sacrifices which they by design or accident, were unable to make. Nor would it be farfetched to suspect each may have suffered psychic abrasions no less grievous to him than real wounds incurred by real soldiers on real battlefields.

Of the four, only Howells spoke out with relative candor about his disinclination to enlist. In his case, timidity, aversion to the company of rough men, and consuming literary ambition probably contributed to his decision. Adams and James could claim parental pressure or family responsibilities or a physical ailment as excuses for staying out, but their misgivings over the propriety of their conduct and attempts to include themselves however indirectly in the Great Adventure signified moral uneasiness. Mark Twain's relation to the War was the most complex of all, for he began by taking up arms against the federal government, then assiduously cultivated the military leaders who crushed the Confederacy, and ended up hurling thunderbolts against wars in general. Not one of the four writers ever condemned the American War openly or disparaged the contestants, but each covertly resented the demands of the War on his mind and body and felt guilt of some sort about his failure to meet them.

Although the "malingerers" differed markedly in their personal responses to the War and its aftermath (as might be expected of men so unlike in temperament, social background, politics, and culture) they held certain attitudes in common. The War dug a deep trench between the old America of their youth—provincial, comparatively innocent, and unthreatening—and the new continental nation to which they successfully but still precariously accommodated themselves. Hence their nostalgia for what the War destroyed or made obsolete, their shared hostility toward the plutocracy, their oblique sympathy for the beaten South, and their fear and awe of the Machine both in its civil and military manifestations.

Chapter 6

Henry Adams

We write, not to those who have gone, but to those who stay behind,—
those who, rich or otherwise, of "Beacon Street" or any other street,
sound in wind and limb, with time to spare, and no strong ties to
constrain them, can yet linger at home. With the country ringing to the
note of war, hosts mustering to the fray from far and near, the nation's
life and honor trembling on the ordeal of battle, these worthless young
imbeciles still follow, as far as they may, their wonted round of
amusement and ease; watering places, races, streets, theatres, drawing-
rooms. Their dull blood will not stir at the blast of the trumpet. Neither
the impulses of patriotism, nor the love of adventure, nor the thirst for
honor, nor the fear of shame can rouse them from this miserable
lethargy. Those who no less now than of old are the inspiration and the
reward of youthful valor, will well know how to punish cowardice and
sloth. The scorn of men, and of women, should pursue all who, without
cogent reason, stand idle lookers-on in this time of peril.

FRANCIS PARKMAN, 1862

The Young Strategist

FOR men of Henry Adams's generation, the War separated the
old and loosely confederated America from the new centralized
nation into which they found themselves unceremoniously flung.
Adams described his "failure" to cope with and adjust to this post-
War world in his *Education*—part history, part autobiography, part
Bildungsroman. But it remains an unsatisfactory source, not because it contains lies but because of its omissions and reticences.
His fear of biographers, those murderers of reputation, induced
him (as he told Henry James) to write his apologia as "a mere
shield of protection in the grave."[1] The Henry Adams who criticized
Gladstone for "confessing" a part of his "gross impropriety" as a

93

way of concealing a greater one might himself be accused of "confessing" in order to obfuscate.

Why did he fear exposure? What was there to conceal? The retrospective story of the War years as told in the *Education* is impressionistic but not inaccurate. The old man looking back at his young self recalls authentic emotions, analyzes blunders and humiliations, recreates "historic" occasions; and yet his "manikin" has taken on an extra dimension in the process. Just as the "I" in Whitman's original "Song of Myself" is more than the author, and the voice in *Walden* is an extension of Henry Thoreau, so the antihero of the *Education*—half Goodman Brown, half Bartleby the Scrivener—is something more or other than the private secretary of the American Minister to England, 1861–68. To distinguish the secretary from his double, we must turn to the letter-writer who disburdened himself in private and public utterances during the War and who is reflected in the unworshipful eyes of family and friends.

As his brother Charles once angrily reminded him, Adams had enjoyed far better chances to witness the War and to acquaint himself with "great historic events"[2] than most of his contemporaries. In Germany, where he spent two years after graduating from Harvard, he saw his country drifting toward the "irrepressible conflict," that provocative phrase coined by William H. Seward, the man whom all the Adamses had hoped would be the next President. He came home in time to vote for Lincoln, professedly unfrightened and prepared for "luck or unluck."[3] Already he displayed a proprietary feeling toward his country not unnatural in a recent descendent of Presidents and intimate of the politically powerful. In Washington, where he hastened after his arrival, he busied himself on behalf of the moderate Republicans, at loggerheads both with treasonable disunionists and radical abolitionists. Throughout the "Great Secession Winter" of 1860–61, Adams and his brother Charles fired letters at each other filled with stratagems, political gossip, and prophecies and cunningly planted their father's view in the New York and Boston press.

In later years Adams concluded that neither the politicians nor any American "wanted the Civil War, or expected or intended it." Certainly "none planned it."[4] Young Adams in the winter of 1861 simply took it for granted that Southern "traitors" plotted to secede after the Democratic party schism in June 1860 foreshadowed a Republican victory. The Adams men, father and sons, trusted in coolness and firmness to prevent the Border States from following demented South Carolina and expected the delinquents to return shamefaced to the fold. But if the Slave Power "in the fury of its unbridled license"[5] did ignite a war, then Henry Adams planned "to take such a part in it as is necessary and useful." In his daydreams, he envisaged the ideal Massachusetts regiment to serve in, a Cromwellian army composed of troops "who fight because there is no other way; not because they are angry; men who will come with their bibles as well as their rifles and who will pray God to forgive them for every life they take."[6]

He doubted affairs would reach such a pass even after South Carolina seceded; war postponed was war averted, as the Fire-Eaters well knew. A Southern blunder might sustain the delay—for example, if the secessionists attacked the relief ship en route to supply Fort Sumter. Such an act would put the South in the wrong and "raise the North to fever heat and perhaps secure Kentucky." The twenty-three-year-old strategist who less than a year before had adjured himself and Charles "to blow up sophistry and jam hard down on morality" now recommended a little bloodletting for policy's sake. To compromise the South, he wrote, "the North ought to be worsted in the fight. . . . If Major Anderson and his whole command were all murdered in cold blood, it would be an excellent thing for the country, much as I should regret it on the part of those individuals."[7]

Qualms and Indecisions

The bombardment of Fort Sumter probably caused less consternation in the Adams household than the telegram bearing the message of the senior Adams's appointment to St. James's. Mrs. Adams, who, according to Charles, Jr., "took a constitutional and sincere pleasure in the forecast of evil," predicted "all sorts of evil consequences" and refused to be comforted.[8] Her husband fully realized the perils of his assignment but as yet did not suspect the magnitude of the insurrection. He anticipated the possibility of some "violence and civic convulsion,"[9] but like most of his friends he expected a short war and for the moment worried more about his sons than his country. Of all of his children, only the eldest, John Quincy Adams II, seemed to have any aptitude for the military. When Charles announced his intention to join the army (how disgraceful for a historic family so "prominent in the contest of words" to "stand aloof from the conflict")[10] his father complained in his diary: "He has now taken to an occupation for which he has little fitness, simply from family pride. But none of his predecessors have been soldiers, why should he?"[11] At any rate, Henry, now assisting him in London, was putting his powers to more sensible use. Several years before, Adams Senior had warned him against "studious idleness," an affliction particularly affecting young men who removed them-

selves "from the scenes of action at home."[12] Yet once again Henry
was living in a foreign land, employing "his powers beneficially,"
perhaps, but still an ocean's distance from the conflict. Or so it
appeared to the Minister's secretary until he managed after a certain amount of rationalization to quiet his misgivings.

The reconstruction of the London years in the *Education* plays
down the frequency and intensity of these qualms. Rather, the
author suggests that his part in the diplomatic sallies made him no
less a veteran than his comrades in the field. "On April 13," he
writes, "the storm burst and rolled several hundred thousand young
men like Henry Adams into the surf of the wild ocean, all helpless
like himself, to be beaten about for four years by the waves of war."
He, too, had been thrown into "a fury of fire," although it might not
appear so to an outsider who had seen "the solitary private secretary
crawling down to the wretched old Cunard steamer" on his way to
Liverpool. Adams was sailing into a "hostile world without defense
—or arms." Soon he would be scratched and mauled by English
lions, retreat from bloody diplomatic reverses, gorge on gloom, wear
his humiliations like wounds. "The war alone" (the author of the
Education recalls) "did not greatly distress him; already he could
plainly discern in history, that man from the beginning had found
his chief amusement in bloodshed."[13] His battlefield was England,
where a hostile society put him under continual strain and pres-
sured him into a soldierly response. "To appear confident in times of
doubt," he wrote in 1863, "steady in times of disaster, cool and quiet
at all times, and unshaken under any pressure, requires a continual wakefulness and actually has an effect to make a man that
which he represents himself to be."[14] The thought of his friends
dying in the Richmond swamps might tempt him momentarily to
desert his unsung and risky post, but Charles's exhortations to stick
it out and the prospect of his parents abandoned to "the wild beasts
of the British amphitheatre" checked his halfhearted resolves to
enlist. He stayed and suffered. In time, Union successes convinced
him the army did not require his services. The end of the War found
Adams and his friends "set adrift in a world they would find altogether strange."[15]

To appreciate what the War chapters in the *Education* omit or
gloss over one must consult the letters Adams wrote and received
between the start of the London mission and the death of Lincoln.
The process by which he came to accept his indispensability and his
dramatizing of the derring-do on the diplomatic front are there
recorded—as in the *Education*—along with a good deal of pertinent
detail Adams selectively blotted out of the later book.

For one thing, the letters show a young man tremendously
moved and anxious about the bloodletting at home but plainly

disinclined, despite his periodic outbursts of military fervor, to share the lot of his soldier friends. Before Bull Run, he idly speculated about the military life. "Pain is the only thing I should fear, but after all one's health is just as likely to be benefitted as to be hurt by a campaign, bullets and all." Still, since he was "hardly the material for a soldier," he resigned "the hope of becoming a hero." The debacle at Manassas prompted a reconsideration, and a letter to Charles set down just what kind of military berth he was willing to accept. He wanted nothing more than a commission from the Governor together with a promise that he would have a friend as his Captain: "I would serve under him and perhaps other Boston fellows would be mustered under him so as to make it pleasant." Tactfully Charles pointed out why Henry was "not particularly well fitted for the army" and while berating him for funking his job ("You want to run home because our reverses make the post abroad in which fortune has thrown you very uncomfortable"), he provided him with a rationale for civilian valor.[16]

Now Adams could stay out of uniform in good conscience—he could not "leave the chief and the family in the lurch"—and he was free to magnify the terrors of his English "prison-house." When Charles described to him how mutual army friends "opened their eyes wide with astonishment" at the thought of Henry's enlisting, he let it pass without comment. Still a slave to his moods, and oscillating uneasily between elation and despair, he professed at times to envy his brother: "Hard as your life is and threatens to become, I would like well to share it with you in order to escape in the consciousness of action a little of the struggle against fancied evils that we feel here." Or again: "I feel ashamed and humiliated at leading this miserable life here, and since having been blown up by my own petard in my first effort to do good, I haven't even the hope of being of more use here than I should be in the army." But he had no stomach for the soldier's life, no faith in the army as an instrument of national redemption:

> I dread the continuance of this war and its demoralizing effects more than anything else, and happy would be the day when we could see the first sign of returning peace. It's likely to be hard enough work to keep our people educated and honest anyway, and the accounts that reach us of the wholesale demoralization in the army of the west from camp-life, and of their dirt, and whiskey and general repulsiveness, are not encouraging to one who wants to see them taught to give up that blackguard habit of drinking liquor in bar-rooms, to brush their teeth and hands and wear clean clothes, and to believe that they have a duty in life besides that of getting ahead, and a responsibility for other people's acts as well as

their own. The little weaknesses I speak of are faults of
youth; but what will they become if America in its youth
takes a permanent course toward every kind of idleness, vice
and ignorance?[17]

In time the vicissitudes of battle engaged his attention, buoyed
up or depressed his hopes, but he never agonized over the human
costs of the War as Whitman did or pondered like Melville its tragic
import. "For my own part," he wrote to Charles, "I confess that I
value human life at a pretty low price, and God knows I set no
higher value on my own than on others."[18] Such sentiments may be
put down to youthful bravado and cynicism. Very likely reports of
friends killed and wounded shook him more deeply than he let on.
Yet his very distance from the War necessarily blurred its actualities.

The perceptiveness of the older Henry Adams is already prefigured in the young "inside dopester" transmitting his epistolary
analyses of diplomatic gambits while interpreting military-political
developments at home. So is the catastrophist, alternately shudder-
ing and rejoicing, constantly snuffing disaster and quick to
prophesy; so is the Hamlet confessing his irresolution and fondling
his faults; and so is the student drawn to important men and ideas,
constantly observing and reflecting.

The House of Adams Victorious

Henry Adams's version of the War as seen from the London cockpit
(both at the time and later) was factual and impressionistic. It
began when a shockingly incompetent politician-President, as a
favor to his Secretary of State, unceremoniously appointed Charles
Francis Adams Minister to England. The importance of the assignment entirely escaped Lincoln. Adams Senior and family settled in
London expecting a sympathetic welcome from the self-declared
enemies of slavery. They discovered instead that "no one in England—literally no one—doubted that Jefferson Davis had made or
would make a nation, and nearly all were glad of it, though not
often saying so."[19] The American Minister, snubbed and lied to,
proved more than a match for his disingenuous hosts. Although
embarrassed by the gaucheries of Seward and the polite hostility of
Whitehall, he adroitly confounded the pro-Confederate interven-
tionists. The Minister did not entirely lack allies. He could count on
a handful of nonconformist liberals and sections of the working
class, and he was aided by the stupidity of rebel emissaries, the
Emancipation Proclamation, and timely Union victories. Neverthe-

less, this epitome of New England rectitude, more reserved, more English than the English, was the real hero of the diplomatic war.

Henry Adams's family interpretation does less than justice to the English people. He indicted a nation for the rudeness of Yankee-phobic journalists and the ill-will of Tory aristocrats anad minimized the early and continuous support of the North from many influential quarters. Confederate agents had no comparable group of public men so "heartily and intelligently attached" to their cause.[20] Apparently it never occurred to him that some even pro-American Englishmen offered good reasons for opposing the War or that (until the Emancipation Proclamation) skeptics might suspect the sincerity of a government so solicitous of slave property. Part of his job, of course, was to mold English opinion, not palliate it, and in his gadding about he must often have met the type of anti-Union man John Stuart Mill described to Motley: "the type of Tory to whom slavery is rather agreeable than not, or who so hate your democratic institutions that they would be sure to inveigh against you whatever you did, and are enraged at being no longer able to taunt you with being false to your own principles."[21] How disenchanted he became with Thackeray and Carlyle after hearing or reading their slanderous outbursts against his government we know from the *Education*. Neither that book nor the letters, however, convey the strength and composition of what he referred to as America's "active and energetic allies here,"[22] or more than allude to the manifold efforts by other Americans in and outside of England to justify the Union cause. It was more dramatic to focus on the Minister and his son in embattled isolation, to describe how Yankee morality and shrewdness (with the assistance of local recruits like John Bright) overcame at last a mean but fortunately maladroit opposition.*

Prospects and Portents

Henry Adams subsequently treated the War as an event and a spectacle, an ordeal to be lived through. What it cost the country in blood and suffering seemed of less moment to him than the lessons

---

* Charles Hale, editor of the *Boston Advertiser* and intimate of the Adams family, reported to his mother an example of Henry's "shrewdness" in November 1861. He was dining with him and Mary Adams when some one called "with a written memorandum" requesting the address of William Lowndes Yancey, the recently appointed Confederate commissioner to England and France: "Henry Adams endorsed on the back 'No *American* by the name of Yancey is known at this legation!'—an impudent answer to an impudent question" (Charles Hale to Sarah Preston Everett Hale, Nov. 19, 1861, Hale Papers, Smith).

it furnished for the social philosopher. From his English vantage point, it had the grandeur touching all titanic events, and Adams in his euphoric moods yearned for some uncivilized Homer to chronicle the "Cyclopean battles." Gettysburg awed him. "There's a magnificence about the pertinacity of the struggle, lasting so many days, and closing so far as we know on the eve of our single national anniversary, with the whole nation bending over it, that makes even these English cubs silent." At such moments he felt "like a King" and asserted his "nationality with a quiet pugnacity."[23]

The extinction of the slave system, it might be supposed, would have prompted Adams to reflect a little on the society being pounded into submission, but the written evidence discloses no consuming interest either in the South or the Negro. Southerners were brutes and paranoids

> haunted by suspicion, by *idées fixes*, by violent morbid excitement; but this was not all. They were stupendously ignorant of the world. As a class the cotton-planters were mentally one-sided, ill-balanced, and provincial to a degree rarely known. They were a close society on whom the new foundations of power had poured a stream of wealth and slaves that acted like oil on flame. They showed a young student his first object-lesson of the way in which excess of power worked when held by inadequate hands.

In 1860, they stood for "bad temper, bad manners, poker, and treason."[24] Had he fought against these "cranks" and "barbarians," probably he would have come to think better of them, as Charles and many of his soldier-friends did. The young civilian-diplomat, however, seeing in every Confederate success a boost for the partisans of intervention, wanted to pulverize the South. One thing had become clear to him, he wrote Charles in 1862,

> which is that we must not let them as an independent state get the monopoly of cotton again, unless we want to find a powerful and bitterly hostile nation on our border, supported by all the moral and social influence of Great Britain in peace; certain in war to drag us into all the European complications; sure to be in perpetual anarchy within, but always ready to disturb anything and everything without; to compel us to support a standing army no less large than if we conquer them and hold them so, and with infinite means of wounding and scattering dissension among us. We must ruin them before we let them go or it will all have to be done over again. And we must exterminate them in the end, be it long or be it short, for it is a battle between us and slavery.[25]

To destroy the Rebels, Adams recommended a strangling blockade (let the South choke on its own cotton) and the unleashing of Negro guerrillas. Here, as in some of his other ventures into military strategy, he spoke without knowledge or experience. The "Negro," both for Henry and his father, was an "issue," one to be handled with circumspection. They considered themselves "abolitionists"—which is to say they regarded the slave system as iniquitous and barbaric—but they gave little serious or informed thought to the possible consequences of its elimination. The Emancipation Proclamation delighted Henry as a propaganda measure, because, he wrote to Charles, it "has done more for us here than all our former victories and all our diplomacy."[26] The Negro was a weapon in the Northern arsenal, his liberation a strategic coup to hasten the downfall of the South and to discredit the London *Times*.

It can only be guessed what passed through the mind of Charles when Henry, momentarily bored with London society, expressed a wish in 1863 "to go home and take a commission in a negro regiment." Day by day contact with the "Contrabands" had dampened Charles's optimism about the future of the American Negro. Slavery, he was coming to believe, had turned the blacks into a docile and morally corrupted people. The only way to protect this "indolent" and "shiftless" peasantry and to make it self-supporting was to put it under government direction, exacting from the Negro "that amount of labor which he owes to the community and the cotton market." But he had no faith in the Negroes' ultimate prospects and looked upon their sudden emancipation as a calamity. Even if it had been postponed, the coming economic revolution would have soon compelled their owners to junk them like "antiquated and unprofitable machines." Conceivably they might survive throughout some indefinite period of villeinage; without care they would perish. For who would nurture them after they had been displaced by machinery or by more efficient forms of labor? Charles foresaw enormous benefits deriving from the War—but for the Caucasian, not the African: "He is the foot-ball of passion and accident, and the fit of freedom may prove his destruction."[27]

Henry Adams, needless to say, did not broadcast his brother's gloomy projections lest Southern sympathizers in England seize upon them to strengthen their case. Besides, he disagreed with Charles's surmises. The demand for American cotton and the shortage of labor, he reasoned, guaranteed a continued demand for black farmworkers. Agreed that "instantaneous" emancipation was not the answer. But why not take a leaf from the Roman annals and colonize the South with settlements of old soldiers who could instill the moribund social system with their Northern energy, establish schools and churches, create new industries, and expiate the "old crime"?

> It is the only means by which we can insure our hold on the South and plant colonies that are certain of success. It must be a military system of colonies, governed by the Executive and without any dependence upon or relation to the States in which they happen to be placed. With such a system I would allow fifty years for the South to become ten times as great and powerful and loyal as she ever was, besides being free.[28]

He was a little vague about the Negro's role in this reconstruction process (the "emeriti" were to form "common cause with the ne-groes in gradually sapping the strength of the slave-holders") and made no further mention of his scheme.

Charles in his letters to his father and Henry continued to harp on the Negro's incapacity and to reiterate his conclusions about slavery as "a patriarchal institution" and its baneful effect on the black man. Slaves, he said, "were not, as a whole, cruelly treated or over-worked." Therein lay slavery's most sinister aspect: its mild-ness made Negroes "as supine as logs or animals." Would the War at last "revolutionize this miserable, and the more miserable be-cause contented, race of slaves"? While not denying black intelli-gence, adaptability, and courage, he took Negro inferiority for granted and recommended the army as the best training school to prepare the black citizen for survival.[29]

By this time Henry Adams, who offered no rebuttal to his brother's racial pronouncements, was more than ever concerned with the question uppermost in his mind from the very first—his career. The War had "stirred up" his generation, placed its stamp on every member, and saddled his class with a "great burden."[30] An assiduous disciple of Tocqueville and Mill, Adams accepted their view of his country's potential magnificence or degradation. "If," Mill had written to J. L. Motley,

> you have among you men of calibre to use the high spirit which this struggle has raised, and the grave reflections to which it gives rise, as means of moving public opinion in favor of correcting what is bad and of strengthening what is good in your institutions and modes of feeling and thought, the war will prove to have been a permanent blessing to your country such as we have never dared to hope for, and a source of estimable improvement in the projects of the hu-man race in other ways besides the great one of extinguishing slavery.[31]

Adams had this obligation in mind when he admonished himself and his generation: "We cannot be commonplace." As early as 1862, he was calling for a national "school" directed by a young elite "like ourselves or better, to start new influences not only in politics, but in literature, in law, in society, and throughout the whole social organism of this country."[32]

The Unwanted Man

Such thoughts were openly bruited in 1862 by men of Adams's class. Francis Parkman had already told readers of the *Boston Advertiser* it was time "men of a high and finished manhood" supplanted the "dextrous politicians" and "fluent demagogues" who featured "log-cabins, raccoons, and rail-splitting" in their degrading campaigns. Before the War, gentlemen—perhaps overly fastidious—had shrunk "from the mean contacts and repugnant compliances" exacted by public life. Their country's crisis enabled them to "listen to the call of patriotism without compromising self-respect." Presumably these same soldier-gentry ("who by education and associations have gained a more liberal and balanced development than falls to the general share") could be counted on to manage national affairs when the fighting was over, although Parkman did not attempt to predict the post-War fate of the Brahmin class. His point in 1862 was simpler: either the political wirepullers and Bowery Brigadiers would be replaced by trusty officers or "we must resign ourselves to an inglorious war and a ruinous peace."[33]

When Adams returned to the United States in 1868 after his father had resigned his ministry, it seemed possible that the "men of calibre" Mill and Parkman referred to might indeed provide the managerial expertise required by the fractured nation. Whether Adams at this time thought the War had proved a "blessing" is not clear, but some of his letters during and after the War intimate a confidence that he, too, as part of the patrician-intelligentsia, would become a force in Washington by influencing men of power.

The story of Adams's discomfiture (his rueful discovery that coarse-grained politicoes, greedy for boodle, Radical Reconstructionists waving the "Bloody-Shirt" to distract attention from their ruinous policies, and the rank and file who elected them no longer needed or wanted men like himself) is the story of his class. Not only had the masses, scarcely known to him, been shaped and disciplined by a complex military machine in four years of war; they had also been shaped and manipulated by a political machine composed of people very much like themselves and directing itself to the

bread-and-butter issues disdained by high-minded gentlemen re-
formists. In 1865 the country teemed with energetic and ambitious
materialists—sons of Grant—who did not share the concerns of
Adams: conservative and statesmanlike rule from the top by the
honest and the able, civil service reform, low tariffs.[34] Hence there
was a symbolic truth in Henry Adams's remark to his brother:
"Grant wrecked my own life, and the last hope or chance of lifting
society back to a reasonably high plane. Grant's administration is to
me the dividing line between what we hoped for, and what we got."[35]
His novel *Democracy* (1879) is among other things a fictional obit-
uary on the "Brahmin caste" as a political entity and a confession
(like his *Education*) that Henry Adams lacked the ability and the
will to cope with society in post-War America.

Parkman had spelled out the scenario of *Democracy* in one of
his public letters. The "well-instructed class," he wrote, which
proved its patriotism and mettle on a dozen battlefields, had been
"jostled from political life far less from its own shortcomings than
by action of our political machine." How could this elite survive in a
country "where the bought vote of the unlettered boor" neutralized
"the vote of the wisest and best"? No other class was so supremely
equipped to rule, yet no other class was less accepted on its own
terms. It faced the alternative of falling into line with the self-
seekers or leaving public service.[36]

Democracy poses this dilemma. Post-War Washington has
been taken over by "those vast aggregations in which, under the
covering mantle of professed principle, self-interest and petty ambition hunt their game." In such a political sewer, the "gentlemen" are
no match for Adams's spoilsman, Senator Ratcliffe, wallowing in
corruption as he professes to save "this glorious Union" from "the
blood-stained hands of rebels."[37] In 1863, Parkman, for all of his
criticism of the multitude, believed in the "great national heart" still
beating "under the surface of froth and scum."[38] In 1879, Henry
Adams's gullible heroine makes a comparable affirmation: "Underneath the scum floating on the surface of politics, Madeleine felt
that there was a sort of healthy ocean current of honest purpose,
which swept the scum before it, and kept the mass pure."[39] Her
creator was less positive. Adams's various spokesmen in the novel
(each a facet of himself) accept democracy as inevitable, but they
do not enthusiastically endorse it. It is still a risk, a problem, an
experiment—"the only direction society can take that is worth
taking."[40] In fact *Democracy* rather shrilly underscores the implication that the War's outcome boded ill for Adams's nation, his
class, and himself. Like Melville and Henry James, he also chose a
Southerner to say the last word about the War and democracy.
Carrington, his Virginian hero, does not go so far as Ungar and

stigmatize democracy as "arch strumpet of an impious age,"[41] but he, too, is an Isolato encircled by demagogues and ignorant masses. In 1879, having made his peace with the Rebels, Adams felt closer to a Confederate veteran, the friend of the Lees and treasurer of eighteenth-century values, than he did to Washington City's new barbarians.

Adams's references to the War in *Democracy* (he resees the struggle through the eyes and consciousness of Sybil, the heroine's sister) are tender and elegiac. Gone are the vengeful and acerbic anti-Southern asides of the London years. As Sybil and Carrington ride through the cemetery at Arlington, they are "suddenly met by the long white ranks of head-stones, stretching up and down the hill-sides by thousands, in order of battle; as though Cadmus had reversed his myth, and had sown living men, to come up dragons' teeth." Here is war without glamour: "wounds, disease, death." As Carrington speaks of his experiences, her imagination rushes "with him down the Valley of Virginia . . . or gloomily toiling back to the Potomac after the bloody days at Gettysburg, or watching the last grand *débâcle* on the road from Richmond to Appomattox." The girl is drawn to Carrington even while she stands at "the graves of her own champions," and Adams apparently is as well. For like Melville, he had begun to think of himself as a covert "rebel" against a society that outraged his sensibilities and rejected his services.[42]

Eventually the War came to signify for him a point in his country's history when the old "moral law expired—like the Constitution" and thousands of his kind were driven "into active enmity, not only to Grant, but to the system or want of system, which took possession of the President." By temperament a catastrophist, he had predicted in 1862 a time when engines would control their makers and the human race blow itself up,[43] but he had not expected doomsday to come so quickly. The duality of science, its services and disservices, its capacity for good and ill, and the incapacity of man to cope with the social dislocations it produced, haunted sensitive minds in Adams's generation as it had in Hawthorne's and Melville's. In the advancing years, the War—whose sound and fury had been too distant to touch him deeply—faded out of his consciousness, but he continued to study the currents of energy it had accelerated.

Chapter 7

Henry James

There comes back to me out of the distant past an impression of the citizen soldier at once in his collective grouping and in his impaired, his more or less war-worn state, which was to serve me for long years as the most intimate vision of him that my span of life was likely to disclose. This was a limited affair indeed, I recognize as I try to recover it, but I mention it because I was to find at the end of time that I had kept it in reserve, left it lurking deep down in my sense of things, however shyly and dimly, however confusedly even, as a term of comparison, a glimpse of something by the loss of which I should have been the poorer; such a residuary possession of the spirit, in fine, as only needed darkness to close round it a little from without in order to give forth a vague phosphorescent light.

HENRY JAMES, 1916

The Wound

LIKE that other second son and onlooker, Henry Adams—uncomfortably safe in his London redoubt and watching his uniformed older brother expand a little ostentatiously into manhood— Henry James kept his distance from the War. Only James had not one but two brothers both younger than himself fighting in the Union Army while he observed the conflict, as he says, from "the almost ignobly safe stillness"[1] of a Newport garden or in the libraries of Cambridge.

Still, the years of the War remained for him, as they were when he was experiencing them, "indescribably intensified." Or, as he put it in the language of the "late" style: "as a more constituted and sustained act of living, in proportion to my powers and opportunities, than any other homogeneous stretch of experience that my memory now recovers."[2] The frequency of his references to these years is one measure of their impact, even though his reminiscences are often suspiciously blurred, as if he were trying to screen the story of his nonparticipation behind a fog of words.

James returned to that time in *Notes of a Son and Brother* (1914), an extraordinary example of his recollective powers yet more evocative than explicit when it came to himself and the War. It conveys the intensity of his perturbations, his heavy heart and inner stress; his own secondary and derived view of the War does not prevent him from sharing "in the generalized pang of participation." But exactly what he thought and did throughout "the huge procession of those particular months and years" remains vague, for all of his volubility.[3]

As he recalled it after a long interval, the firing on Fort Sumter and Lincoln's summoning of volunteers coincided with a private "physical mishap" which he obliquely and confusingly described. He referred to it as a "horrid if obscure hurt." Somehow he knew immediately it would remain an affliction, although he gave no reason why he should have made this instant prognosis. It was enough to have suffered, in James's portentous phrase, "a single vast visitation."[4]

James's ambiguous account of this episode has provoked some dark speculations from Jamesians. (Had the Master experienced the same fate as Hemingway's Jake Barnes in *The Sun Also Rises*?) According to James's loving and relentless biographer, Leon Edel, it seems likely that the "wound" acquired while helping to put out a "shabby conflagration" in Newport amounted to hardly more than a strained back. The Boston specialist who examined him found nothing organically wrong and pooh-poohed the whole thing. Edel concurs with the Boston doctor's diagnosis, or at least part of it. What James had been overwhelmed by, he conjectures, was a malign invasion of the spirit, something akin to what his father had undergone seventeen years earlier. The Swedenborgians, whose doctrines the elder James professed, described this phenomenon as a "vastation," a portmanteau word for Henry James's "vast visitation." In other words, he had neither castrated himself nor developed a hernia, but he had suffered a psychic wound.[5]

In reporting his misadventure, James hinted that the "obscurity" (a word frequently linked with "horror" in his tales) of the wound lay in the mystery of its origins. It might have come, he guessed, "most from one's own poor organism, still so young and so meant for better things, but which had suffered particular wrong." Long after, though not at the time, he noted the parallel between his private hurt and the nation's—"the enclosing social body, a body rent with a thousand wounds." The "willing youth" of his own generation had not held back when the President issued his call to

save the Union. To have "trumped up a lameness at such a juncture," James keenly felt, "could be made to pass in no light for
graceful." But a genuine hurt at least entitled him "to the honour of
a sort of tragic fellowship"; unable to carry a rifle, he could at least
vicariously and literally suffer. It almost comforted him when the
back pain (which might have been diagnosed as the organic mani-
festation of an unconscious wound or wounded conscience) persisted.[6]

Father and Sons

James had a good deal to say in his reminiscences about the role of
his younger brothers in the War, for their activity and courage
shamed his own passivity: they *engaged* themselves in the titanic
struggle. On the other hand, he kept eloquently silent about the
nonparticipation of William James, who like himself was eligible for
the military but who found other duties to preoccupy him.* And he
had hardly anything to say about his father's attitude toward his two
elder sons and the War.

James Sr., for all of his geniality and charm, was an opinionated and strong-minded man. At times it looked as if he were
seeking his own salvation through his children. How else to explain
his almost excessive concern for their education, his habit of keeping them jumping from one school to the next, the restless shuttling
of his family back and forth across the ocean? Was the fear that his
boys might display the "extravagance and insubordination" of
American youth a reflection of his own suppressed guilt toward *his*
father whose desires he balked at and whose will he had helped to
break?[7] Did he transfer this guilt feeling in some way to William
and Henry?

Neither was easygoing. Both felt the need to justify themselves, to suffer, to undergo martyrdom, and to display a pacifistic
heroism morally equivalent to the military sort. Both adopted in
later life heroic postures and placed themselves (and in Henry
James's case, his characters) in "morally interesting" situations.
The War caught them unprepared for the national crisis.

---

* "There is no evidence . . . that William was in the autumn of 1861 preoccupied by the public questions of the day, as he was in later life—for example, at the time of the Spanish War. He expressed himself eloquently on
the issues of the Civil War in his oration of 1897 at the dedication of the
monument to Colonel Robert Gould Shaw, but this was retrospective and detached rather than contemporary. In 1861 physical frailty precluded the
possibility of enlistment" (Ralph Barton Perry, *The Thought and Character
of William James* [Boston, 1935], I, 202–3). See also Fredrickson, 158–60.

Living abroad during the turmoils of the fifties, they had not been exposed to "the rising hysteria" over the great evil their father trusted Providence to eliminate. His two darling cosmopolites were interested in other matters. Outwardly sophisticated but inwardly unsure, neither was prepared to line up with the ardent volunteers. Whether they were physically qualified to endure the rigors of marching and fighting is beside the point. Numbers of young men did enlist who in all likelihood were no more robust. But that they were temperamentally unsuited for battle and the rough camaraderie of camp life, and terrified by the prospect of physical violence, is readily conceivable, even though William James never bothered to explain why he did not enlist and Henry James fell back not too convincingly on the excuse of an injured spine.

Letters written by the elder James during this period mention the devilish time he was having trying to keep his hotheads out of uniform. "I have had a firm grasp upon the coat tails of my Willy and Henry," he wrote to a friend in 1861, "who both vituperate me beyond measure because I won't let them go. The coats are of very staunch material, or the tails must have been off two days ago, the scamps pull so hard." Or again:

> The way I excuse my paternal interference to them is to tell them, first, that no existing government, nor indeed any now possible government, is worth an honest human life and a clean one like theirs; especially if that government is likewise in danger of bringing back slavery again under our banner: than which consummation I would rather see chaos itself come again. Secondly, I tell them that no young American should put himself in the way of death, until he has realized something of the good of life; until he has found some charming conjugal Elizabeth or other to whisper his devotion to, and assume the task if need be, of keeping his memory green.[8]

Nothing in either William or Henry James's recollections, however, indicates that they ever importuned their father to allow them to run off to war. He had no intention of permitting them to enlist even if they had wanted to, and he held to this decision after he had changed his own position on the War and delivered some powerful attacks against the "diabolic pretension" of slavery.[9]

Curiously enough, the protective attitude toward his eldest sons did not seem to carry over to his younger boys. He put no obstacles in their way after they decided, still in their teens, to enlist. When Robertson James, the baby of the family, sailed with his regiment for the South in July 1863, his father was exalted:

He went off in good spirits, and though it cost me a heart-
break to part with one so young on a service so hard, I cannot
but adore the Great Providence which is thus lifting our
young men out of indolence and vanity, into some free sympathy with His own deathless life. I seem never to have loved
the dear boy before, now that he is clad with such an aureole
of Divine beauty and innocence; and though the flesh was
weak I still had the courage, spiritually, to bid him put all his
heart in his living or dying, that so whether he lived or died
he might be fully adopted of that Divine spirit of liberty
which is at last renewing all things in its own image.[10]

How James Sr. reconciled such thoughts with the inactivity of his
two oldest boys we can only conjecture.*

"The Consecrating Sentiment"

As for Henry James, Jr., the example of his soldier-brothers filled
him with remorse and humiliation: he, the older and feebler, had to
nourish himself on the crumbs of their experiential feast. Decades
later, he measured his loss and speculated on what Garth Wilkinson
and Robertson James must have gained "in wondrous opportunity of
vision, that is *appreciation of the thing seen.*" They were the actors
in "portentous and prodigious" events, he the observer, "seeing,
sharing, envying, applauding, pitying, all from too far-off." He

---

* Henry Junior could only attribute the willingness of his tender parents to
"surrender their latest born" as proof "that we were all lifted together as one
wave that might bear us where it would." As for himself, he professed to envy
his younger brothers for being "eager," "ardent," "strenuous" (*Notes of a Son
and Brother* [New York, 1914], 375–76). Garth Wilkinson (Wilky) James's
recollection of his father's "offerings" to the War is somewhat different from
Henry's: "When I went to war I was a boy of 17 years of age, the son of
parents devoted to the cause of the Union and the abolition of slavery. It
seems unnecessary to tell you that my experiences of life were small. I had
been brought up in the belief that slavery was a monstrous wrong, its destruction worthy of a man's best effort, even unto the laying down of life. I had
been spending the summer in Newport, Rhode Island, when the war got
fairly under way. To me, in my boyish fancy, to go to the war seemed
glorious indeed, to my parents it seemed a stern duty, a sacrifice worth any
cost. Not for glory's sake, nor for the vantage of a fleeting satisfaction then,
did they give me to the cause, but altogether for the reverse of these, from
the sad necessities of a direful evil, from which the alarmed conscience of
the North was smiting her children into line for the defense of the country's
life. . . . My father accompanied me to the recruiting station, witnessed the
enrollment, and gave me, as his willing mite, to the cause he had so much at
heart" (Paper read before "The Loyal Legion" and reprinted in the Milwaukee
Sentinel, Dec. 2, 1888).

remembered their letters, full of the sound and color of war. The references they contained to battles and great commanders affected him "from afar off as a vast epic vision."[11]

Rereading these letters, he conjured up the faces he had known in his youth. Memories came in clusters. The richest of them, his "nearest approach to a 'contact' with the active drama" of the War, was a visit he paid in the summer of 1861 to an encampment in Portsmouth Grove, Rhode Island. This, he recalled, was "my first and all but sole vision of the American soldier in his multitude, and above all . . . in his depression, his wasted melancholy almost." He may have been reading his own melancholy into the scene, which he likened to Walt Whitman's "tender elegiac" commemorations. Indeed, he described the few moments he spent with the convalescent soldiers in Portsmouth Grove as if he had been another Whitman. Their talk seemed to him "the very poetry of the esoteric vernacular." It pleased him to think he had to some extent "coincided with, not to say positively anticipated dear old Walt— even if I hadn't come armed like him with oranges and peppermints." Given the shortness of time, he displayed no "less of the consecrating sentiment" than the "good Walt" did—this same Whitman whose *Drum-Taps* Mr. Henry James, Jr., had superciliously reviewed in 1865.* By the time he wrote *Notes of a Son and Brother*, James had adopted a compassionate and admiring view of Whitman the "wound-dresser."[12]

He had also come to think differently about what he called "my 'relation to' the War." While it raged it seemed "a sore and trouble, a mixed and oppressive thing." By 1914, it had become "a thing exquisite to me, a thing of the last refinement of romance," and in his visionary moments he re-created the camp at Readville, Massachusetts where brother Wilky and his fellow officers temporarily congregated. There he had gaped at the beautiful and absurdly young soldiers, handsome, bearded, and tawny, and enjoyed their "shining revels." One of them, Wilky's friend and superior, Robert Gould Shaw, who would soon die with his black troops at Fort Wagner, epitomized the martyrdom of his generation: "Dark eyed, youthfully brown, heartily bright, actively handsome, and with the arrested expression, the indefinable shining stigma." So, at any rate,

---

* "Mr. Walt Whitman," *The Nation*, I (Nov. 1865), 625–26. This review may explain Whitman's dismissal of James in his conversations with Traubel. "Howells, James, and some others appear to think I rest my philosophy, my democracy," he told him, "upon braggadocio, noise, rough assertion, such integers." He forgave Howells, who seemed "to have something to say," but James remained "only feathers to me." His vogue would not last because "he don't stand permanently for anything" (*With Walt Whitman in Camden* [New York, 1915], I, 78, 271–72, 233).

the "young figures of the fallen" appeared to the older writer. They had surrendered themselves, he intimated, to a race on whose behalf his family's sympathies had also been enlisted, but he recalled his impression "vaguely sinister and sad" on seeing the Negro regiment at Readville. Although arming the blacks had been "a tremendous War measure," observing their strange collective presence made him wonder whether their white commanders had not been asked to pay an inordinate price.[13]

He never ceased wanting "to do something" for these upright and clear-faced young men, to set up each in a "sacred niche."[14] But how could he celebrate their feats of arms? He knew nothing of bivouacs and skirmishes and would not trust his imagination or secondhand reports. Deliberately or accidentally, he had missed almost every chance to study military life. Prevented by illness, he was not even present when Wilky's Negro regiment paraded in Boston en route to war.

Yet he could not have been ignorant of Wilky James's feelings as he lay wounded near to death after the repulse of his black troops at Fort Wagner. As related by James Sr. in a letter, the convalescent asked his father to preach him a sermon. The elder James, never at a loss for analogies, chose the Twenty-Third Psalm as his text. Wilky, the innocent sheep abandoned on the battlefield, had been rescued by the all-seeing Shepherd—at which point the wounded son interrupted the exegesis:

> "Ah father, it's easy preaching faith in God's care, but one night it was hard to practice it. I woke up lying in the sand under my tent, and slowly recalled all that had happened, my wounds, my fall, the two men that tried to drag me to the rear, their fall one after the other, my feeble crawling to the ambulance—when memory slept, and I here woke up to find myself apparently forgotten by all the world, and sick & faint from loss of blood. As I lay ignorant of all that had happened meanwhile and wondering whether I should ever see my home again, a groan beside me arrested my attention, and turning my head, I discerned by the dim camp a poor Ohio man with his jaw shot away, who finding that I was unable to move, crept over me and deluged me with his blood. At that moment, I felt"—here he stopped too full to proceed, and I suppose he was going to say, that then he felt how hard it was to hope in God. But the story made me realize some of the horrors of this dreadful war.[15]

One wonders whether the stay-at-home's response was the same, and whether the sufferings of his brother exacerbated his private anguish.

"A Poor Worm of Peace"

Henry James, inexperienced and averse to violence, would never be the novelist of this side of the War. Besides he held a low opinion of historical fiction as a genre and dismissed it in a letter to Sarah Orne Jewett as mere sleight-of-hand:

> You may multiply the little facts that can be got from pictures, & documents, relics & prints, as much as you like—*the* real thing is almost impossible to do, & in its essence the whole effect is as nought. I mean the evolution, the representation of the old CONSCIOUSNESS, the soul, the sense, the horizon, the action of individuals, in whose minds half the things that make ours, that make the modern world were non-existent.[16]

Even at its best, it was all "humbug that *may* amuse."

These subsequent reservations did not prevent him from trying to capture what he defined in one of his prefaces as the "visitable past," a past still resonant and palpitating. Three of his early stories do, in fact, deal with the War, but not with "the bugle's blare, the waving of banners, the marching of men." They tell of the only War he knew, the War on the home front as seen by the civilian or convalescent soldier.

What distinguishes them from the conventional romantic War story is their conscientious avoidance of the sentimental and their dry tone. What makes them interesting are the clues they contain to the author's state of mind during the War years when, in uneasy isolation, he observed his peers en route to battle or returning from it, all gallantly accoutered and bursting with a self-confidence and energy notably missing in himself. He had seen them in camp. He had visited his cousins, the Temples, in the company of two golden heroes, Oliver Wendell Holmes, Jr., and John Gray—all three enamored of the lovely Minny Temple. He had sat by poor wounded Wilky. These incidents, all flavored with his private guilt and misgivings, may have furnished ingredients for his three tales. In each, a soldier dies, a victim of duplicity yet somehow abetting the malign forces by a perverse passiveness. Clearly the alien ones are the masculine self-assured men uninhibited by Hamletism; and clearly the characters with whom James most closely identifies are invalids or noncombatants who do not have to fight and who betray the men who do.

In "The Story of a Year" (1865) a young officer, John Ford,

becomes engaged to his mother's ward, Elizabeth Crowe, a match frowned upon by Mrs. Ford, who dotes on her son and thinks the girl is shallow. Ford goes off to war, writes Elizabeth long letters which she at first vastly admires and then finds boring, is severely wounded, and returns home still clinging to life. During his absence, "Lizzie," egged on by the grim mother, goes visiting, meets an attractive civilian, and—after hearing that Ford is mortally wounded—pledges herself to the other man. Upon learning that her fiancé is alive and home, the shocked and guilt-ridden Lizzie is ready to chuck the civilian, but Ford has been told of her "betrayal." Presumably he no longer cares to live, and after blessing Lizzie, he dies. She goes through the ritual of repudiating her live lover, but he refuses (and with success, we are led to believe) her rejection.

"Poor Richard" (1867) has even fainter links with the War. Richard Maule, a moody, undisciplined young man, is in love with Gertrude Whittaker, rich, cool, and self-composed. Captain Severn, recovering from a war wound, and Major Luttrell, a pleasant if scoundrelly recruiting officer, are also interested in Gertrude, much to Richard's annoyance. As a civilian, inexperienced and at a disadvantage in having to compete with the two soldiers, he is enraged with himself and the world. Rightly suspecting that Severn has won Gertrude's love, he prevents him from declaring it on the eve of his departure by telling him that Gertrude is not at home. Severn returns to his command only to be killed by a "beastly guerrilla." Luttrell, who has connived in the deception, is accepted by Gertrude until Richard melodramatically discloses his and Luttrell's part in the shabby piece of treachery. Gertrude breaks her engagement with the Major and Richard goes to war.

"A Most Extraordinary Case" (1868) is probably the best of the three stories. Colonel Ferdinand Mason, a "war-wasted" young invalid, is rescued from his grimy quarters in a New York hotel by his aunt and transported to her country place where he can get proper care. There his aunt and her niece, Caroline Hofmann, an attractive wholesome girl, take charge, aided by a former army doctor, Horace Knight, an old acquaintance of Mason. Mason falls in love with Caroline, his health waxing with his passion. Meanwhile, Caroline and the bouncy doctor have pledged their affections. When Mason learns of this, he loses all zest for living and quietly expires, much to the doctor's amazement.

If the theory is correct that James when excluded from masculine territory would express himself through feminine surrogates, then the man who sat through the War, an invalid suffering real pain from imaginary ills, might be inclined to contemplate it from a feminine perspective.[17] Like pretty Lizzie Crowe, who received letters from her soldier-lover containing "long details of movements, plans of campaigns, military opinions and conjectures, expressed with the emphasis habitual to young sub-lieutenants," James's vision of the War was formed by similar letters written home by his two soldier brothers. Lizzie's most intimate contact with the battle scene is a rug brought by her wounded fiancé.

> A strange earthy smell lingered in that faded old rug, and with it a faint perfume of tobacco. Instantly the young girl's senses were transported as they had never been before to those far-off Southern battlefields. She saw men lying in swamps, puffing their kindly pipes, drawing their blankets closer, canopied with the same luminous dusk that shone down upon her comfortable weakness.[18]

So, perhaps, the incipient novelist imagined the distant war during the "red months." And perhaps the author of "Poor Richard" is not wholly detached from his heroine when she remarks to Luttrell: " 'War is an infamy, Major, though it *is* your trade. It's very well for you, who look at it professionally, and for those who go and fight; but it's a miserable business for women; it makes us more spiteful than ever.' "[19] James's invalids are reduced to shadows by the "detested war," but their malady lies deeper than wounds and fevers. They know from firsthand experience about a war their creator avoided, but they must yield to more robust and masculine rivals and virtually will their own deaths. However much or little subliminal history of Henry James these stories contain, it is not unreasonable to connect their passively suffering antiheroes with the young civilian who observed the "break-up of the vast veteran army" and knew he would be forever excluded from its "unprecedented history."[20]

Unconsciously he was preparing himself to be the elegist and mourner of "fine fierce young men" and rueful preserver of selected memories. The details of the triumphal day when Lee surrendered went unrecorded; the President's assassination (he associated it with Hawthorne's death a year before, at the news of which he wept) he vividly retained. In James's random recollections, Lincoln, Hawthorne, the War, and his own literary career are intertwined. Hawthorne, grieving over the War and discomfited by it, might qualify as a kind of war casualty like his spiritual heir, Henry James, who had been rediscovering him in Newport. Hawthorne's example assured James one could be a writer in America; his death may have symbolized to him the ever-widening gulf between the old republic and the new nation he would have to make his way in.[21]

The War as it reshaped the country also complicated the American consciousness. Before it ended, James knew he was going to be a writer in this different America despite the discouragements of his parents and his brother William. He shared the general air of expectation, the awareness of "big things" on the horizon, as General Grant ("no light-handed artist he!") slowly pounded his way to victory. Grant, the soldier, "was at all events working to an end, and something strange and immense, even like the light of a new day rising above a definite rim, shot its rays through the chinks of the immediate, the high-piled screen of sacrifice behind which he wrought."[22] In his own unmilitary way James, the more light-handed artist, was beginning to see the light. These grand events, culminating in Lincoln's assassination, were as important to the budding writer—victim and beneficiary of the War—as they were to Walt Whitman.

"Ashburton Place [his family's Boston residence] resounds for me with a wild cry, rocks as from a convulsed breast, on that early morning of our news of Lincoln's death by murder," James wrote in his autobiography. His memory of the springtime of 1865 was a Whitmanesque out-of-doors vision, all light and movement, until the "unforgettable death" of the President condensed everything to blackness on April 15—James's birthday:

> I was fairly to go in shame of its being my birthday. These would have been the hours of the streets if none others had been—when the huge general gasp filled them like a great earth-shudder and people's eyes met people's eyes without the vulgarity of speech. Even this was, all so strangely, part of the lift and the swell, as tragedy has but to be of a pure enough strain and a high enough connection to sow with its dark hand the seed of greater life. The collective sense of what had occurred was of a sadness too noble not somehow to inspire, and it was truly in the air that, whatever we had as a nation produced or failed to produce, we could at least gather round this perfection of a classic woe.[23]

He never came closer to making a pronouncement on the significance of the War for the artist: the legacy of Lincoln and his "mould-smashing mask."[24] War memories kept welling up in his mind throughout the rest of the century, especially during times of stress. The Anglo-American crisis over Venezuela in 1895, the Boer and Spanish-American wars, and finally World War I all aroused associations and feelings "buried under all the accumulated emotions and years." The "poor worm of peace,"[25] as James once called himself, also took pleasure in the company of old soldiers and acquired a special taste for military memoirs. But virtual expatriation insulated him from the American scene, and the enchantment of Europe, wicked and benign, dimmed the red sixties. Between the beginning of his long European sojourn in 1875 and a ten-month stay in the United States a decade later, James gave little thought to the War and its meaning.

The Blighted South

Next to *Notes of a Son and Brother,* the most revealing passages of the War's impact on Henry James are to be found in *The American Scene* (1907), which includes an account of his pilgrimage to the South in 1905. He made the visit when he was emotionally stable enough to cope with the painful recollections of the War and had already exorcized the demons that harassed his early and middle years. At least he no longer brooded over his inglorious role in wartime. James gave no hint why the South should occupy a special place in his itinerary. Probably he did not really know himself. But in traveling to the scene of a War in which he had not participated yet passionately *experienced,* he may very well have been trying both to recapture and confront half-forgotten memories.

He carried to the South some clearly defined preconceptions. The secessionists, with their grandiose and preposterous ambitions, had endangered members of his family, menaced his country, inadvertently exposed his weakness. The very prospect of visiting Richmond evoked the War years when to his "young imagination the Confederate capital had grown lurid, fuliginous, vividly tragic—especially under the process through which its fate was to close round it and overwhelm it, invest it with one of the great verberating historic names." To go southward after nearly half a century was to taste,

> mystically, of the very essence of the old Southern idea—the hugest fallacy, as it hovered there to one's backward, one's ranging vision, for which hundreds of men had ever laid down their lives. I was tasting of the very bitterness of the immense, grotesque, defeated project—the project, extravagant, fantastic, and to-day pathetic in its folly, of a vast Slave State (as the old term ran) artfully, savingly isolated in the world that was to contain it and trade with it. This is what everything round me meant—that that absurdity had once flourished there; and nothing, immediately, could have been more interesting than the lesson that such may remain, for long years, the telltale face of things where such absurdities *have* flourished.[26]

Having crossed into the territory of the "enemy," he discovered to his wonder not the "ancient order," not the "masculine, fierce and moustachioed" South of his boyhood fancies, but a feminized invalid South resembling "at the most a sort of sick lionness who has so visibly parted with her teeth and claws that we may patronizingly walk all round her." The recurring image throughout the Southern chapters of *The American Scene* is that of a pale female figure much spent by excessive bloodletting. Baltimore, Richmond, Charleston—all appeared "adorably weak," beautiful, charming, touching, and dead. In their deficiency of life, these cities (as seen through James's "inquiring" eye) bring to mind the moribund ladies in the tales of Poe. Thus he can compare Charleston, the hatchery of rebellion and quintessence of Southernness,

> to the image of some handsome pale person, a beauty (to call her so) of other days, who, besides confessing to the inanimate state from closed eyes and motionless lips, from the arrest of respiration and gesture, was to leave one, by the day's end, with the sense of a figure prepared for romantic interment, stretched in a fair winding-sheet covered with admirable flowers, surrounded with shining tapers.[27]

The discrepancy between his expectations and what he found was both poignant and anticlimactic. Once the thought of these cities had made his imagination wince; he had come to savor all of his horrendous associations of the War. What now impressed him was the enormous vacuum it had left. He pondered the absence of visible symbols, "the mercilessly small"[28] mementos of the Confederacy, the pathetic museums and meager public buildings. In contrast to the dense texture of Europe, the emptiness of the Southern scene struck him as all the more vacant, emptier even than the empty North.

This very absence of effect dramatized for him as nothing had before the exploded expectations of the Southern megalomaniacs and their plans for a slave empire with its own values and culture. It had never occurred to them that they were doomed from the start, that the rest of the world would never have recognized the achievements of a parochial slave society. Hence the statue of General Lee dominating the emptiness of Richmond suggested to James "something more than the melancholy of a lost cause. The whole infelicity speaks of a cause that could never have been gained."

> We talk of the provincial, but the provinciality projected by the Confederate dream, and in which it proposed to steep the whole helpless social mass, looks to our present eyes as artlessly perverse, as untouched by any intellectual tradition of beauty or wit, as some exhibited array of the odd utensils or divinities of lone and primitive islanders.[29]

This realization did not prevent him from being deeply affected by "such pathetic victims of fate" or sympathizing with a people "so played upon and betrayed, so beaten and bruised, by the burden of their condition." He no longer felt any rancor toward the South or judged it morally; it had become, among other things, an aesthetic problem.[30]

His artist's eye was attracted by the spectacle of a defunct and defeated section nurturing "the flame-colored *idea*" that "flowered out of the fact." He observed with fascinated interest the process whereby it tried to disengage "itself, as legend, as valuable, enriching, inspiring romantic legend," and settled down "to play its permanent part." Practically, the South was linked with the rest of the country, but theoretically, ideally—especially for the priestesses of the past (Confederate ladies with their "gentle, florid reverence"), it burned "with a smothered flame." And James perceptively observed in a sentence that presages the coming of William Faulkner: "The haunting consciousness thus produced is the prison of the Southern spirit."[31]

The culturally poverty-stricken South had been disinherited from the tradition of art and letters, but if the only music it produced was the weird chants of emancipated blacks, and if few monuments existed to serve as flares for the altars of memory, this very deprivation was a challenge. Given the South's "rich heroic past" and "fierce avenging future," how would one respond, he asked, "if one had this great melancholy void to garnish and to people"?[32] How could the present be made artistically palatable?

James himself had no interest in the blueprints of the "New South." More to his taste was the South "before the great folly" and the vestiges of the "great folly" itself—the unreconstructed South. He felt so not because he relished the vindictive, although he suspected the South (like the young country fellow he met in the Richmond museum who was ready to fight the North again) would have a "poor and unfurnished" consciousness "without this cool platonic passion." The "purged" and "renovated" were likely to become "comparatively vulgar," whereas those parts of the social organism scorched and scarred in the kiln of the "great artist," History, had happily lost their "cheerful rawnesses" in the process and "been baked beautiful and hard."[33]

Such aesthetic considerations dignified what James regarded as a "queer and quaint and benighted" culture and softened an early anti-Southern bias. Quite possibly his sympathy for the prostrate South reflected self-sympathy. Time enabled him to forgive his own failures and to sublimate his fantasies of adult tyranny; time also quieted old antipathies to the point where even beholding Fort Sumter in the company of Owen Wister (a sight that made his companion's heart "harden again to steel") left his mood of tenderness unchanged. An event that raised a host of armed men was too dim to stir his imagination, and Sumter's flag, as seen from the Charleston battery in 1861, must have been "such a mere speck in space that the vice of the act" lost something of its grossness. Besides, the lapse of forty years completely altered the scene; the innocent forts had been washed clean by time. To rage against South Carolina in 1905 would be like punishing a child for his naughtiness a week before.[34]

Elsewhere in *The American Scene,* James associated the South with images of relaxation and permissiveness. Moving from North to South had always struck him "as a return, on the part of that soul, from a comparatively grim Theistic faith to the ineradicable principle of Paganism: a conscious casting-off of the dread theological abstraction." Perhaps in this metaphorically permissive South, he found a temporary escape from the "multiplied, lurking, familiar powers" of his youth.[35]

The pervasive image of the blasted South may have had an even more personal application. He could not explain, he confessed, why he saw the South in a "painful image—that of a figure somehow blighted or stricken, discomfortably, impossibly seated in an invalid-chair, and yet fixing one with strange eyes that were half a defiance and half a deprecation of one's noticing, and much more of one's referring to, any abnormal sign."[36] To the reader, however, the Southern invalid bears a recognizable likeness to young Henry James nursing his "obscure hurt" and defiantly (though not without self-deprecation) resisting domestic and social pressures.

Rejecting Southern braggadocio, he identified with Southern pain. The South he easily moved back to was not the militant South of wartime but a South objectified in charming old Charleston houses. They spoke to him of the "less vitiated past that closed a quarter of a century or so before the War, before the fatal time when the South, monomaniacal at the parting of the ways, 'elected' for extension and conquest."[37] This was also the period when the Washington Square of his boyhood emanated a comparable charm, a time when his New York was still relatively uncomplicated and his soul unfettered.

Henry James did not exaggerate when he declared the years of the War to be the most intense period of his life. The War itself was only a distant sound to him, a glare on the Southern horizon, but few writers registered its vibrations more sensitively. Not so much the frequency but the import of his allusions, buried and overt, signifies the profundity of its impact.

Chapter 8

William Dean Howells

You might get a series of sketches by substitutes; the substitutes haven't been much heard from in the war literature. How would "The Autobiography of a Substitute" do? You might follow him up to the moment he was killed in the other man's place, and inquire whether he had any right to the feelings of a hero when he was only hired in place of one. Might call it "The Career of a Deputy Hero."

WILLIAM DEAN HOWELLS, 1890

M ost biographers of William Dean Howells have felt obliged to say something about his involvement (or lack of it) in the War, although few have reckoned it a matter of vast literary import. Howells never wrote at length about his decision not to enlist, but he dropped enough hints in passing to suggest a subsequent discomfort about his reluctance to wear a uniform. Was he psychologically unsuited for soldiering, and did he wince with guilt for the rest of his life? The question is an interesting and valid one but less important, perhaps, than the impact of the War on the man and writer.[1]

Howells never modified his belief in the centrality of the War in the American experience or doubted that militarily, morally, and politically it "was one of the grandest series of events the world ever witnessed."[2] Nonetheless, his views on its issues and consequences changed significantly between youth and maturity. In 1861, the twenty-four-year-old poet, temperamentally unsuited to hurly-burly adventure and wholly preoccupied with his literary ambitions, was an unreliable observer of the great crisis. In the post-War years an older and wiser Howells found new meanings in the War, modified his opinions of the South, and abandoned untenable convictions. By 1900 he had grown skeptical of all wars, including the "dreadful war" which had violently crushed a perhaps remediable wrong.[3] All his references to the War must thus be tallied with his state of mind at the time he made them.

The Inglorious Assignment

"Every loyal American who went abroad during the first years of our great war," Howells wrote in 1881, "felt bound to make himself some excuse for turning his back on his country in the hour of her trouble."[4] What his "excuse" was, he never made clear, but according to his own testimony, he did not seek the Venice consulship out of patriotism. "If I hoped to serve my country there and sweep Confederate cruisers from the Adriatic [part of his job was to report the presence of Rebel privateers], I'm afraid my prime intent was to add to her literature and to my own credit."[5] His letters written during 1860–61 corroborate this candid admission.

Howells's almost unseemly haste at this time to escape his military obligations, his self-solicitude, and his irritation with a war that threatened to derange "all my literary plans" are hardly endearing. Here was a young man, reared like James and Adams in an antislavery home, who as a journalist in the 1850s had found it "undeniably amusing" to play the game of "firing the Southern heart."* He had celebrated John Brown in verse ("If I were not your son," he declared to his abolitionist father, "I would desire to be Old John Brown's—God bless him!"), and he had written a campaign biography of Abraham Lincoln. But even before the shooting began, the circumspect reporter had second thoughts and changed from partisan to observer. The uproar in Columbus, Ohio, as the barracks went up and the recruits drilled did not stir him, nor did he share the elation of the young volunteers, most of them "not over eighteen," infected by "the mad and blind devil of war." To the son of Dr. Oliver Wendell Holmes (soon to bleed on the battlefields) whom he had met in Boston during the previous year, Howells wrote:

> I hear by circuitous route that you have enlisted. If so, how?, why?, when? For myself, I have not yet gone in. But who knows himself now-a-days? I certainly contemplated a zouave company now forming line of my young men friends, who

* "When they [the Southern editors] made some violent proclamation against the North, or wreaked themselves in some frenzy of pro-slavery ethics, we took our pleasure in shredding the text into small passages and tagging each with a note of open derision or ironical deprecation. We called it 'firing the Southern heart,' in a phrase much used at that time" (Howells, *Years of My Youth* [New York, 1916], 148).

offer me a privacy, on favorable terms. But as I said, who
knows himself? The hot weather comes on. The drill will be
very hot and oppressive. And whatever valor I have had in
earlier years has been pretty well metaphysicked out of me,
since I came of thought.[6]

The facetious tone of this letter and the studiedly antiheroic
pose Howells struck then and later do not suggest the riven mind.*
Even before his short visit to Boston early in 1860—a glimpse of the
paradise he aspired to[7]—Howells had consecrated himself to a
literary career that would take more than a civil war to interrupt.
Thanks to his Lincoln biography and the good offices of the President's secretaries, John Hay and John G. Nicolay, he sat out the
War years in Venice without allowing his consular duties to interfere with his literary exercises. His letters of 1862–63 tell the story
of an ambitious writer indefatigably pushing his literary wares for
the Boston market. He worries about his salary, complains of the
high cost of living, bemoans European immorality, studies Italian,
exchanges literary chitchat with his fellow writers. He basks in
Venice with his recently acquired wife after recovering from an
initial disgust with what he first regards as a class-ridden and
impure society, yet frets over his inactivity. By the summer of 1864,
America is far away. He scarcely alludes to the political and military
crises threatening his country. His head is full of negotiations with
the *Boston Advertiser*, about to publish his Venetian sketches, and
with schemes about his literary future. He is determined to capi-
talize immediately on the standing he has acquired from his European sojourn and to make a "pecuniary success."[8]

Not that he succeeded in banishing the War completely from
his mind. News from family and friends telling of Federal disasters
confirmed his doubts about its outcome and quickened his fears, and
his references to the War from 1861 to 1863 sound petulant and
despairing. The North did not really care about slavery as an issue.
Had the South been permitted to secede in peace, "we should to-day
have been a stronger and freer and better people than ever we were
before." If only Garibaldi would take command of the Union
armies—"that is, if we shall have any armies by the time he could
reach America." "Divided politically in the north, everywhere beaten
with dreadful slaughter in the field—it's sickening to read the
accounts from home, and moves one to wonder if there *is* not divine

---

* "Aren't you sorry the Atlantic goes so gun-powerfully into the war? It's
patriotic; but do we not get enough [blot] in the newspapers? I would rather
have the honey of Attic bees" (Howells to John Piatt, Aug. 4, 1861, quoted in
William Dean Howells: Representative Selections, ed. Rudolf and C. M. Kirk
[New York, 1961], lv).

interest in a good cause, and if we are fatally mistaken after all, and ours is a bad cause."[9]

For all of his bleating, Howells could not really convince himself that the War was a "bloody farce," although such an interpretation might have palliated his "desertion" from what he at first took to be a needless and hopeless struggle.* Too many people he respected were grimly optimistic and ready to justify its heavy price. And the predicament of his soldier-contemporaries, in contrast to his own civilian safety, may have given him a twinge or two even if none of his correspondents chided him for electing the pen instead of the sword. At least a degree of uneasiness is detectable in a letter written to General John G. Mitchell, in which he protested that "a certain *reluctance* (I am loth to call it a harder name) in my blood" did not unfit him, despite his "weak, irresolute faith," for appreciating heroism in others. The experience of Mitchell and other Ohio "Roundheads" seemed to underscore the ingloriousness of his Venetian assignment.[10]

He never confessed as much in so many words, but in a slight and rather silly novella, *A Fearful Responsibility* (1881), a character generally conceded to be the author "had once almost volunteered as a private soldier," but "sternly discouraged" by his doctor and urged by the president of the college at which he is a professor to complete his "projected history of Venice," he sails for Italy. He is "grieved and vexed" that no one expected him to enlist "and that his inward struggle on that point had been idle so far as others were

---

* His pessimistic reflections may have been in part inspired by Moncure Daniel Conway, a hot antislavery man and persistent critic of the administration's cautious emancipation policy. Conway wrote to Howells: "I fear it is a very atheistic war, when the Union is put above Humanity as an object. I still think that if the South should sue for terms & negotiations anything they required as a guarantee of Slavery in the Southern States would be conceded. . . . It is quite probable that the South *will* propose negotiation if Lincoln is re-elected. They *cannot* hold out, & will try & get their heel on the nation's neck again. So you see I cannot find much joy in military victories yet. To see people dying for a Union I may yet have to attack & try to break up is not pleasant" (Conway to Howells, Oct. 18, 186?, Houghton Lib.). Yet encouraging letters came from J. L. Motley predicting the destruction of slavery *"by the sword"* (Motley to Howells, Aug. 7, 1862) and from Salmon P. Chase heralding the establishment "of universal free labor as the basis of all our institutions." Chase continued: "We, that is all your friends, are expecting some grand things from your sojourn in Venice. If you do not give us a very charming book, we shall be greatly disappointed. You must beat Ruskin" (Chase to Howells, Aug. 25, 1863, Houghton Lib.). In the same vein, Charles Hale wrote: "Congratulate yourself that you have bright sunny days, and are three or four thousand miles away from the cares that are perplexing us at home. You must do something to lighten our load & light up our darker days" (Charles Hale to Howells, April 29, 1863, Houghton Lib.).

concerned." Like his creator, the professor defends his country against the slights of Englishmen friendly to the Southern cause, but he still feels pangs of guilt. When a young girl visitor tells his wife how everyone at home despises the young men who have escaped to Canada and congratulates her on having a husband "honorably out of the way," he blurts out: "I'm *dis*honorably out of the way; I can never forgive myself for not going to the war."[11]

Rediscovering the Enemy

Howells neither extenuated nor deprecated his opting out in his reminiscences and remained ambivalent about the War. The shamed stay-at-home whose literary success left something unfulfilled paid homage to action and took a critical if not remorseful view of his younger self. The elder man—pacifist, Tolstoyan convert, and espouser of Christian socialism—was both more charitable toward the Venetian consul and wryly skeptical of his early political convictions.

Howells returned to the United States in 1865 to resume his literary career. When he became assistant editor of the *Atlantic Monthly* a year later, he reviewed a number of books by Northern and Southern writers which dealt with various phases of a war he knew only by hearsay. Given his animus against slavery, class distinctions, and physical violence, his fear and dislike of Southern civilization were predictable, and although too gentle to howl for retribution, he struck out repeatedly during the 1860s against "a people inured to the practice of cruelty by slavery and all the more abominable because they believed themselves Christians and civilized." Sarcastically he complimented a West Point officer for his delicacy in refusing to accept captured Confederate cannon. Were the young gentlemen-cadets to learn that "some of the most distinguished chiefs of the treason" graduated from the Academy, or worse, allude to the "utter and inglorious defeat" of the South, it might wound the "high-toned sensibilities" of Southern students. The "truculent patricianism" of Admiral Raphael Semmes, the quixotic commander of Confederate privateers, made him wonder whether the Southerner "was not created with some important mental differences from other men." He deplored the memoirs of ex-Confederates, mainly the chronicles of rogues and poltroons, because they would poison the minds of a generation that needed to learn, if not repentance, at least to distinguish between what was "truly heroic" and base in Southern resistance: "There can be no hope for the South until it is ashamed of the cruelty, the rapacity, and the bravado which such books applaud."[12]

These animosities gradually yielded to his abiding common sense. They had not prevented him from publishing Southern writers in the *Atlantic* even before his disenchantment with Reconstruction policies. By the mid-seventies the anti-Southern fusillades had ended. Along with his liberal Republican friends who may have influenced him, he stopped blaming Horace Greeley for his part in releasing Jefferson Davis; he no longer referred to Confederate soldiers as Arkansas savages, Georgian peasants, and Carolinian vassals. Later he would find redeeming traits (piety, honesty, "some old-fashioned love for literature," "a high ideal of womanhood") in the men "who got drunk, and swore like pirates, and slashed on one another with knives." An oration by the South Carolinian diplomat William Henry Trescot made him realize in 1871 how little he knew "of that South Carolina civilization which substituted a local for a national patriotism, and finally produced the war."[13] George Cary Eggleston's *A Rebel's Recollections,* serialized in the *Atlantic* in 1874, taught the same lesson about Virginia.[14] In time he learned to distinguish between "the chivalry" (which he continued to detest no less fervently than his friend Mark Twain) and the "good Southerners" whose virtues he gradually discovered.*

Yet if he came to see "that those opposed to the Union . . . were as sincere as its friends, and were moved by a patriotism which differed from ours only in being mistaken," that not "all union soldiers were as good as their cause, or all rebels as bad as theirs," he did not exculpate the slaveholders for demanding "that conscience itself should come to their help in making their evil our good."[15]

The War Assessed

The War continued to serve as a touchstone for his broadening social consciousness and at the same time a subject for unemotional

---

* See his tribute to the antislavery Kentuckian and onetime minister to Russia, Cassius Clay, who stayed in Kentucky, risked his life, and battled his opponents in the Southern way—with guns and knives. Like the other planters, he was an anachronism, "purely mediaeval," but he had a "magnificently generous side." He shamed the scholar: "When others, who knew art and literature so very much better, were cowering before that hideous idol of slavery, he rose and dealt it a deadly blow in its sanctuary, among worshippers whose hands were instantly lifted against his life. About a book or a statue we can let him be mistaken, since he was right about humanity . . . we can fitly recognize in him the moral sense, which, if sometimes too strongly qualified by a virile force, was yet an extraordinary moral sense" (*Harper's,* LXX II [Nov. 1886], 966–67).

reappraisal. After more than a half-century, Howells could look back at his abolitionist days still convinced that slavery was the root cause of the American War. He was neither ashamed nor sorry to have written his "hymn or ode to John Brown" but admitted that the disclosure of new facts about his former hero spoiled his rapture. Brown now appeared less of a saint than some sort of Old Testament Samuel "who hewed Agag in pieces before the Lord." Howells no longer believed, as did the men of fifty-nine, in ferocious heavenly agents, nor could he condemn John Brown's trial, a fair one "as these unfair things called trials go." Virginia's response to the "invasion" of Harper's Ferry was as inevitable as the invasion itself. Indeed, the South understood Brown better than the North, for "he was of the make of its own sons in his appeal to violence."[16]

In drawing up a balance sheet on the War, Howells the realist found reasons for gratification and dismay. It had toppled slavery and with it state rights, "the superstition of the pro-slavery South," yet something precious vanished in the process: "the dignity which once clothed the separate existence of the States." War dramatized the best and worst in the nation—examples of courage, resourcefulness, and self-sacrifice and of dishonesty, stupidity, and shortsightedness. Why had he and his friends never let their concern for the slave interfere with their private pleasures? Why had they simply assumed slavery would disappear one day and been so blind to the succession of portents? Custom and submission to law, he decided, deadened apprehension, and he found "something pathetic" in the situation of a people caught in an "inexorable labyrinth." Ignorant and trustful, the nation counted upon "the good ending, as if our national story were a tale that must end well" and the "suspenses" and "thrilling episodes" were ephemeral anxieties before "the morrow's consolations." Howells, the "educated" fatalist, knew otherwise. "There is a doom for nations as there is for men, and looking back upon our history, I cannot see how we could have escaped."[17]

Possibly such thoughts grew out of his dissatisfaction with the capitalist ethos and his doubts about a war ostensibly waged to save freedom and democracy but which provided in his opinion only a modicum of liberty for blacks and precious little "economic democracy" for the poor.

Howells's ignorance of the black man on whose fate the whole War turned was no less deep than that of other humanitarian whites. Early and late the Negro was an ethical problem for him, and a troubling one, for although he despised coarse racial and ethnic prejudices from the start, he could not completely divest himself of a sort of benign racism.* In 1866 he ridiculed the Alabama Negrophobe Dr. J. C. Nott† and approved the usage "colored people" as a "legitimate euphemism" to substitute for the contemptuous term "nigger." During Reconstruction he wrote indulgently about amiable and docile Negroes (Colonel Higginson's troops were "those picturesque, brave black soldiers" and "simple childlike warriors") but condemned the "ignorant Negro rulers" who "carried into their legislation and administration the spirit of the servile raid on the plantation hen-roost and smoke-house" and were unfit to make the laws or "to do anything save to steal the public money."[18]

He was too honest and self-distrustful, however, not to question his stereotypical opinions, and further acquaintance with distinguished "Afro-Americans (I did not invent the term, I am glad to say, but I am glad to use it)" unsettled his conception of blacks as childish, meek, irresponsible people who laughed a good deal and possessed a doglike fidelity. Men like Paul L. Dunbar, Booker T. Washington, Frederick Douglass, and Charles W. Chesnutt proved to him that there was "no color line in the brain." The Negro problem, he told his readers, "may be more complex than we have thought it." Did the amiability of the blacks veil their contempt for white absurdities? He recognized how hard it was for them to achieve "industrial and economic equality" with their "limbs manacled and fettered by cruel prepossessions." The continued discrimination against black people and the ferocious disregard of their rights and liberties remained for him a disturbing legacy of the War.[19]

He had come a long way from the time when political issues seemed to him perfectly self-evident, and he no longer trusted his own or others' recollections of the past. The obscurity of motives and the unanticipated consequences of actions, planned and unplanned, struck him forcibly after the mid-seventies and colored his response to the War in all its aspects. What might be called a

* For evidence of his unconscious "primitivism," see Ann W. Amacher, "The Genteel Primitivist and the Semi-Tragic Octoroon," *New England Quarterly*, XXIX (June 1956), 216–17, and T. W. Ford, "Howells and the American Negro," *Texas Studies in Language and Literature*, V (winter 1964), 530–37, which analyze Howells's novel about a mixed marriage, *An Imperative Duty* (1891).

† "Dr. Nott makes some statements so new and important that they deserve attention. He says that the colored preachers are the worst class in the South; that the negro who cannot read and write is more moral than one who can; that the recent Jamaica troubles were caused by the colored preachers; that Frederick Douglass is a pestilent fellow and spits out the venom of a blackguard; that negroes make their nearest approach to civilization in slavery" (*The Nation*, II [Feb. 22, 1866], 228–29).

Tolstoyan vision of war was accompanied by a Tolstoyan aversion to all killing and cruelty and violence—the more organized, the more hideous. The lesson of the holiest and wickedest war was peace.[20]

This being so, it seems paradoxical that Howells, like his friends William James and Edward Bellamy, should be aroused by military heroism and fascinated by army organization. The pacifist, however, was seeking analogies between military and civilian life. As an organization, the army refuted the clichés about human nature; it was an answer to cynics who insisted that human selfishness invariably defeated nobler impulses. Soldiers competed against each other "in devotion and daring," not for "place and money." He allowed himself to speculate in 1891, as Bellamy had done in *Looking Backward* four years before, about a society organized like soldiers in which selfish actions would amount to treason and social malefactors be held "guilty of conduct unbecoming a citizen and a gentleman."[21]

Literary Consequences

Under the mask of fiction, Howells occasionally intimated his misgivings about the War and its consequences, but he knew he was not the person to attempt a major novel on this complex theme. Memories of farm boys' "wild hilarity" after Sumter stayed fresh in his mind. The very excitement of his language in recalling the first weeks of the War denotes the strength of the original impression. At the time, however, he had no inclination to write about such matters. His passions were literary, not political. He disliked speeches, rallies, meetings.[22]

"For a future novelist, a realist," he later acknowledged, "this was a pity, I think, but so it was." The scenes which so vividly unfolded themselves to the older man—the swaggering boys with their Garibaldian red shirts "bursting from their fields and shops as for a holiday," and the mystery and sublimity of their transfigurement—did not get into his fiction. Melville and Whitman were moved to write about the outpouring of boy soldiers; Howells had other matters on his mind. "But possibly," he reflected in *Years of My Youth,* "if I had written that forever-to-be-unwritten novel I might have plucked out the heart of the moment and laid it throbbing before the reader; and yet I might rather have been satisfied with the more subjective riddle of one who looked on, and baffled himself with the question of the event."[23]

This last sentence is the telling one. Whenever Howells refers directly to the War in his fiction, it is never the battleground that draws his attention (the advocate of human reasonableness dis-

trusted heroics), but the War's effect on men and culture. A character in one of his short novels loses his faith in immortality after his
first sight of a battlefield where the dead riders look as dead as their
horses, and he vows to go to Canada if there is another war.[24] The
professor in *A Fearful Responsibility* worries more about his private
shame than the War itself. And Howells in his most prolonged if
oblique look at the War is concerned with its sordid aftermath.

When Howells returned from Europe in 1865, he noted many
changes in American life—some of them deplorable—but it took a
much longer time for him to discover how the flexible society of
antebellum times had solidified into a plutocracy and how with the
disappearance of the slavery issue ("the highest . . . that ever
divided a people, or parted the just from the unjust") politics lost its
capacity "to engage the idealist's fancy or the moralist's conscience."[25]

One of his most trenchant critiques of plutocratic values, *A
Hazard of New Fortunes* (1890), links the Civil War directly with
the class war of the Gilded Age, chattel slavery with wage slavery.
Two characters in the novel are War veterans: Berthold Lindau,
who stood behind the Berlin barricades in forty-eight, and in
America lost a hand fighting to unshackle the black slaves, and
Colonel Woodburn, a Virginian and author of a book proving "that
slavery was and is the only solution of the labor problem." Both men
are cranks, yet the facts of the novel support their diatribes against
capitalist practices. Lindau's disgust for business chicanery, which
impels him to renounce his War pension, is complemented by the
Colonel's condemnation of the commercial spirit, although the Colonel is a neofeudalist. Commercialism, he tiresomely reiterates, prevented slavery from developing into "the mild patriarchalism of the
divine intention." His plan to end social disorder resembles the
benevolent and scientific authoritarianism of George Fitzhugh: a
responsible elite and a disciplined and submissive underlying population willing to accept its regimentation in turn for a guaranteed
security. Howells is obviously closer to the German than to the
Southerner, but he sides openly with neither. He covertly suggests,
however, that the post-War spoilsmen—Lindau's "oligarchy of
traders and tricksters"—may have been spawned by the War itself.
The basest mercenary motives, both Lindau and Woodburn agree,
often "led men to the cannon's mouth."[26]

Yet if Howells had deep reservations about the War's impact
on American society as a whole, he was sure its influence on American literature would be incalculable, not because it inspired much
writing of permanent value, but because it signalized a victory of
nationality over provinciality. It "fertilized the fields of thought
among us," he concluded, "as well as the fields of battle with the

blood of its sacrifice." Before the War, Howells argued, American literature was New England literature; after 1865, a truly native literature nourished by European vitality animated the American consciousness.[27]

The War provided him, as it did Whitman, with valuable evidence for his social and aesthetic credo. Howells's subsequent campaign against romanticism in literature employed some of the same words and arguments he used against the chivalric creed of the professional "Southrons." Read in this light, the defeat of the South inadvertently assured the triumph of literary realism, for the War's authentic record was embodied in the annals of the common soldier, in the careers of a handful of officers unbeguiled by military glamour, and in the lives of a few statesmen.

Not surprisingly, the War leaders with whom Howells felt in closest accord—Grant and Lincoln—were the least posturing and "heroic" in their demeanor. Neither was a "genius" in the false sense that self-flattering poets (according to Howells) passed themselves off to "the inarticulate classes" as being "on peculiar terms of confidence with the deity." True genius he defined as "the mastery that comes to natural aptitude from the hardest study of any art or science."[28]

Grant, the great soldier, moved through great events as if they were ordinary affairs. He had no love of war. He fought because it was his duty. His memoirs, "written as simply and straightforwardly as his battles were fought, couched in the most unpretentious style," bore out Howells's credo: "Great literature is nothing more nor less than the clear expression of minds that have something great in them, whether religion, or beauty, or deep experience."[29]

The natural and unspectacular aptitude epitomized in Grant's deeds and words Howells found even more remarkably exemplified in Lincoln. He embodied the national ideal because he was *not* a soldier. "Despite what ignorant poets might pipe of the glory and splendor of war," it was "only sublime in its necessity and purpose." Lincoln, the civilian, more appropriately memorialized the meaning of the War in his role of emancipator than the "military despotism of martial statues." Howells never forgave himself for failing to gauge Lincoln's "historical quality," and having missed the chance of his life in deputing a substitute to interview Lincoln in 1860, he made up for his dereliction by a lifetime of tribute. In his eulogistic vein, he sounded like most Lincoln-lovers, but characteristically, instead of dwelling upon the mystic and man of sorrows, he celebrated Lincoln's good sense and lucidity of mind. The "dateless" Lincoln incarnated sublimity—but "sublimity without spectacularity." He likened him to Tolstoy's portrait of General Kutusev. Both gave the lie to "the infernal pretension that 'genius' of whatever sort, or virtue of being a 'genius,' is a law to itself in morals and politics." Neither of these "simple, modest, and therefore truly grand" figures was "cast in the ready-made factitious mould employed by history for the manufacture of European heroes." And Lincoln especially provided the perfect model for a "democracy whose ideal is the realization in its chiefs of the same virtues which sweeten and enlighten the lowest life in the commonwealth."[30]

Like Grant, Lincoln also corroborated Howells's literary philosophy, for what was "realism" if not the honest treatment of the average and the commonplace Lincoln sanctioned and sanctified? To achieve his "simple and manly style" and "artistic sense of words," he must have "trained himself, to the study of expression, till he felt through all his consciousness the beauty of simplicity." He demonstrated that "good literature" need not depend solely on literary culture. Unlike poets and fiction writers who tended to stumble over their cultural baggage, Lincoln (and the same was true for other unlettered men who wrote of their War experiences) somehow found the right style of expression. Howells did not equate bad writing and bad ethics, but he speculated whether the slavery apologists' "habit of declaring wrong right, in defiance of reason" had not resulted in a good deal of "bombast and swagger."[31]

Perhaps his literary credo, which declared men neither saints nor monsters, enabled him ultimately to excuse his own withdrawal from the War and to judge the motives and conduct of the South with some detachment. He had not met the challenge of the War with gallantry, but he had at least been instructed by it and later aspired to a civic courage and simple humanity which he deemed superior to military glory. One is tempted to see his defense of the Chicago anarchists in 1887, when no other American writer of comparable reputation took this unpopular stand, as an unconscious desire to cancel out his unvalorous withdrawal in 1861. Although Howells never overcame his timidity or revulsion from ugly facts (violence, sordidness, brutality sickened him) his fiction—seldom entirely free of blandness and tepidity—is stubbornly controversial. It can be read in part as a sustained analysis, and sometimes a dark and mordant one, of the cultural and social dislocations that followed the war he beheld from afar.

Chapter 9

Mark Twain

*I was a soldier two weeks once in the beginning of the war, and
was hunted like a rat the whole time. Familiar? My splendid Kipling
himself hasn't a more burnt-in, hard-baked and unforgettable
familiarity with that death-on-the-pale-horse-with-hell-following-after
which is a raw soldier's first fortnight in the field—and which,
without any doubt, is the most tremendous fortnight and vividest he is
ever going to see.*

MARK TWAIN, 1890

The Comic Mask

O F the four "malingerers," Mark Twain was the only one who
could have spoken to Billy Yank and Johnny Reb in their own
languages and conceivably have written the great War book critics
like his friend Howells were calling for. He knew men and ways of
life existing beyond the hedged boundaries of Adams, James, and
Howells. Southern born, he ranged the New World and the Old, di-
vesting himself of Hannibal parochialism in the process. He mastered the American vernacular and converted it into a literary language. No author of his time understood better the appetites and
dreams of the audience he commanded and entertained. Yet the
man so happily equipped to write the national "epic" studiedly
avoided doing so. When he did turn to the War, he usually burlesqued his own connection with it.[1]

Mark Twain never studied the Civil War as war since he never
experienced it nor developed sufficient interest in it to get it up
second hand as Melville did. He was never moved to write about its
righteousness or holiness or to speak of it as a "fiery crucible" in
which a sinful nation was purified. He remained evasive about his
opinions and activities during the opening months of 1861 (only a

few sentences in *The Autobiography* touch upon the period), and subsequent allusions, with few exceptions, are sparse and offhand. Later he satirized what might be called the social consequences of the War, not hesitating to goad a whole herd of his country's sacred cows, but he resisted the impious and impolitic urge to be *openly* irreverent about the War itself. Even so, enough external and internal evidence exists to link his diatribes against war in the abstract and some wars in particular with the Civil War.

For all of his splenetic rhetoric and fascination with the macabre, Mark Twain, like most sensitive and imaginative men, disliked and feared violence. That he joked about his own cowardice or at least his reluctance to risk his life did not mean he took war lightly. His mask of antihero enabled him to escape the responsibility of stating his true feelings about what his readers believed to be a sacred cause. Americans have always granted their humorists a certain license to skirt the limits of propriety. If Mark Twain sometimes resented his ascribed role as national jester, there must have been times when he appreciated the immunity granted to clowns. He dared not reveal his private misgivings about the War and his reasons for declining to fight. The War after all did end slavery, preserve the Union, and remove the last obstructions to America's triumphant advance. But he remembered that thousands of men, North and South, had loathed it as he did and fought only because they had been conscripted or because fear of public disapproval overmastered personal fears. They would subsequently relish someone like Mark Twain, who openly confessed himself a coward like most men and sniped at the twin watchdogs—Conscience and Public Opinion.

Such an assumption is not necessarily at odds with his remark to Howells that he was "entirely satisfied with the result of the Civil War and . . . eager to have its facts and meanings brought out at once in history,"[2] or with his assertion that the emancipation of the slaves freed both white and black men.

Mark Twain's "Campaign"

The War ended Mark Twain's career as a river pilot and closed a period of his life he was always to look back upon with intense nostalgia. He might have offered his skill either to the Confederacy or the Union,[3] as did one of his pilot friends he wrote about who "died a very honorable death."[4] Instead, he returned to Missouri, where for a few weeks he served in a volunteer company organized to defend the Confederacy. After an interval of feckless campaigning, he joined his brother, Orion, and traveled by stage coach to Nevada.

Orion Clemens, as a reward for supporting the Republican campaign, had been appointed Secretary to the Governor of the Nevada Territory. What his brother's political opinions were at the time is not clear. Apparently he retained a furtive sympathy for the Confederacy until 1862. Two years later, his slanderous if unserious allegation that money raised for the Sanitary Commission had been diverted "to aid a Miscegenation Society"[5] indicated, if nothing else, a want of patriotic piety. But possibly his innuendoes against particular Unionists while on the staff of the Virginia City *Enterprise* were prompted by journalistic rivalry, not by political conviction.* Be that as it may, he steered off national issues during his prospecting and reporting days in the West, offered no comments on military campaigns, associated freely with Northern and Southern partisans, and kept silent about his own abortive adventure in soldiering.

A blend of fact and speculation surrounds Mark Twain's War career because of his inventions and exaggerations as much as his reticence, but this much seems fairly certain: early in April 1861 he left New Orleans for St. Louis, arriving there on the nineteenth— that is, one week after the attack on Fort Sumter. He stayed in St. Louis until June, after which he made a short trip to Hannibal where he and some friends formed a company of Confederate sympathizers, the inglorious Marian Rangers. For approximately two weeks these amateur soldiers played at war until bad weather

---

* For varying opinions on this matter, see Paul Fatout, *Mark Twain in Virginia City* (Bloomington, Ind., 1964); L. J. Budd, *Mark Twain: Social Philosopher* (Bloomington, Ind., 1962); J. M. Cox, *Mark Twain: The Fate of Humor* (Princeton, 1966); H. N. Smith, ed., *Mark Twain of the Enterprise* (Berkeley, Cal., 1957). Fatout argues that Mark Twain was never a secessionist and always remained loyal to the Union. As proof, he cites a letter Mark Twain wrote to a friend in September 1862 expressing a genuine concern for the future of the United States. Although certainly no abolitionist and at the outset still holding the racial bias of his section, he never advocated the Confederate cause (67–68). Budd notes that Mark Twain voted for the Constitutional Union Party in 1860, "composed mainly of former Whigs and Know-Nothings who straddled the slavery question by appealing to the symbols the new party label invoked" (66). This would suggest that even then he clung "to his old Whiggish devotion to national unity" (*ibid*). Perhaps his experience as a river-boat pilot diluted his local and sectional ties. Cox emphasizes Mark Twain's Southern leanings and interprets both his arrival in and departure from Nevada as acts of evasion, in keeping with his evasion of the Civil War itself. Smith believes that Mark Twain went to Nevada to avoid being entangled in the secession cause, but that he considered himself a Southerner and had no love for Yankees. In time he identified with the Northern side, but during the Nevada sojourn "he avoided public reference to the War or to the issue of loyalists versus Copperheads" (19).

and the rumor of Union troops in the vicinity sapped their martial zeal and they disbanded. Mark Twain retired to St. Louis after the escapade (for it was scarcely more than that) and from there headed westward with his brother on July 18.

Seventeen years later, he made his first public reference to the event at Hartford, Connecticut, and thereafter retold the story with humorous variations. Its classic formulation, "The Private History of a Campaign That Failed" (1885), is the lengthiest and perhaps most covertly revealing of all the unreliable accounts. This sketch, which he contributed to the *Century Magazine*'s "Battles and Leaders" series, describes in some detail the "history" of his military fiasco. A tissue of fact, misstatement, and invention, it is also a belated defense and apology.[6]

He begins his story with the news of South Carolina's secession on December 20, 1860. A quarrel erupts between him and his copilot, who challenges the loyalty of a slaveholder's son. Mark Twain weakly counters that his father had acknowledged the wickedness of slavery and resolved before he died to free the one Negro he owned if only he could persuade himself it was right to impoverish his family by doing so. The pilot is unconvinced. A mere impulse means nothing. But a month later, as Mark Twain relates it, "the secession atmosphere had considerably thickened on the lower Mississippi, and I became a rebel; so did he."

The origins of the Marian Rangers and the swearing in of the troop is followed by a burlesqued account of himself and his fellow soldiers as they clumsily maneuver to avoid contact with the foe. The climax occurs after several weeks of skylarking and comical misadventure when the boys mistake a stranger for the enemy and shoot him down. Horrified by the deed, Mark Twain and some of his friends decide the War is not what they bargained for, a decision encouraged by the rumor that a Federal Colonel and his regiment are about to descend upon them. The Colonel's name is U.S. Grant.

So much for the story itself, which, if it tells very little about Mark Twain's actual war experiences, raises some interesting questions about the farcical author. Why did he present himself and his companions as if they were Tom Sawyer and his carefree gang (he was close to twenty-six at the time), and how could Sam Clemens who held the responsible post of steamboat pilot ("the only unfettered and entirely independent human being,"[7] he boasted elsewhere) be related to the callow recruit of the "History"? He may have remained a boy at heart, but the so-called story of the Marian Rangers is utterly unconvincing unless read as the apologia of one who is trying to explain what he thinks might be taken as a discreditable episode. Only then does the account of himself and friends as witless innocents become understandable.

The "History," in fact, is more than an exercise in self-justification; it is also a seriocomic attack on militarism and war. Notwithstanding the breezy tone of the piece, Mark Twain is using the jester's license to undercut the reverential and celebratory *Century* series. The young Confederates, like the boys in *The Mysterious Stranger*, are a cross section of the "damned human race" in embryo, some of them infected with the false and ridiculous virus of chivalry, all of them boastful, proud, thoughtless, cowardly. And he belongs to the company he treats with contempt and affection. Like them he is gay and fearful by turn, self-deluded, ready for horseplay and frolic—that is, until the prospect of a shameful death "occurred to us as being among the possibilities of war. It took the romance all out of the campaign, and turned our dreams of glory into a repulsive nightmare."[8]

Such thoughts had not entered their minds when Colonel Ralls harangued them in a speech "full of gunpowder and glory, full of that adjective-piling, mixed-metaphor and windy declamation which were regarded as eloquence in that ancient time and that remote region." The fierce equalitarianism offered as one cause of the Rangers' incompetence typified antebellum America in general and the Southwest in particular. Missouri was dotted with "camps composed of young men who had been born and reared to a sturdy independence, and who did not know what it meant to be ordered around by Tom, Dick, and Harry, whom they had known familiarly all their lives, in the village or on the farm." Time would transform these masterless young men from ignorant yokels into "valuable soldiers" who having learned "the grim trade" would "obey like machines."[9]

In describing the death of the stranger, Mark Twain suddenly stopped his spoofing; he was offering a valid reason for his want of heroism, an excuse for his retirement. The incident, inserted into a series intended to glorify military prowess, dramatized a war not waged by idealists fighting for what they deemed to be a just cause or even by intrepid adventurers. It was a war fought by bumpkins and fanatics who pointlessly murdered each other:

> The man was not in uniform, and was not armed. He was a stranger in the country; that was all we ever found out about him. The thought of him got to preying upon me every night; I could not get rid of it. I could not drive it away, the taking of that unoffending life seemed such a wanton thing. And it seemed an epitome of war; that all war must be just that— the killing of strangers against whom you feel no personal animosity; strangers whom, in other circumstances, you would help if you found them in trouble, and who would help

you if you needed it. My campaign was spoiled. It seemed to me that I was not rightly equipped for this awful business; that war was intended for men, and I for a child's nurse. I resolved to retire from this avocation of sham soldiership while I could save some remnant of my self-respect.[10]

So Mark Twain, the humanitarian, reasoned in 1885. What Samuel Clemens of 1861 thought about such matters or why he deserted from the Marian Rangers (if his particular form of opting out can be called "desertion") will never be known. He may have told himself that he was not "equipped for the awful business," as thousands of volunteers and draftees might have told themselves with equal justice. Resenting subordination, panicky, as most raw recruits would be at the prospect of fighting, and unconstrained by a relentless military apparatus, he ran off to freedom. Given the chance, many other men undeterred by sectional loyalties or ideological commitment would have done the same. Only later, presumably, did he show any uneasiness about his decision.*

By the mid-eighties, he had reached the point where he could equivocate about War, but not then or later would he write irreverently of the military chieftains who masterminded it.† Sherman, who believed that "War is hell" and devastated Georgia, and Grant, whose alleged squeamishness at the sight of raw meat did not deter him from lavishly expending his manpower, were soldiers whose friendship he eagerly sought.

As Justin Kaplan has shown, his association with Grant is especially interesting. Grant's career fascinated Mark Twain for many of the reasons it did Howells. An ordinary man, the General performed extraordinary deeds without heroics; and although as a politician he was (to use one of Mark Twain's favorite epithets) a "chucklehead" whose administration ushered in one of the gaudiest

---

* "I was troubled in my conscience a little, for I had enlisted, and was not clear as to my lawful right to disenlist. But I remembered that one of the conditions of joining was that the members of the Guard should not be required to leave their homes except in cases of invasion of the States by an enemy. The Confederate forces had invaded southwest Missouri. I saw at once that in accordance with the terms of enlistment I was required to leave the State, and I left at once by the overland route for Nevada" (quoted in Fatout, *Twain in Virginia City*, 66–67).

† The closest he came, and this very guardedly, was his comment on "a fine oil painting representing Stonewall Jackson's last interview with General Lee." Since it lacked a title, he offered the following suggestions: "First interview between Lee and Jackson. Last Interview between Lee and Jackson. Jackson Introducing Himself to Lee. Jackson Accepting Lee's Invitation to Dinner. Jackson Declining Lee's Invitation to Dinner—with Thanks. Jackson Apologizing for a Heavy Defeat. Jackson Reporting a Great Victory. Jackson Asking Lee for a Match" (*Life on the Mississippi*, Chapter XLIV).

and most corrupt periods in American history, he was also the Great Soldier, the Hero to Mark Twain's antihero. By attaching himself, so to speak, to the General's regimentals, entertaining him, and finally by publishing and marketing three hundred thousand sets of Grant's *Memoirs*, he acquired a kind of derived honor: the man of peace linked in the public's eye with the man of war and gaining credit by this affiliation. As Whitman needed Lincoln to legitimize his pronouncements and prophecies, so Mark Twain may have seen in Grant a respectable front for a subversive author.

Thus, at a mammoth testimonial to Grant held in Chicago in November 1879, Mark Twain, coming at the end of an orgy of oratory, arose to speak to his own toast: "The babies—as they comfort us in our sorrows, let us not forget them in our festivities." In this speech, he drew a dangerously irreverent picture of the infant Ulysses trying to get his toe into his mouth—but then adroitly won his audience and Grant himself with the clincher: "And if the child is but a prophecy of the man, there are mighty few who will doubt that he *succeeded.*" Mark Twain considered his affectionate diminution of the General not only a tribute but a personal victory over a man of iron whose defenses he dissolved with laughter. This was the same Grant, so he pretended, who nearly captured him sixteen years before. He originally planned to call his War burlesque "My Campaign Against Grant," and bearing in mind the tenor of that sketch, "that war was intended for men, and I for a child's nurse," then the Chicago speech reinforces the connotation of the abused child striking back at the inflexible adult, only there he reversed the roles: the soldier was converted into the infant.[11]

Huck and Tom

An authentic part of Mark Twain belonged to the America of successful men—big generals, big capitalists, big politicians. He enjoyed mixing with Carnegie and the Standard Oil executives and religious tycoons like Henry Ward Beecher as much as they did with him. He seldom lost his impatience with mass democracy (usually depicted as cowardly and sheeplike), adhered to a stake-in-society theory of government, and distrusted enemies of the American-Way-of-Life whether they be crooks or reformers. On such questions as government and business, universal suffrage, poor relief, labor agitation, and left-wing socialist movements, his views were remarkably close to William Graham Sumner's—another War dodger.[12]

This side of his nature he incorporated in Tom Sawyer, putative entrepreneur, go-getter, and organizer who accepts the ruling code while pretending not to. In reality Tom is the aggressive male, hostile to newcomers, eager to excel, and given to daydreams in which he executes his coups with the maximum of stage effect. Appropriately, at the end of his adventures Tom is slated for West Point, after which he will be trained in the best law school in the country to prepare himself for either career, or both. He is the perfect recruit for the business campaigns of the Gilded Age: ebullient and practical and filled with a craving not only to succeed but also to humiliate his competitors.

Mark Twain's opposing self found expression in Tom's confidant, Huckleberry Finn, unbusiest of loafers, who resists scrubbing and discipline and strangles in the noose of convention that Tom is quite content to place around his own neck. As Tom Sawyer, Mark Twain slipped easily into the rapidly mechanizing post-War United States. As Huck Finn he turned into the wry observer of his own disenchantment and a dissembling rebel.* He came to see the War, which he sometimes publicly celebrated and which occasionally tempted him into sentimentality, as the nursery for pension-grabbing GAR veterans and as a prelude to the scandals of the Gilded Age.

One of the hallmarks of his humor is disenchantment, the disparity between expectation and reality; no wonder the words "fraud" and "fraudulent" appeared so often in his pages. Like Adams, James, and Howells, his response to the War was personal. The great and ennobling struggle ended for him in "the moral rot" of Jay Gould,[13] whose fraudulence exposed the fraudulence of Mark Twain's idyllic pre-War hopes.

The Fable of Catastrophe

No single work of Mark Twain's deals exclusively with his blasted dream, but one—*A Connecticut Yankee in King Arthur's Court* (1889)—may very well have sprung from the War and its aftermath.

There is no evidence he had the War in mind when he first began to work out the details of the novel. Its germ appears in a

---

* "Insofar as *Huckleberry Finn* represents history—and it represents it by creating it—it treats the Civil War as a childish adventure in which a romantic schoolboy pompously stages the freeing of a stereotypical Negro from Uncle Tom's Cabin. The whole performance is the absurdity from which Huck Finn can, after rather half-heartedly playing the part allotted him, retreat to the territory in a marvelously alembicated reenactment of Samuel Clemens' ignominious desertion from the Confederate army and flight into Nevada twenty-three years earlier" (James M. Cox, "Walt Whitman, Mark Twain, and the Civil War," *The Sewanee Review,* LXIX [spring 1961], 202).

notebook entry of 1885 (the same year he published his "Private History"), in which he imagines a battle between a modern army, replete with automatic weapons, and a medieval host.* A year later he read the introduction and first three chapters to a select group, the Military Service Institution, which included General Sherman, and then disclosed to a New York reporter the plot of the remaining chapters:

> He [the Connecticut Yankee] took a contract from King Arthur to kill off, at one of the great tournaments, fifteen kings and many acres of hostile armored knights. When, lance in rest, they charged by squadrons upon him, he behind the protection of a barbed wire fence charged with electricity, mowed them down with Gatling guns that he had made for the occasion. He found that the "education of the nineteenth century is plenty good enough capital to go into business in the sixth century with," and the next year he was running the kingdom all by himself on a moderate royalty of forty per cent.[14]

Mark Twain modified this version considerably (for example, he postponed the destruction of chivalry until the end of the book), but not its pervasive violence. The ferocious burlesque concludes with a vast slaughter and reflects his ambivalent response to the new America that emerged after the murderous battles of 1864–65. His Gatling guns, torpedoes, and mines that blow the knights to bits are the not-so-disguised correlatives of a real war fought in the upper South where (as Mark Twain says of the smashed and exploded squadrons of Merlin), the dead could not be counted because "they did not exist as individuals, but merely as homogeneous protoplasm, with alloys of iron and buttons." The chivalry of medieval Britain and of nineteenth-century America were both swept away by the machine of war "like chaff before the gale."†

* Some years before (1868) he visited an arms factory in Hartford, Connecticut, and described for his California readers the formidable properties of the Gatling gun: "a cluster of six to ten savage tubes that carry great conical pellets of lead, with unerring accuracy, a distance of two and a half miles. It feeds itself with cartridges, and you work it with a crank like a hand organ" (quoted in H. N. Smith, *Mark Twain's Fable of Progress: Political and Economic Ideas in "A Connecticut Yankee"* [New Brunswick, N.J., 1964], 111).

† *A Connecticut Yankee in King Arthur's Court* (New York [Modern Library edn.], 1949?), 434, 444. The battle of the Sand-Belt in *Yankee* resembles some of the eyewitness descriptions of the explosion of the Petersburg mine, July 1864. See Bruce Catton, *A Stillness at Appomattox* (New York, 1954), 242–43. If Mark Twain read the popular memoirs of General Taylor published in 1879, he might have been struck by Taylor's description of New England cavalrymen "strapped to their steeds" and wearing iron breastplates: "We did not know whether the Federals had organized cuirassiers, or were recurring to

Ostensibly, *A Connecticut Yankee* satirized the mind and mores of the Middle Ages as well as answering the anti-American slurs of Matthew Arnold, who had patronizingly dismissed America's lack of "distinction" and complained of the grammatical blunders in Grant's *Memoirs*,* but the theme is blurred by Mark Twain's uncertain and divided attitude toward his hero and his "New Deal." Insofar as Hank Morgan stands for the spirit of progressive democracy, humanitarianism, and enlightenment, he speaks for the author. It is less clear how he regards the brash Yankee developer, the Tom Sawyerish Hank, the "cute trickster." Whatever significance he placed on Hank's plans for renovating a backward civilization when he first dreamed up the novel, there is no mistaking their disastrous outcome.

The Old England partially transformed by the "Boss" is rural, encased in superstition, innocently cruel—an England fabricated out of books yet similar to the antebellum South. Before and after the War, Northern writers often coupled "South" with "barbaric," and Mark Twain was hardly unfamiliar with the Northern view of the War as a struggle between barbarism and civilization. In *A Connecticut Yankee* he specifically compares Arthurian "freemen" —the "big children," "modified savages," "great simple-hearted creatures," animallike, slothful, dirty, improvident, irrational, who made up "seven-tenths of the free population of the country"—to Southern "Poor Whites."† Implicit but unmistakable are the parallels he draws between the Knights (those "titled fine gentlemen who could fight better than they could spell, while religion was the passion of

---

the customs of Gustavus Adolphus. I saw a poor fellow lying dead on the pike, pierced through breastplate and body by a rifle ball. Iron-clad men are of small account before modern weapons" (Gen. Richard Taylor, *Destruction and Reconstruction*, ed. Richard Harwell [New York and London, 1955], 59).

* Justin Kaplan, *Mr. Clemens and Mark Twain* (New York, 1966), 274, 299. Despite his distaste for Grant's neologisms, Arnold found him less boastful than most Americans, and he approved of Grant's prose: "straightforward, nervous, firm, possessing in general the high merit of saying clearly in the fewest possible words what had to be said, and saying it, frequently, with shrewd and unexpected turns of expression" (*Civilization in the United States* [Boston, 1888], 6).

† *A Connecticut Yankee*, 14, 22, 88, 99, 111, 102–3, 298–99. Hank (and perhaps Mark Twain) did not scant the attractiveness, manliness, and benignity of the "big boobies." Launcelot is not unlike Henry Adams's portrait of Robert E. Lee's son, "Roony"—handsome, genial, a natural leader but "simple beyond analysis. . . . No one knew enough to know how ignorant he was; how childlike; how helpless before the relative complexity of a school. As an animal, the Southerner seemed to have every advantage, but even as an animal he steadily lost ground" (Henry Adams, *The Education of Henry Adams* [Boston and New York, 1918], 57). See R. B. Salomon, *Twain and the Image of History* (New Haven, 1961), 115.

their ladies")[15] and the self-styled planter aristocracy. The Arthurian elite, though not irredeemably bad, is hopelessly benighted. The manhood of the common folk they exploit has not been entirely extinguished, but mentally as well as physically they are in thralldom to their betters. The slave class, of course, is despised by freeman and aristocrat alike.

In this primitive land, the bulk of the inhabitants lives in huts not unlike those found in the rural South. The children of both sexes run around naked. All in all, this panorama of innocence and violence, credulity and backwardness is a touched-up composite of scenes from *Huckleberry Finn, Pudd'nhead Wilson,* and *Life on the Mississippi.* The last, in fact, could be read as a companion piece to *A Connecticut Yankee.*

Both books are littered with corpses, and although the mayhem is made ridiculous by its extravagance, Mark Twain does not conceal his anger and revulsion. When he visited the scenes of his childhood in 1882, he revived old terrors: memories of drowned boys, grotesque horrors of the Vicksburg siege, lurid steamboat explosions, atrocities of river pirates, murderous vendettas. It was as if he had never really detached himself from this world. The War simply organized and systematized the violence he found everywhere in the United States but most unadulterated in the South.

In neither *A Connecticut Yankee* nor *Life on the Mississippi* did his assault on chivalry always dissolve into comedy. Its prerogatives, whether Arthurian or Southern, enraged as much as amused him. Dixie's "wealthy, well-born ignorant swells," counterparts of King Arthur's Court, were "tinselled with the usual harmless military and judicial titles of that old day of cheap shams and windy pretense."[16] Blaming the War on the romances of Walter Scott was more than a piece of Twainian hyperbole. The post-War South still suffered from "the debilitating influence of his books" with their "fantastic heroes," "grotesque 'chivalry' doings," "romantic juvenilities," "inflated language," and "other windy humbuggeries," even while "the wholesome and practical nineteenth-century smell of cotton factories and locomotives" was "already perceptible."[17] Symptomatic of the Scott disease was the style of the statehouse at Baton Rouge, a pathetic and phony symbol that ought to have been dynamited like Arthur's knights rather than restored. "By itself," Mark Twain reflected, "the imitation castle is doubtless harmless, and well enough; but as a symbol and breeder and sustainer of maudlin Middle-Age romanticism here in the midst of the plainest and sturdiest and infinitely greatest and worthiest of all the centuries the world has seen, it is necessarily a hurtful thing and a mistake."[18]

By implication, *A Connecticut Yankee* makes the same point. Hank Morgan, the voice of Efficiency, Organization, Invention,

Progress, is the Promethean capitalist bringing intellectual light and technological power to a backward people; the Tom Sawyer part of Mark Twain believed in the aggressive entrepreneur and in his optimistic moods he was ready to celebrate him. But never unqualifiedly and never without irony. For all his pillorying of Southern stagnation and approval of Northern get-up-and-go, he displayed a not always hidden hostility to what he praised and affection for what he scorned. If he abandoned the undeveloped South, became a success, hobnobbed with millionaires, a part of him knew that the ethos he espoused bred unscrupulous men who vied with one another in devising ways to cheat their customers. His clownish Yankee tycoon, aided by a corps of fifty experts, appears to be on the brink of succeeding, but the transformation of England from "backwardness" to "progress" occurs between chapters. Anticipating Henry Adams's dire prophecy to his brother about the coming explosion of the world, Arthur's newfangled realm blows itself up.

Mark Twain does not fully support either the progressive or nonprogressive sides in the final showdown of England's civil war. The people cling to the nobility as the poor whites clung to their leaders centuries later. They may be stupid and cloddish and naïve, but they are loyal. What is more, if Merlin's civilization is primitive and superstition-ridden, is the "new deal" of the Boss with its soap and telegraph wires vastly superior? Tom Sawyer would say it was, but not Huckleberry Finn, through whom Mark Twain conveys his affection for preindustrial America and his misgivings about the technological society of the post-War years.

There are grounds for supposing he was unable to commit himself to either side in his home-grown civil war. The South charmed and repelled him. He saw it as a frontier pocket, a kingdom of slipshod loafers blighted by slavery before the War and cursed after the peace by the legacy of the master class. Resisting everything new and experimental, it clung to its punctilios and asinine codes. But by 1900 it had become the friendlier and less rigid "delectable land" of his boyhood, backward and "chuckleheaded" yet the nourisher of his imagination, a South excessively punished for its childlike presumption.[19]

If Mark Twain loved and hated the South, he admired and resented the busy and prosperous section that honored and rewarded him. According to Henry Nash Smith,[20] he first envisaged Hank Morgan as a kind of folk hero who would transmogrify a sleepy backwater society into a mechanized utopia. Between the start and finish of A Connecticut Yankee his confidence soured. The America he hoped for, modern and progressive but still imbued with antebellum virtue, had gone whoring after dollars, and it sanctified success no matter what methods were used in obtaining it. The transformation of Hank Morgan, liberator, into Morgan the vengeful "abolitionist" midway through the book reflects the author's changing point of view. What began as a good-humored burlesque of chivalry ended in a ferocious assault against the agencies of industrialism from which he had once hoped so much. It was as if he were recoiling from the Yankee enterprise* and rebelling once again, as he had in 1861, against the aggressive idealism of the North. Faced at that time with the choice of fighting with one of the two armies or "lighting out for the territories," he chose the latter course. Neither then nor later would he submit himself to the mechanical discipline (symbolized by the army) he at once admired and despised.

In some notes he wrote for an essay on history, Mark Twain jotted down the steps of America's degradation. The decline set in with the consolidationist schemes of Cornelius Vanderbilt and the discovery of gold in California. Next came the War, followed by the swindling practices of Jay Gould, a personification of national degeneracy. It culminated in further industrial consolidation (epitomized by the Standard Oil Company), an imperialist war, the seizure of the Philippines, and the financial hegemony of Morgan— not Hank Morgan but J. P.[21]

He never weighed the importance of the War in this sequence. Whether cause or symptom of change, principle or agent, he did not say. By the early 1870s, however, he seems to have realized the War was not going to produce the millennium even though it had destroyed an iniquitous institution. Inadvertently, it turned him from a proud and contented steamboat pilot into a great writer and a ravaged spirit. Post-War expansion, particularly the growth of the mass media, created a huge audience for him which he captured with a tactical skill he had never shown in his private campaign.† It also hitched him to a system that compelled his loyalties while it violated the truths of his secret self.

* Mark Twain's shifting attitude in *A Connecticut Yankee* was paralleled by the abrupt change of Northern opinion toward the South during the first year of the War. Before Bull Run, Northern writers found Southern opinions and manners comical if not always endearing. Then Northern ridicule of the South turned into hatred. Southern chivalry no longer provoked smiles; it was an evil to be extirpated. Perhaps the triumph of Merlin over Hank at the conclusion can be said to symbolize the success of Southern writers in romanticizing the Old Cause in their fiction and the rehabilitation of the chivalric myth in the books of Thomas Nelson Page and others.

† "It is easy to see, when one travels around, that one must be endowed with a great deal of genuine generalship in order to maneuvre a publication whose line of battle stretches from end to end of a great continent, and whose foragers and skirmishers invest every hamlet and besiege every village hidden away in all the vast space between" (*Mark Twain's Letters to His Publishers, 1867–1894*, ed. Hamlin Hill [Berkeley and Los Angeles, 1967], 31).

Part Four

DRAWING-ROOM WARRIORS AND COMBATANTS

WILLIAM DEAN HOWELLS WROTE TO JOHN W. DE FOREST, JUNE 1, 1887, enclosing an editorial from the Boston *Transcript* "in which you will find yourself pleasantly mentioned." Observing "more in sorrow than in anger" that neither Howells nor Henry James had written a military story like Prosper Mérimée's "Taking of the Redoubt," the nameless critic continued:

> The remark is elicited by reflections on the few really good works of fiction bearing on the American civil war, and not by any failure on the part of Messrs Howells and James to live up to any promise to write stories of the Rebellion. Those gentlemen, like Thackeray, probably feel that they would be in the way as military novelists. When the fighting begins they go below and leave the gallant fellows above unobstructed to work the guns and do all other things warlike for such cases made and provided.

Howells, with his "power of minute observation," might still "write something with drums and trumpets in it" if he wanted to. "He came home when the heat of the contest still glowed in the face of the country, and no one better than he could sketch a society born and reared civilian profoundly stirred out of its old hum-drum, peaceful ways by the sudden intrusion of the military element." Yet even Howells would have to make the War scenes incidental to his story, for he had lived in Italy during "those eventful years." The only troops he saw were Austrian. As for James, "no body more martial than the Home Guard, and that of a section very exclusive," would hold his "analytical attention." Only a few works of Civil War fiction were "both good stories and good literature," and of these the editorial ranked De Forest's War novel among the best.*

The paucity of "good" War literature was not unrelated to the paucity of novelists and poets instructed or concerned enough to write it. Most Northern writers hated slavery, despised Southern traitors, and welcomed the centralized nation they felt destined to emerge from the War, but their self-appointed roles as bards and prophets removed them too effectually from the theaters of conflict. For reasons of age (many were in their thirties), temperament, health, family responsibilities, they disqualified themselves (as the poor could not) from military service and supported the Great Cause as soldiers of the pen.

A small number of their peers, however—educated men for the most part from roughly the same social background—came by choice or accident to look into the face of war and were able to convey something of its hard reality. A few of the combatants mentioned in this section could be described as primarily men of letters. Some reported the War objectively; others wrote private responses to killing and dying or tried to communicate to nonparticipants the ecstasy of sacrifice. The attitudes these gentlemen-soldiers displayed both consciously and unconsciously, what they saw and did not see, recognized or were oblivious to, say a good deal about the class aspects of the War.

For the three writers singled out for extensive treatment, John W. De Forest, Ambrose Bierce, and Albion W. Tourgée, the War in which they fought and suffered was the most important event in their lives. Each in his own way was obsessed by it and tried, occasionally with considerable success, to write truthfully about the experience of war itself and in particular of its implications.

* J. W. De Forest Papers (Beineke Lib., Yale).

Chapter 10

Gentlemen of Peace and War

*At this point the war got the floor again—the ten minutes quite up.
I was not sorry, for war talk by men who have been in a war is always
interesting; whereas moon talk by a poet who has not been on the
moon is likely to be dull.*

MARK TWAIN, 1883

*It happens rarely that poets put their delicate-fibred brains in the
paths of real bullets, but it does happen.*

OLIVER WENDELL HOLMES, 1865

If you cannot shoulder a musket, you can blow a bugle.

MRS. C. M. KIRKLAND, 1863

The "Elevated" View—Stedman, Taylor & Co.

THE effusions of warriors in mufti like Richard Henry Stoddard, Thomas Bailey Aldrich, George Henry Boker, and Edmund Clarence Stedman are forgotten with good reason. Talented and in many ways sympathetic men, their elegies, eulogies, satires, and ballads on the theme of war were largely rhymed propaganda ground out for the home front. A few of them made some effort to see the real War. Bayard Taylor, traveler, lecturer, and poet, visited some military camps before accepting a diplomatic post in Russia. Stedman wrote a vividly "literary" account of the Bull Run disaster for the New York *World*[1] and reported the Union defeat at Ball's Bluff—his last glimpse of real battle. Neither they nor the vehemently patriotic civilian writers broke through the smoke of ideology to behold the larger dimensions of the War.

For literary men who took small interest in politics, the War was an annoying interruption,* and it was task enough to water the gardens of the Muses during the four-year drought. "These war times are hard on authors," Bayard Taylor complained; "the sword of Mars chops in two the strings of Apollo's lyre!"[2] It was also hard not to be caught up in the issues of the War or to ignore its presumed consequences. Whatever their political and aesthetic differences, the literary publicists belonged to the elect of "acute large-active minds" who saw in the War a chance to establish "a centralization of thoughts, feelings, and views on national subjects." They were the conscious or unconscious adjuncts of those scientists, scholars, clergymen, political theorists, journalists, and politicians bent upon converting "a loose aggregate of sovereign or semi-sovereign states" into "a single central object of love and devotion."†

The dream of a nation directed by an "ideal aristocracy" gave them what George Godfrey Leland, author and editor, called an "elevated"[3] view of the War. It encouraged them not only to write poetic exhortations but also to campaign on the home front against Copperheads, to write and disseminate "correct" opinion to the nation's press, to address meetings and assemblies. Toward the Southern enemy they presented a stern collective face. None would have disagreed with Norton's description of enemy leaders as "men in whom passions have usurped the place of reason, and whose understanding has been perverted, and well nigh, in moral matters, extinguished by long training in the seclusion of barbarism, and long use in the arts of self-deception."[4] Slavery appeared to them an ugly stigma of barbarism, and while differing in their notions on the Negro and his capacities, they were ready to prolong the War if necessary to assure slavery's extinction.‡ All, after first misgivings

---

* Stoddard remarked almost petulantly that an anthology "of amatory verse from the best English and American poets" which he and Bayard Taylor were preparing might have succeeded but for the "impending shadow of our great Civil War" (*Recollections Personal and Literary*, ed. Ripley Hitchcock [New York, 1903], 274). Some years later, Stedman recalled how Stoddard, Taylor, and others "found their music broken in upon by the tumult of a national war" (*Poets of America* [Boston and New York, 1885], 379).

† Wolcott Gibbs to F. L. Olmsted, Nov. 6, 1861, Olmsted Papers, Library of Congress. In the same spirit, Stedman wrote to his mother in 1861: "So soon as this fight is over, we propose to shoot ahead of Great Britain in arms, navies, art, literature, health, and all other elements and appendages of national greatness" (E. C. Stedman, *Life and Letters of Edmund Clarence Stedman*, ed. Laura Stedman and G. M. Gould [New York, 1910], I, 245).

‡ Writing from St. Petersburg, June 19, 1862, Bayard Taylor declared: "since I am again in Europe I don't want the war to end *too soon*. The longer it lasts, the more certain is the doom of slavery. And if the war is over without slavery being utterly crushed, we shall have a second war in ten years" (Stedman, *Life and Letters*, I, 388).

about the "ignorant, ungainly, silly, Western Hoosier,"[5] President Lincoln, eventually backed him and in the end exalted him. He figured in their poems and orations as a benign distillation of the common man. It is hard to imagine many of them any more socially at ease with Uncle Abe than with the common soldiers they sincerely but distantly applauded.

Edmund Clarence Stedman might serve as the prototype for the "squires of poesy" who "entered on the vocation of literature" in the "savagely unpropitious" fifties.[6] Yale man, journalist, stockbroker, and poet, he professed to have been *"rejuvenated"* by a war that gave significance for the first time to "the hackneyed stars-and-stripes." Heretofore, he wrote to his mother in 1861, politics disgusted him. Now the "Homeric grandeur of the contest" and the heroic conduct of the "lowly" and "simple-hearted" soldiers restored his faith. The "right and noble" War, besides providing an outlet for his adventurous spirit, promised to redeem the nation physically and morally* and chastise the "domineering insolent, irrational, haughty" slaveholders. Their "bitter and criminal hatred" had touched off the conflict, not slavery: *"we are not fighting the negro's cause.* Slavery has been the cause of the war in no sense other than that it has added another distinctness to the line betwixt North and South which climate and race had already drawn."[7] Reversing himself two years later, he held the "great slavery cause" responsible. But neither then nor after did he allow the Negro to be the equal of the Caucasian.[8]

During his brief stint as war correspondent, Stedman came closer to the real War than any of the drawing-room poets, but from 1862 to 1865 he and his friends remained patriotic bystanders† who memorialized the War in derivative verse. "O Brother bards," George Henry Boker cried out,

---

* "The base passions attendant upon scheming and money-grubbing are laid aside for simple, chivalric, national love and hate, and henceforth the sentimental and poetic will fuse with the intellectual to dignify and elevate our race" (*Life and Letters,* I, 242). Stedman echoes here the sentiments of his favorite poet, "Tennyson, my master" (*ibid.,* 188).

† Until January 1863, when he left the Attorney General's office in Washington to take a Wall Street job, Stedman professed to be emotionally involved in the War. "I do my duty from day to day," he wrote to R. H. Stoddard, "according to my strength, daily thinking more of the affections, their culture and enjoyment—and less of ambition. Who, indeed, amongst the suffering and devotion here present, can be so base as to think of self. The humanities here developed by lowly men are grand and worshipful, whether wasted in a mismanaged cause or destined to win it finally. So Walt Whitman seems to think; he is in town, and for a month has devoted himself to the hospitals. I don't know him, though he passes me daily; but I guess he has a good heart and is a noble fellow, despite his erratics" (*Life and Letters,* I, 308–10).

Now is the time, if ever there was,
    To strike aloud the sounding lyre,
To touch the heroes of our holy cause
    Heart-deep with ancient fire.[9]

His brother bards needed no encouragement to "fill with passion" the "Nation's choral mouth."[10] They sent congratulatory messages to each other on the publications of their ballads, hymns, and elegies*—verse possessing less vitality and concreteness than the newspaper stories that prompted them. The War, in fact, seemed hardly more to them than a timely source for heroic themes, the death of Lincoln the subject for an ode.

Lincoln's assassination, the report of which transformed New York City into a "vast mausoleum," aroused in the amiable Stedman more wonder than grief. "You know," he wrote to Bayard Taylor, "that a *vulgar* woman appears a lady *in mourning;* and that a lady is never so elegant as when in black." Like Whitman he dramatized Lincoln's death as the climax of a national tragedy that "faultlessly preserved" the unities. Unlike Whitman, he read into Booth's deed "the unpardonable sin" of the South and claimed for himself and his friends "whose eyes were ever anointed to discern the right and the sure," the prophetic vision to divine the effects of this last somber act "on the future of human progress."[11]

War Poets on Sea and Land—H. H. Brownell and N. S. Shaler

Frederick Law Olmsted wrote to his wife, June 11, 1862, of the suffering he witnessed in his work with the United States Sanitary Commission. "The horror of war," he told her, "can never be known but on the field. It is beyond, far beyond all imagination."[12] Certainly it was beyond the imagination of the genteel poets, some of whose "perpetual, pistareen, paste-pot work," as Whitman described it, "sung" the War. Even Melville and Whitman, vicariously suffering with the fighting men, barely suggested the terrors of the field. Their best war poetry tended to be philosophical and personal.

* "Poets are the heroes who proclaim through their golden trumpets, the coming of the host that is to make their warnings good by its deeds," Oliver Wendell Holmes wrote to George Boker in 1863. Thomas Bailey Aldrich confessed himself so overcome by the swelling rhythm of one of Boker's poems that he had to brace himself against the mantel. The soldier-reader, Aldrich assured him, would feel "he'd got an encouraging letter from home" after reading one of Boker's poems (E. S. Bradley, *George Henry Boker, Poet and Patriot* [Philadelphia, 1927], 112). Civilian War-poets apparently believed that their versified propaganda fired the hearts of soldier and civilian alike.

Two poets wanting the genius of either composed scenes and episodes of the War with unusual graphic power. They had watched or engaged in the events they versified, and they possessed sufficient skill and passion to make them come alive. One transcribed his impressions while they still palpitated in his mind; the other waited many years before he set them down. Both, for all their roughness and clumsiness, depicted the face of war.

Henry Howard Brownell never considered himself a real "poet" until Dr. Holmes designated him "Our Battle Laureate" in 1865.[13] Reared and educated in East Hartford, Connecticut (he graduated from what is now Trinity College in 1841), he taught school in Alabama, practiced law, wrote popular history, and published two volumes of undistinguished verse before the War gave him a subject and a cause to kindle his small poetic flame.* He watched the approaching convulsion with more prescience than most ("World, art thou 'ware of a storm?/ Hark to the ominous sound,/ How the far-off gales their battle form,/ And the great sea swells feel ground!"),[14] and his strong antislavery convictions found increasing outlet just before and after secession. These poems, more earnest than artful, appeared in the Hartford press and attracted little attention. Brownell's fortunes changed when his ingeniously rhymed reconstruction of Captain David G. Farragut's orders to his ships before the assault against New Orleans led to an exchange of letters between the two men. An invitation from Farragut, after Brownell had expressed a wish to watch a naval engagement, resulted in his joining Farragut's staff as master's mate at the end of 1863.

Brownell wrote a number of poems included in his modestly titled *Lyrics of a Day, or Newspaper Poetry, by a Volunteer in the U.S. Service* (1863) aboard Farragut's flagship, *Hartford*. He had always loved the sea and was something of a sailor before he served his "grand old Senior, strong and mild,"[15] but it took a series of minor engagements and the stunning battle of Mobile Bay to demonstrate his poetic mettle. Farragut, who assigned him the task of "taking notes of the action," mentioned in his dispatches that Brownell had performed his duty with "coolness and accuracy."[16]

"The Bay Fight," Brownell's most impressive War poem, commemorated the successful penetration of Farragut's fleet into Mobile Bay and the subduing of the Confederate forts guarding the approaches. It told at length in irregular stanzas and in pulsating

---

* "I have often thought that the uplift of enthusiasm and incentive which the Civil War brought to so many was a leaven to the whole nation, that more than compensated for all the tremendous cost" (J. T. Trowbridge, "An Early Contributor's Recollections," *Atlantic Monthly*, C [Nov. 1907], 588).

three- and four-beat lines the full story of "the glorious deed." In his
zeal for accuracy, Brownell followed the sequence of battle almost
too faithfully. Nothing of importance mentioned in the official
report escaped his attention: the deployment of vessels against the
forts, the perilous passage through the mine fields and the explosion
of the ironclad *Tecumseh,* and the final assault on the monstrous
Confederate ram, the *Tennessee,* when "Half the fleet, in an angry
ring/ Closed round the hideous Thing," and "the huge Sea-Hog/ Lay
on the tide like a log" and "vomited flame no more."

Farragut's flagship would be out of place in any romantic sea-
scape. Scarred from the "River-Wars" after running the Confederate
batteries below New Orleans in April 1862,* its wounds

> . . . were leeched with clamorous skill,
>   (Surgery savage and hard,)
> Splinted with bolt and beam,
> Probed in scarfing and seam,
>   Rudely linted and tarred
> With oakum and boiling pitch,
> And sutured with splice and hitch.
>   At the Brooklyn Navy-Yard!

The guns—Dahlgren, Parrott, and Sawyer—are likened to bluff old
sea lawyers who "talk" to the Rebels; the ship shudders as the great
guns leap. "Clouds of splinters" fall in "oaken showers"; decks
slicken with blood:

> Red, from main-mast to bitts!
> Red, on bulwark and wale—
> Red, by combing and hatch—
> Red, o'er netting and rail![17]

All of Brownell's sea battles resound with "crashing, splinter-
ing, and pounding." The steam-pumps throb; broadsides pound
away; the "long gun-deck" of the *Hartford* is "Two hundred feet of
hell!"[18] Dr. Holmes pardonably exaggerated when he wrote in the
Atlantic:

If Drayton had fought at Agincourt, if Campbell had held a
sabre at Hohenlinden, if Scott had been in the saddle with
Marmion, if Tennyson had charged with the six hundred at
Balaklava, each of these poets might possibly have pictured
what he saw as faithfully and as fearfully as Mr. Brownell

---

* The *Hartford* received thirty-two hits. See Bern Anderson, *By Sea and
River. The Naval History of the Civil War* (New York, 1962), 124.

has painted the sea-fights in which he took part as a combatant.*

A fervent antislavery man, Brownell did not mince his abhorrence of Southern secessionists. The foe is "valorous" but "villainous." They are "pirates," "tyrants," and "traitors." But in his poems "flung up by the strong Tide-Rip of Public Trouble," he explained in 1864, "I have chanted of Treason and Slavery, sometimes fancifully or passionately, perhaps—always fairly, in effect, I hope." He knew good men in the South who had managed to convert slavery "into something at least not absolutely shocking to the senses," and he refused to blink away Northern complicity. "It is now these many years," he bluntly told his readers, "that we have held an uncommonly large Candle (saving your presence,) to the Devil. It is going out, and the snuff and smoke come under our noses pretty strongly —but he won't let us drop it, as long as a spark remains to light his work withal. Let us bear it as we may, and not make matters worse by trying to puff it alight again."[19]

A reviewer in 1866 criticized with some justice Brownell's "mishapen" stanzas, his unnecessarily rough versification, the lines "as turgid as a city gutter after a heavy rain," but acknowledged the strength of his "uneven genius," his "general disregard for what passes as poetry among the present school of minor versifiers."[20] The same might be said of the equally rough but "poetically impressive" War poems of Nathaniel Southgate Shaler, dubbed by a *Nation* critic as "the Crabbe of the battlefield."[21]

Shaler, an eminent Harvard geologist in the post-War years, was born in Kentucky and educated at Harvard, where his Connecticut-born father had preceded him. His mother's Virginia ancestry and his close ties with friends and kinsmen who chose the Confederate side complicated but did not confuse his loyalties when he joined the Union army in 1862. Although his sympathies at the time "were altogether with the South,"[22] his reason kept him Unionist, and he resisted the arguments of his secessionist comrades—some of them fellow-students—to line up with the Confederacy. As a self-styled "Unionist of the States'-Rights group," Shaler convinced himself that state prerogatives were only safe in a strong Union and that Lincoln's government rightly warred to preserve it. Slavery, which he regarded as "mainly an ancient

* *Atlantic Monthly*, XV (May 1865), 589. "I do not wish to waste words, nor to exaggerate. In my opinion these poems of yours are master-pieces,— unequalled for picturesque brilliant detailed descriptions of sea-fights; hardly to be paralleled for vigor and effect in any poems that I know" (O. W. Holmes to H. H. Brownell, Jan. 13, 1865, Houghton Lib.).

unhappiness" imposed upon the South, was nonetheless (as he wrote to a Southern correspondent) an anachronism.

> There is a civilization possible having negro slavery for its foundation, and a cultivation not wanting in many elements of moral and intellectual beauty; but it is a civilization and society of the Middle Ages with the lighter circumstances of the nineteenth century—a feudal castle with modern furniture. Such is the society south of Mason and Dixon's Line. The North, on the contrary, is the creature of the day, never behind the march of nations but a pioneer.[23]

So said his head. In his heart, he felt an alien in Cambridge where he was enrolled in the Lawrence Scientific School under Professor Agassiz. An "intangible something" chilled familiarity although a few hospitable families friendly to the South received him. George Ticknor, "more of a Southern sympathizer than I was myself," Shaler later recalled, went out of his way to welcome him. He seemed to like Southern "tone," perhaps because Ticknor's "studies of Spanish history and literature had developed in him a fancy for the mediaeval type of man and society." Shaler understood the coolness of the anti-Southern faction, especially after the "dastardly assault on Sumner," an act "as much execrated in Kentucky as in Massachusetts." Nevertheless, the "hard things" he constantly heard against his people made him feel as if he were "in a hostile country, where toleration was a matter of courtesy and not of right."* When he returned home to enlist, he did so without enthusiasm. War was a business to be handled "in a hard, reckoning way." He would do his best "to support the Union, as I would do the like for any business institution in which I was concerned." At the same time, he would try to defend "the rights of the several States."[24]

He was commissioned captain in 1862 with orders to raise an artillery battery. His war activities were pretty well confined to the Kentucky theater, where he took part in the defense of Cincinnati against the threatened invasion of Braxton Bragg in September 1862 and helped to intercept the thrust of Morgan's Raiders into Ohio the following year. Ill-health compelled his retirement in 1864,

---

* "I am inclined to think it is a secondary effect of Puritanism, which offsets the method of contact of man with man. Some slight, but yet important peculiarity in the way people look at or greet you or pass you on the street with no sense of your existence—matters of no weight, save for the fact that primitive-minded folk are as blindly sensitive as are dogs and other animals to the manners of folk about them" (*The Autobiography of Nathaniel Southgate Shaler* [Boston and New York, 1909], 200).

but he saw enough fighting to know what authentic war was like (always for him "Satan's work") and to learn its terrible lessons.

These experiences he incorporated in *From Old Fields,* a post-humously published volume of poems which related in "unmusical blank verse" his autobiography of battle and presented "the sordid, tragic, commonplaces of war with an undeluded eye."[25] Without ever questioning the justice of the side he fought for, Shaler spurned mean partisanship and treated his adversaries with compassion and respect. Many of them were boyhood chums, possessors of "a certain fine negligence and prodigality of nature" always attractive to him, and as a Kentuckian, proud of his state, he could admire their courage and devotion if not their cause.[26]

In his vignettes of Kentucky's civil war, Shaler aspired to rescue the past from "enduring silence," but he also intended to counteract romantic stereotypes of military life by emphasizing the unglamorous side of war. He spurned the spit-and-polish soldiers "tricked-off" in holiday gear for the grubby veteran, "a burthened, dirty peddler" with "half-hundred weight upon his back." His armies, commonwealths in motion, resembled a rabble. Under pressure "this mob/ of farmers, shopmen, smiths, a folk in arms," coalesced into destructive machines. His veteran brigades confronted each other

> Not as you see them pictured in fair rows
> Like garden plants, but scattered creeping men
> By ones and twos and threes that slip right on,
> Kneeling to shoot, running to win their way,
> And sometimes toppling when the way is lost
> For this world's faring.[27]

Shaler knows war's "infernal splendour," but charging men and exploding caissons only provide the background for grim or farcical incidents. "Near the Front" discloses a village street at midnight. A harvest moon illuminates the burned and gutted houses. Corpses line the sidewalks, their feet in "dusty gutters" and "shaped as they'll lie/ Within the trenches ere the shovelers/ Have done their part." Wagons, guns, and ambulances pass by them to the front: "The creaking wheels/ Crunch on the loosened stones two feet away/ From outer line of heads, and send the dust/ Upon their senseless eyes." A soldier, his blood seeping from a loosened bandage, quaveringly cries for water. A woman moves stealthily among the dead men, "scanning the faces upturned to the sky"—then disappears.[28]

In "The Marksman's Work," two "silent lines" are poised for battle, each side waiting reports from "belated scouts." Sheep browse between the Federal and Confederate pickets a thousand yards apart while on a housetop a young officer sketches the Yankee position, a fleck against "earth and sky" yet "with the glass" changed to "near neighbor." At orders from the commander, a Minnesota sharpshooter, "A lank grizzled fellow, with the eye,/ Blue-grey and strangely steadfast, of the sort/ Who have the slaying habit," pots the sketcher:

> There he goes
> Backward behind the ridgepole, while his sketch
> Flits down the roof towards us. As the face
> Slips out of sight, we see the startled look
> That comes upon it when the man knows death.

Silent and uneasy, the Yankee soldiers "Keep eyes from others' faces and seek out/ Some trifling thing to do."[29]

Not all of Shaler's anecdotes deal with "Satan's work." A number dramatize interludes when Johnnies and Yanks momentarily halt the killing and comfortably fraternize. Firing stops when a country girl insists on crossing a contested field to join her mother and is escorted by a Federal general to the Confederate lines. A young artillery officer modeled after Shaler beats three mutinous soldiers with his sword, ties a rum-soaked demon to a caisson wheel, and blasts his men with fiery curses before they accept him. One poem anatomizes the army mule. Another relates the decision of a Federal officer to permit a coffin filled with surgical instruments to pass over to the Rebel lines.[30]

From Old Fields is amateur poetry, often long-winded and repetitive yet redeemed by its hard fidelity to what Shaler saw and heard. His Confederate troopers, "centaurs, knit of man and horse," are authentic, and so is his description of an attack against a fort

> When half a mile up fellow veterans crouch
> In grinning patience, waiting till you come,
> What's left unrent by cannon, blown and spent
> For last hard greeting at the rifle's mouth,
> Or spit of bayonet that hurls a chap
> A ragged bundle down the way he came.[31]

William James was right when he observed in a letter to Shaler's wife that her husband's poems, with their nobility of sentiment and vulgar realism of detail, copied "no special model."* Few Civil War

---

* "It is a most moving and grasping work, with a great epic wind of sadness blowing all through it in spite of so many lively individual touches. These all seem to me cut on a vast background of landscape, and human

writers evoked the heroism and animality of battle with comparable power.

Gentlemen-Soldiers—Captain O. W. Holmes, Jr., and Others

The hero of Henry James's novel *The Bostonians* resembles Shaler's chivalrous Southerners in character and spirit. In one scene James takes his ex-Confederate Mississippian on a visit to Memorial Hall in Cambridge, Massachusetts, a huge pile—"buttressed, cloistered, turreted, dedicated, superscribed"—erected in honor of Harvard men who died in the War. He and his escort linger longest "in the presence of the white, ranged tablets, each of which in its proud, sad clearness, is inscribed with the name of a student-soldier." James interpolates:

> The effect of the place is singularly noble and solemn, and it is impossible to feel it without a lifting of the heart. It stands there for duty and honor, it speaks of sacrifice and example, seems a kind of temple to youth, manhood, generosity. Most of them were young, all were in their prime, and all of them had fallen; this simple idea hovers before the visitor and makes him read with tenderness each name and place— names often without other history, and forgotten Southern battles.[32]

For Basil Ransom, "a generous foeman," the monument transcends partisan loyalties, overarches the defeated as well as the victors. For James it is a reminder of the golden lads he had seen and talked to at Readville, as well as, perhaps, a melancholy self-reproof.

The slain collegians, "aureoled," "gleaming," "high-hearted," and "beautiful," had already been publicly mourned by James Russell Lowell in his "Harvard Commemoration Ode" (1865). They were elegized even more affectingly in 1866 with the publication of the *Harvard Memorial Biographies*, edited by Thomas Wentworth Higginson, whose words against the wicked insurrection may have strengthened the resolves of Harvard boys to volunteer.

Higginson, who became a dedicated if not particularly competent officer in a black regiment for eighteen months, cautioned

---

multitudes fulfilling what was fated, that dim twilight in which the memories of those early 60's lie now in so many of our minds. There are 'anecdotes' in plenty, but they all swim in that atmosphere of landscape and heroic fate, and moral sadness in the life of man" (quoted in *The Autobiography of Nathaniel Southgate Shaler* [Boston and New York, 1909], 444).

young writers as late as April 1862 not to overrate the charms of
military life. Great writers, he reminded them, outlasted "great
military chieftains." War interrupted "all higher evocations" and
blasted the cultured minority.[33] Four years later he detected no
such malign consequences. The collegians, large numbers of them
"of Puritan and revolutionary descent," had thrown themselves
"promptly and heartily into the war," unaffected by lures of power
and glory and governed "by solid conviction and the absolute law of
conscience."[34] The War ended once and for all the myth of the
cultivated American's alienation and torpor.

The most striking thing about these Harvard biographies written by friends and relatives (ninety-five in all and twelve contributed by Higginson himself), is the idealism of the young patricians.
Some were inculcated with the abolitionism of their families; the
majority were not abolitionists at all. Most of them enlisted in order
to put down "horrid Rebellion," and although war violated the religious convictions of many, the peril to the Union overcame their
scruples. "What is the worth of this man's life or of that man's
education," one of them wrote, "if this great and glorious fabric of
our Union, raised with such toil and labor by our forefathers, and
transmitted to us in value increased tenfold, is to be shattered to
pieces by traitorous hands, and allowed to fall crumbling into the
dust?"[35] "If I die," wrote another, "it will be with conviction, as firm
as eternal truth itself, that our country will be finally saved."[36] The
letters, journals, and speeches of the Harvard martyrs echo the
sentiments and periods of great classical orations from the Greeks
to Daniel Webster. They fell on the battlefields before their hopeful
faith had darkened into the wisdom of Melville's "College Colonel."

Higginson's collegians became the subject of a war literature
they died too soon to write themselves. The lamentations aroused by
the death of Colonel Robert Gould Shaw were both personal and
symbolic. That "truly beautiful boy" shot down on the parapet of
Fort Wagner and buried with the black soldiers whom he had led in
a bootless assault became the exemplar for all the unmonumented
lives mowed down by "inexorable war." So William James implied in
1897 at the unveiling of Augustus Saint-Gaudens's bronze relief
commemorating Shaw and his Negro troops. Shaw's "moral service," not his acknowledged fortitude, drew James's accolade, the
"lonely courage" he demonstrated when he exchanged his commission in a respected white regiment for the "dubious fortunes" of a
black one.[37]

Shaw's friend and fellow Harvardian, Oliver Wendell Holmes,
Jr., saw him as one of those "single romantic" figures—another
Sidney, Wolfe, or Montcalm—who added a touch of glory "to the

bare fact that the strongest legions prevailed."* Holmes, three times wounded by the time he was twenty-three and familiar, as William James was not, with organized killing, made no mention of Shaw's "moral service" in behalf of a despised race. His distinguishing merit in Holmes's eyes was his membership in the company of gentlemen who went to the battlefields and "died there becomingly." Other Harvard men, many of them snobs and Copperheads, fought as bravely and died as gloriously.[38]

Thoroughly imbued with abolitionist doctrine, Holmes had enlisted eight days after the President's call for troops. The issues seemed clear enough in April 1861. He was a crusader "in the cause of the future of the whole civilized world"[39] and already pledged to a personal code of "manly and heroic conduct."[40] The War strengthened that code while it shook his faith "in the Christian Crusade of the 19th century,"[41] for many of the officers he admired most were gallant disbelievers of the Lincoln government. Moreover, Holmes had no religious faith to sustain him. Wounded for the first time at Ball's Bluff, he worried less about his salvation than his style of behavior. How would he be regarded by his family, by the world? Was he upholding the chivalric ideal of Sir Philip Sidney? Unconsciously he was formulating a value system to shape a course of permissible conduct unsustained by religious belief, by patriotism, or by the comfort of a conviction. For the Christian credo, the son of the Puritans substituted a samurai-like code of loyalty and pride.[42]

The test of a faith was how the adherent behaved under extreme tension, how he responded to disaster. Holmes was shot through the left breast in October 1861. Taken to an improvised hospital, he closed his eyes on the bloody spectacle: "a red blanket with an arm lying on it in a pool of blood . . . and near the entrance a surgeon calmly grasping a man's finger and cutting it off— both standing—while the victim contemplated the operation with a very grievous mug." In time he learned to look on such scenes with indifference: the piles of uniformed corpses, the night marches when he stumbled over "swollen bodies, already fly-blown and decaying," the wounded men "shot in head or bowels." He grew

---

* Compare Whittier's response to Shaw's death: "The only Regiment I ever looked upon during the war was the 54th on its departure for the South. I shall never forget the scene. As he rode at the head of his troops, the very flower of grace and chivalry, he seemed to me beautiful and awful as an Angel of God, come down to lead the host of freedom to victory. I have longed to speak the emotions of that hour; but I *dared* not, lest I should indirectly give a new impulse to War" (quoted in letter of Lydia Maria Child to Francis G. Shaw, May 21, 1876, Massachusetts Historical Society).

accustomed to the sounds as well as the sights of war. "A bullet," he noted, "has a most villainous greasy slide through the air." He never forgot "the long roll of fire from the main line." By July 1864 not even his carefully contrived soldier's code could medicine his "exhausted spirit" and "doubting mind." He was honorably mustered out and once again became the student, but he continued to travel on the track he had been following since before Antietam when his heart, he said, was "touched with fire."[43]

In the "collapse of creeds" following the War, Holmes translated his "soldier's faith" into a warrior-mystique that enabled him to embrace any friend or former foe who shared "the passion and action of his time at peril of being judged not to have lived." But in his recollections the rank and file are seen distantly, if at all. Like most other collegians, Holmes had eyes only for his fellow-officers whose exploits and misfortunes and "splendid carelessness for life" illuminated his war.[44]

The literary gentry regarded these gentlemen-soldiers—Theodore Winthrop is a good example—as representative men of the hour. Winthrop, a Yale graduate and a traveler and author of some reputation, died at Great Bethel in his thirty-third year. (See Supplement 3.) He personified, in his sister's words, "the promise, beauty, culture and patriotism that were crowding to the front."[45] He also viewed the War like others of his class as a means to stamp out anarchy as well as slavery, and the army as the *"Police of the Nation"* which "must hold the South as the Metropolitan Police holds New York."[46] His sketches, two of which described for *Atlantic Monthly* readers the progress of the fashionable New York Seventh Regiment from Broadway to Washington in the spring of sixty-one, suggest more than the dreamy poet, literary adventurer, and society man he was reputed to be. Winthrop was a dashing fellow with a lively and sometimes sardonic cast of thought. He fell before he had outgrown his boyish romanticism, but nothing in his rather extensive publications supports the critic John Macy's opinion that Winthrop might have become the most talented chronicler of the War.[47]

Not surprisingly, the literary-minded gentlemen volunteers resorted at times to romantic flourishes now suspect in any would-be realistic portrayal of battle. We have come to accept the view of the War as an amalgam of whisky and blood, and so it was. But it was also exhilarating, and the eyewitnesses who reported dramatic scenes and episodes romantically preserved at least one true version of it. "In addition to the usual sights of a battle," Charles Francis Adams, Jr., wrote to his father in 1863,

I saw but one striking object—the body of a dead rebel by the road-side the attitude of which was wonderful. Tall, slim and athletic, with regular sharply chiseled features, he had fallen flat on his back, with one hand upraised as if striking, and with his long light hair flung back in heavy waves from his forehead. It was curious, no one seems to have passed the body without the same thought of admiration.[48]

A witness of Colonel Barlow's death might have been describing a battle panorama of Horace Vernet:

He was on foot. Instead of the linen coat, he had a splendid uniform on, which seemed to shine with newness,—pants inside high-topped boots, an army hat, and yellow regulation gloves. It seemed as if a new suit must have dropped on him from the skies. And then he rushed up the hill at the head of his little regiment, looking so handsome, facing his men to cheer them, moving with such grace and elasticity, that it seemed as if he were dancing with delight. I have seen brave men and brave officers; . . . but I never saw such a sight as Barlow's advance, and never expect to again. It was a picture, —it was poetry.[49]

It was these gallant fellows who were featured in the War romances so popular after 1865 although, as Howells remarked in his review of the *Harvard Memorial Biographies,* none of the "brilliant and generous young men gave more than the simplest and obscurest soldier whom patriot impulse drew from the shop and furrow." The few attempts even to approximate "the martyrdom that crowned the silent tens of thousands"[50] met with small favor, as John W. De Forest was to discover.

Chapter 11

John W. De Forest

Nevertheless, if something of this sort is absolutely required, we will instance Mr. J. W. De Forest, in his very inadequately named Miss Ravenel's Conversion, *as presenting an image of American life during the late rebellion, both North and South, at home and in the field, which does not "shrink to pitiful dimensions" even when "put by the side of Tolstoï's"* War and Peace; *it is an admirable novel, and spacious enough for the vast drama glimpsed in it.*

WILLIAM DEAN HOWELLS, 1887

War. Permanence of the Institution of War.—*The history of war is the history of the human race. It is one of the natural functions of the savage, and the most honored profession of civilized society. The ancient Scandinavian looked forward to a perpetual state of war in paradise, and the enlightened American republic gives to its successful warrior the first place in its councils and its heart. All civilized men regard it as a great evil, yet some one of the leading nations of the world is nearly always engaged in it; and it may safely be said that the sun never sets upon a world wholly at peace. We have recently seen in our own land the philanthropist urging on a hesitating government, the minister of the Christian religion exchanging the gown for the sword, and the fairest and gentlest of "the sex" instilling energy into the uplifted arm. War must therefore be recognized as an instinct of humanity, of divine origin, not to be replaced, as idealists hope, by any human device like tribunals of arbitration or submissive trust in the generosity of competitors.*

FROM O. H. ERNST, "WAR" IN Johnson's New Universal Cyclopaedia (FIRST EDITION, 1877); CITED BY JOHN W. DE FOREST IN A LETTER TO WILLIAM DEAN HOWELLS, MARCH 11, 1879

A Volunteer's Adventures

" Counting service in war and peace, I was six and a half years under the colors. I was on three storming parties, six days of field engagement, and thirty-seven days of siege duty, making forty-six days under fire."* So John W. De Forest succinctly summarized his military career in the preface to his revealing but unremarkable volume of verse. He regretted having missed Gettysburg and Chickamauga. He was glad to have taken part in the Port Hudson campaign and to have been present at the final victories in the Shenandoah Valley. He did not say, perhaps out of modesty, that thirty-five years earlier he had published the best novel about the War to be written by a veteran or, for that matter, by anyone.

No more unlikely prospect for a successful war novelist could be imagined than the unmilitary and bookish man from New Haven, Connecticut, who "commenced recruiting a company for the Twelfth Connecticut Volunteers" in the fall of 1861.[1] Considerably older than most recruits mustered into the Union army (he was thirty-five), ever threatened "by the fretting enmity of monotonous invalidism,"[2] a bit hypochondriacal, a husband and father, he had more legitimate reasons for staying out of the War than most of his younger literary contemporaries. He was not an abolitionist nor did he hate the South. He was cool, conservative, and undoctrinaire, with just a touch of the prig and the snob. His writing already exhibited an irony toward the world, and toward himself, a disdain for untidy emotions, and a mixture of fastidiousness and hardness that was to pervade so much of his post-War work. It took a debacle like the defeat at Bull Run to quicken his latent patriotism into action. For the youngest of four sons and the scion of a civic-minded family that had distinguished itself in the War for Independence,[3] it was almost *de rigueur* to seek a commission.

Luckily, examinations for a captaincy in a volunteer regiment were perfunctory,† since De Forest had no military qualifications to

---

* *Poems, Medley and Palestrina* (New Haven, 1902), ix. De Forest was in active service between February 1862 and December 1864. During this period, he was field officer, inspector general, chief of ordnance, and staff officer. His chief, Major-General Godfrey Weitzel, considered him "one of the best volunteer officers that I have ever had under me" (John W. De Forest, *A Volunteer's Adventures* [New Haven, 1946], xvii).

† He received his commission on January 1, 1862, in General Benjamin Butler's "New England Division." For the next three years, he served as a field officer in Louisiana and Virginia. He was mustered out in December 1864. Disabilities incurred during his campaigning qualified him for a com-

speak of save intelligence and gentlemanly pride. A sickly youth, he had spent a good part of his early manhood traveling in the Near East and Europe in quest of health and dreaming of a literary career. By 1861 he had published a history of the Indians in Connecticut, two chatty books about his foreign wanderings, and two novels. The War broke up the lazy rhythm of his life. It also provided him with his most wrenching personal experience as well as a mighty subject for his pen.

Whites and Blacks in Pre-War Dixie

Although De Forest had not publicly involved himself in politics during the 1850s, he knew where he stood on the sectional issues of the day ("I believe in Free Soil, Kansas squatters, Sharp's rifles, and Mr. Seward," he declared in 1855),[4] but unlike most of the Yankee literati, he also knew something about the South and particularly about the citadel of Secessia, Charleston, South Carolina.

His wife's father, Charles Upham Shepard, Emerson's first cousin and an eminent mineralogist, divided his time in the fifties between Amherst College and the Charleston Medical College. De Forest got his first glimpse of Charleston in 1855 when he visited his bride-to-be. He saw it again in January 1861, only a few weeks after South Carolina seceded. The opinions of Southerners and the South he formed in these pre-War years never substantially changed; further acquaintance during and after the War simply amplified and deepened his convictions.

De Forest then and later looked at the South more objectively than most Northern men of letters did, but he never allowed his appreciation for Southern manliness and simplicity or his fondness for particular types and persons to alter inbred preconceptions. He retained a kind of half-amused, half-contemptuous attitude toward what he continued to regard as a childish and anachronistic people.* Charlestonians he found to be polite and accommodating

---

mission in the Veterans Reserve Corps ("known first as the Invalid Corps") in February 1865. De Forest remained in Washington "until the Provost Marshal General's Bureau was abolished in July 1866 and was then moved to South Carolina where he served with the Bureau of Refugees, Freedmen, and Abandoned Lands as a Sub-Assistant Commissioner in charge of activities in three South Carolina counties. Here he remained until the end of 1867" (Charles South, "Truly Your Humble Servant," *Prologue*, II [spring 1970], 25, 30).

* A sentiment shared by many New Englanders, even those who like De Forest respected the fighting capacities of the Southern soldiers. Oliver Wendell Holmes, Jr., expressed similar views some years after the Civil War

to the outsider so long as he was untainted by abolitionism or Black Republicanism, to the South Carolinian one and the same thing. Parochial "beyond anything known in the North, even in self-poised Boston,"[5] they showed little curiosity about Northern civilization, so convinced were they of the superiority of their own. Every reported disorder in the Free States they attributed to free institutions, and although Unionist sentiment still prevailed among the Charleston leadership during De Forest's first visit, he complained even then that he had to be somewhat guarded in his letters: "The post office here has sometimes had the scoundrelly meanness to open letters written by persons suspected of free sentiments."[6]

He spent only ten days in Charleston on his second visit, but his account of "Charleston Under Arms" is sharp and observant. Charleston had grown shabby since South Carolina's secession, the citizens prepared for war but hoping the federal government would let them go in peace. Meanwhile, wharves stood empty and economy was "the order of the day." Young men in homespun gray garrisoned the ring of protecting fortresses, all save Sumter whose imminent seizure, capitulation, or destruction dominated the discussion in the rumor-ridden city. The overaged formed the home guard "in training," a malicious citizen assured De Forest, "to take Fort Sumter by charging upon it at low water." Grandiose prophecies of Northern doom and Southern affluence should Washington try coercion alternated with anxieties over the costs of independence and the prospect of the South's "handsome, genteel, educated young fellows" being pitted against "a gang of Irishmen, Germans, British deserters, and New York roughs, not worth killing, and yet instructed to kill to the best advantage."[7]

While discounting secessionist hopes, De Forest admired the candor and directness with which the Charlestonians blurted out their erroneous beliefs. Lincoln's election signified to South Carolina's oligarchy the impossibility of sectional harmony. The North would never concede slavery was "right"; the South insisted the good of slavery had to be not only asserted but also believed. Hence the unpatchable schism. Such were the considered views of the

---

in a letter to Senator A. J. Beveridge: "I hope that time will explode the humbug of the Southern Gentleman in your mind—not that there weren't a few —and not that their comparatively primitive intellectual condition didn't sometimes give a sort of religious purity of type, rarer in the more civilized and therefore more sceptical northerner. But the southern gentlemen generally were an arrogant crew who knew nothing of the ideas that make the life of the few thousands that may be called civilized" (quoted by Mark De Wolfe Howe, *Justice Oliver Wendell Holmes. The Shaping Years, 1841–1870* [Cambridge, Mass.], 70–71). De Forest subscribed to this view as well as to Holmes's hard military code.

"men of standing and property," remarkable for their physical beauty "and almost invariably distinguished by a fearless, open-eyed frankness, in some instances running into arrogance and pugnacity."[8]

They were no less talkative if somewhat less frank about one consequence of Lincoln's election: its effect on the blacks. "Our slaves have heard of Lincoln," one man said to De Forest, "—that he is a black man, or black Republican, or black something,—that he is to become ruler of this country on the fourth of March,—that he is a friend of theirs and will free them. We must establish our independence in order to make them believe that they are beyond his help. We have had to hang some of them in Alabama,—and we expect to be obliged to hang others, perhaps many." Fear of a servile insurrection, "prevalent though not a universal fear," was understandable, De Forest thought, and without condoning lynch law, he could see why "suspected incendiaries" received short shrift in the South. "If you live in a powder-magazine, you positively must feel inhospitably inclined towards a man who presents himself with a cigar in his mouth."[9]

De Forest seems to have vacillated in his opinion of Negro character and intelligence, although he professed to be unwaveringly antislavery. Some ten years before his first visit to Charleston, he had closely observed a black man in Smyrna who dramatically challenged his stereotype of Negro-ness,

> a negro, who, dressed handsomely in the Turkish style, lounged quietly on a bench near the door, and occupied himself with smoking a meditative pipe. "Do you see that fellow?" said the captain. "He is as good as any of them here." Coming from a country where individuals of this color bear all the marks of a depressed and despised people, I saw in this man the first of a species. No sneaking, no grinning, no small impertinences; but self-possession, self-respect in every feature, dignity and ease in every motion. No Turk in the room had more calmness, gravity, and intelligence in his air; or looked more like the gentleman, Hamlet, than he did like the gentleman, Othello. I saw at once that he had been treated like a man all his life, and that not the least suspicion had ever entered his brain that he was not a man. He gave me new ideas of the possibilities of the African race, and made me look forward to a supposable time when negroes shall have a chance with the rest of us.[10]

No such thoughts occurred to him in Charleston where the "darkies" looked stupider and more childish than he had imagined:

In fact, my present feeling is that they are not worth all the hulabaloo that is made about them. They are left ignorant & animal, say the Abolitionists. Granted. But their great, great grandfathers in Africa were four times as ignorant & at least twice as animal.—They are small, for the most part, much inferior in size & appearance to us, & even to the Irish & Germans. Indeed they are decidedly below the free blacks of the North, & particularly so in their air & expression of countenance.[11]

These were first impressions, he admitted, and shortly after he corrected himself on their size. "Black, you know, tends to make things appear smaller than they are, and in consequence I think I rather underrated the colored population as regards length and breadth individually." But he thought the Negroes' "inexpressible gaiety" belied "any condition of unhappiness" and was even disposed to quarrel with "these sable philosophers" for submitting to their conditions so contentedly.[12]

When accused by his brother and sister-in-law of succumbing to the "seductions of slavery," he told them not to worry. He had jotted down his notes without considering the "matter of right and wrong." For one who had heard only the antislavery side, it was a "novelty" to hear the opposite point of view: "But I am stiff as far as the politics of the matter are concerned, as well as on the remote question of justice and injustice."[13] From this time on, De Forest met and wrote about a variety of Negroes, some of whom shared the manliness of the Smyrna "Hamlet" and others who might have appeared in the Negrophobic novels of Thomas Dixon.[14] Eventually he fell back upon an environmentalist or Darwinian interpretation of a race warped by its long servitude yet capable of slow improvement if not betrayed by white misleaders or sentimental visionaries. He had not become a soldier to free the slaves (in 1862 he turned down a colonelcy in a Negro regiment, a decision he later half-regretted)* but his observation of Southern blacks during the War rather raised than lowered his hopes for the Negro's future.

---

* De Forest was dissuaded by the argument that black troops would only be "called on for fatigue duty" of the most menial kind and that his fellow officers would not be gentlemen (*A Volunteer's Adventures*, 50–51). "At that time," he wrote to his brother in 1864, "those positions were in bad odor there, partly because the government had not yet sanctioned the movement, & partly because of the exceedingly bad character of the officers whom Butler put into his colored regiments. I thought it more respectable to be a captain of the 12th than to be a colonel along side of Jack Nelson the pugilist & Daniels the Mississippi-river gambler, both since dismissed the service" (J. W. De Forest to Andrew W. De Forest, Sept. 16, 1864, De Forest Papers, Yale).

The War in Document and Fiction

De Forest wrote two sustained accounts of the War*—one documentary, the other fictional. The first, assembled from letters, articles, and journal entries written during his army years, was posthumously published as *A Volunteer's Adventures* (1946). The second, *Miss Ravenel's Conversion from Secession to Loyalty* (1867), incorporated many of the same incidents, but in addition to invented scenes and episodes, contained a running authorial commentary on the issues of the War. A blend of irony and humor, anger and disdain, faith and skepticism infused them both.

What distinguishes *A Volunteer's Adventures* from other competently written eyewitness chronicles is its conscious literary intention. De Forest was already a professional writer when he exchanged his civilian dress for a uniform. The letters he dispatched from camp and battlefield comprised a record of the War which he hoped to exploit for literary purposes should he survive. In them he sketched and scrutinized the panorama of war with an incredulous eye.

The novelist is evident in the swift impressions of men in the higher and lower echelons: the general-politician Benjamin F. Butler, who flashed his smile "after the mechanical fashion of Edward Everett, as if he meant to make things pleasant to us and also to show us his handsome teeth";† the abolitionist general John

---

* Two other works of De Forest relating to the War are minor but important. A number of verses in *Poems, Medley and Palestrina* recall in rough but sometimes memorable lines the fierce actions he participated in, the dreary routine of campaigning, and his professional attitude toward a brave foe. These poems are grim, exultant, and sad, but they justify a war that washed away with blood "the scrolls of shame" (20). "The Brigade Commander" shows De Forest at his best and worst. Despite its melodramatic, not to say preposterous, plot, the story of the demonic but brilliant tactician contains a superb description of a battle and celebrates the veteran soldier, the survivor "of marches, privations, maladies, sieges, and battles" (18). The men adore their commander because he is a professional soldier and because he wins. "If a man," De Forest writes, "will win battles and give his brigade a right to brag loudly of its doings, he may have its admiration and even its enthusiastic devotion, though he be as pitiless and wicked as Lucifer" (*Stories by American Authors* [New York (Charles Scribner's Sons), 1884], VIII, 5).

† De Forest later portrayed Butler in the character of the coarse and witty General Daniel Bangs in his novel *Playing the Mischief* (New York, 1875): "His constant stumbling-block was this, that he believed that all his countrymen were rogues, and could be moved by merely roguish motives" (223). Bangs's colleagues relished his "impudent mendacity" and his jokes as they would "the droll exaggerations of Mark Twain or the whimsies of Artemus

W. Phelps, grizzled, shambling, sarcastic, a splenetic disciplinarian laughed at and liked for his oddities; Sergeant Weber, De Forest's "crack soldier," formerly of the Hanoverian army and veteran of the Seminole War, who after being demoted and sentenced for drunkenness redeems himself in battle; one of the "unsanctified" Billy Yanks besieging Port Hudson, who, seated on a stump and grimly masticating "his hard rations while a comrade tried to dig a buckshot out of his skull with a jackknife," grumbles to his mate: "G—d damn it! Can't you start it? . . . Dig in like hell!"[15]

De Forest always saw the rank and file as "they" and kept a mental as well as officer's distance from them. In time, however, he came to regard common soldiers with a kind of awe, not so much because of their physical courage (he encountered "poltroons" as well as heroes and conscientiously noted manifestations of battle terror)* but because of their "patience under hardship, privation, and sickness" and their heroic submission. If in general he considered officers braver than those they commanded, that was only because their responsibilities crowded out their fears. Exhausting marches and skirmishes quickly salted the green recruit. De Forest noticed with satisfaction how quickly his men lost their "innocent pacific air" and acquired the veteran look. "Hardened by exposure and suffering, they had a stony, indifferent stare and an expression of surly patience, reminding me of bulldogs and bloodhounds held in leash. It was impossible to divine from their faces whether they expected battle or a peaceful march."[16]

The sufferings and emergencies that tested them tested him, although a Puritan disposition had armored him against the outrages of army life. Sometimes he appeared to be amused as much as shocked by his miserable state, his uniform frayed and threadbare,

---

Ward" (226). Although he was never under fire, his claque transformed him into a hero. He might have been more successful as well as more honorable if he had had "morality enough to perceive that most of his countrymen are moved by moral sentiments" (227–28). De Forest in the same novel had even harsher things to say about General Hornblower (modeled after the political general N. P. Banks), "another of those martial civilians who leaped from the platform of the popular orator into the stirrups of the general, and whose strategy and tactics lent to the solemn tragedy of our civil war a few scenes of farce, alas! dearly paid for" (270). All references to the Monument Edition, State College, Pa., 1961.

* "This last man, on hearing the Rebel bullets, faced about and started rearward. I never saw anything done more naturally and promptly. He did not look wild with fright; he simply looked alarmed and resolved to get out of danger; it was the simplest and most persuaded expression of countenance imaginable. He was not a thorough coward, and never afterward turned tail that I know of; but he was confounded by the peril of the moment and thought of nothing but getting away from it" (*A Volunteer's Adventures*, 63).

punctured with bullet holes and pipe burns, his trousers "stiff with a mixture of dust & rain."[17] Exposure to dirt, disease, and hunger taught him to distinguish between the words "discomfort" and "suffering," as he explained to his brother in 1863:

> We waste unnecessary sympathy on poor people. A man is not necessarily wretched because he is cold & hungry & unsheltered; provided those circumstances usually attend him, he gets along very well with them; they are annoyances, but not torments. I remember now with a sort of amused contempt how I used to think it a terrible hardship to have a single bad night's rest. Day before yesterday, I was twenty-four hours on picket, snoozing a little under a tree, starting up at every sound to see who was approaching, making long midnight rounds to be sure of the watchfulness of the videttes, and watching uninterruptedly from midnight till daybreak. It was not very bad, and I came in at morning feeling quite bright, nor did I take a nap during the day.[18]

Here spoke the professional who had been repeatedly under fire, had seen men smashed and blown apart before his eyes, and controlled his fear. "Try our best, we never shall realize completely that the dead are dead, or that the living are to die."[19]

Once he, too, had been a civilian with a civilian's misconceptions about war. Now, leading his men against the Butternuts for the first time, he "expected a severe hand-to-hand struggle; not having learned that bayonet fighting occurs mainly in newspapers and other works of fiction." It did not take him long to discover, with due respect to "military authors" who had never heard a bullet whistle yet who found fighting "delightful," that barring "a few flashes of elation" in moments of triumph, war was "much like being in a rich cholera district in the height of the season." Here and there dashing equestrians gesticulated with their sabres, but for the most part those painterly scenes of troops converging in massive columns seldom materialized. Instead Reb and Yank tried to kill each other from behind fence and thicket. Southern troops lost fewer men than the Federals, because they fought more like redskins or hunters.[20]

All of his disgust and fascination with the war spectacle De Forest poured into *Miss Ravenel's Conversion*. Captain Colburne, the hero, dogs the steps of his creator, and although the hand of Thackeray, Balzac, and possibly Stendhal can be detected in character and plot, the war scenes of the novel duplicate those of *A Volunteer's Adventures*. If anything, the "multitudinous agony" of fighting and dying is even more graphically depicted, and so too are the cheerful ferocity and toughness of an enemy invariably presented without rancor.*

But the novel is also private and symbolic where the documentary is not; and its ostensible burden—the victory of righteousness, civilization, progress, and science over barbarism and reaction—is constantly undercut by De Forest's ambivalent feelings toward both the angelic hosts and the squadrons of Satan—and toward the Civil War itself.

Lily Ravenel is a charming and inconsequential heroine whose so-called "conversion" is peripheral to the deeper import of the novel. The prolonged and interrupted love affair between her and Captain Colburne (a touched-up model of De Forest) is only a sop to romantic readers. His real subject is Colburne's transformation from a promising but untested young man full of self-doubt into a veteran "educated" by events.

To his dehydrated New Boston (New Haven)—decent, bloodless, and cloistered—come three outsiders from the South: Dr. Ravenel, a loyalist recently of Louisiana but South Carolina born and Northern educated; his bewitching daughter, loaded with Southern charm and Southern prejudice; and Colonel Carter, a "high-toned" Virginian and Union officer whose masculinity almost overwhelms the male and female virgins of New Boston's academic community.† Colburne falls unreflectively in love with Lily, but he is amused and instructed by her father's running disparagement of Southerners and Southern institutions; and he reluctantly learns to respect if not to admire the morally obtuse but still enormously brave and competent Colonel who steals his girl from him, breaks her heart through his philandering, and dies like a hero. At the end of the novel, Colburne, still a captain because he will not truckle to politicians and tempered by the fires of war, marries the young widow, much to his own and her father's satisfaction. Like the nation, he has learned his powers. A mighty evil has been eradi-

---

* "As he reached the top he stared in astonishment and some dismay at a man in butternut-colored clothing mounted on a rough pony with the double-barreled gun of Greene's mosstroopers across his saddle-bow, who was posted on the road not forty feet distant. The Butternut immediately said in the pleasant way current in armies, 'Halt, you son of a bitch' " (*Miss Ravenel's Conversion from Secession to Loyalty* [New York (Holt, Rinehart and Winston Paperback), 1964], 293).

† In his review of *Miss Ravenel's Conversion*, Howells described Carter as belonging to the "type of officers of the old army . . . true to the semi-civilization of the South." He appreciated the satiric picture of New Boston's academic society, "pure, colorless, and cold" but savored its "rich and wholesome juices" more enthusiastically than De Forest did. A more authentic type of Puritan than Howells, he had a greater relish for certain kinds of wickedness or impropriety. See *Atlantic Monthly*, XX (July 1867), 120–22.

cated. Conquerors and conquered have survived a ruthless surgery, the North that sinned by abetting slavery and profiting from it and the South free at last from its cancer.

Dr. Ravenel interprets the War as "the fifth act of the grand drama of human liberty."

> First, the Christian Revelation. Second, the Protestant Reformation. Third, the War of American Independence. Fourth, the French Revolution. Fifth, the struggle for the freedom of all men, without distinction of race and color; this democratic struggle which confirms the masses in an equality with the few. We have taught a greater lesson than all of us think or understand. Once again we have reminded the world of democracy, the futility of oligarchies, the outlawry of Caesarism.

Presumably De Forest agrees, as he does with Colburne's reflections on the dignity of sorrow and the benefits of adversity, on how the "soldier's life cultivates some of the Christian virtues . . . especially resignation and obedience."[21] Yet one hesitates to accept these affirmations as the unqualified gospel of the author or to agree unreservedly with Edmund Wilson that De Forest reflected "the complacency of the cockily victorious North."[22]

Nowhere, to be sure, does he try to justify what Dr. Ravenel called the "stupid, barbarous Ashantee rebellion." Southern ideas and manners always seemed to him, as they did to Henry James, slightly ridiculous. But the vehement and exaggerated way in which the Doctor assails the Southern devils and ranges the contending forces on the sides of good and evil is not De Forest's, who was not given to hyperbolical pronouncements. Dr. Ravenel sees the War as a struggle between the Judean North and Babylon, Tyre, and Sodom; and it is he, not De Forest, who likens John Wilkes Booth to Judas Iscariot, Lincoln to Christ, and who exclaims: "I can now understand the *Paradise Lost*, for I have beheld Heaven fighting against Hell."[23]

In fact, De Forest makes the rank and file of Satan's myrmidons as likable as their angelic opponents.* If they are primitive and animallike in contrast to Yankees like Colburne, they are less rigid and certainly no less brave. The three most flawed characters in *Miss Ravenel's Conversion,* and the most passionately alive, are the least ideological. Their zestful relish for the sensual, though

---

* It may be significant, however, that the "last prayer" of the heroic Negro slave, Major Scott, after exchanging fatal shots with a Rebel, is "My God!" and the "last curse of the Rebel" is "Damnation!" (*Miss Ravenel's Conversion,* 292).

unchecked by rectitude, gives them an attractive dimension sadly wanting in the frigid Puritans. Even more than Colburne, broadened as well as toughened by the War, De Forest savored if he did not embrace people whose habits and values violated his ancestral creed. He could not openly condone the transgressions of his Creole, Mrs. Larue, who compromised the Colonel and said shocking things in French—the language of the most corrupt of nations. He could not excuse the drunkenness, profanity, and callousness of Lieutenant Van Zandt or the pliable conscience of Colonel Carter. He could and did recount their escapades uncensoriously and with gusto.

Dr. Ravenel thought the planters deserved to be blown up, or as he put it in language similar in spirit and content to the sentiments of Mark Twain, " 'razed and got out of the way, like any other obstacle to the progress of humanity.' "* If De Forest agreed, he had mixed feelings about the brutal and filthy way Providence went about disposing of them. Nor was he entirely optimistic about the consequences of a War that left such rascals as the politician Major Gazaway to flourish in the redeemed Union of Grant, Sherman, and Farragut. He only knew that for himself, the War had been the most thrilling as well as degrading experience of his life, a nightmare he was privileged to share with courageous men in both armies.

In one of his frequent authorial asides, De Forest remarked of an occasion after the War when the sounds of rock blasting

> reminded him of the roar of artillery; of the thunder of those signal guns which used to presage battle; of the alarums which only a few months previous were a command to him to mount and ride into the combat. Then he thought almost with a feeling of sadness, so strange is the human heart, that he had probably heard those clamors uttered in mortal earnest for the last time. Never again, perhaps, even should he live to the age of three-score and ten, would the shriek of grape-shot, and the crash of shell, and the multitudinous whiz of musketry be a part of his life. Nevermore would he hearken to that charging yell which once had stirred his blood more fiercely than the sound of trumpets: the Southern

* "It was time. The world had got to be too intelligent for them. They could not live without retarding the progress of civilization. They wanted to keep up the social systems of the middle ages amidst railroads, steamboats, telegraphs, patent reapers, and under the noses of Humboldt, Leverrier, Lyell, and Agassiz. Of course they must go to the wall. They will be pinned up to it *in terrorem,* like exterminated crows and chickenhawks. The grand jury of future centuries will bring in the verdict. 'Served them right!' " (*Miss Ravenel's Conversion,* 50, 233–34).

battle-yell, full of howls and yelpings as of brute beasts rushing hilariously to the fray: the long-sustained Northern yell,
all human, but none the less relentless and stern; nevermore
the one nor the other. No more charges of cavalry, rushing
through the dust of the distance; no more answering smoke
of musketry, veiling unshaken lines and squares; no more
columns of smoke, piling high above deafening batteries. No
more groans of wounded, nor shouts of victors over positions
carried and banners captured, nor reports of triumphs which
saved a nation from disappearing off the face of the earth.[24]

Nothing in his civilian life ever matched the terrible fullness of
those days. There was no "moral equivalent" for De Forest's War.

The Recorders—Trashy and True

Miss Ravenel's Conversion was not De Forest's last word on the Civil
War; two articles he wrote for Howells in 1879 can be considered
postscripts to his fine novel.

In "Our Military Past and Present," he underscored his case for
a national army led by professionals in place of the politics-ridden
state militias that had maddened Colonel Carter. The militia system, he argued, had signally failed since its inception in the Revolutionary War, not for want of courageous men but for want of
discipline and leadership. During the Civil War, volunteer troops
gradually learned their business despite shameful disorganization
and the incompetence of dastardly superiors. "Self-respect, a noble
feeling of comradeship, earnest purpose, and common sense supplied in great measure the lack of complete discipline and of trained
regimental officers."[25] Volunteers absorbed into regular army units
quickly became excellent soldiers.

De Forest went so far as to recommend popular instruction in
the science and art of war in schools and universities. In addition,
he called for good military histories, "not the trashy, misleading
ones which prattle of 'billows of cavalry' and 'infantry standing like
rocks;' not such stuff as the world has had about war from a host of
ignorant romancers calling themselves historians; but books which
show just what war is, and what to do amidst its difficulties and
perplexities."* He captiously corrected popular misconceptions

---

* Later he found in Tolstoy a true reporter of war who dared to set down
what even he had feared to reveal lest he be thought a coward: "the extreme
horror of battle and the anguish with which the bravest soldiers struggle
through it." Only Tolstoy, he wrote to Howells, had "written the whole truth
about war and battle. His story of Borodino,—the soldiers sitting hungry &
white under that storm of death,—the desperate struggle to keep the mind

about battle. Cavalry usually fought dismounted and behind cover unless the enemy was in flight. Infantry stood firmest when lying on the ground and taking advantage of every bush, rock, and ripple of ground:

> It stands, not in solid masses, but in fragile groups or slender lines, swaying backwards and forwards unexpectedly, gaping open here and there with slaughter or sudden quailing, cobbled into temporary form by hoarse and anxious officers, supported hastily by panting reinforcements, doing its suffering best perhaps, but not at all like a rock. The columns of attack which one reads of are frail and fluctuating threads, for the most part dragging wearily along as if on a march, though sometimes breaking forth in brief, partial spurts. What they advance against the spectator can seldom discern with the eye; he only guesses it when a long, light roll of smoke leaps from the earth in front, followed by a continuous harsh roar; something invisible and perhaps altogether unexpected is causing regiments and brigades to vanish away. Or if the charge succeeds, it seems marvelous that the defeated should have fled, the conquerors look so scattered and few. A return attack will surely sweep them backward, and the master of the science of war is still needed, or victory will be turned to defeat.[26]

De Forest wanted to ban from military shelves in school libraries all the civilian historians filled with "rhetorical generalities." The best military writers, he thought, were Carlyle, Napier, Napoleon, Kinglake, and, of course, Caesar—writers who "give a faithful picture of war and a clear explanation of its giant mechanism and sublime logic."[27] His own essay, significantly titled

---

away from the horrors of the situation,—the poor brave prince pacing the meadow, counting his steps . . . it is the actual truth about the glories of war. I swear it on the faith of a man who has seen it all by the hour together a great many times. No such tremendous wrestle as Borodino, indeed, has come within my experience. But a less obdurate & bloody one enlightens the participator. I lay for eight hours once under a cannonade. . . . Nothing is more confounding, fragmentary, incomprehensible, than a battle as one sees it. And you see so little, too, unless you are a staff officer & ride about, or perhaps a general. No two spectators ever fully agree in their story of a battle. Tolstoi must have been engaged many times. There are a thousand touches which nobody could have guessed. The general who gives Pierre an angry glare & goes; the staff officer who yells, 'What are you here for?' & rides off; the view of the charging enemy whom Pierre supposes to be Russians, & wonders why they are coming back;—are touches which go to make up the picture of the haste, flurry, confusion which battle is" (J. W. De Forest to W. D. Howells, Jan. 24, 1887, Houghton Lib.).

"Caesar's Art of War and Writing," not only contains some implicit parallels between the Gallic wars and the American Civil War but also shows how closely De Forest related truth and style.

It was not surprising, De Forest observes in this essay, that Caesar should "thrash and crush" a people like the Gauls in order "to end the countless, fruitless, noxious uproars arising from their character and institutions." Gallic communities were founded on

> "the narrow and enfeebling idea of blood relationship [here read 'the Southern kinship system']. The principle that if a man is your tenth cousin you must stand by him, right or wrong, and that if he is not your cousin you may rob and kill him, is obviously incapable of producing a quiet, industrious, populous, and civilized community [Dr. Ravenel couldn't have put it better]. In the Gallic wars [read 'Civil War'] a nation founded on the broad idea of contract encountered a host of states founded on the limited idea of cousinhood. The former was sure to crush the latter, and mankind should be thankful that it did so."[28]

Caesar's style, De Forest continued, was an accurate measure of the man, a "compact, lucid, business-like way of writing" characteristic of all great soldiers who had no need to resort to the "artifices of rhetoric." Translated into English, he read "more like DeFoe than like Addison."

> Nor is there ever the slightest attempt at impressiveness, or what the French call *emphase*. Caesar never "bears on" and never struts, not even when he is relating sublime deeds of heroism,—not even when he is explaining wonderful strokes of genius. At first it strikes one with complete astonishment that any human being who had taken a leading and passionate part in such great performances could write about them in a tone of such entire simplicity. We can understand it only when we remember that here was a very extraordinary man, who necessarily looked upon his extraordinary labors and achievements as the most natural things in the world. On the whole, taking into consideration the professional value of the matter in the Commentaries, and the perfectly perspicuous and gracefully simple manner in which that matter is presented, we must allot to Caesar the singular distinction of having produced the best military narrative that ever was written.[29]

In praising Caesar, De Forest defined his own literary aesthetic and inadvertently if not by design called to mind another soldier-author, whom he admired as sincerely as Mark Twain* and Howells did and whose views on war and writing supported his own.

The *Memoirs* of General Grant may not be the greatest prose epic of the Civil War, but it is a story told without heroics and with firmness, dignity, and simplicity. "The constant composition of orders and instructions," De Forest said, "teaches a general to be lucid and short, and leads him to look upon the contrary qualities with distaste.† Moreover, the great soldier is by birthright a clear and quick thinker, and his literary utterance is naturally a reflex of his mental operations."[30] Grant says as much when he praised Zachary Taylor for expressing "what he wanted to say in the fewest well-chosen words" and refusing to "sacrifice meaning to the construction of high-sounding sentences."[31]

Grant's writing is relaxed, but it does not slouch. Pomposity is foreign to his nature. He has a trained eye, a fine topological sense, an uncluttered mind, a dry humor. There is no more irresolution in his prose than in his deeds. Some of his laconic summaries of horrendous episodes suggest Hemingway—or De Forest:

> In this last move there was a brisk fire upon our troops, and some execution was done. One cannon-ball passed through our ranks, not far from me. It took off the head of an enlisted man, and the under jaw of Captain Page of my regiment, while the splinters from the musket of a killed soldier, and his brains and bones, knocked down two or three others, including one officer, Lieutenant Wallen,—hurting them more or less. Our casualties of the day were nine killed and forty-seven wounded.

* "By chance, I had been comparing the memoirs with Caesar's 'Commentaries' and was qualified to deliver judgment. I was able to say in all sincerity that the same high merits distinguished both books—clarity of statement, directness, simplicity, unpretentiousness, manifest truthfulness, fairness and justice toward friend and foe alike, soldierly candor and frankness, and soldierly avoidance of flowery speech. I placed the two books side by side upon the same high level, and I still think they belonged there. I learned afterward that General Grant was pleased with this verdict. It shows that he was just a man, just a human being, just an author. An author values a compliment even when it comes from a source of doubtful competency" (*Mark Twain in Eruption*, ed. Bernard DeVoto [New York and London, 1940], 183).

† Reviewing Grant's letters, "as hard and dry as sandpaper," Henry James said of them: "These few bald little letters have a ray of the hard limpidity of the writer's strong and simple Autobiography—they have nothing more." Their tone reminded him "of the quality that, when we meet its equivalent in an old, dry portrait or even in an angular piece of furniture, affects the historic, not to say enthusiastic sense" (*Henry James. The American Essays*, ed. Leon Edel [New York, 1956], 208–9).

And like De Forest he is often dry and deflationary: "A great many men, when they smell battle afar off, chafe to get into the fray. When they say so themselves they generally fail to convince their hearers that they are as anxious as they would like to make believe, and as they approach danger they become more subdued."[32]

De Forest also saw eye to eye with Grant on the causes and meaning of the War. A Unionist and a moderate—certainly no abolitionist—Grant blamed the War on slavery, not on "a blundering generation." There would have been no cause to fight had Southern leaders not tried to push slavery beyond the original slave states. A fair vote in 1861, Grant believed, would have shown a majority of Southerners opposed to secession, but demagogues too old to fight persuaded or coerced those who had to do the fighting: "They denounced the Northerners as cowards, poltroons, negro-worshippers; claimed that one Southern man was equal to five Northern men in battle; that if the South would stand up for its rights the North would break down." Jefferson Davis even promised "to drink all the blood spilled south of Mason and Dixon's line if there should be war."[33]

Grant and his admirer De Forest were immersed in a war that choked several millions with blood. Both came out of it convinced, in Grant's words, that "it was worth all it cost." Grant wanted no anniversaries or victory celebrations, no days of humiliations to commemorate defeats. He asked only for "truthful history" which did "full credit to the courage, endurance and soldierly ability of the American citizen, no matter what section of the country he hailed from, or in what ranks he fought."[34] There is no evidence that he ever read De Forest's novel or any fictional account of the Civil War, but of all the novels of the War, De Forest's came the closest to meeting Grant's specifications.

Chapter 12

Ambrose Bierce

Abatiss, n.   Embarrassing circumstances placed outside a fort in order to augment the coy reluctance of the enemy.

Army, n.   A class of non-producers who defend the nation by devouring everything likely to tempt an enemy to invade.

Bayonet, n.   An instrument for pricking the bubble of a nation's conceit.

Bomb, or *Bomb-Shell,* n.   A besieger's argument in favor of capitulation, skillfully adapted to the understanding of women and children.

Foe, n.   A person instigated by his wicked nature to deny one's merits or exhibit superior merits of his own.

Freedman, n.   A person whose manacles have sunk so deeply into the flesh that they are no longer visible.

AMBROSE BIERCE, 1881 . . . 1906

"Salad Days"

AMBROSE BIERCE not only choked on the blood of the Civil War, he practically drowned in it. For the remainder of his life it bubbled in his imagination and stained his prose.

Toward Grant, the "Butcher," in some of whose campaigns he had taken a microscopic part and whom he had seen shedding "the blood of the grape and grain abundantly" with his staff during the battle of Missionary Ridge,[1] Bierce maintained a reserved respect. He knew from experience, as Grant's toadies did not, that the General blundered on occasion. Nonetheless, in 1886 he memorialized the "admirable soldier"[2] as a hard and cruel agent for a hard and cruel God. Presumptuous civilians might try to invest the Civil War with divine intentions, to see "what the prophets say they saw." Too

181

"simply wise" to dispute chance or fate, Grant submitted without any inward struggle to duty:

> The cannon syllabled his name;
>   His shadow shifted o'er the land
>   Portentous, as at his demand
> Successive bastions sprang to flame!
>
> He flared the continent with fire,
>   The rivers ran in lines of light!
>   Thy will be done on earth—if right
> Or wrong he cared not to inquire.
>
> His was the heavy hand, and his
>   The service of the despot blade;
>   His the soft answer that allayed
> War's giant animosities.[3]

The eighteen-year-old Ambrose Bierce from northern Indiana, the second in his county to enlist after Lincoln's call to arms, was not the author Ambrose Bierce who wrote these lines. "When I ask myself what has become of Ambrose Bierce the youth, who fought at Chickamauga," he told a friend, "I am bound to answer that he is dead. Some little of him survives in my memory, but many of him are absolutely dead and gone."[4] The "deceased" Bierce was a country boy with a patchy education. Possibly some of the bookishness of his father, an ineffectual farmer, rubbed off on the son. A two-year apprenticeship as a printer's devil and several terms in a Kentucky military school may also have disciplined his mind. But when he was mustered into the Ninth Regiment of the Indiana Volunteers, nobody expected very much from him. His friends and neighbors knew him only as a solitary undemonstrative boy who preferred books to games and who showed few signs of ambition or ability.

"At one time in my green and salad days," he later recalled, "I was sufficiently zealous for Freedom to be engaged in a four years' battle for its promotion. There were other issues, but they did not count much for me."[5] That was Bierce's way of saying he had once had illusions. The Bierce clan was antislavery and none more so than Lucius Verus Bierce, Ambrose's favorite uncle and the only member of the family of any public distinction. This same General Bierce of Akron had furnished his friend John Brown with supplies and weapons* for Brown's Kansas business. On the evening of Brown's execution, he addressed a mass meeting in which he equated the martyr's alleged fanaticism, folly, madness, and

---

* "These were the identical weapons used in the Pottawatomie affair" (Carey McWilliams, *Ambrose Bierce* [New York, 1967], 28).

wickedness with virtue, divine wisdom, obedience to God, and piety. John Brown, he predicted, would "rise up before the world with his calm, marble features, more terrible in death, and defeat, than in life and victory."[6] Whether or not his nephew read the oration, he applauded its sentiments. Eventually an older and disenchanted Bierce conjured up some retributive ghosts of his own.

War Internalized

Bierce's biographers agree the War was the central experience of his life to which he constantly returned, a time of bale and bliss, and an ordeal that brought some coherence to the hitherto random pattern of his youth. Of all the literary combatants of the Civil War, none saw more action* or steeped himself so completely in the essence of battle. For no other writer did it remain such an obsessive presence. "To this day," he wrote in 1887, "I cannot look over a landscape without noting the advantages of a ground for attack or defense. . . . I never hear a rifle-shot without a thrill in my veins. I never catch the peculiar odor of gunpowder without having visions of the dead and dying."[7] The sight of Richmond in 1912 dejected him as it had Henry James when the author of *The American Scene* visited the city seven years before. "True, the history is some fifty years old, but it is always with me when I am there, making solemn eyes at me."[8] There is no reason to question his quiet assertion that prefaces a recollection of Chickamauga, the graveyard of his idealistic youth: "I had served at the front from the beginning of the trouble, and had seen enough of war to give me a fair understanding of it."[9]

Outside of a few letters and diary notes, very little remains of Bierce's on-the-spot recording of the War years. His account of them is largely retrospective, often glazed with nostalgia, and set down after he had trained himself to write. Yet thanks to an almost uncanny visual sense cultivated by his wartime duties as topographical engineer, he managed to fix in his mind the terrain he had traversed and to map his stories and sketches so that the reader can visualize every copse or ravine or stream he mentions. He also

---

* At Shiloh, Murfreesboro, Stone River, Chattanooga, Kenesaw Mountain (where he was seriously wounded), Missionary Ridge, and Franklin and in lesser engagements. Enlisting as a private, he rose to first lieutenant and upon his mustering out in January 1865 was brevetted major for distinguished service. He was often cited for bravery in the dispatches; experienced the excitement of capture, brief incarceration, and escape; and as a Treasury agent in post-War Alabama he once again participated in a kind of sporadic war.

absorbed the "business" of war, the details of the soldier's "trade" conspicuously missing from the War chronicles of those who picked up their information secondhand. This "solidity of specification," as Henry James might say, gave his War fiction the "illusion of reality."

The word "illusion" is used advisedly here, because Bierce's tales of war are not in the least realistic; they are, as he doubtless intended them to be, incredible events occurring in credible surroundings. Triggered like traps, they abound in coincidences and are as contemptuous of the "probable" as any of Poe's most bizarre experiments. Bierce's soldiers move in a trance through a prefigured universe. Father and son, brother and brother, husband and wife, child and parent, separated by chance or conviction, murderously collide in accidental encounters. The playthings of some Power, they follow a course "decreed from the beginning of time."[10] Ill-matched against the outside forces assailing them, they are also victimized by atavistic ones. Bierce's uncomplicated men-at-arms, suddenly commandeered by compulsive fear or wounded by shame, destroy themselves.

Yet each of Bierce's preposterous tales is framed in fact and touched with what Poe called "the potent magic of verisimilitude." Transitions from reality to surreality seem believable not only because the War was filled with romantic and implausible episodes but also because of the writer's intense scrutiny of war itself. The issues of the War no longer concerned him by the time he came to write his soldier stories. They had practically disappeared in the wake of history. But the physical and psychological consequences of constant exposure to suffering and death, the way men behaved in the stress of battle—these matters powerfully worked his imagination, for the War was only meaningful to Bierce as a personal experience. If war in general became his parable of pitifully accoutered man attacked by heavily armored natural forces, the Civil War dramatized his private obsessions.

The Volunteer Remembers

Like De Forest, Bierce smuggled personal experiences into his fiction (the tales are usually laid in localities he had fought over), but he left no personal records so complete as *A Volunteer's Adventures. Bits of Autobiography*, composed some time after the events described, touches only a few of the high points in Bierce's career as a soldier. All the same, it complements the War fiction and hints of his fiery initiation.

From the moment he enlisted, Bierce conducted himself like

the trusty and competent soldiers who figure in his stories. The sketches are not self-celebrations, however, and tell little of his personal exploits; they are the emotion-tinted memories of an untranquil man. He looks back to "the autumn of that 'most immemorial year,' the 1861st of our Lord, and of our Heroic Age" when his regiment from the Indiana lowlands encamped in the Cheat Mountain country of West Virginia. During the first months of his " 'prentice days of warfare," he and his friends in the "Delectable Mountains" assumed the responsibility of personally subduing the rebel fiends. They felt omnipotent and free, in charge of their respective destinies. The proximity of the enemy added just the necessary "spice of danger." Only a few incongruities marred the idyll: a soldier named Abbott killed by "a nearly spent cannon shot" on which his name was stamped (an incident scarcely less improbable than one of Bierce's horrendous fictional coincidences) and the discovery of "some things—lying by the way side" whose "yellow-clay faces" would soon be made anonymous by rooting swine.[11]

Subsequent campaigns in the West seasoned the green recruit, and unremitting encounters with death raised first doubts in his mind about the propriety of dying "for a cause which may be right and may be wrong."[12] Bierce was attached to the Army of the Ohio under General Buell and took part in the dash from Nashville to assist Grant's mauled divisions at Pittsburg Landing. Shiloh, his first major battle, began with a sequence of exhilarating bugle calls, reached a climax in a tempest of hissing lead and "spouting fires," and ended in "desolation" and "awful silence." War was no longer new to him, but his surcharged recollection of confusion, of troops demented by shell shock, of the night march when he and his men, soaked to the skin, stumbled in darkness over the bodies of the dead and near dead, testify to the sustained intensity of the impact:

> Knapsacks, canteens, haversacks distended with soaken and swollen biscuits, gaping to disgorge, blankets beaten into the soil by the rain, rifles with bent barrels or splintered stocks, waist-belts, hats and the omnipresent sardine-box—all the wretched débris of the battle still littered the spongy earth as far as one could see, in every direction. Dead horses were everywhere; a few disabled caissons, or limbers, reclining on one elbow, as it were; ammunition wagons standing disconsolate behind four or six sprawling mules. Men? There were men enough; all dead, apparently, except one, who lay near where I had halted my platoon to await the slower movement of the line—a Federal sergeant, variously hurt, who had been a fine giant in his time. He lay face upward, taking in his breath in convulsive, rattling snorts, and blowing it out in sputters of froth which crawled creamily down his cheeks,

piling itself alongside his neck and ears. A bullet had clipped a groove in his skull, above the temple; from this the brain protruded in bosses, dropping off in flakes and streams. I had not previously known one could get on, even in this unsatisfactory fashion, with so little brain. One of my men, whom I knew for a womanish fellow, asked if he should put his bayonet through him. Inexpressibly shocked by the cold-blooded proposal, I told him I thought not; it was unusual, and too many were looking.[13]

When Bierce wrote "What I Saw at Shiloh," he was already practicing to disguise the violence of his revulsion of organized killing by irony, understatement, and bravado. He succeeded no better than Hemingway. Like Sergeant Byring in "A Tough Tussle," the repugnance he felt toward the mangled dead was at once physical and spiritual, and his bitter joking about spilled guts and brains, his facetiousness in the presence of corrupted flesh, betrayed "his *unusually* acute sensibilities—his keen sense of the beautiful, which these hideous things outraged." Neither Bierce nor his sergeant found any dignity in death. It "was a thing to be hated. It was not picturesque, it had no tender and solemn side—a dismal thing, hideous in all its manifestations and suggestions."[14] The half-buried corpses at Shiloh angered him:

> Their clothing was half burnt away—their hair and beard [sic] entirely; the rain had come too late to save their nails. Some were swollen to double girth; others shriveled to manikins. According to degree of exposure, their faces were bloated and black or yellow and shrunken. The contraction of muscles which had given them claws for hands had cursed each countenance with a hideous grin.

And at the conclusion of this disgusting tableau, he burst out: "Faugh! I cannot catalogue the charms of these gallant gentlemen who had got what they enlisted for."[15]

The sight of men tumbling over like tenpins as the lead thudded against flesh, the piling up of bodies in "a very pretty line of dead," the postures of soldiers flattened out beneath "showers of shrapnel darting divergent from the unassailable sky," parodied the fracas between men and nature. Their fate and his was to wait "meekly to be blown out of life by level gusts of grape—to clench our teeth and shrink helpless before big shot pushing noisily through the consenting air." Neither Blue nor Gray was made to stand up to this kind of chastisement. In Bierce's War, lead always scores "its old-time victory over steel," and the heroic invariably breaks "its great heart against the commonplace."[16]

At Chickamauga, the setting of one of his most macabre and powerful tales, he observed a fragment of the fierce seesaw battle as a staff officer in General W. B. Hazen's command.* And at Pickett's Mill, too minor a disaster to find a place in Sherman's memoirs but important enough to be "related by the enemy," he stored up additional facts about the art of war. Here ignorant armies clashed by day. The Indiana veterans, unaware of what was going on in front of or behind them, fought alongside regiments of strangers. Their commander—"aggressive, arrogant, tyrannical, honorable, truthful, courageous"—had not flinched at the "criminal" order that would sacrifice his feeble brigade. His valorous troops though virtually cut to pieces pushed to the "dead-line," the stretch of "clear space—neutral ground, devoid of dead" beyond which men vulnerable to bullets could not pass. Veterans of this caliber and experience had by now learned almost instinctively to divine the hopeless and to retire in good order.[17]

Bierce survived a number of other engagements, only some of which he wrote about. "There are many battles in a war," he remarked, "and many incidents in battle: one does not recollect everything." The War itself, however, had pressed so deeply into his consciousness that he did not need to recollect it. Again and again he came back to it, sometimes to the accompaniment of rhetorical music. "Is it not strange," he asked, "that the phantoms of a blood-stained period have so airy a grace and look with so tender eyes?— that I recall with difficulty the danger and death and horrors of the time, and without effort all that was gracious and picturesque?" One suspects that it was not all that difficult for him to recall the terrors so meticulously and relentlessly recorded in his prose. What he desperately yearned for were his adventurous youth and his lost illusions. ("Ah, Youth, there is no such wizard as thou! Give me but one touch of thine artist hand upon the dull canvas of the Present; gild for but one moment the drear and somber scenes of to-day, and I will willingly surrender an other life than the one that I should

* "In such circumstances the life of a staff officer of a brigade is distinctly 'not a happy one,' mainly because of its precarious tenure and the unnerving alternations of emotion to which he is exposed. From a position of that comparative security from which a civilian would ascribe his escape to a 'miracle,' he may be despatched with an order to some commander of a prone regiment in the front line—a person for the moment inconspicuous and not always easy to find without a deal of search among men somewhat preoccupied, and in a din in which question and answer alike must be imparted in the sign language. It is customary in such cases to duck the head and scuttle away on a keen run, an object of lively interest to some thousands of admiring marksmen. In returning—well, it is not customary to return" ("Killed at Resaca," in *Collected Works of Ambrose Bierce* [New York, 1966], II, 96).

have thrown away at Shiloh.") But he could not reproduce the ecstasy as authentically as the pain.[18]

Soldiers v. Civilians

The War left Ambrose Bierce stranded in a civilian world. He ungraciously adjusted to it, but between his retirement from the army and his disappearance into Mexico in 1913, he remained a prickly alien. The unformed (and he would have said "misinformed") youth emerged after four years of fighting as one of those "hardened and impenitent man-killers to whom death in its awfulest forms is a fact familiar to their every-day observation; who sleep on hills trembling with the thunder of great guns, dine in the midst of streaming missiles, and play cards among the dead faces of their dearest friends."[19] In short, he was a "veteran," and no "civilian" who had not undergone this terrific initiation could claim membership in Bierce's mystic company.

The "civilian"—untested, insulated from the quintessential experience of violence and death—inhabited a different country and spoke in a different tongue. He was likely to be a "patriot," an idealist, an amateur; he believed in God and Providence, hated the enemy, and had not an inkling of the soldier's austere trade.

"An Affair of the Outposts" personifies the civilian in the Governor who for strictly political reasons comes from the "peaceful lands beyond the sea of strife" to visit Grant's bedraggled army after the battle of Pittsburg Landing. The Governor misreads the hieroglyphics of war. To his unpracticed eye, the apparent disorder of the camp suggests "carelessness, confusion, indifference" whereas "a soldier would have observed expectancy and readiness."* Trapped in a melee, he is just unterrified enough to appreciate "the composure and precision" of the troops, but he is more shocked than enlightened by the sordidness of battle: "Even in his distress and peril the helpless civilian could not forbear to contrast it with the

---

* Elsewhere Bierce observes: "An army in line-of-battle awaiting attack, or prepared to deliver it, presents strange contrasts. At the front are precision, formality, fixity, and silence. Toward the rear these characteristics are less and less conspicuous, and finally, in point of space, are lost altogether in confusion, motion, and noise. The homogeneous becomes heterogeneous. Definition is lacking; repose is replaced by an apparently purposeless activity; harmony vanishes in hubbub, form in disorder. Commotion everywhere and ceaseless unrest. The men who do not fight are never ready" (*Collected Works*, II, 198). Here, perhaps, is an allegory of war and peace. After Appomattox, veteran and nonveteran alike wanted to instill some of this military discipline and precision into civilian life. Edward Bellamy's "Industrial Army" in *Looking Backward* is an example of such thinking.

gorgeous parades and reviews held in honor of himself—with the brilliant uniforms, the music, the banners, and marching. It was an ugly and sickening business: to all that was artistic in his nature, revolting, brutal, in bad taste." The "great man" is rescued from capture by the heroic sacrifices of the Tenth Company but passes off his near misadventure with a witticism whose irony he is too obtuse to recognize: "At present—if you will permit an illusion to the horrors of peace—I am 'in the hands of my friends.' "[20]

In a society where such men held high place, war seemed superior to the indecencies of peace. The veterans bestialized by battle and forced into the imbecile business of killing evoked in Bierce a tenderness notably absent in his dealings with the rest of the world. It made no difference to him whether they broke under the ordeal or survived it; they contended against the uncontendable. The strong in his stories are always broken in any case. The men he most admired were stern paternal figures like General Hazen, who made a religion out of duty, lived what they preached, and shared the fate of all who lived "a life of strife and animosities."[21] Such men were out of place in post-War America where civilian precepts and values suffocated the soldierly ones.

Bierce's idealism, although not completely extinguished at the end of the War, was already guttering. His work as a Treasury agent in Alabama in 1865 and a glimpse of corruption in New Orleans snuffed it out. Once he had believed in "a set of infinitely precious 'principles'—infallible criteria—moral solvents, mordant to all base materials." The carpetbaggers who enriched themselves and the ex-soldiers who looted "the people their comrades had offered their lives to bring back into the Union" helped to rout such fancies from his mind.[22] "O Father of Battles," he begged in later years, "pray give us release/ From the horrors of peace, the horrors of peace!"[23]

Corrupt civilians aroused his contempt, bloody-minded civilians his rage. Bierce never sympathized with the Southern cause, but like Whitman he honored Confederate veterans as unfeignedly as he did his Northern comrades in arms, for they belonged to his bloodied fraternity. "What glorious fellows they were. . . . These my late antagonists of the dark days when, God forgive us, we were trying to cut one another's throat." So Bierce wrote long after when battle seemed to him a "criminal insanity."[24] He regretted his role of death-dealer and looked upon his former enemies as superior to the breed who survived them:

> They were honest and courageous foemen, having little in common with the political madmen who persuaded them to their doom and the literary bearers of false witness in the

aftertime. They did not live through the period of honorable
strife into the period of vilification—did not pass from the
iron age to the brazen—from the era of the sword to that of
the tongue and pen. Among them is no member of the
Southern Historical Society. Their valor was not the fury of
the non-combatant; they have no voice in the thunder of
civilians and the shouting. Not by them are impaired the
dignity and infinite pathos of the Lost Cause. Give them,
these blameless gentlemen, their rightful part in all the
pomp that fills the circuit of the summer hills.[25]

Bierce's tribute concluded his plea to provide markers for the
shallow and forgotten graves of the Confederate dead. "Is there a
man, North or South," he asked, "who would begrudge the expense
of giving to these fallen brothers the tribute of green graves?"
Apparently there were, just as there were the "Vindictives" of the
"Bloody-Shirt" unwilling to return captured Rebel flags. He gently
chided GAR veterans for fearing that concessions to old foes
smacked of treason. He and his fellow soldiers had not fought to
capture banners but to teach the South "better manners." Let kings
keep trophies, he said. "The freeman's trophy is the foeman's love,/
Despite war's ravage."

> Give back the foolish flags whose bearers fell,
>   Too valiant to forsake them.
> Is it presumptuous, this counsel? Well,
>   I helped to take them.[26]

He was less genial to the superpatriots and self-righteous
moralists, inflexible judges of right and wrong. Rejected ideas, he
warned them, constantly double back to "mock the new"; they run
"Recurrent in an endless track." And angered by one who opposed
the decorating of Confederate graves, Bierce wrote:

> The wretch, whate'er his life and lot,
>   Who does not love the harmless dead
>   With all his heart and all his head—
> May God forgive him, *I* shall not.[27]

"A Land of Peace and Pensions"

The War educated Bierce, "enlightened" or "undeceived" him in the
same sense that Melville's shattered veterans were enlightened by
exploding shells and undeceived by bullets. It also left him a
casualty, permanently warped and seared like one of Hawthorne's

damned seekers who is crushed rather than tempered by revelation. A universe where such atrocities could happen remained hostile to him as did the God who allegedly managed human affairs. Once he had swallowed the "fascinating fallacy that all men are born equal,"[28] believed that words meant what the dictionary said they did. He had heard the cry for help when he was "young and full of faith," and in keeping with others of that "sentimental generation" had willingly taken more than his fair share of hard knocks. But "The Hesitating Veteran" asked himself in the light of the aftermath whether it had been worth it:

> That all is over now—the reign
>   Of love and trade still all dissensions,
> And the clear heavens arch again
>   Above a land of peace and pensions.
> The black chap—at the last we gave
>   Him everything that he had cried for,
> Though many white chaps in the grave
>   'Twould puzzle to say what they died for.
>
> I hope he's better off—I trust
>   That his society and his master's
> Are worth the price we paid, and must
>   Continue paying, in disasters;
> But sometimes doubts press thronging round
>   ('Tis mostly when my hurts are aching)
>
> If war for Union was a sound
>   and profitable undertaking.
> No mortal man can Truth restore
>   Or say where she is to be sought for.
> I know what uniform I wore—
>   O, that I knew which side I fought for![29]

Bierce the veteran did know what side he fought for even though Bierce the devil's lexicographer might treat the pastime of war with Biercean irreverence. If he knew little about the controversies leading up to the War when he enlisted, according to his friend and confidant, Walter Neale, he decided "after he had reached years of discretion . . . that he had fought on the right side."* But the War turned him into a "hired assassin" and a bleak

---

* Walter Neale, *Life of Ambrose Bierce* (New York, 1929), 102. According to Neale, Bierce enlisted to free the slaves: "There was besides, the moral urge, the chivalric impulse, and the excuse to justify bloodshed. Of course, the dominating urge was lust for war, the opportunity for adventure, the call to the blood of youth" (193–94). Had Bierce known the Negro as well in 1861, as he did in 1906, "he might have been tempted to fight for the South—

determinist. In his last visits to the battlefields—once in 1903 and again in 1913—retracing "old routes and lines of march" and standing "in my old camps," he tried but only partially succeeded in recapturing the elation of what he called "my Realm of Adventure."[30] The ache of despair overmatched the pleasures of nostalgia.

By this time, Bierce's misanthropy was not "a reasoned philosophy of despair but a conditioned reflex."[31] His response to the War had always been intensely personal, never philosophical, and he generalized his pessimism into universal law. The War remained for Bierce hardly more than a lurid stage set for a private drama. It left the grander drama untouched and unfelt, but few writers registered the shock of war's terrors with a comparable fidelity.

---

this jocosely" (190). And again: "He grew to dislike negroes intensely as a race, despite his fascination, although he did not extend his antipathies to individuals. But how he 'loathed their black hides, their filthy persons, and their odiferous [sic] aroma!'" (189). Neale, a Virginian, was deeply prejudiced against Negroes himself. His allegations about Bierce's distaste for blacks, Hindus, American Indians, Chinese, and Japanese must be taken with this in mind.

Chapter 13

Albion W. Tourgée

He saw the war from the inside; was a private soldier in the Federal army at the outset, several months in Confederate prisons and still bears the unpleasant reminders of a service which was earnest if insignificant. For fourteen years after its close he lived among those whose best sentiment the poem is intended to reflect. He may be entirely wrong, but he has an intense pride, as an American, in the achievements of those men, has a profound pity for any ex-confederate who cannot endorse the sentiments of the poem and an unfathomable contempt for any man who would have them feel otherwise.

ALBION W. TOURGÉE, 1882

Carpetbagger

THE War itself turned out to be less important to Albion Winegar Tourgée than either its causes or consequences. Like Bierce, he enlisted in 1861 and fought in a number of important battles before he resigned under pressure in December 1863. Unlike Bierce, he was not an exemplary soldier, although just as truculent, opinionated, and brave. Bierce honored his former foes, detested the sleazy materialism following the peace, and remained loyal to the brotherhood of veterans. So did Tourgée. Bierce, soured and disenchanted, came to regret his youthful idealism about the Union and the slave and spurned uplifters and do-gooders. Tourgée, converted to Unionism and antislavery shortly before the War, stubbornly kept the faith as soldier, Carpetbagger, novelist, and publicist.

According to his biographers,[1] he sometimes confounded his causes with personal advancement. At times he cut ethical corners, played down embarrassing episodes in his post-War political activities, and glorified his public image to the point of distortion. He could be vain, pompous, self-righteous. Yet for all that, he was a

193

dedicated and self-sacrificing man. Few of his contemporaries studied the history of the sectional rift so attentively or tried more disinterestedly to plumb its meaning. None was a more unflinching and persistent advocate of Negro rights.

In his own day Tourgée won wide popularity as the self-advertised "Fool" whose adventures and misadventures in North Carolina after the War exposed the fallacies of Republican Reconstruction policies. Like other reformers of his time, he chose the novel to convey his social message, even though he wrote as if there had been no advance in its technique since Fenimore Cooper. His readers must suffer through ridiculous plots and the clumsiest fictive devices before encountering passages of vigorous exposition in which Tourgée, the lawyer, historian, and prophet, overshadows the concoctor of chases, murders, captures, conspiracies, haunted houses, and secret wills. These interpolations deal with questions that preoccupied Tourgée in his nonfiction writing as well. How did the War come about? Why did the North prove unfaithful to the Sacred Cause after 1865 and contrive the folly of Reconstruction? Why did the South resent Northern overtures? And what was to become of the Negro in the nonmilitary phase of the War that continued long after Appomattox?

Soldier

The Civil War was another violent episode in the life of a young man whose adolescence had already been troubled by emotional and physical injuries. He lost his mother at five, the same year a fall from a ladder temporarily paralyzed him. At ten, he was badly injured when a harrow rolled over him; at fourteen, an explosion cost him the sight of one eye. None of these misfortunes seems to have dampened his gusto or to have taught him prudence.

Tourgée's family were antislavery but not actively abolitionist. Young Albion thought politics a waste of time until the arguments of his sweetheart and the pull of the times converted him in the fall of 1860 into an enthusiastic captain of the Rochester Wide Awake Club. University authorities discouraged student participation in national politics, but Tourgée, his ambitions quickened by the prospect of approaching war, impatiently rejected the interdict. A month before Sumter, he enlisted in a company of dragoons commanded by his mathematics professor and shortly after was transferred to the 27th New York Volunteers.

Bull Run was an inauspicious start for an aspiring soldier. His regiment performed better than most of the other raw levies, but it, too, broke up in the general rout. "Military discipline," his fictional counterpart explains in *Figs and Thistles*, "had not yet superseded the necessity of individual knowledge, nor obedience become so habitual as to supply the want of confidence."[2] Tourgée escaped a Confederate bullet in this instance, but in the retreat he suffered another of the bizarre injuries that bedeviled his career. As an artillery battery passed through the lines during the disorderly retreat toward Washington, Tourgée was struck in the back by a gun-carriage wheel and paralyzed from the waist down. It took a year for him to recover, and the injury plagued him for the rest of his life.

He resumed his soldiering in the summer of 1862, newly commissioned lieutenant in the 105th Ohio Volunteer Infantry, and for the next year and a half traversed the same ground and took part in some of the same engagements Bierce and Shaler had fought in. Months of marching and training lay ahead before the 105th saw bloody action at Perryville, where Tourgée was slightly wounded. During the late fall of 1862, the Ohioans chased Morgan's Raiders in Kentucky and Tennessee. Then, in January 1863, Morgan's men captured a wagon train commanded by Lieutenant Tourgée and temporarily halted his none too glorious military career.

He spent the next four months in a series of Confederate prisons. Letters he wrote to his fiancée at this time contain his only references to that unhappy interval, but he does not appear to have suffered excessively. After he had been exchanged, he stopped off at Columbus, Ohio, long enough to marry and from there rejoined his regiment, now poised for the Chattanooga campaign. At Chickamauga, he took part in a wild charge against the flank of General Longstreet's corps, the last major engagement of his military career. Recurring back ailments kept him out of the battles of Lookout Mountain and Missionary Ridge, and it was plain to Tourgée's superiors that he was no longer fit for combat. In December 1863 he retired (not without rancor) from the Union Army.

All reports indicate Tourgée's bravery and competence, but he seems to have been a chronic troublemaker from the moment he enlisted. He irritated his superiors by complaining about maggoty beef or by organizing protests against what he considered unjust decisions. Repeatedly passed over for promotion because of his crotchety independence and contempt for military protocol, Tourgée angled for a commission in a Negro regiment, but nothing came of it. He left the army as much a civilian as when he entered it, and the history of the Ohio 105th—his most revealing statement about the War years—is really a celebration of civilians in uniform, the farm boys who nobly submitted to war's indignities.

We see them first through Tourgée's eyes at the swearing in.

The newly constructed barracks at Camp Taylor are made out of rough boards with the sweet smell of the forest and the sawmill about them, dripping "the amber of the riven hemlock." The volunteers stand in two long uneven lines as "the sun beats hot on the glowing napes, which the military caps, just donned for the first time, have left unprotected—the sweat drops creep down hot, flushed faces." Eyes glance longingly at blue Lake Erie sparkling in the distance. The collective oath of allegiance is clumsily sworn, but the men are moved by the great occasion. Of the original thousand, only a handful have had any military experience; the majority are untrained and undisciplined. Yet these rural greenhorns are immediately dispatched by the governor to repel the seasoned invaders of Kentucky.[3]

Tourgée indignantly replied to the Southern taunt that Federal troops were "Lincoln's hirelings" or mercenaries. His Ohioans could have earned double their wages of $13 a month, and their enlistment sometimes brought real deprivation to their families. Two-thirds of the volunteers were farmers, most of them from staunchly antislavery counties. Some had seen John Brown whose absurd and impotent mission was "predestined to failure, and . . . could only have succeeded through failure."* An antislavery Colonel led the antislavery regiment through terrible marches in what was to most of the recruits a "foreign land." Exposure to fire turned them into veterans before they had learned tactics and drill. "Once the recruit 'stood up to be shot at,'" Tourgée observed, "all the rest of his education" was a matter of form. It gave him "the inexpressible something" which transformed him into a veteran. He knew "that which lies beyond drill and discipline and is the real marrow of the soldier's life."[4]

Tourgée in Fact and Fiction

But the "real marrow" was strangely absent from his fiction, and only one of his novels contains authentic battle scenes. Nowhere, save in his regimental history, does he show much interest in the

* One of the recruits had met John Kagi, a John Brown guerrilla, after Kagi's return from the Kansas wars, his hair graying, his skull creased by a bullet. Tourgée quotes the recruit as saying: "I was, however, so impressed with his [Kagi's] earnestness and the thrilling recital of events in Kansas that it has been difficult for me to regard the firing on Sumter as more than an episode in the war which had begun years before on the western plains" (Tourgée, The Story of a Thousand. Being a History of the 105th Ohio Volunteer Infantry, in the War for the Union from August 21, 1862, to June 6, 1865 [Buffalo, 1896], 33).

machinery or psychology of war. The War neither satisfied his hunger for personal glory nor stamped him as it did De Forest and Bierce; it injured his body but left his spirit unaffected. By the time he came to write his historical survey of the great sectional conflict, fourteen years of "education" had not altered his old convictions. As early as 1863, he rejected the "oft repeated maxim of the Administration—'We are fighting for the Union as it was'" as a "most sublime hoax."[5] But he knew that the national euphoria of 1861 when "the whole people were lifted to a higher plane than they had ever trod before"[6] could not be sustained. The "great war of yesterday" no longer mattered. What both citizen and statesman needed to remember, Tourgée wrote in 1884, was *"not the battles, the marches, the conflicts,—not the courage, the suffering, the blood, but only the causes that underlay the struggle and the results that followed from it."*[7]

The young veteran who settled in Greensboro, North Carolina, in October 1865 did not yet entertain such notions. Like many Northerners of comparable background, he took it for granted that with slavery expunged, the future would be "as bright and busy within the conquered territory as it had been along the ever-advancing frontier of the West." What better place to recoup his fortunes and his health and possibly to realize his political ambitions? "Of the true character of the South," Tourgée observed from hindsight, he was "almost as ignorant as the men who made the Nation's laws."[8] He assessed the results of that ignorance in his best novel, *A Fool's Errand* (1879).

The hero is a touched-up portrait of the author and the story a misleadingly selective account of Tourgée's North Carolina years. Both the "Fool" and Tourgée were Carpetbaggers. Both came to Greensboro to set up a nursery business and practice law, and both embroiled themselves with the local people and Ku Klux Klan by upholding Negro rights. But Comfort Servasse is a disinterested humanitarian whose harassment springs from Southern vindictiveness and racial bias, whereas Tourgée became an outspoken political partisan almost from the moment he arrived in North Carolina. He wrote and spoke against former secessionists, preached the gospel of radical Republicanism, demanded suffrage for the blacks, and spread reports—some of them highly exaggerated—of atrocities against Negro and white victims of the Klan.

Tourgée's views on racial equality and his preconceptions of Southern benightedness would have aroused animosities had he been as mild and as politically inactive as his fictional alter ego. It would have been out of character, however, for this headstrong and combative crusader to try to win over his adversaries by tact or compromise. He flung himself into the political melee and thrust out at both the die-hard conservatives and moderates of his party. By the time Tourgée abandoned his Southern mission, he was one of the most detested persons in the state. Lawyers respected his legal competence and irreproachable conduct while serving on the bench of the Superior Court,[9] but such scraps of approbation were sorry fare for the man who had come South with higher expectations. He left certain that no outsider could dissolve the thick accretions of intolerance. Any Northerner residing in the South was automatically ticketed as a Carpetbagger, any opinion not in harmony with Southern public truths disregarded. He had not appreciated, he told an interviewer in 1879, the impossibility of persuading a Southerner to accept the Negro as a political element or to weaken his certitude on the undying hostility of the North. He blamed the South for its obduracy. He blamed himself for thinking he could live among a people whom even during his army days he had liked and sympathized with.

Tourgée's "History"

Tourgée worried over the implications of his bootless errand for the rest of his life. He saw it as another setback in a long series of personal failures, yet the "failure" enabled him to achieve at least a brief popular success. Northern readers found *A Fool's Errand* and its "key," *The Invisible Empire* (1880)—Tourgée's documentary exposé of the Ku Klux Klan—an exciting interpretation of a topical theme. The widespread response to these books encouraged him to believe Americans might accept his diagnosis of the causes of the still unsettled Civil War and agree with his solution: "the pressing necessity of national education, as a remedy for the evils now afflicting the South."[10]

So what began as a fictionalized autobiography lengthened into an unpremeditated six-volume "history" that spanned the years between 1840 and 1877,* "the most serious attempt ever made," Tourgée boasted, "to portray the various phases of a climacteric era."[11] Judged even by his own aesthetic standards, the series fell short of his claims. The novelist, he said, is bound by the same requirements as the historian. He must write only about the life he knows. He may be forgiven for defective analysis of motives, faulty perspective, "but the novelist who does not seek honestly and faithfully to make his work true in every sense, is a libeler who is all the

---

* In historical sequence: *Hot Plowshares* (1883); *Figs and Thistles* (1879); *A Royal Gentleman* (1881); *A Fool's Errand* (1879); *Bricks Without Straw* (1886); *John Eax* (1882).

more contemptible because he stands beyond the pale of the law."[12] Tourgée was at his best when writing about what he had directly experienced, at his most romantic and "literary" when trying to re-create the antebellum South which he only knew through books and hearsay.

Even so, the "history," when supplemented by his miscellaneous writings, was a suggestive and in some ways novel interpretation of the War by a writer whose exposure to both sections provided him with a double vision. Pieced together from his collective works, Tourgée's version of the sectional war might be summarized as follows.

The events of 1861–65 can be seen as the military phase of a war that long antedated them. Two nations, speaking the same language, worshipping the same God, and professing "to revere the same ideals," had been growing up together under the aegis of a single government, each earnestly denying the ever-widening gulf between them. "Year after year they bridged it with mutual falsehoods." Glorying in their distinctiveness, they publicly proclaimed their oneness although only a "flimsy pact" held them together. Northerners who dared to lift "a little way the veil that hid the facts" were declared public enemies.[13] When at last the irreconcilable antagonisms could no longer be plastered over, the two hostile powers fell apart "as if they had never been united. Before the sword was drawn, the separation was as complete as if the ocean rolled between."[14]

The guns of Sumter exposed the cleavage hitherto camouflaged by rhetoric. Now the long estranged North and South "taunted and jeered each other, both unconscious of the bloody destiny that lay before them." The War itself, seeded in the past, was of no great moment "whether ten or ten thousand lives were lost." It took half a dozen years for the rain to "wash away the blood," the grass to "hide the bleached bones," and the grain to "obliterate the track of charging squadrons." But why Americans slaughtered each other, "which impulse prevailed and which was forced to yield"—these were matters of great consequence indeed.[15]

The imaginary line dividing the two sections separated kingdoms of light and darkness, one dedicated to the ideal of individual liberty, the other to caste. "They spoke the same language, but they did not think the same thoughts. The ideal of one was liberty: the corner-stone of the other, servitude. Humanity was the pass-word in one; mastership was essential to authority in the other. The one made intelligence the right hand of liberty; the other accounted knowledge its chiefest enemy." In the North, education, sciences, and the arts flourished, foreign populations welcomed and assimilated, commerce and trade encouraged. In the oligarchic South,

strangers were distrusted and every institution geared to strengthen
and to justify Negro slavery. Each people "was a constant menace
to the peace and security of the other."[16]

Abolitionists may have exaggerated slavery's visible evils—"the
cruel lash, the impossible task, and whatever of opportunity for
malice the system gave rise to"—but "in the heat of partisan
advocacy" they rather underplayed "the *unconscious* evils of the
system—those which warped the brain and heart of the master as
well as dwarfed the soul of the slave."[17] The master race paid a
spiritual penalty for holding other human beings as chattels. To
justify their dominion over "dumb driven brutes, deprived of all
volition and hope," they had to train themselves to believe in "their
own innate and unimpeachable superiority" and in the "unalterable
inferiority of the slave-race." It took the exertions of the subtlest
Southern minds to prove the fictions that slaves were the most
contented and light-hearted people on earth, "carefully nourished,
protected, and guarded from error as well as evil,"[18] and to demonstrate how law, science, and religion sanctioned the system.

Yet everyday realities of Southern life mocked the pastoral
idyll of the apologists. Happy slaves perversely "desired to escape
from the paternal institution which had thrown around their lives
all these blissful and beautifying circumstances."[19] Such palpable
contradictions of Southern apologetics as fugitive slaves and Black
Codes did not disturb Southern leaders until the militancy of antislavery signaled to them "a portentous mustering of uncounted
forces against their Moloch."[20]

Abolition sprang up independent of party or region. Long
before it surfaced, "it had entered the pulpit, the home, the school"
and touched off an intellectual conflict affecting "almost the entire
branch of human knowledge." Every institution opposed it, as did
both major parties, the one declaring it wicked, the other absurd.
Yet marvelously it spread, not following any boundary but growing
imperceptibly "in streaks and spots" and silently working even in
the hearts of its enemies. No detested cause ever claimed more un-
self-seeking advocates; no public question in the world's history ever
involved a whole people "so intensely sincere in their convictions."
Each side mistook the motives of the other. Abolitionism to the
slaveholder was cruel fanaticism; the abolitionist—"beaten, incar-
cerated, maligned"—looked upon the slaveowner as the base and
selfish upholder of an evil "that grew blacker with every ray of light
thrown upon its real character."[21]

As abolitionism spread, the struggle between its friends and
foes grew increasingly bitter, for the single-mindedness of the antislavery people "made them valuable allies and dangerous enemies."
By the 1840s they had long since discredited the American Coloni-

zationist Society as a weak and vacillating body whose "prime object was to remove that demoralizing and disturbing element, the free Negro," while leaving the slave in bondage. Abolitionists now risked their safety and defied the law by assisting fugitive slaves, and they found converts among their revilers and persecutors:

> Then, too, there was mystery and daring and unlawfulness to charm the brave and pique the curious. The colored orator was in his own person at once a show and an argument. The woman, who stood by her husband on the platform while dangerous and offensive missiles flew about his head, was, of course, a heroine. The tragedy was so deep that no one could withhold his sympathy from the victims. The hopelessness of the old Greek drama was in every hour of the struggle that marked the decade of which we write. The slave was an Edipus whose woes were forever enacted within the sight of all. The old saw and pitied. The young heard and shuddered. The nation's heart echoed his moans. The nation's life leaned daily more and more to his relief. Hourly the conflict of ideas grew more intense. Momently the decisive struggle grew nearer. While Time lagged in his flight, men and women were growing up in whose hearts liberty was enshrined above all other thought. The conflict that then raged was but a forerunner of a mightier revolution; the slave who fled to freedom but an antitype of the slave to whom liberty should come almost as an unsought boon. The uprising of freemen against an unjust law was but a precursor of the wrath that should sweep away the foundations of that law. Time mocked at the Statesman's wisdom and justified the folly of the Malcontents.[22]

Curiously neither section made slavery the root of the contention. The South insisted it fought for "the collective right of a people to govern themselves according to their own ideas," to "live and die in Dixie"; the North said it fought for the Union, a "base and mean" cause in comparison to the one it "denied and tried to conceal." Call the War what you will—"Rebellion," "The War Between the States," "The War for Separation"—it boiled down to two opposing issues: "the right of man to self-direction" and "the right of one man to control and modify another's actions without his consent and against his will." In short, Federal soldiers died for a nobler cause than to restore national power: "We counted our cause supremely holy because success could add little to our own honor, prosperity, or ease, but offered all its rich harvest of blessing to other ages and an alien and oppressed people."[23]

Songs sung by both armies disclosed that slavery was the primary cause of the Civil War. Although the North announced its intention not to disturb slavery where it already existed, its "chosen battle-song" (the true index of popular feeling) was animated by "the soul of John Brown, hidden beneath the specious words and subtly grotesque phrasing." The South, in its turn, marched under "the quaint Africo-American strains of 'Dixie,' " the "mystical and equivocal ode" it "caught from the slave's lips," to express its pride of land and life. Paradoxically, both songs, expressing the ethos of two nations, derived from Negro melodies, "those curious blendings of exaggerated sentiment and pathetic drollery which permitted the marriage of minor chords and a jig movement." Each expressed "in a quaint and unique manner the dominant thought of a distinct and peculiar people": "Dixie," the South's "real national anthem" which "with strange inconsistency constituted also the battle-cry of a conflict waged for the perpetuation of slavery,"* and "John Brown's Body," that "weird anthem of universal liberty" chanted hourly by soldiers whose government for two years denied any hostility to the institution of slavery.[24]

The North finally won the War, the real purpose of which it had been ashamed to acknowledge, and proceeded to apologize thereafter to the vanquished. It taught its children to forget, not to forgive, and in its self-abasement effaced "all possible records of the strife." While the North forgot to honor its heroes, flattering them instead as if they had been mercenaries "rather than representatives of its thought and deserving types of manhood,"[25] the South deified theirs. "Dixie" continued to be sung from the Potomac to the Rio Grande. The North, absorbed in dollar-chasing, had no time for the past; the South, where past and present were one, celebrated the past less as an exercise in nostalgia than an affirmation of un-changed belief. The victors' failure to appreciate how deeply former passions and prejudices still gripped the Southern populace largely explained the debacle of Reconstruction.

Having settled the question of national power and slavery, the North awaited the fusion of the fractured nation. It counted upon emigration, foreign and domestic, to bring new vitality to a depleted

---

* "And over all rose and fell the rollicking strains of Dixie—Dixie, strange child of bondage and burlesque—the refrain of the plantation negro, caught and linked with livelier bars to suit the purpose of the simulated African, in whose hands the guitar became a banjo, and whose minstrelsy was a satire worthy of Cervantes; Dixie, snatched from the slave and the mountebank and sanctified and exalted by the passion of a whole people; Dixie, the casket which the slave gave to the master, in which to enshrine his holiest thought, the strain which fired the Southern heart, the Grecian horse which was brought within the citadel of slavery, and spawned a brood which broached the walls to the beleaguring fanatics" (Tourgée, A Royal Gentleman [New York, 1881], 258–59).

society and the "healing efficacy of trade" to restore its economy. The South "would rejoice in the new fellowship of liberty and the wonderful impetus that free thought and free labor should give to enterprise and prosperity." But such expectations did not take into account the depth of the rift. The origins of secession lay not in differing interpretations of the Constitution or in the alleged machinations of conspirators, but "in the hearts of the people." In Southern eyes, Northern armies were invaders from a foreign country. Bayonet-backed Reconstruction governments simply solidified the old Confederacy, and Southern submission signified no change of heart. The South resented being "forgiven" for what it considered its well-justified resistance to force. The new battle line it established was the "color-line," which before had "marked only the distinction of caste" but which now became "the line of demarcation between hostile forces." Northern indifference and ignorance enabled the unrepentant South to win this last phase of the War.[26]

Racism and the Future

So much for Tourgée's subjective chronicle. He felt obliged to write it, perhaps, because his historic diagnosis contained the clue to the solution of a continuing war. His backward glance did not lead him to condone Southern racism, only to recognize it as a fact. Whether racial prejudice was a natural instinct or a disease seemed to him at this time beside the point. He simply wanted to restrain its manifestations. But critics of the South first had to absolve the Southerners from blame for an attitude so deeply ingrained in their culture and be made to see that removing the Negro's disabilities by fiat only moved him *"as a man"* further away from the Southern white than he had been before the War. Southerners categorically denied the Negro's capacities, because they had never looked behind "his black face, servile manner, and mirthful proclivity" that "hid the man."[27]

Tourgée's stay in North Carolina taught him to appreciate Southern fears of black envelopment. As one of his characters observes:

> "Your ancient Puritan rage for individual right blinded the eyes of the people of the North to the fact that we acted only from the impulse of self-preservation. The South, as a people, does not wish to oppress or injure the colored man, either individually or collectively considered; but we stand face to face with the alternative of repression or surrender. We must prevent the colored man from exercising the power which

your humanitarian zeal for the individual and curious disregard for the aggregate bestowed upon him, or yield ourselves to his dominion—*if not to-day, certainly in a very near
future.*"28

But for Tourgée, the certainty of black retribution only heightened
the urgency of the crisis. Descendants of slaves were certain to burn
with rage at the oppression of their ancestors. In a hundred years,
he predicted, black orators and poets would dwell on the wrongs of
slavery more fervently than the slaves did themselves. "The colored
man who to-day looks back on slavery with feelings very far removed from unmixed bitterness will have great-great grandchildren
to whom the wrongs which he has suffered will constitute a ceaseless impulse to concerted action with their fellows in the interest of
their race."29

To prevent or at least soften the clash that was bound to come
from Negro demands for equality and the white man's determination to keep him in his place, Tourgée repeatedly advocated in novel
and tract the necessity for a federally supported crash program to
educate black and white illiterates of the South. Afro-Americans
needed time "to learn very much and forget still more" if Lincoln's
proclamation was to have any meaning.30 White Americans had to
be warned of the fearful consequences of racial bigotry. His plan
would not produce a sudden change in minds "moulded by the
influences of centuries."31 It might reverse a dangerous tendency
and mitigate the ferocity of racial strife.

Tourgée's hopefulness lessened in the last three decades of the
century as events disproved the possibility of his solution. Deserted
by both major parties and subjugated in the South, the Negroes lost
heart. The once burning "problem" had become a national bore.
Tourgée's unwavering efforts on behalf of equal rights for blacks
coincided with their virtual re-enslavement; and, unfortunately,
with the marked decline of his literary powers. His journalistic
enterprises collapsed; his moralistic tracts grew tiresome. In 1897,
as a reward for supporting McKinley, he obtained the consulship at
Bordeaux and held the post until his death in 1905. By then he had
abandoned his educational panacea for blacks as another chapter in
the "Fool's Gospel" and discarded both education and Christianity as
dissolvents of racial injustice. Once, he wrote to a friend in 1902, he
had made "the spelling-book the scepter of national power!"

Now I realize its folly, though I am glad that I then believed.
Now, I realize the terrible truth that neither Education,
Christianity, nor Civilization, mean [*sic*] justice or equality be-
tween man and man, when one is white and the other

colored. White Christianity twists with enthusiasm the Master's words to excuse wrong to the colored man individually and collectively. There has never been a white Christian people who were willing to give a colored people equal opportunity, equal right and security to enjoy "life, liberty and the pursuit of happiness." Even our American Christian slavery was the worst ever known on earth.[32]

It was an especially bitter conclusion for one who had invested so much of himself, and over such a long period, on the real issue of the War.

Part Five

THE WAR
AT SECOND HAND

LESS THAN A QUARTER-CENTURY AFTER THE CONFEDERATE SUR-
render, veterans of the victorious and defeated armies began to
commemorate the War in concert. Old hatreds dissolved into nostalgic recollection. Northern and Southern orators vied with one
another in praising the courage and nobility of their former
enemies; newspapers in both sections gave columns to ceremonies
of reconciliation. To survivors of the dark years who could see
beyond the era of "railroad-wrecking millionaires" and "unscrupulous demagogues" (some of them metamorphosed from soldiers
and civilian patriots "into a middle-aged band of robbers of the
public tills"), the encampments where Blue and Gray fraternized
and reminisced seemed the culmination of some predestined
chronicle, another example of good mysteriously evolving from
evil. The once sundered land was now "a mighty and swiftly increasing nation."*

Partly to enlighten the younger generation on events too

* *Century Magazine,* XXVIII (Aug. 1884), 630.

quickly "enveloped in accident and mystery," the editors of *Century Magazine* launched in 1884 their immensely popular illustrated series on the War. The time had come, they believed, when former foes could discuss without rancor or political prejudice the battles and leaders and teach the post-War generation "how the men who were divided on a question of principle and State fealty, and who fought the war which must remain the pivotal period of our history, won by equal devotion and valor that respect for each which is the strongest bond of a reunited people."*

Not everyone fell in with what John Hay called in a letter to his collaborator, John G. Nicolay, "the present tone of blubbering sentiment." Nicolay's assertion that "Lee ought to be shot" (an opinion that "horrified" the *Century*'s editor, Richard Watson Gilder) seemed to Hay "a simple truth of law and equity." He also decided "that Stonewall Jackson was a howling crank." Such views were impolitic in 1885. In their monumental life and times of Lincoln, Hay and Nicolay took pains not to show themselves to the public "in the attitude of two old dotards fighting over again the politics of their youth."† Very likely the *Century* would not have published the abridged version of their ten-volume work if they had.

The panorama unfolding month after month in that magazine bore little resemblance to Bierce's war or De Forest's or Whitman's. "Not one of its varied, vivid, thrilling pages," in the words of Paul H. Buck, "told of a war where men went mad with hatred, starved in prison camps, and invoked God's aid in damnation of the enemy. The history that the veterans told was a war in which valor countered valor, and each side devotedly served the right. The blood that was shed was baptismal blood, consecrating the birth of a new and greater nation."‡ Tourgée remarked in 1884 that the War itself was less important than its causes and consequences. The public's "unbroken response of welcome" to the *Century* series suggests most Americans thought the opposite was true.§

Young naturalists like Stephen Crane or Frank Norris knew the War only by hearsay. Neither the cool post-mortems of surviving generals nor the pessimism of aging ex-abolitionists excited them. They regarded the War not as a cosmic drama written and

---

* *Ibid.* (Oct. 1884), 944.
† W. R. Thayer, *The Life and Letters of John Hay* (Boston and New York, 1915, II, 32–33.
‡ *The Road to Reunion* (Boston, 1938), 248.
§ *Century Magazine*, XXIX (March 1885), 788.

directed by God but as a textbook illustration of Darwin's laws or a spectacular "tale of the death grapple of millions."* Secession and slavery, issues supposed to have animated the common soldier,† did not touch the imagination of writers fascinated by the color and violence of battle and the animallike behavior of men under terrible stress.

* Frank Norris died before he could write his projected trilogy on the battle of Gettysburg, but his disparaging review of Winston Churchill's *The Crisis* (1901) conveys his own conception of the War. Churchill, he said, had an "immense public" and a subject "in a sense made to hand, already dramatic, picturesque, interesting; whose theme is enwoven with the career of the most loveable of great men, Lincoln, and yet who has thought it advisable to be cautious, to exercise an undue restraint, to use gray colors. So large a stage, so heroic a theme, so vast an audience . . . and such a meager performance" (Donald Pizer, *The Literary Criticism of Frank Norris* [Austin, Tex., 1964], 182).

† "They saw it, from the start, as a hideous evil they had to grapple with, and to kill or be killed by; and while politicians of the 'Conservative class' were poring over law-books and parchments to find 'constitutional authority' for this or other act; and while graduates from *West Point* were painfully, and—I have no doubt—conscientious· debating whether *any* emergency could arise in which the laws of war would justify a liberation of slaves—the quicker and homelier sense of the private soldiers saw that the rebellion was a crisis for which the Constitution had made no adequate provision—doubtless holding it as a crime too horrible to be contemplated; while as regarded liberating the slaves, & finally arming them when requisite—if not prepared for it from the outset, they were at least far earlier in accepting such results than were too many of their officers" (Charles G. Halpine, "The Marching Soldier. His Joys and Sorrows," unpublished lecture, c. 1865, in Halpine Papers, Huntington Lib.).

Chapter 14

Stephen Crane and Harold Frederic

There was no real literature of our Civil War, excepting the forgotten "Miss Ravenall's [sic] Conversion" by J. W. De Forest, until Stephen Crane wrote "The Red Badge of Courage."

ERNEST HEMINGWAY, 1942

Was ever a man before who wrote of battles so abundantly as he has done, and never had a word, never a word from first to last, of the purpose and justification of the war?

H. G. WELLS, 1900

There is not only the individual mind in the battlefield, but there is the mass mind also. Crane watches the merging of the individual with the herd.

V. S. PRITCHETT, 1947

There was not much else to tell. Marthe had had what they call brain fever, and had emerged from this some weeks afterward a pallid and dim-eyed ghost of her former self, sitting for hours together in her rocking-chair in the unused parlor, her hands idly in her lap, her poor thoughts glued ceaselessly to that vague, far-off Virginia which folks told about as hot and sunny, but which her mind's eye saw under the gloom of an endless and dreadful night.

HAROLD FREDERIC, 1893

Recruits and Veterans

S TEPHEN CRANE did not think of the War as a national tragedy nor was he ever tempted to examine its causes and consequences. The incidents of *The Red Badge of Courage* might have occurred at Sevastopol or Sedan.* Yet critics in his own day acclaimed it the finest novel of the War, and so it is still judged by many.

Why did he write it? In 1893, he knew nothing of actual war, had "never smelled," so he said, "even the powder of sham battle." His famous novel (if Crane is to be believed) may even have begun as an act of bravado, a boast that he could write a better book than Zola's *La Débâcle*. More likely, however, his self-declared "potboiler" had been incubating for some time before he finished the first draft, and "almost every impression was preconceived."[1]

Given his obsession with war in general, his choice of the American War as a setting for his story was natural enough. Anyone growing up in Crane's America could hardly have remained deaf to the echoes of that event. Memoirs, biographies, regimental histories, multivolumed chronicles, pamphlets, poems, diaries poured from the presses. The land swarmed with veterans more than ready to reminisce about the most exciting years of their lives. Had Crane read none of the books whose impress has been detected in *The Red Badge*, he could have pieced together his novel from the spoken and pictorial accounts of the War. Any number of nonfiction works by the survivors contain the archetypal "plot" or situation Crane so brilliantly adapted for his special purpose.[2] In brief, it dealt with the transformation of raw volunteers into soldiers, or, to put it another way, with the conversion of the freest of the free, the collectivity of "sovereigns," into a group-animal obedient to the commands of some unseen master.

One version of this classic experience can be found in an issue of the *Century Magazine* Crane almost certainly read. A simple country boy—his patriotism inflated by marching bands, oratory, and pretty girls—enlists in the Union Army without quite knowing why. The recruit feels uneasiness, even fear, but takes some comfort in the prospect of a short and unterrible war. As he marches off

---

* Bernard Weisberger sees the hero not in some "universal setting" but as a "simple fighting man of a pastoral republic in 1861" and the novel as "specifically an epic of America's national tragedy, the Civil War" (*Twelve Original Essays on American Novels*, ed. Charles Shapiro [Detroit, 1958], 123). As will be seen, my own view differs.

to the tune of cheering crowds and weeping mothers, he throbs with self-engendered heroism. Then comes the awakening: pain, boredom, misery. He finds he must abandon civilian notions of independence and submit unthinkingly to the military machine. After blunders and rebuffs and exposure to bullets, he is transmogrified into a veteran trained to survive and to kill.[3]

The evolution from recruit to veteran is paralleled by the collective experience of the regiment or brigade. Group-men, as regimental histories bear out, repeat the same cycle as individual soldiers. The seasoning or winnowing of a regiment becomes a central theme in a good many military recollections. They tell of green levies hastily assembled, hastily trained by officers no less ignorant of military art than those they command, and hastily dispatched to the battlefields within a few months, perhaps even weeks, from the time of enlistment. And they describe the process by which an undisciplined pack of men toughens and shrinks into a formidable aggregate.

An unusually acute record of this collective transformation is Ira Seymour Dodd's *The Song of the Rappahannock*. The author, who like Crane's Henry Fleming fought at Chancellorsville, set down his War experiences a few years after the publication of *The Red Badge*.* The "song" of the title is the song of bullets:

> Preceding a distant detonation from beyond the river a faint quavering whistle would come, growing louder as with apparently increasing hurry it drew near. It seemed to speak in fascinating insinuating tone of some very special message to you alone; then suddenly, with venomous buzz in your very ear while your heart stood still it would speed by and die away in the farther distance. It was the voice of a minie bullet from the rifle of some sharpshooter in the Confederate picket line.[4]

Dodd touches on most of the familiar sidelights of field and camp— first encounter with the enemy, the look of the wounded,† the

---

* "In every battle," Dodd wrote, "there are a few heroes of the type with which Stephen Crane has made us familiar, whose ingenuity in finding safe places is amusing, and whose antics make life a burden to officers and file-closers" (*The Song of the Rappahannock* [New York, 1898], 160).

† "And I remember that every one of those wounded men whether his hurt were great or small, was pale as death and wore a fixed expression, not of terror but of stony despair. They all walked slowly and wearily and if you asked one of them, 'How is the battle going?' you got the invariable answer, 'Our regiment is all cut to pieces'; and they said it in a tone of tired reproach as though you ought to know and had insulted them by asking, or else with an inflection which meant, 'Presently you will catch it yourselves.' It was a

humor and fatalism of enlisted men—but his key chapter is "The Making of the Regiment."

For Dodd's New Jersey regiment, the "making" began with the euphoria after Sumter and the rush to the colors in the few weeks following Lincoln's proclamation—especially among the young. Bull Run ended the holiday mood. Then local pride responded to the urgent call for troops as village vied with village in meeting enlistment quotas. Bounties, after the draft enactment, added another incentive to sign up. "And yet the chief impulse was that imperious spirit of the hour which had begotten the feeling in every man's heart that until he had offered himself to his country he owed an unpaid debt." It was hard for a man to stay behind when he saw his friends and neighbors in uniform.[5]

Most of the recruits were boys and young men between the ages of sixteen and twenty-five (the Civil War was fought largely by boy-men), and only a few of the oldsters in their forties or over survived the long ordeal. Although they had never fired a shot in anger, the majority of them were familiar with some kind of drill. "It would have been hard at that time," Dodd observes, "to find a young American who did not know something about the rudiments of infantry tactics. The political campaigns immediately preceding the war, with their semimilitary organizations and their nightly processions, were a preparation for what followed which has been too little noticed." Civilian drill companies formed in the spring of 1861 used Hardee's and Casey's *Tactics* as texts.[6]

After a few weeks at camp, the men marched pretty well and performed the rudimentary maneuvers, but they looked more formidable than they were. The regiment took the field ignorant of real soldiering, raggedly disciplined, and unconfident. Then began the grueling regime of twenty-mile marches over rough terrain, the contests with mud and dust almost equal to battles. The weeding out of weaklings and misfits in all ranks accelerated as the regiment brushed with the enemy and as hostile cavalry lurked on its flanks, ready to pounce. By this time the men had learned how to survive in the field, how to sleep comfortably, cook in the rain, forage skillfully. In time skirmishes and full-scale engagements turned them into veterans not remarkable for spit and polish but tough and resourceful fighters. They had become "a cog in the wheels of a remorseless machine."[7]

Spontaneous eruptions of unsoldierly behavior continued. Reckless boys turned the air "blue with blasphemy." They chased

---

procession of spectres and cold cheer it furnished for us, hurrying forward toward the ever-nearing and now frightful tones of the Song" (*Song of the Rappahannock*, 21).

rabbits while under fire and carried on fist fights (sometimes flat on the ground in order to avoid enemy bullets). But gradually the regiment settled down, the ranks thinned by death and tempered by privation. Ghastly retreats in mud and rain, more demoralizing than enemy fire, completed its education. "The process," Dodd concedes, "was not ideal; it was in many ways illogical, unmilitary and wasteful; yet its results have seldom been surpassed."[8]

Crane managed to apprehend this "process." It would be hard to find in *The Red Badge* a single episode, a single observation related to the talk and conduct of the common soldier not recorded elsewhere in the immense compilation of the War. The authenticity of Henry Fleming's behavior in battle was vouched for by his real-life counterparts;* but although Crane's soldiers might have stepped out of a Winslow Homer sketch and assumed the postures of the living and dead in Brady's photographs,† they are Crane's automatons nonetheless. They fear, exult, banter, worry, complain, boast, swear like all soldiers, but they have no antecedents to speak of, no politics, no prejudices.

* Compare the following, for example, with *The Red Badge:* "Men found themselves in action, and without much thought, before they knew it. While yet unaccustomed to the sounds and scenes of such an occasion, and chiefly so, while idle, preparing to engage, but not yet engaged—green hands would experience a cold shrinking of the diaphragm, an uneasy moving of the eyes, a tremor in the joints of the knee and a choking in the throat caused by the nervous swelling of the apple. Then would come the scattering sounds of musketry, or the sharp crack of rifles, as we drove in their picket-lines, or they ours; sharp and growing vollies would next announce the skirmishers had begun to amuse each other; a few red flashes and white puffs from whatever earth-works or advantage ground was opposite, would next give information that their artillery was beginning to feel for us; and in another moment the screaming shell or humming round-shot would come along; sometimes passing over us, and striking far beyond; sometimes bursting over-head with a crash that would make the bravest crouch in their saddles, or draw down their heads between their shoulders; and sometimes striking the earth just in front of us, and ricochetting either over the ranks or through the ranks . . . for we then cared not much which; the blood being by that time warm; the stomachs of the men settled; the ears having grown rapidly accustomed to the music; & the eyes, lately roving uneasily, being now lighted by what is called the 'joy of battle'—for I know no other term to express it; and in a very brief time more, the throats lately twitching and swelling with nervous anxiety or uncertainty, would be distended to their utmost in the Union cheer,—the old 'hurrah' our boys gave with such a will as we charged bayonets against the enemy, or stood in line to receive them with withering vollies as their yelling lines advanced" (Charles G. Halpine, "The Marching Soldier. His Joys and Sorrows," unpublished lecture, c. 1865, in Halpine Papers, Huntington Lib.).

† For a pertinent comment on Winslow Homer and Crane together with pictorial illustrations, see John Wilmerding, *Winslow Homer* (New York, 1972), 44–47, 54–63.

Negroes and Lincoln and hospitals and prisons are not to be found in Crane's theater; these and other matters were irrelevant to his main concern—the nature of war and what happens to people who engage in it. What is heroism? How does a man behave under extreme battle stress? Is there any larger meaning or purpose behind mass killing? Questions of this kind preoccupied him, not the War already too distant for his generation to view as their elders did. He was not historically minded. The War served only as his setting for an antiwar tour de force in which deluded people misread the laws of the universe and were overwhelmed.

Henry Fleming's "Conversion"

The verisimilitude of *The Red Badge* is partly gained by Crane's painterly panoramas, partly by concrete facts of actual war quarried out of uncountable sources. Its style, tone, syntax are expressionistic. Crane not only describes the scenery of a particular battle; he also discharges his emotional antipathy toward war itself in the barbarous and violent imagery he uses to represent it. By involving soldier types—a "Youth," a "tall soldier," a "tattered soldier" in his own version of "Earth's Holocaust," he adds an abstract Hawthornean dimension to his naturalistic novel.

Ambrose Bierce may have had some such intimation when he said of Crane: "This young man has the power to feel. He knows nothing of war, yet he is drenched with blood."[9] Both Bierce and De Forest knew a great deal about war, but their realistic rendition of battle never caught on with the reading public as Crane's less authentic and highly subjective descriptions did.* "He naturally underestimated the checks placed by physical strain and fatigue on the faculties," wrote one contemporary reviewer, "as well as war's malignant, cold ironies, its prosaic dreadfulness, its dreary, deadening tedium," but he was "essentially true to the psychological core of war—if not to actualities."[10]

The Red Badge is usually read as a tale of initiation: a youthful hero, after having been overmastered by fear, regains self-confidence and acquires a juster view of his importance in the cosmos. Less obviously, it is a profane parable against war and against its glorifiers and apologists.

Like the "wise" youths in the stories of Hawthorne and Mel-

---

* R. H. Stallman notes that Bierce's other references to Crane were disparaging. Crane, on the other hand, extravagantly extolled Bierce's "The Occurrence at Owl Creek Bridge" (*Stephen Crane: Letters,* ed. R. H. Stallman and Lillian Gilkes [New York, 1960], 140).

ville, the hero is an inveterate innocent before he leaves his rural Eden, where the very cows are haloed in happiness, for the fields of war. There he hopes to capture at least a shred of glory, although he knows perfectly well the days of bloody conflict and "Greeklike struggle" are long past: "Secular and religious education had effaced the throat-grappling instinct, or else firm finance held in check the passions."[11]

Symbolically cut off from the safe civilian community by his new uniform, Henry Fleming joins the community of soldiers only to find that soldiering can be dull and pointless. He and his fellows have been regimented into the business of war against an enemy with whom they enjoy fraternizing and who presumably harbors no hostility to them. Eventually the "rebel" in blue is converted into a "veteran" and "educated" into espousing the military mystique. Crane's pervasive religious terminology underscores the theme of rebirth, but the "baptism of fire" is of a distinctly unchristian kind, for the Church into which Henry is admitted is the Church Militant with a vengeance, and the blood-swollen god to be propitiated bears a remarkably close resemblance to the devil.

Henry's conversion to the "true faith" follows the wavering course traced out in many spiritual autobiographies. He, too, must undergo periods of despair, flee like Jonah from his obligations and vainly hide, complain about the hard chastisements visited upon him, and be practically dragged to salvation. At the outset he and his comrades are "fresh fish," the designation applied to them by veterans already baptized with blood and immune to the trepidations of the unregenerate: anger and fear. But Henry's regiment is in the process of becoming like the veteran-elect. They form a kind of infernal congregation of their own, making "low-toned noises with their mouths," cheering, snarling, praying, their barbaric song blending in "an undercurrent of sound, strange and chantlike with the resounding chords of the war march."[12]

A God deaf to the canticles of his congregation presses harder tasks upon them. The reluctant unheroic hero "skedaddles," but powerful feelings of anguish and guilt preserve him from damnation. In the "religious half-light" of a forest chapel, he stares into the dead eyes of a decomposing corpse, a sacrifice to the war god and perhaps a hint of divine retribution. At any rate, the criminal gravitates compulsively toward the holy ground from which his legs have taken him, only now the battle has amplified from the "perfunctory popping" that accompanied his maiden fracas to a "celebrated battle." Amongst the sprawling dead and the "blood-stained crowd streaming to the rear," he feels like a profane interloper.[13]

In the next scenes Henry plumbs the ultimate in despair, a crucial moment in all conversion experiences. He joins the retinue of the wounded, God's bloody anointed, and must hear the solicitude of the desperately wounded "tattered man"—his "homely face suffused with a light of love for the army which was to him all things beautiful and powerful"—who assumes Henry to be one of his sanctified company. " 'Where yeh hit, ol' boy?' " he asks "in a brotherly tone." The "letters of guilt" now "burned into his brow," he meets Jim Conklin, the "tall soldier," wounded to death and already "a stalking specter of a soldier." He and the "tattered soldier" watch Jim Conklin go through the ceremony of dying: "There was something ritelike in these movements of the doomed soldier. And there was a resemblance in him to a devotee of a mad religion, blood-sucking, muscle-wrenching, bone-crushing." Jim expires in "a sort of hideous hornpipe," waving his arms wildly "in expression of implike enthusiasm." Henry acknowledges himself a "craven loon" forever banned from Valhalla. At this juncture, God intervenes for the prodigal. Henry suddenly acquires the faith of the "tattered soldier."

The sign from his Redeemer, a buffet from a gun, produces the bloody sign of election; and with that he returns to his comrades whom he finds drunk with the wine of war and sleeping off the effects of their holy debauch. Saved himself, he detects the signs of salvation in the "new eye" of his twice-born friends. Higher-ups may still call his regiment mule-drivers and mud-diggers, but they are not the same boastful boys who enlisted in the 304th New York. They no longer fight like pestered beasts, fire their guns just to reassure themselves, or disguise their fear by bravado. The "methodical idiots" move forward as a unit, shoot carefully, and take advantage of cover. They have become "men."[14]

Unruffled by the "song of the bullets" and shells snarling in the treetops, Henry Fleming can smile at the men who "dodge and duck" when the shells explode. He bears the marks of grace. In his transcendent state, he sees microscopically like the enraptured speaker in Whitman's "Song of Myself." He shares in full measure the "wild battle madness" that animates the regiment and feels in himself "the daring spirit of a savage, religion-mad."[15]

At the conclusion, Henry is resting comfortably in the regimental bosom and reading his own seraphic contentment into the universe, but the world Henry has at last come to terms with is hellish and irrational, inhabited by smudged jabbering creatures "with their swaying bodies, black faces and glowing eyes, like strange and ugly fiends jigging heavily in the smoke."[16] The words Crane repeatedly falls back upon to describe the man-made clamor of war are "wild," "mad," "insane," "crazy," "delirium," "enthusiasm," "frenzy," "frantic."

A picture of war that resembles a religious revival in hell, all sound and fury, seems to place Stephen Crane on the side of the debunkers and against the participants who saw it as a holy crusade. His War is cruel and purposeless, especially for the foot soldiers. It turns men into animals or machines and blurs the distinction between fools and heroes.* Nonetheless, he finds something awesome and admirable in his remnant of veterans.

His tribute to that chastened and seasoned brotherhood is "The Little Regiment," which Crane considered one of his best stories. The plot is of no importance although both amusing and psychologically perceptive. It tells of two brothers who mask their concern for each other's safety behind a barrage of rudeness, but the real subject is the veteran regiment made "little" by decimation and rooted "deeply into the mud, precisely as almighty nature roots mullein stalks" by "the machinery of orders." Experience has taught them to accept these "orders." They may "swear piously," but they have no illusions about their importance to the universe, and they assume the disorder surrounding them is at least coherent to unseen superiors. "Even if they had been convinced that the army was a headless monster, they would merely have nodded with the veteran's cynicism. It was none of their business as soldiers. Their duty was to grab sleep and food when occasion permitted, and cheerfully fight wherever their feet were planted until more orders came. This was a task sufficiently absorbing."[17]

Dan and Billie, the warring brothers, are both authentic veterans, Bierce's "impenitent man-killers." Each is an integral part of the regiment which he venerates. Dan, a nerveless "muscular machine," has learned to exterminate the enemy automatically, almost absent-mindedly. Listening to the "wild surf sounds" of the guns, Billie feels no fear: "The terrible voices from the hills told him that in this wide conflict his life was an insignificant fact, and that his death would be an insignificant fact." Men like Billie and Dan make up the Little Regiment which like other corps, brigades, or regiments is "as pregnant with individuality as the names of cities."[18]

The Little Regiment, "a splendid thing of steel and blue," has been welded into a graceful "steel-backed machine" by the flame of discipline, loyalty, and experience. New regiments break up and scatter under intensive fire. The Little Regiment moves on past "the relics of other assaults" and crashes into "iron entrenchments" with that "singular final despair which enables men coolly to defy the walls of a city of death." Crane did not glorify or sentimentalize the "fierce elation in the terrors of war, catching a man's heart and making it burn with such ardour that he becomes capable of dying"

---

* The theme of one of the best stories with a War setting: "A Mystery of Heroism."

nor would he have subscribed to "the soldier's faith" of Captain Oliver Wendell Holmes, Jr.* All wars were hateful to him, including the Civil War, but he was not indifferent to contests in which men victimized by external powers and internal drives and duped by their illusions managed somehow to go under without cringing.[19]

Mutual Admirers

The January 26, 1896, issue of *The New York Times* carried a dispatch from its London correspondent, Harold Frederic, reporting the literary triumph of Stephen Crane. Frederic, himself a writer of some importance, called *The Red Badge of Courage* "a deathless book," "the best of its kind," "outside of all classifications." It defined, he said, the "actual truth about battle" more exactly than Tolstoy or the French realists did by projecting it through the "starry eyes" of a sensitive participant:

> The regiment itself, the refugees from other regiments in the crowded flight, and the enemy on the other side of the fence are differentiated only as they wear the blue or gray. . . . This exhausts the dramatic persona of the book, and yet it is more vehemently alive and heaving with dramatic human action than every other book of our time. The people are all strangers to us, but the sight of them stirs the profoundest emotions of interest in our breasts. What they do appeals as vividly to our consciousness as if we had known them all our life.[20]

Coming as it did from one who had already written a novella and six stories with a War setting, this tribute was no uncritical panegyric. Frederic, like Crane, knew that combatants did not make the best reporters of war. "It seems," he observed, "as if the actual sight of a battle has some dynamic quality in it which overwhelms and crushes the literary faculty of the observer. At best he gives us a conventional account of what happened, but on analysis you find that this is not what he really saw but what all his reading has taught him that he must have seen." Like the camera which ex-

---

* "I do not know what is true. I do not know the meaning of the universe. But in the midst of doubt, in the collapse of creeds, there is one thing I do not doubt, that no man who lives in the same world with most of us can doubt, and that is that the faith is true and adorable which leads a soldier to throw away his life in obedience to a blindly accepted duty, in a cause which he little understands, in a plan of campaign of which he has no notion, under tactics of which he does not see the use" (*Speeches of Oliver Wendell Holmes, Jr.* [Boston, 1934], 59).

posed the romantic distortions of generations of battle painters, Crane's "photographic revelations" suddenly illumined the authentic face of war.[21]

The same cannot be said for the static and studied battle scenes in Frederic's war fiction, but his stories convey at least one dimension of the War's anguish and strangeness more compellingly than anything written by Crane or, for that matter, by any one of his literary contemporaries—a fact to which Crane generously testified.

The two met in London in the spring of 1897 and were soon unfeigned admirers of each other's work. An appreciation Crane wrote the next year praised his new friend's disciplined craftsmanship and likened his mind to a "sensitive plate exposed to the sunlight of '61–'65." It wonderfully reproduced, Crane thought, the "voluminous life" in rural New York State when "the North was sending its thousands to the war"—the "great country back of the line of fight—the waiting women, the lightless windows, the tables set for three instead of five . . . a land elate or forlorn, triumphant or despairing, always strained, eager, listening, tragic in attitude, trembling and quivering like a vast mass of nerves from the shock of the far away conflicts in the South."[22]

Frederic's War stories expressed all that Crane said they did. They also reflected a tacit bias that Crane left unmentioned. Far from celebrating the War as a holy cause, Frederic treated it as unmitigated disaster, and his stories are probably among the earliest examples of fiction written by a Northern writer of distinction which was not simply against war, as Crane's was, but against *the* War.

The War in Dearborn County

Frederic's country was the Mohawk Valley—Oneida County to be exact, Dearborn County in his fiction—a region as distinct and self-contained as Yoknapatawpha or Anderson's Winesburg. Farmers and villagers and townspeople bearing such names as Beech, Whipple, Parshall, Hornbeck, Turnbull, Parmalee, Hagadorn, Pulsford, and Trimble stare out of Frederic's collective portrait. Decidedly York State in their manners and ideas, their responses to the War were not very different from comparable rural communities in the North. The same fluctuations of misery and joy, consternation, and rage which kept the inhabitants of Dearborn County in turmoil during the War years must have shaken villages and farms in other districts hundreds of miles from the battle lines.

Unlike Crane, fifteen years his junior, Frederic did not have to get his facts about the War from books. He was nine when the War ended, old enough as he wrote later for "the pictures of that period" to "stick in my recollections" and "by comparison, make all the later things blurred and indistinct."[23]

Utica, where he was born in 1856 (the "Octavius" of his War stories), had sent more than its required complement of sons to faraway Southern places with outlandish names. The first recruits entrained to the accompaniment of band music and speeches. No one expected a long war. Even after a year of fighting, the Uticans shared the illusion widely held in the North that "the Rebels cooped up in Yorktown—the identical place where the British had been compelled to surrender at the close of the Revolution,"[24] would at any moment yield.* When they easily broke out of McClellan's ineffective trap and began to slaughter the Federals, Oneida County's hopes and elation changed to despair and anger.

Frederic is at his best in depicting the confused reactions of the villagers to the distant savagery. The ferocious casualties suffered by Oneida County contingents in the Peninsular campaigns alone stunned their families and friends. How much of these times Frederic actually remembered and how much he simply reconstructed from latter-day recollections of others it is hard to say, but he recreates as few writers have ever managed to do the atmosphere of a bereft community mourning its dead and swept up "in a hysterical whirl of emotions—now pride, now horror, now bitter wrath on top." His Octavians gather silently around the post office waiting for the dispatches from Antietam or Gaines's Mill or Malvern Hill to arrive. They scan the "long strips of paper posted up beside the door" listing the names of the dead and wounded. After every battle, the whole town seems to wear "a single face, repeated upon the mental vision at every step—a terrible face with distended empty eyes, riven brows, and an open drawn mouth like the old Greek mask of tragedy."[25]

The people of Dearborn County do not understand why they should have to suffer such an affliction. The "half-frenzied shriek" of an old farmer, one of the densely packed mass around the telegraph office, expresses the collective anguish and feeling of outrage: " 'Wa'nt the rest of the North doin' anything at all? . . . Do they think Dearborn County's got to suppress the whole damned

---

* In Frederic's fine story "Marsena," the young lady poet who in the thrilling days of April 1861 had contributed "an original and spirited poem on 'Pale Columbia, Shriek to Arms!' to the local paper now caught the optimistic mood in her second effusion, 'The Dove-like Dawn of White-winged Peace'" (*Harold Frederic's Stories of York State*, ed. T. F. O'Donnell [Syracuse, 1966], 186, 198).

rebellion single-handed?' " Although their regiments have brought
honor to the county, the citizens take no comfort in that "empty and
heart-sickened pretence." They move homeward burdened with the
miserable news, passing blackened shuttered houses. They speak in
low tones.[26]

Gradually the names of Southern rivers—Rapidan, Rappahannock, Chickahominy, Chattahoochee—become as familiar to the
Dearborn County farmers as their own gentle streams. But in their
fancies, these rivers mentioned so often in the battle reports turn
into "dark, sinister, swampy currents, deep and silent, and discolored with human blood." Virginia arouses no romantic associations of the "hot and sunny" Southland. It is a place where
handsome New York boys sink up to their waists in mud, a battle-
ground "under the gloom of an endless and dreadful night." In less
than a year, the popular image of the South as a kind of holiday
resort where soldiers have nothing to do except to live "snug and
warm in sort o' little houses built into the ground" and watch horse
races and cockfights every day is transformed into the picture of a
vast graveyard. The carpet looms in Dearborn County spin "only
long depressing rolls of black and blue" as the weavers come to rely
on two sources for rags: blue woolen strips from army uniforms
and shreds from "the black of bombazine or worsted mourning into
which the news in each week's papers forced one or another of the
neighboring families."[27]

Copperheads and Deserters

Frederic's most searching study of Oneida County in wartime is *The
Copperhead* (1892), a short novel about a dissenter persecuted by
his neighbors for openly opposing what he regards as a war against
fellow-Americans.

Until the fifties (according to the narrator, adopted at this time
into the Beech household and recalling people and events through a
haze of years), Abner Beech was the recognized leader of his neigh-
borhood, "a tremendous worker, a 'good provider,' a citizen of
weight and substance." He was also "a great hand for reading." He
possessed the largest library for miles around, the bulk of which
"related exclusively to American history and politics" and featured
campaign biographies of illustrious Democratic politicians. From
these partisan "histories" as well as from conversations with the
austere patriarch himself the young narrator acquired two convictions: that Hamilton and Marshall were monsters, and "that every
true American ought to hold himself in daily readiness to fight with

England." These truths prevailed in his consciousness until a more impending evil—the abolitionists—supplanted defunct Federalists and the hereditary foreign foe.[28]

The narrator explains how Abner Beech enlightened him about the "wickedness of these men who desired to establish negro sovereignty in the Republic, and to compel each white girl to marry a black man." To be sure the only Negro he has ever seen was a wandering "old darky . . . incredibly ragged, dirty, and light-hearted, shuffling through 'Jump Jim Crow,' " but it appalls him that the loafers who laugh at the black man are unaware of their precarious fate. What is even worse, the abolitionists who formerly "lived and wrought their evil deeds in distant places" have now spread into New York like a pestilence.[29] Their malign presence is dramatized for him when Abner Beech wrathfully consigns the sermons of Theodore Parker to the wood-stove. A terrible sequence of events—John Brown's raid, Lincoln's election, Fort Sumter—is capped by a terrible fact: some of Abner Beech's neighbors are abolitionists. The virus of abolitionism spreads, and soon Abner Beech is a pariah.

Before the novel is completed, Beech the Copperhead has disowned his son for enlisting in a Dearborn County regiment, quarreled angrily with the leading abolitionist, Jehoida "Jee" Hagadorn (a "tiresome fanatic of the 'fifties" who became the "inspired prophet of the 'sixties"), brawled with his neighbors on election day, and been burned out of his dwelling by village incendiaries. Eventually, and not very plausibly, he is reconciled with his persecutors. His son who returns from battle minus an arm is reunited with the long-suffering daughter of silly "Jee" Hagadorn. His neighbors, by this time mollified and guilt-ridden, rally around the "Copperhead," and Beech decides that "right down't the bottom, their hearts was sound an' sweet as a butternut." This contrived ending cannot disguise Frederic's obvious sympathy for Lincoln's loyal opposition and his devotion to Horatio Seymour.[30]

"The Old Governor," always a hero in the Frederic household,[31] had been branded a Copperhead by his political enemies during the War. He narrowly won the governorship in 1862, a year when Union military defeats and the President's Emancipation Proclamation alienated many voters in New York State, and the next summer he was unfairly blamed for inducing the draft riots in New York City. George Templeton Strong and his Republican friends branded Seymour an "unprincipled politician," "utterly base and selfish," the "representative of a platform of treason and national disintegration," as bad as Benedict Arnold and Aaron Burr.[32] To Frederic, he remained the "venerable friend" and "foremost citizen" of the state,[33]

and although Frederic never openly subscribed to Seymour's position on the War in *The Copperhead* or in other War stories, his
point of view was implicitly "Seymourite."

Seymour condoned neither slavery nor secession and after
Sumter wholeheartedly backed the policy of military force to restore
the Union, but he rejected the "irrepressible conflict" explanation
for the War and accused bigots and intriguers in both sections of
engineering it. When he thought the Washington government endangered civil and political liberties, he challenged it, and throughout the War continued to speak out against the "vindictive piety"
and "malignant philanthropy"[34] of the Radicals.

Something of Seymour's animus against uncharitable abolitionists and authoritarian government can be detected in *The Copperhead,* although Frederic himself ·is only recreating "the peculiar
mixture of patriotism and disaffection" characteristic of Oneida
County during the War. Abner Beech's ridiculous Negrophobia and
scorn of "Lincoln's nigger-worshippers" voting the "Woollyhead
ticket" are obviously not his own, but Abner's support of Seymour,
and his denunciation of "this wicked war between brothers" is not
gainsaid by the author. " 'Why, just think what's been a-goin' on!' "
Abner exclaims. " 'Great armies raised, hundreds of thousands of
honest men taken from their work an' set to murderin' each other,
whole deestricks of country torn up by the roots, homes desolated,
the land filled with widows an' orphans, an' every house a house of
mournin'.' "[35]

A Dissenting Voice

"Jee" Hagadorn's howl of exultation on hearing of Lincoln's Emancipation Proclamation is drowned out by the "terrible babel of
chorused groans and prayers and howls and curses" rising over
Malvern Hill where Marsena Pulford, the onetime photographer of
Octavius, is mortally wounded. Frederic's descriptions of carnage in
"Marsena" and in "The Day in the Wilderness" are unremarkable,
but they convey his intense disgust of war and its "pestilential
abominations." No cause, however noble, is worth the cost of this
man-made butchery. "Foul," "savage," "wild," "sinister," "barbaric,"
"frightful" are the adjectives he uses to describe it—never "grand,"
"glorious," "awesome." The misery on the Southern battlefields is
only exceeded by the "tortured hearts" and "desolate homes" in
Dearborn County. Frederic's War drags on for the first three years
without any end in sight. In successive springs, the "trees burst
forth into green," the strawberries appear, but warm weather brings
no joy or hope to wives and parents, for they know it means "more

awful massacre." In their imaginations they see "two great lines of armies . . . scowling at each other, still on that blood-soaked fighting ground between Washington and Richmond where they were three years before." Their only hope lies in General Grant, a savage man fit to end a savage contest. "He was going in, with jaws set and nerves of steel, to smash, kill, burn, annihilate, sparing nothing, looking not to right or left, till the red road had been hewed through to Richmond."[36]

Characteristically, Frederic found the soldier at the front a less interesting subject than the deserter, the type of poor man who hired out as a substitute to pay his debts. Mose Whipple, denied a furlough to visit his ailing father, lights out for the Adirondacks. Thanks to the connivance of a sympathetic deputy marshal, he is allowed to remain undiscovered and is even diverted from attempting to rejoin his regiment slogging it out "between the Wilderness and Cold Harbor,"[37] for the marshal knows Mose would be immediately executed. Frederic takes no sides, but Mose is justified by the values of Dearborn County if not the War Department's in honoring the obligations of kinship. In this story as in his other tales of the War, Frederic's sympathies lie with the inglorious ones: grimy uncelebrated foot soldiers whose names are never mentioned in the dispatches and who are shoveled into unmarked graves; dissenters like Abner Beech, "that indomitable and ferocious farmer," as Stephen Crane puts it, "with his impregnable disloyalty or conscience, or whatever"[38]; and most of all the farmers and townspeople of Dearborn County who wait and mourn.

Frederic's stories ("in large part," he says, "my own recollections of the dreadful time—the actual things that a boy from five to nine saw or heard about him, while his own relatives were being killed and his school-fellows orphaned")[39] play down both heroics and issues. The South is only a place. Confederate soldiers, the few times he mentions them, are faceless, whooping, mud-colored forms flitting through a "gloomy and sinister wilderness." Neither side operates under divine orders, nor does Frederic ever intimate that a mighty nation is being formed in the kiln of war. He refers only sparingly to national politics; slavery and the Negro receive slight notice. Frederic's War is simply a ghastly predicament worsened if not engendered by "the pressure of philanthropists"[40] and seen almost exclusively through the woeful eyes of a New York county.

Part Six

THE SOUTH:
ONLOOKERS
AND PARTICIPANTS

THE GREAT WAR NOVEL OR EPIC EVERYONE WAS CALLING FOR OR predicting during the War and thereafter ought to have been written by a Southerner. The South was the "theater" of the battle action, the *mise-en-scène* distinctive and romantic, its principal actors appropriate to the magnitude of the tragedy. Moreover, a story of exploded expectations and of military and social disaster lends itself to literary treatment more readily than the vulgarity of victory. In retrospect, the fall of the Confederacy seems emblematic of the human tragedy—an outraged, self-deceived, vainglorious, brave people (not without fear and apprehension) tilted against the ever replenished armies of the North and against impersonal forces that organized and equipped them.

Today it is possible to construct the ideal author of the unwritten masterpiece: a man old enough to have fought in some of the campaigns; an insider, yet sufficiently unbeguiled by Southern preconceptions of caste and race and culture to appraise the parochialism of his section; a humorist and ironist gauging without cynicism the comic disproportion between Southern claims and performance; a student of human behavior who relishes the variety of types that flourished in the eleven "countries" of the Confederacy and records with Chekhovian nostalgia the passing of a way of life.

No such writer appeared until Faulkner. Between 1861 and 1900, a number of men and women, Southern in background and point of view, spoke for their section and their cause, but only a small amount of fiction and poetry produced during those forty years had any permanent literary value. Even less of it deeply and seriously explored the War. The literature of the embattled Confederacy was a patriotic literature, predominantly polemical and shrill, occasionally elegiac. After the War no Southern De Forest or Bierce or Crane or Frederic emerged to document and analyze the tragic experience, no Whitman or Melville to universalize the American catastrophe.

Perhaps the War was too omnipresent and too stunning for Southern writers to comprehend at the time. During Reconstruction and after, old hatreds and humiliations blurred understanding, and rather than attempt to write truthful accounts of the real War, many preferred to veil hateful realities in legend and romance. A few dared to question the legend and were roughly handled by its priests. Others chose the safer course of confining their recollections to memories, diaries, and letters, a repository that would ultimately contribute to the Southern literary harvest in the next century. A high percentage of nineteenth-century Southern writing about the War (fiction and poetry especially) was shot through with sentiment, moonshine, and special pleading. A lesser amount (much of it private and personal) was down-to-earth, sharp, humorous, observant. Among the Southerners who wrote about the War unrhetorically and with some detachment and insight, three names stand out: Henry Timrod, poet; Mary Chesnut, diarist; and George Washington Cable, novelist.

Chapter 15

Writers in the Confederacy

The country craves literary food with an insatiable hunger, for it has fasted long. But no namby-pamby, every-day fiction will appease that craving. Light reading is eagerly desired, but it must smack of war, for all our wishes, hopes, and fears—every breath we breathe by day or night—

> *All thoughts, all passions, all delights,*
> *   Whatever stirs the mortal frame,*
> *All are but ministers of War,*
> *   And feed his horrid flame.*
>
> The Southern Literary Messenger, JUNE 1862

> *No longer shall the darksome cloud*
> *Of Northern Hate and Envy shroud*
> *The radiance of our Poets proud.*
>
> *They come, a glorious Band, to claim*
> *The guerdon of their poet-fame—*
> *Their brows with heavenly light aflame!*
>
> *Unshackled by the Northman's rule,*
> *Freed from the Bigot's canting school,*
> *The maxims of the knave and fool,*
>
> *The Genius of this youthful Land*
> *Like some rare blossom, will expand,*
> *Upflowering to the Fair and Grand!*
>
> PAUL HAMILTON HAYNE, 1862

Was it King Henry whose son was lost at sea, whereafter he never smiled? In the weight he carried to suppress all joy forever, he was but a fool to this Lee. When you and I are white haired and tell huge stories about these times to awe struck youngsters white haired around us then the shadow of Lee lengthening through the years behind him will mark a continent with a giant form.
Big thing ! ! !

229

*Why is it that I can never let myself loose and write on without
feeling somehow ashamed? There must be some taste of the
ludicrous in high degree of emotion of whatever kind the instant we
cease to sympathise with it.*

FROM *Ham Chamberlayne—Virginian. Letters and Papers of
an Artillery Officer in the War for Southern Independence,
1861–1865*

South Carolina Quixote

W ILLIAM GILMORE SIMMS, first among the writers of the antebellum South, had been prophesying "the destruction of this
once Grand Confederacy" at least a decade before the outbreak of
the sectional war—a war he thought the North would never be rash
enough to fight. During the nullification crisis in the 1830s, Simms
had been abused for his Unionism by South Carolina ultraists.
Later, for reasons not always clear to himself or his intimates, he
rode northward as knight-errant for his "disdainful state." In her
behalf, he offended New York audiences in 1856 by turning a historical talk into an assault on Massachusetts, Charles Sumner, and
all others who impugned the honor of his "Mother Country." Should
"this great empire be doomed to the convulsions of Civil War," he
warned the startled Northerners, then South Carolina "with her
lithe and sinewy limbs & muscles—will twine herself around the
giant caryatides which sustain the anchor of the great Confederacy,
and falling like the strong man of Israel, will bring down with her,
in common ruin, the vast and wondrous fabric, which her own
prowess has so much helped to raise."[1]

Because his reading public was largely Northern, Simms, of all
Southern writers, had the most to lose by this gratuitous gasconade.
As his blunt friend, James Henry Hammond, pointed out to him, he
martyred himself for a people who would not even buy his books
and for a vainglorious Preston Brooks who would accept his sacrifice as "a slight oblation." Hammond continued: "It is thought your
attempt to take the North by the nose, in its state of highest excitement & utmost exasperation and to subdue to your will by rhetoric &
argument & even *old* fact, was a little Quixotic—rather beyond
Shakespeare & Petruchio." Of course he had lost nothing in the
South, but neither had he gained much: "for *we* always expect Self-
sacrifice & hardly praise—never *pay* it." Simms could only reply
that "his mind followed his heart."[2]

Four years after his lecturing fiasco, Simms concentrated all of his prodigious energies in support of the beleaguered South he had alternately celebrated and chastised. No other Southern writer more diligently and frankly scored the citizens of his section for their backward and ruinous agronomy, their indifference to the mechanical arts, and their intellectual indolence.[3] At the same time he projected the vision of an agrarian society rejuvenated by industry and a diversified agricultural system and fostering education and art. Unified "by the cohesive bond of African slavery" and governed by a fluid elite constantly refreshed by able and ambitious recruits from the yeomanry, the South would have the parasitical and disorderly North at its mercy. As Simms watched the bombardment of Fort Sumter and "the expulsion of the enemy from the sacred soil of Carolina," his long deferred hopes seemed about to be realized.[4]

The Promised Renascence

Not all of Simms's literary contemporaries in the South agreed with his politics. Only a minority considered slavery a truly humane or stabilizing institution and a good many were reluctant disunionists. The majority of them, however, shared Simms's ardent cultural nationalism and his detestation of the Northern literary establishment (especially Boston's) which originated and perpetuated the slander of Southern cultural inferiority.

While denying that the South lay "in a long lettered eclipse . . . mitigated only by the beams of Boston, or such benignant illuminations as is diffused therein by the Northern monthlies and weeklies," Southern apologists offered a variety of reasons to account for the apparent lag in their section's literary production. Admittedly, Northern writers, sustained by a large population and by "a centralization toward the towns and cities which is a prominent feature of their society," won glittering rewards, but the trash pouring out of Yankee Grub-Streets contributed little to civilization. Admittedly, too, the South possessed virtually no professional writers, but it abounded with gifted gentlemen amateurs "with a taste for study." This minority "of cultured gentlemen, trained in the liberal arts and in the law, who turned to literature for refreshment and relaxation,"[5] was symptomatic, as Simms knew only too well, of the plight of Southern letters, but it would have been impolitic to say so. Instead, these casual contributors were called upon to provide the South with a wholesome substitute for the poisonous pap dished out by Northern periodicals.

Among themselves the Southern literary vanguard questioned the possibility of creating an authentic literature printed by Southern publishers and supported by a loyal agrarian readership. "No *purely* agricultural people, anywhere," Simms wrote, "has ever produced a national literature; has ever triumphed in the Arts, *belles lettres,* or the Drama; though they have produced great orators, politicians, warriors, and even philosophers." Men of ambition and talent in the South followed politics and the professions, not literary pursuits. They were more likely to spend their leisure moments in field sports, travel, and talk than in sampling the local literary wares. Until the War shut off communication with the North, Southerners with a taste for reading patronized Northern periodicals at the expense of their own struggling publications glutted with voluntary contributions—"fatal poison to any literary enterprise."[6]

Southern literary nationalism came to a boil with the Confederacy. Liberals who had rather timidly questioned the excessive attention to the defense of slavery (must the claims for "cotton culture," they wondered, rule out consideration for literary culture?) now took for granted the primary importance of sectional independence. Perhaps the politicians would at last appreciate the writer's role in that struggle and the penalty the South already paid for the failure of its fiction to delineate a true picture of slavery with the power of Mrs. Stowe's lying but persuasive novel. "Had a Southern poet painted in beauty, and idealized into still higher fascination the domestic ties that breed devoting affections in our negroes— painted the negro nurse, and the negro playmates, remembered by all of us with thrills of affection," then the baneful effect of Longfellow's exquisitely versified but false and fanatical antislavery poems might have been mitigated.[7]

As for the cultural and intellectual prospects of the new nation, every sign seemed propitious. Secession silenced Northern dictation "on all points of literature and art," and in the general euphoria of the first weeks of the War, magazines and newspapers rang with expostulations on the grand destiny of the Confederacy, the sovereignty of King Cotton, the benevolence of slavery, Southern womanhood, and the military prowess of the "Southron." Once again polemicists quashed Yankee claims of cultural superiority, sneered at New England's "rotten and phosphorescent literature" tinged with "unbelief and infidelity," and contrasted invidiously the celebrated "smartness" of the North with the *"public intelligence"* of the South. Yankees were "Imitators, counterfeiters, forgers on all things and at all times," an anonymous South Carolinian charged, and nothing illustrated "their native baseness" more egregiously than "those contemptible, puerile, worthless productions, which they complacently styled their 'literature.' "[8]

Freed at last from the "shackles of Northern literary bondage," Southern ladies and gentlemen would correct European misconceptions of Southern backwardness and demonstrate in their poems, essays, and novels that

> the fairest land is the home of Genius; here, where pure and loving hearts throb, amid enchanting landscapes, whose inhabitants love to listen to the wildest tale of imagination; here where the day-star of Independence is dawning on the horizon and the Southern Republic is marching forward to take a proud place among the nations of the world. Another star shall twinkle in the literary firmament. The garden of Knowledge shall have one more flower planted within it, to bloom in perpetual vigour and unfading beauty, whose fragrance shall be exhaled throughout our happy clime.

The "immense treasures of intellectual wealth" so long "hidden in the Southern mind" were certain to emerge even more remarkably after the literary character of the country had time to develop, for the planter class possessed both the attributes and the opportunities to create "a noble literature"—independence of thought, dignity of character, and leisure. It was only wanting in inclination.[9]

The "inclination" might not exhibit itself "whilst the battle of liberty is being fought" and war "the one engrossing topic." It required time before an unborn school of artists distilled the annals of old battles into poems and romances. Present actors and spectators, disqualified by "passions and prejudices," were incapable of "impartial judgment." Only after future "Humes and Robertsons, Guizots and Gibbons" had traced "our national progress," would Southern literature pass from its imitative stage into a creative type of its own. But first the South had to "throw off the yoke of Puritan domination" and arouse itself "from the lethargic stupor that broods over our literary energies." A talking people had to transform themselves into a reading people and provide for themselves a more solid and durable kind of education than they had previously settled for. Adhering to correct models, the new literature would neither yield to morbid and trashy sentimentalism nor scorn "a healthy popular taste." As one hopeful essayist expressed it in 1862: "As the tree of our national existence becomes deep-rooted . . . its soul enriched by the gallant dead, and hallowed by inspiring associations, the growth of letters will become healthy and vigorous."[10]

These comments and others no less fervent and florid reflect an intense sectional jealousy, an almost paranoid response to an alleged Yankee conspiracy against Southern genius. They can also be read as an attempt to wring some recognition for the profession of letters from a heretofore indifferent political leadership. At a time of national crisis, supporting Southern literature could be defended as a patriotic duty.

For a brief period the War did provide an impetus to Southern letters. Deprived of Northern and European books and magazines, the South had to patronize its own publishers and printers as well as its own authors. Scores of new magazines, all dedicated to the cause of independence, competed for public attention. A few enjoyed a temporary success, but a chauvinistic temper and the paucity of foreign literary imports were not enough to insure excellence or hold a diffident clientele. Very little fiction or poetry written in the South during the War came to much—including the songs and poems once pronounced as perhaps "the greatest and most lasting contributions of the Southern Confederacy to the literature of America."[11]

" 'As dolphins show their most brilliant hues, and swans give forth their most precious odors when crushed,' " wrote a Virginia editor in 1861, " 'so a people, stricken with the calamity of war produce their most melodious poetry.' " Only a handful of the patriotic effusions written on either side during the War bear him out. Noncombatants usually composed the fiercest calls to battle—versified exhortations to defend sacred soil and to shoot, stab, kill, and expel the invader—but few civilian songsters ever saw a uniformed corpse lying, in the words of an English observer, "stark and stiff, his brave clothes all dabbled in gore, his mouth wide open, grinning awful, the bloody foam on his lips dried into a purple crust."[12]

Although the War was less remote to Southern authors than to their Yankee counterparts, with few exceptions the ballads, calls to arms, prayers, battle odes, and dirges published in the Southern press were poor stuff and of no interest to fighting men. Soldiers in both armies preferred elegiac songs like "When This Cruel War Is Over" and "All Quiet on the Potomac" or hymns or doleful love songs like "Lorena." Confederate magazine verse tended to be more sanguinary and bitter than Northern verse but less comprehensive and topical. Northern poets, both amateur and professional, chronicled the entire War: the announcement of secession, Sumter, Lincoln's first call for troops, defeats and victories, attacks on Copperheads, heroic acts, vignettes of life behind the lines. Southern occasional verse usually celebrated the gallantry of individual leaders, lamented the deaths of heroes, and execrated the craven foe.[13]

Timrod's War

Among the poets of the Confederacy, Henry Timrod stands out as the single authentic talent and the only one who appears to have been "educated" by events in the Melvillean sense. One turns with relief from the declamatory, truculent, and diffuse verses of the superpatriots to Timrod's thoughtful and somber poems. He is more reflective and serious than most of his fellow Southerners and less frequently touched by the insular meanness that creeps into so much Confederate War poetry.*

Timrod belonged to the same Charleston literary circle that included Simms and Paul Hamilton Hayne. Simms had encouraged Timrod's literary ambitions at least as early as 1854 and thereafter hovered over him with officious solicitude that both irritated and touched his protégé. Never robust and a chronic invalid throughout the War years, Timrod was sometimes hard-pressed to cope with Simms's bossy and self-centered personality. Simms in his turn persisted in regarding Timrod as a languorous melancholiac, "slow, timid, sensitive, and always suffering," a little lazy, and physically and spiritually delicate. His impatience with what he took to be Timrod's morbid temperament and his inattentiveness to Timrod's bite and irony did not diminish his affection and sympathy. Timrod might carp at the older man's thick-skinned manner and artless vanity, but he knew him to be generous and kindly. "Somehow or other," he confessed to Simms, "you always magnetize me on to a little strength."[14]

Timrod felt easier with Hayne, his old schoolmate and future biographer, who deserves a place in American literary annals if only

---

* Born in Charleston, South Carolina, the son of a bookbinder with literary leanings, Timrod was Charleston schooled before matriculating at the University of Georgia in 1845. He left the University after one year, presumably for health and financial reasons. A short period studying law convinced him and his mentor that he was unsuited for the bar. Nor was he any more successful in obtaining a position as professor of classics. As early as 1846, he began to contribute to literary publications, supporting himself rather skimpily between 1850 and 1861 as a tutor on various plantations. The Boston publishing house Ticknor and Fields issued a volume of his poems in 1859. Although already a consumptive, Timrod joined a militia company in July 1861 and enlisted without much enthusiasm as a private in the Confederate army one year later. He did not take part in any military engagements but served as a private secretary, was briefly detached to cover the war in the West as a correspondent, and received a medical discharge at the end of the year. In July 1863 he re-enlisted, but a serious hemorrhage forced him to resign after only one day. Between 1863 and 1865, Timrod helped to edit newspapers in Charleston and Columbia, barely eking out a livelihood. He had married in February 1864, and the death of his son in the early fall of 1865 all but completed a procession of misfortunes which ended in his death from tuberculosis in 1867. Sick and impoverished at the end of the War and barely able to sustain himself by intermittent and ill-paid jobs and the occasional liberality of friends, he was prepared, he wrote to Hayne in 1866, "to consign every line I ever wrote to eternal oblivion for one-hundred dollars in hand" (J. B. Hubbell, *The Last Years of Henry Timrod, 1864–1867* [Durham, N.C., 1941], 61).

for his unstinted devotion to his more gifted friend. Hayne possessed modest abilities, but his poetry—safe, trite, and derivative—
is mostly feeble stuff. ("Dear Mr. Hayne," Sidney Lanier once
exclaimed in a letter praising one of Hayne's narrative poems, "thou
hast here made death *dainty!*") Adversity stirred in him self-pity
and resentment. He constantly blamed the South for neglecting him
while describing it to Northern correspondents before and after the
War as a cultural Sahara. The *"very profession"* of poet, he complained to Lowell in 1859, "is looked upon with contempt." South
Carolinians, he wrote to another Yankee, were narrow-minded and
provincial: *"Literature* they despise . . . I have lost my *patriotism,*
because it is impossible to maintain patriotism in Purgatory." In
1866 he attributed whatever reputation his verses enjoyed to Northern readers and dubbed Southerners as an "uncultivated, soul-less,
& grovelling set of yahoos" so far as poetry and letters were concerned. As he composed flattering testimonials to eminent Yankee
poets, he would abuse the North to his cronies and glory in his role
of the last of the literary cavaliers. But despite his passion for
recognition, flashes of spite, and unconquerable vanity, Hayne invariably deferred to his "brother" Timrod, treating him tenderly and
pushing his poetry ahead of his own. Timrod's wife did not exaggerate when she thanked Hayne for "your unremitting efforts to *secure*
the fame of your dead friend."[15]

Neither Hayne nor Timrod wanted to get involved in the
"sectional difficulties" agitating their state in the 1850s. "I hear
nothing about me now but politics—slavery, & anti-slavery ad
nauseam," Hayne complained to R. H. Stoddard in 1855. "Fat old
gentlemen catch me by the button, & want to know with a fierce
look what I think about Nebraska. My days are rendered wretched
by such persecution." Timrod, bored with schoolteaching and entirely absorbed in writing poetry, was if anything less interested in
politics and less sectional in his views than Hayne. He neither
favored secession nor defended slavery. To judge by his letters,
literature, nature, and pretty girls absorbed him until 1861. "Up to
this date," he wrote to a favorite woman correspondent in July
1861, "four letters have passed between us, and yet neither of us
has said a single word upon the state of the country! Let us continue
to ignore the subject. Each confident of the other's patriotism, we
can afford, I think, to dally with pleasanter topics, without incurring
mutual suspicions of indifference to the great events going on about
us."[16]

These "events," in fact, affected him more than he cared to
admit, despite his relative indifference to the hot sectional issues
and the claims of Southern nationalism. Some conception of Timrod's state of mind can be deduced from his essay on Southern

literature published in 1859. Ostensibly beyond politics, it struck at bogus Southern culture, at old fogyism, at what he called "Southernism." Thus, it could be read as a political statement in a non-political form.

The subject or victim of this essay was the Southern writer, patronized in the North and ignored and criticized at home by a mixed congress of Southern "bigots," "slaves," "autocrats"—and chauvinists. The bigot refused to acknowledge any writer after Pope; the slave waited for a Northern or European imprimatur before daring to acknowledge a Southern writer; the autocrat exalted or condemned a writer irrespective of "his real position in the world of letters" whose works pleased or offended "*him*"; and the chauvinist demanded of the Southern author that he "confine himself in the choice of his subjects to the scenery, the history, and the traditions of his own country." Timrod softened his attack by paying a conventional tribute to Southern geography and institutions, to cultured gentlemen, and to the charm and purity of Southern womanhood, but his essay implicitly flouted the cant of Southern nationalism.[17]

His South had no monopoly on genius. The true nationalist, he argued, could be distinguished by the originality of his thought, not by the "false and narrow criterion" of subject matter. Some Northern authors achieved reputations by the "art of puffing," but the Northern reading public had "a well-founded faith in its capacity to judge for itself, a not inconsiderable knowledge of the present state of Poetry and Art, and a cordial disposition to recognize and reward the native authors who address it." It was not so in the South, and it would never come about by legislative fiat or so long as the "ill-judged clemency" of amateur cliques continued to flatter mediocrity and reject the South's few genuine artists. "After all," he observed, "the chief impediment to a broad, deep, and liberal culture" was Southern self-complacency. "With a strange inconsistency, the very persons who decry Southern literature are forever extolling Southern taste, Southern learning, and Southern civilization."[18]

Secession and war temporarily interrupted this line of speculation. Timrod welcomed neither, but as a South Carolinian, he felt obliged to sink himself in a cause he was too feeble to fight for. If lung hemorrhages and general debility drove him from the ranks ("How very little the country will have owed me at the end of this war!" he wrote in 1863), he could at least "pitch in" with his pen.[19] His War poetry provides a pretty clear outline of his shifting moods between 1861 and 1866.

Southern nationalism triumphed in the formation of the Confederacy, but no poet or novelist had as yet succeeded in dignifying its mission. Not yet a nation and largely defined by what it opposed rather than what it stood for, the new government needed a laureate to make clear to itself and to the world that it represented something more than the last bastion of slavery.

Timrod never saw himself in that role. "The lyre of Tyrtaeus is the only one to which the Public will listen," he wrote to a friend in 1861, "and over that martial instrument I have but small command." But he had already demonstrated, in "Ethnogenesis," his imaginative if unrapturous celebration of the birth of a nation, an ability to speak persuasively for the Confederacy. Had this poem merely ranged an untainted South against a polluted and unchristian North, it would have done no more than repeat the sentiments of patriotic scribblers. Timrod did draw the invidious sectional contrasts, but he also envisaged an Eden embosomed in cotton fields, as secure as if it "lay entrenched behind/ Whole leagues of Russian ice and Arctic storm!" Peering into the future, he foretold of a wealthy and powerful nation radiating warmth and goodness beyond its borders:

> The hour perchance is not yet wholly ripe
> When all shall own it, but the type
> Whereby we shall be known in every land
> Is that vast gulf which laves our Southern strand,
> And through the cold, untempered ocean pours
> Its genial streams, that far off Arctic shores
> May sometimes catch upon the softened breeze
> Strange tropic warmth and hints of summer seas![20]

"The Cotton Boll," published in the same year, continues the strain of prophecy. As the poet idly pulls "soft white fibers" from the "cloven sheath," he conjures up an endless landscape of cotton: "To the remotest point of sight,/ Although I gaze upon no waste of snow,/ The endless field is white." Timrod is speaking of real cotton, the kingly staple that will enrich the South, but he also turns it into an emblem of Southern largesse: cotton will sustain and humanize the world. He becomes the poet he asks for, the one who will "fitly sing" of the "mighty commerce" that "hushes hungry lips/ In alien lands" and "only bounds its blessings by mankind!" The sound of war is heard throughout the poem as the poet chants "the days to come, unsilenced, though the quiet summer air/ Stirs with the bruit of battles." Even eventual victory will not extinguish accumulated woes: ". . . we cannot all forget/ That there is much even Victory must regret." Yet after the Goth has been crushed and leniently judged, "the half-dead dream of universal peace" will be revived.

The theme of peace present in most of Timrod's War poems became more insistent as the War progressed and Confederate expectations sank. Melancholy, no doubt enhanced by ill-health, raised in his fancy images of banners "drooping in the rain/ And meadows beaten into bloody clay," but until the catastrophes of 1863, he tried his hand at those martial airs he thought himself unqualified to write. Two of his hortatory efforts, "A Cry to Arms" and "Carolina," succeed better than the usual sanguinary nonsense written to heat up the boilers of patriotism—including that empty and overpraised "My Maryland"*—but Timrod rightly distrusted his own or anyone else's attempts to compose a national song that expressed "the whole great soul of a nation within the compass of a few simple and melodious verses."[21]

He had given considerable thought to the problem, noting as early as 1861 that both "The Star-Spangled Banner" and "Rule Britannia" failed as poetry and that "all the Yankee poets (and it cannot be denied that there are some noble ones among them)" had "signally failed" to produce a national song even with the incentive of a prize.† To succeed, the song

---

* In spite of the accolades heaped upon James R. Randall's famous poem and Dr. Oliver Wendell Holmes's pronouncement ("the greatest of all war songs") it is an exercise in rhetoric, and bad rhetoric at that ("She is not dead, nor deaf, nor dumb—/ Huzza! she spurns the Northern scum!/ She breathes! she burns! she'll come! she'll come!/ Maryland, my Maryland!—" lines comically reminiscent of Longfellow's "She starts,—she moves,—she seems to feel/ The thrill of life along her keel,/ And, spurning with her foot the ground,/ With one exulting, joyous bound,/ She leaps into the ocean's arms!"). J. W. Davidson noted in his *Living Writers of the South* (New York, 1869) that Confederate soldiers were more amused than inspired by bloodthirsty civilian verse—"humorous" poetry, they called it—and burlesqued and parodied "My Maryland." It is hardly to be wondered at. Randall served briefly in the army before receiving a medical discharge, but throughout the War he excoriated the Yankees ("that mangy race . . . the codfish poltroons!") and prayed "that the black invaders may be hurled to the earth they have polluted, bleeding, butchered and hopeless" (J. R. Randall to Kate S. Hammond, Oct. 16, 1863 and April 15, 1864, Randall Papers, University of North Carolina). As might be expected, Augusta Evans Wilson, the celebrated author of *Beulah, Macaria,* and *St. Elmo* and an intimate of Timrod's friend Rachel Lyons, preferred Randall to Timrod, " 'shrinking and sensitive as a mimosa.' " She described Randall to Miss Lyons in 1862 as "the very antipode of your quiet friend. Randall is a rich, rare, tropical, luxuriant soul, whose beautiful thoughts and glowing images overflow continually, like a silver winecup whose amber and purple foam oozes over the brim" (W. P. Fidler, *Augusta Evans Wilson, 1835–1909* [University of Alabama Press, 1951], 100).

† Timrod was referring to the efforts of a New York Committee, including such names as George W. Curtis and George Templeton Strong, to set up and judge a competition for the writing of a national hymn not less than sixteen

must run glibly on the tongue; it must contain somewhere, either in a stanza or a refrain, a sentiment, tersely and music-ally expressed, which appeals to some favorite pride, prej-udice or passion of the people; it must be married to an effective, but not complicated air, and it must be aided by such collocations of accidents as may not be computed.

The South, in "Dixie," and the North in "John Brown's Body," already possessed such songs, and Timrod was not the man to write another. He felt more deeply than most the "pathos and grandeur" of the Southern struggle while he distrusted the unreflective emo-tions impelling inspired poetasters to burst "at once into anapaests." It took composure and recollective distance to write a true account of any deeply felt experience, a mental climate only possible in times of peace.[22]

Such a happy consummation seemed ever more remote as the War lurched on. His beloved Charleston, tense underneath the calm, girded by forts without and garrisoned within, waited "all untroubled in her faith . . ./ The triumph or the tomb."[23] Timrod did not share her calm, and premonitions of disaster disturb his verse after the summer of 1862. In April of that year he covered the Confederate retreat from Shiloh for the Charleston *Courier*, his first taste of real war. He left no record of the experience, but the testi-mony of his friends intimates how it shocked and sickened him.[24] Unlike Stephen Crane, another consumptive poet who hated war and died young, Timrod, sadly miscast as a war correspondent, lacked both the knack and the curiosity to describe it.*

Thenceforth his poems played down the heroics of war; he tempered his few celebrations of victory "with the lofty woe/ That wails above the noble dead." A bleak Christmas day in Charleston turned his thoughts to "some loved reveler of a year ago" now

---

lines or over forty, patriotic in spirit, simple in form with a marked rhythm, and suitable for ordinary voices. Among the twelve hundred entries, none was judged deserving of the $250 award or the gold medal of equivalent value. Richard Grant White, prominent New Yorker and member of the Committee, acknowledged the primitiveness and simplicity of the offerings but confessed his admiration "at the dexterity with which the writer has worked sound political and moral truth into them. Such men as this," he declared, "are worth more to a nation than colonels and poets." The following is a sample: "All hail our country great,/ May she never falter;/ But every damned Seces-sionist/ Be hung up by the halter" (Richard Grant White, *National Hymns. How They Are Written and How They Are Not Written. A Lyric and National Study for the Times* [New York, 1861], 142, 114–15).

* According to J. R. Randall, who met Timrod in Mobile in 1862, Timrod's absent-mindedness and night-blindness, not to mention his temperament and illness, "unfitted him for such rude employment" (E. W. Parks, *Henry Tim-rod* [New York, 1964], 38–39).

keeping "his mute Christmas" under the snow-covered "Virginian earth." The coming of spring "with that nameless pathos in the air" advertised a universal resurrection. Who, he asked, could think of war at such a time or hear death calling "in the West Wind's aromatic breath?" Yet this same spring (personified as a girl kneeling on the desecrated ground, "Lifting her bloody daisies up to God") would raise "A million men to arms" and stain the earth with gore. The sound of rain beating on his sill reminded him of spadefuls of earth dropping "like lead/ Upon the coffin of the dead." An indifferent Nature presided over the mounds of forgotten soldiers.[25]

The peace Timrod yearned for so ardently came at last, "Peace in the quiet dales,/ Made rankly fertile by the blood of men," but it was a peace observed by a shattered poet in a shattered land. One year and a few months after the War ended, a choir sang Timrod's "Ode" commemorating the Confederate dead at Magnolia Cemetery in Charleston. Poetic genius, he had remarked in February 1864, languished in "the tumult of revolution," but the poet who survived it, "his mind filled with recollections of deeds of heroism and self-sacrifice which he had witnessed," would do justice to grandeur of the struggle. The very quietness and simplicity of the "Ode" account for its eloquence. It stirs the heart "more than the roar of a thousand patriot cannon," because it leaves so much unsaid that is at the same time hauntingly intimated. Modest and beautiful like Whitman's lilacs, Timrod's verses memorialized "defeated valor," the buried soldiers' and his own. A year later he was dead.[26]

Launching the Legend

Secession, Timrod said in one of his infrequent public statements, "was the logical consequence of all that had gone before—the legitimate result of God's own divine political economy." William Gladstone erred when he told Parliament that Jefferson Davis created a Southern nation. North and South differed as markedly from each other as England and France, because "time, distance, diversities of soil and climate, opposition of interests and antagonistic traits, habits, sentiments, opinions, and institutions" made them so. As for the ultimate meaning of the War itself, here Timrod echoed the Northern writers who discovered the nobility in what seemed to have become a gross and dispiriting contest. Time would fit its meanness, cruelty, cowardice, chicanery, and selfishness into proper perspective:

> A hundred years hence, and we, too, in spite of the belittling influences of that demoralization which prevails among a

portion of our people, will assume the proportions of Paladins, and with ghostly hands thrust from our unforgotten
graves, challenge future generations to prove themselves
men by measuring their strength, their virtue and their
heroism with our own.

Timrod miscalculated the time it would take to mythologize the
past by about ninety-nine years. It began almost immediately after
the surrender of the Confederacy and quickened as Northern occupation and Reconstruction solidified a hitherto fragmented South.
Faced with a dismal present and the prospects of an even bleaker
future, men and women who lived through the War years looked
back rather than ahead. "It is not often given to a people to suffer as
the Southern people have suffered," one of them wrote years later,
"and whether the war was their own fault, or whether it was a
judgment on them for their sins of omission and commission, of
'negligence and ignorance,' it is between them and their God. But
whatever was the account against them, it has been wiped out with
a sponge dipped in tears and blood, and the slate is clean for the
score of this new generation—this 'New South,' God help them!"[27]
Suffering did not necessarily bring wisdom or illumination—
much less a change of view. Some literary spokesmen accepted the
results of trial by arms and welcomed fraternal intercourse between
the sections; others continued the old harangues.* Very few indeed
dared to analyze the old order in a critical or even disinterested way.
Those who did, as we shall see, received short shrift from the
priests and priestesses tending the Confederate shrine. "What is
civilization?" asked an editorial in 1866. If it came down to factories, a miraculous agriculture, art galleries, and vast libraries,
then the South was not civilized:

> But if to produce the greatest number of great and good men,
> and good and gentle women, in proportion to her *white* popu-
> lation, of any Christian nation on earth, is civilization, then,
> if our reading of history is not at fault, the South stands first
> amongst the nations of the earth. (The white population! We
> love the word *white*—it is a sweet, beautiful word, made
> doubly dear by the efforts of the negrophilists to blacken
> it.)[28]

---

* "It was the grand drama of history repeating itself, in the eternal conflict that the ages record, ever going on, between the plundering Hun, and the
fiery blood of the passionate Latin. It was the natural war of the eternally
hostile races, brought to the bloody issue by the Romano-Celtic, South Carolina
Huguenot, resisting the grasping and rapacious greed of the piratical Massachusetts Vi-king etc." (J. Quitman Moore, "Modern Armies—Their Organization and Spirit," *The Crescent Monthly,* I [Sept. 1866], 203).

Once again Southern editors asked readers to support local literary productions and to refurbish the Southern Muse, now somewhat bedraggled after four years of war. Promoters of new magazines again explained the neglect of letters in the South, how the War and the blockade brought publishing to a stop, murdered talent, and cast "the genius of the South . . . into a deep sleep." Still, "it would be difficult to find any country where there are more really brilliant minds and brilliant writers." Although deprived of its weapons, the South would triumph in the literary arena as its chieftains had triumphed on the battlefield. Editors called upon Christian authors to provide a literature suitable for Southern households, a literature to counteract the flood of Northern trash and infidelism engulfing Dixie.[29]

To such "undefeated" conservatives, the South remained a "country" with its own distinctive races and culture; the patriotic course was to pursue the old ways. "A day of reckoning and retribution may come," wrote a die-hard editor to Hayne in 1870, "and when it comes! WHEN IT COMES!"[30] In the meantime the magazine counselled its readers to cherish memories of soldierly gallantry, "of our old homesteads, of the patriarchal relations that once subsisted between the master and his dependents," of planter hospitality, field sports, and joyous holidays:

> The South is covered all over with vestiges of romance, which even the tread of the warrior, with garments dyed in blood, cannot obliterate. While the storm-cloud darkens the political heavens, we may turn to the past for consolation, for agreeable and heroic reminiscences. If we are mortified with the changes that have come over the face of American society; if we despair of reform, when the flood-tide of corruption is sweeping over the land with a continually accumulating force; if the present terrifies and alarms us with its prognostications and omens of worse times to come, we may still turn with pride and pleasure to the past. People who feel that they have been deeply wronged never remain stationary. They gather strength from their afflictions. Their intellectual power is quickened by the passions that agitate and the griefs that assail them, and the mind, in its efforts to extricate itself from impending difficulties, strains every nerve, and strikes out new paths to distinction. So the deepest darkness precedes the dawn, and the blackest cloud covers the sun that shines behind it. The simile is an old one, but it inculcates a great lesson. Genius never sleeps when it sheds tears, but plumes itself for some lofty flight.[31]

Chapter 16

The Unwritten Novel

*I have always read the reminiscent literature of and about the late
unlamented Confederacy that I could obtain. Every day the conviction
grows on me that it will never be painted in colors or words with much
fidelity to fact. It will never have a counterpart of Tolstoy's. And it
is a great pity.*

J. D. CALHOUN TO EDITOR OF *Century Magazine*, SEPT. 7, 1888

*The Civil War and the years that followed it undoubtedly offer the most
dramatic and powerful material available to the American novelist,
and above all to the southern novelist. And some day we shall probably
get a really great novel out of it. But we haven't had it yet.*

W. J. CASH, 1940

I detest De Forest," Paul Hamilton Hayne wrote in his diary, "because in his novel of 'Miss Ravenel' he showed himself a mean,
malignant, mischief-making dog, a sort of Cockney-Judas, who
having once kissed our poor South upon the cheek (when he
thought it would pay), must needs afterwards throw mud upon,
and spit at her, when she was down." *Miss Ravenel* was not, as
Hayne called it, a "base, brutal, and one sided caricature of a section," but his revulsion offers a clue as to why so few Southern
novelists until the next century treated the War with any degree of
detachment or openly challenged the furious old pieties of the Confederacy.[1]

De Forest himself exaggerated only slightly in his reference to
the "romances of Dixie, produced under a mixed inspiration of
namby-pambyism and provincial vanity, strong in polysyllables and
feeble in perception of character."[2] A Dixie realist might have put
into enduring form the paradox of the Southern nation, politically
democratic yet crisscrossed by lines of caste, at once hard-headed

and quixotic, idyllic and turbulent. But even if he had improbably appeared, it is doubtful whether Southerners would have tolerated a dispassionate or undecorated chronicle of their recent history— much less an irreverent one. The South had its low comedians whose ungrammatical and misspelled satires on Lincoln the Baboon and the Black Republicans were matched in venom only by the anti-Southern canards of Northern newspapers' humorists; but the defense of the Sacred Cause could not be left to profane jesters.

In depicting their War, the Southern writers, to paraphrase Henry James, dissolved the bitter herbs of defeat "in the syrup of romanticism."[3] The realism of the Howells school went against the Southern grain. Writers of fiction, a large percentage of them women, used the War to glorify the "Southron as the flower of gentility" and to indulge in fine writing. The results De Forest summed up as "powerful weak."[4]

Cooke's Cavaliers

John Esten Cooke wrote the sort of "Dixie romances" De Forest inveighed against. In later life he agreed with the Howellsians that fiction "should faithfully reflect life" and regretted being "too old to learn my trade anew."[5]

It was not the want of firsthand experience that kept him from writing the unwritten novel of the War. An intimate of J. E. B. Stuart, on whose staff he served throughout the Peninsular campaigns, Cooke's articles from camp and field to the *Southern Literary Messenger* raised the hope that he might escape Yankee bullets and become the annalist "of these stirring days." No author, the *Messenger* said, had yet appeared to paint "the scenes in the cities, towns, hamlets in the devastated districts," to describe the hospitals, report "the daily walk and conversation of our great commanders," collect "the deeds of valour of the privates," and authenticate the outrages of the enemy.[6]

The *Messenger*'s confidence in Cooke was not entirely misplaced. He had talked with Confederate leaders and observed "their daily walk," seen Jackson's men "in their dingy uniforms" stretched out "beneath the pines,"[7] and blasted the caitiff foe without exactly cataloging his crimes.* Hospitals, life in the ranks, and the War

---

* His dispatches hardly bear out J. B. Hubbell's claim that Cooke "cherished little hatred of the enemy" ("The War Diary of John Esten Cooke," *Journal of Southern History*, VI [1941], 527). In them, Yankees are "exceedingly crabbed fruit, ground in the cider-press of Southern wrath and giving forth worthless blood." Cooke scorns Federal armies and execrates their leaders.

behind the lines, however, hardly figured in his fiction or nonfiction. Privately he described the War as "fit for brutes and brutish men" and modern war in particular as a mechanical affair devoid of heroism and romance,[8] but in his novels he invited the reader to relive with him the "stormy days of a convulsed epoch," when the cavaliers challenged the invaders.[9]

These boyish glorifications of Confederate arms, a pastiche of Scott, Simms, and G. P. R. James, are cluttered with rhetorical set-pieces and silly mystifications.* Romantic celebrators like Cooke lacked the wisdom, insight, and tragic irony to see the Southern epic for what it was, and their misconceptions and prejudices blinded them to the central issue—slavery and the Negro. Why the War occurred or what it signified did not concern Cooke. "God decreed it," one of his characters says. "God the all-wise, the all-merciful— for His own purpose." He could not repine, but he would at least do justice to the heroes of "that tremendous drama."[10]

Richard Taylor—Ironist

The novel Cooke failed to write lay fragmented in letters, journals, and memoirs. These documents, as Edmund Wilson contended, were "much more imaginative and revealing"[11] than most fiction and poetry of the War. Wilson included the writing of both sections, but his comment applies with special force to Southern nonfiction, the best of which contained dramatic episodes, conversations, portraits, descriptions, and commentary few of the War novelists could match. What is more, the authors wrote of men and events without interlarding their accounts with slabs of tendentious history and romantic derring-do. Some of them had all the qualifications of a

---

General Pope is the prototype of "the powerful Republic which he defended. Liar, coward, bully—'pest, pilferer, puppy, poltroon' as he has been called— what better 'representative man' could be found for the people who employed him, and were humiliated in his person." Lincoln is "the Gorilla King" whose "ugly visage will be removed by his own betrayed countrymen." "Future ages will stand aghast at the madness which made a Baboon, Dictator—and yielded to the clutch of the grimacing animal the purse and sword of a whole nation." The Northern army is composed of stinking foreign hirelings, Yankees whose combined stench is so bad that Southern gentlemen almost have to hold their collective noses (John Esten Cooke, *Outlines from the Outpost*, ed. Richard Harwell [Chicago, 1961], 199, 223, 226, 227, 239, 243).

* In fairness to Cooke, it should be noted that he only half believed in his adventures of Confederate supermen: "Ah, those 'romances of the war'! The trifling specimens will come first, in which the Southern leaders will be made to talk an incredible gibberish, and figure in tremendous adventures." The "real facts" would be collected later by some "Walter Scott" (*Outlines*, xxviii).

novelist—a good ear, an attentive eye, a gift of phrase, a feeling for dramatic incident, irony, humor—except the inclination to write novels. But in the nonfiction writing of a few Southern men and women, the unwritten novel almost seemed struggling to be born.

General Richard Taylor's *Destruction and Reconstruction* (1879), to take one example, is a real book about a real war. Taylor, the son of President Zachary Taylor, might have figured as a character in *Miss Ravenel's Conversion*. He had something of De Forest's cynicism, toughness, and humor and something of his gentlemanly contempt for ignorant inferiors and the social corruptions they tolerated. Although a Confederate partisan and quick to dart malicious shafts at Yankee military and political leaders, he deflated Southern reputations as well. He despised boasters, whether they happened to be General Pope ("Of an effrontery while danger was remote equalled by helplessness when it was present, and mendacity after it was passed, the annals of despotism scarce offered an example of the elevation of such a favorite") or Southerners who dismissed a brave enemy as mudsills and poltroons.[12]

In contrast to Cooke, Taylor tempered his admiration for the paladins of the Confederacy with cool reservation. Cooke's Jackson looked shabby and unprepossessing as he sucked a lemon, but Cooke could not resist adding a few hero-worshipping details: "A childlike purity and gracious sweetness, mingled with indomitable will," or a "slumbering volcano clearly burned beneath that face so calm and collected—the face of Ney or Murat held in leash and waiting."[13] What impressed Taylor about Jackson, under whom he served for a time, was not merely his piety, taciturnity, and determination but also "an ambition as boundless as Cromwell's, and as merciless":

> Like the unhappy wretch from whose shoulders sprang the foul serpent, he loathed it, perhaps feared it; but he could not escape it—it was himself—nor rend it—it was his own flesh. He fought it with prayer, constant and earnest—Apollyon and Christian in ceaseless combat. What limit to set to his ability I know not, for he was ever superior to occasion. Under ordinary circumstances it was difficult to estimate him because of his peculiarities—peculiarities that would have made a lesser man absurd, but that served to enhance his martial fame, as those of Samuel Johnson did his literary eminence.[14]

Cooke's Lee was godlike and immaculate; Taylor's Lee towered over all the War commanders, but his tactics fell below his strategy, and he showed no élan for the offensive. Cooke's cavaliers (Stuart, Turner Ashby, and others) were the flowerhood of chivalry, heroes of "romantic adventures" and "splendid achievements."* Taylor admired their courage while deploring their disdain of "disciplined subordinate valor"—the only valor that counted. The female population, he drily noted, romanticized the graceful young bloods "leaping cannon to sabre countless foes," but Taylor's recollections featured no preposterous tales. "It is not pleasant to think of now," he remarked about a cold rainy night when he dined on some scraps taken from the haversack of a dead Federal, "but war is a little hardening."[15]

David Hunter Strother—Realist

David Hunter Strother, a Virginia Unionist who served with Federal armies from July 1861 until August 1864, also found war "a little hardening."

He was probably the best-known writer in either camp when the War began, and he elected to fight against his friends and kinsmen. Under the pen name "Porte Crayon," he had acquired a nationwide reputation as the author of self-illustrated travel sketches featured by Harper's in the 1840s and 1850s. In 1859 he covered the trial and execution of John Brown (he called him "a greasy old thief") and sketched the face of "Old Ossawatomie" while the martyr still hung from the scaffold,† but much as he despised abolitionists, he chiefly blamed Tidewater demagogues[16] for blowing up a quarrel right-minded men in both sections could have settled. Each side, he thought, created a false-face of the other, the

---

* "Terrible fellows they are . . . with their menacing eyes and floating plumes, who think no more of charging and routing a regiment of Yankees than of going down the middle in a Virginia reel with that inimitable grace and courtesy so peculiarly their own; who are irresistibly alike in bower and battle; who ride into the fray gaily humming a snatch of song, pause long enough to cleave a luckless mudsill from chin to chin with the 'hard steel battle-axe' which they wield so effectively, and finish in a burst of uproarious hilarity; who fight best at odds of four to one and prefer five; who are all so pure and chivalrous and brave, Sir Galahads for chastity, Sir Lancelots for valor. Where shall we look upon their like again? . . . The good die first always; and it was scarcely to be expected that Stuart and Ashby and the rest of them could go on forever with impunity, charging an army while all the world wondered; we knew that some day or other they would surely come to grief. Yet they could scarcely have anticipated the fate of being exposed to Mr. Cooke's merciless admiration" (The Round Table, VI [July 13, 1867], 26).

† C. D. Eby, Jr., "Porte Crayon": The Life of David Hunter Strother (Chapel Hill, N.C., 1960), 166. Harper's suppressed Strother's report on Harper's Ferry after sympathy for Brown swept the North. Edited by Boyd B. Stutler, it was printed for the first time as "An Eyewitness Describes the Hanging of John Brown," American Heritage, VI (Feb. 1955), 4–9.

North positing an effete, pampered aristocracy, the South a mob of timorous hucksters. Having lived and studied in the North and in Europe as well as in the South, Strother knew where such parochial misconceptions could lead,[17] and he suffered on account of his violently Unionist faith. Virginians maligned him as a type of Simon Girty renegade who masterminded Yankee atrocities against his own people. Strother himself felt "something of an alien in the Union army,"[18] but never regretted his decision to place his nation before his state.

When Strother volunteered as a civilian topographer, he was forty-six. When he resigned, with the rank of lieutenant-colonel, he had served under a half-dozen generals and campaigned in Virginia and Louisiana. He saw more actual war than all but a few of his literary contemporaries and recorded in his diaries the backstage action of the War drama with candor and fidelity. A more respectable "literary" version of his experiences subsequently appeared as "Personal Recollections of the War by a Virginian," which ran in *Harper's* (June 1866–April 1868), but as Strother's capable biographer has demonstrated, the diaries presented the same facts without flourish and contained in addition details too shocking and squalid for genteel audiences.[19]

What makes them more satisfying than many better-known War memoirs, apart from their photographic vividness, is the unfolding consciousness of the author. At the outset he was a prejudiced man, contemptuous of the masses, scornful of philanthropists, skeptical of Negro potentialities and prospects. He had no faith in Lincoln or his administration and feared for a nation which with all its moral, intellectual, and industrial strength lacked "a superior class" to direct its power. Northern politicians were either "paltry thieves" or "fanatical ideologists." The Confederacy had its complement of "bullies and blackguards" but "men of power and sagacity" directed its fortunes. Time and again the Rebels proved their superiority "in all matters of soldierly discipline, in vigilance, alertness, fortitude, forced marching, secret maneuvering, strategy, and knowledge of our forces and plans." But like De Forest's Dr. Ravenel, Strother knew the North would win. He saw the War as a contest between "a once great and magnanimous people," now maddened with "senseless pride," and modern civilization. The South had become "a stumbling block in the path of the nineteenth century," as well as the damnable instrument of treason.[20]

In time Strother modified his low opinion of Northern leadership and changed his mind about Lincoln, whom he met in the fall of 1862. He discovered "a deal of wisdom and determination" behind his "western coarseness" and was not put off by the President's "smutty fables" and "hard jokes." The diary entry for July 7,

1863 reads: "I felt warmed toward Old Abe and for the first time felt a sentiment of personal loyalty to a man who under so many disadvantages, through such vituperation, through weakness, indecision, blunders, and ignorance had yet sustained the war with unbending firmness and tenacity. He deserves well of his country and of history."[21]

It took him longer to re-examine ingrained notions about blacks, whom he had regarded as childish and thriftless and capable of improvement only under firm discipline and "within certain limits." National interest required them to go under like the Indian. Then in 1864, after hearing Frederick Douglass lecture, he confessed his astonishment and humiliation "that I, an educated Anglo-Saxon, a traveller, a philosopher, and scholar, should have lived for forty-eight years to receive instruction and feel my prejudice rebuked by a negro and a freeman. . . . I shook hands with the orator and thanked him for the instruction I had received."[22]

Besides their engaging frankness and humanity, Strother's diaries abound with incidents and observations rarely present in the Southern fiction of the period. Taylor surpassed him in the art of portraiture and showed an apter pictorial sense.* But Strother is unsurpassed in reproducing the gritty texture of the War—descriptions of smashed and rotting corpses that out-horror Bierce, of looting soldiers and colossal mismanagement, and examples of the thickening callousness of the troops—all set down in plain vernacular and spiced with equal amounts of disgust and humor.

Strother summed up the War as the tragedy of a self-deceived people, their minds made "gangrenous" on the subject of slavery, who sacrificed their lives and property for their "smutty ideals." The nation survived, but not before rifle and cannon fire and disease had piled the dead of both armies into "filthy and blood-stained heaps" and not before the South was all but destroyed. Although disturbed by the animosities created by his choice of sides, he did not feel the price too high. "We are making history," he wrote in October 1864, "which will make the nineteenth century memorable. It will one day be considered a great privilege to have lived in these days, to have

* Here is Taylor's economical caricature of General Richard Ewell: "Bright prominent eyes, a bomb-shaped bald head, and a nose like that of Francis of Valois, gave him a striking resemblance to a woodcock; and that was increased by a bird-like habit of putting his head to one side to utter his quaint speech. He fancied that he had some mysterious internal malady, and would eat nothing but frumenty, a preparation of wheat; and his plaintive way of talking of his disease, as if he were someone else, was droll to the extreme." Absorbed in the business of battle, Taylor still observed "some insignificant bluebird" flying westward "bearing a worm in its beak" (*Destruction and Reconstruction: Personal Experiences of the Late War*, ed. R. B. Harwell [New York, 1955], 36–37).

played a part in the greatest war that has shaken the earth for many a year, to have been acquainted with the actors, leaders, and localities of so famous a drama—the crushing out of the last traces of feudalism in the United States."[23]

Mrs. Chesnut's South

A far more gifted writer than either Strother or Taylor, and the most likely candidate to write the unwritten Confederate novel, was Richard Taylor's acquaintance Mary Boykin Chesnut, intimate of his brother-in-law, Jefferson Davis, and wife of Davis's aide, James Chesnut, Jr. In another time and place (ladies of her class and breeding did not expose themselves as "authoresses"), she might well have turned to novel-writing. She had the eye and ear of a novelist as well as the temperament, and one feels in reading her remarkable diary that she may have deliberately employed the form of a fictional memoir.* An inveterate reader of novels might conceivably have dramatized her experiences at such a momentous time in history and presented herself and the War novelistically.

Mrs. Chesnut said her avowed purpose in writing her diary was to provide "facts about these times" that might prove useful "to more important people than I am." Her alleged facts sometimes turned out to be wrong, and she had to keep contradicting herself. This did not disturb her: "Because I like to tell the tale as it is told to me. I write current rumor. I do not vouch for anything." She also wrote for her own diversion, because the War furnished "marvelous experiences" she delighted to record, and because she found society "only an enlarged field for character studies." As she gathered facts and rumors, studied the behavior of friends and strangers in the

---

* A *Diary from Dixie* was first published in 1905. The editors, Isabella D. Martin and Myrta L. Avary, based their version on a much larger manuscript Mrs. Chesnut had copied from her original diaries set down between February 1861 and August 1865 and later destroyed. Presumably the original diary was more explicit about names and scandalous episodes than her final copy, and it is not clear when she transcribed the extant version and what was gained or lost in the process. As she remarks on occasion, her diary even at the time of its composition could hardly be described as secret or private, for she permitted a few of her female confidantes (some of them "principals" in her day-to-day narrative) to peruse and amend it. In fact, in November 1864 the journal lay open on her desk for anyone to read who wanted to. So there was something public and contrived about the whole production. A *Diary from Dixie,* ed. Ben Ames Williams (Boston, 1949), is half again as long as the 1905 edition and more accurate. But Williams acknowledged that he transposed and inserted phrases at times to make the text more readable. A complete and accurate edition of the whole diary needs to be published.

Confederate capital and elsewhere, she herself became a character in her own story, the controlling intelligence, or, as she puts it: "Me, the woman who writes here." The chatty but premonitory diary of Mrs. Chesnut ("Cassandra" to her friends) framed the rise and fall of the Confederacy and anticipated many themes of later Civil War fiction.[24]

Biographical details of Mrs. Chesnut are meager.* Yet if the *Diary* contains practically nothing of her life before Lincoln's election, the years it covers vividly adumbrate the unwritten ones. What she did not say explicitly she hinted at or implied: that her domestic life even before the Civil War was not untroubled in spite of her husband's wealth and position, that their childless marriage saddened her, devoted to him as she was; that she was happiest in public life away from her intrusive in-laws; and that she had learned to conceal her anxieties and vulnerability behind a façade of banter. Mrs. Chesnut, no more than Colonel (later General) Chesnut, publicly displayed her emotions, and her few lapses provoked a husbandly reproof: "Hysterical grief never moves me. It annoys me. You think yourself a miracle of sensibility, but self-control is what you need. That is all that separates you from those who look upon you as unfeeling."[25]

He was referring to her alleged cold heart and her reputation for laughing "at everything and everybody." It pained her to be thus judged by those she loved, but she found much to smile and laugh at in her cozy Confederate society, and she was as quick to respond to the ludicrous as she was to the tragic. Intelligence, good manners, and handsomeness in either sex pleased her; pomposity, snobbish-

---

* She was born in 1823, the daughter of Stephen Decatur Miller and Mary Boykin Miller. Her father, a lawyer, politician, and cotton planter, served in the House of Representatives from 1817 to 1819 and in the South Carolina State Senate from 1822 to 1828. Elected Governor in 1828, he did everything in his power to encourage nullification sentiment in South Carolina. Between 1830 and 1833, he represented South Carolina in the United States Senate. In 1833, he resigned his seat for reasons of health and moved to Mississippi. He died in 1838, two years before his daughter married James Chesnut, Jr., the scion of a rich and distinguished Carolinian family, Princeton educated and soon to become one of the leading figures in the Confederate administration. During the period covered by the *Diary*, her mother lived in Portland, Alabama, while she shuttled between Charleston, Montgomery, Richmond, and Columbia with shorter interludes in Camden and in several Virginia and North Carolina resorts. After the War, General and Mrs. Chesnut retired to his plantation near Camden. She died in 1886, one year after the death of her husband. For a more detailed sketch of her life, see Margaretta A. Childs, "Mary Boykin Miller Chesnut," in E. T. James, J. W. James, Paul S. Boyer, eds., *Notable American Women 1607–1950* (Cambridge, Mass., 1971), I, 327–30.

ness (usually the mark of the parvenu), and hypocrisy aroused in her an amused disdain. "I am for the simple rule, the good old plan," she wrote in 1862. "I praise when I love and abuse when I hate." On occasion she satirized both friends and enemies. Richmond's feverish social life, confrontations with relatives at the family plantation near Camden, the flow of the Confederate elite through her hospitable house provided an abundance of subjects for her sharp and funny commentary.[26]

Mrs. Chesnut enjoyed the company of men, especially when they were good-looking or entertaining or intelligent, but she tended to view the War on the home front as a woman and to take women's side in a man-dominated world. Only the cruel, the vulgar, and the disloyal of her sex were excluded from her sympathies. Young beauties widowed after a few weeks of marriage, some of them carrying children their husbands would never see, moved her deeply. So did anguished mothers and sweethearts so hardened to catastrophe before the War ended that they had become incapable of tears. She knew, as Emily Dickinson did, of that "Quartz contentment" following great sorrow; she savored the bitter humor of a friend's remark: "She says her dismay is caused by the thought that the man she is ordained by fate to marry, whoever he is, may be killed before she knows him, or before *he* knows it." The death lists reported in the press after every battle were "enough to kill a well woman, or to age a strong and hearty one." Such jaunty asides came close to gallows humor. Yet how florid and hollow are the tributes to "sainted Southern womanhood" in contrast to Mrs. Chesnut's unsentimental admiration for maidens and matrons who tended the "awfully smashed-up objects of misery" and steeled themselves to "so much suffering, loathsome wounds, distortion, stumps of limbs exhibited to all and not half-cured."[27]

These were the same women whose ridiculous gossip she recorded and who indulged in unladylike talk never encountered in the novels of Southern males. Whether their antics amused or disquieted her, she appreciated the quiet heroism of many of them, the pertinacity and resourcefulness with which they patched up their disintegrating garments, their struggle to keep some semblance of order in a dislocated society. If their men complained of their whining and whimpering, it was because any decibel above a "mendicant's moan" brought upon them the charge of being disrespectful and unwomanly. "And yet they say our voices are the softest, sweetest, in the world. No wonder. The base submission of our tone must be music in our masters' ears!"[28]

Mrs. Chesnut's ambivalence toward men, including her husband, is apparent throughout her journal and relates in a number of

ways to slavery and the War.* As a daughter and wife of nullifica-
tionists and slavery-apologists, she accepted secession as just and
natural. "We separated from the North because of incompatibility
of temper. We are divorced, North and South, because we hated
each other so. If we could only separate politely and not have a
horrid fight for divorce." The Yankees, she sniffed, fought for
Union: "A Union! Let them call it an empire, a kingdom. We in this
Union would be an unwilling bride, a Union where one party is tied
and dragged in, if he can be well-drubbed first!" Such analogies
came readily to one inflamed against the masculine prerogative. In
symbolizing the South as the sacrificial bride resisting legalized
violation, she may have had in mind her outraged sisters' matri-
monial problems. The South, also, would be subordinate in that
regimented union.[29]

So she accepted the schism as inevitable while appreciating the
irony of supporting a cause dedicated to the perpetuation of an
institution she loathed. James Chesnut explained to his fellow
Senators in 1860 why slavery was ordained by God and nature. His
wife rejected abolitionist claims no less vehemently than her husband, but to her, slavery was a curse and an abomination, and she
resented the Northern imputation that all Southerners fought to
preserve it.

The *Diary* makes no systematic case against slaveholding. Mrs.
Chesnut knew, of course, about the dark side—slave auctions, the
random cruelties of masters and mistresses—but the *Diary* expresses less sympathy for the blacks than it does for Southern
wives:

> Under slavery, we live surrounded by prostitutes, yet an
> abandoned woman is sent out of any decent house. Who
> thinks any worse of a Negro or mulatto woman for being a
> thing we can't name? God forgive us, but ours is a mon-
> strous system, a wrong and an iniquity! Like the patriarchs of
> old, our men live all in one house with their wives and con-
> cubines; and the mulattoes one sees in every family partly
> resemble the white children. Any lady is ready to tell you who
> is the father of all the mulatto children in everybody's house-
> hold but her own. Those, she seems to think, drop from the
> clouds. My disgust sometimes is boiling over. Thank God for

---

* As the following might suggest: "Mrs. Johnston remarked that she would
never own slaves. 'I might say the same thing,' I replied. 'I never would. Mr.
Chesnut does, but he hates all slavery, especially African slavery.' 'Why do
you say "African"?' 'Why, to distinguish that form from the inevitable slavery
of the world. All married women, all children and girls who live in their
father's houses are slaves!' " (*A Diary from Dixie*, 485–86).

my country women, but alas for the men! They are probably no worse than men everywhere, but the lower their mistresses, the more degraded they must be.

Southern editors devoted columns to refuting the lies of Mrs. Stowe; Mrs. Chesnut and her friends knew that *Uncle Tom's Cabin* only touched the exceptional cases. They could have cited more common types than Simon Legree; that hypocrite, for example, who ran a black harem in his own household while posing as "a model of all human virtue to these poor women whom God and the laws have given him" and scolding his daughters for reading immoral books like *Don Juan.* "You see, Mrs. Stowe did not hit the sore spot. She makes Legree a bachelor."[30]

What could pious and kindly Yankee ladies know about slavery? They sat "in their clean cool New England homes, writing books to make their fortunes and to shame us" and sent down the John Browns to "cut our throats in God's name." Meanwhile their Southern equivalents, many of them educated in Northern schools, reading the same books, sharing the same ideas of right and wrong, lived like missionaries amidst slatternly Negro villages with no reward save the threat of black insurrections in this world and threats of future punishment "from blacker devils in the next." The Negro servants who tended them seemed both familiar and mysterious, never picturesque. Stories of women strangled in their beds, of slashed throats and poisonings, not all of them fictitious, raised fears that the slaves were simply biding their time.* No wonder Mrs. Chesnut hated slavery worse than Mrs. Stowe did and agreed with her husband's overseer that it was "a thing too unjust, too unfair to last."[31]

Mrs. Chesnut Maps a Story

On New Year's Eve, 1863, Mrs. Chesnut drank two cups "of strong, good coffee . . . and so did not sleep a wink. Like a fool I passed my whole life in review, and bitter memories maddened me. Then

---

* After the murder of "Cousin Betsy Witherspoon" by her servants, Mrs. Chesnut wrote: "Hitherto I have never thought of being afraid of Negroes. I had never injured any of them; why should they want to hurt me? Two thirds of my religion consists in trying to be good to Negroes, because they are so in our power, and it would be easy to be the other thing. Somehow today I feel that the ground is cut away from under my feet. Why should they treat me any better than they have done Cousin Betsy Witherspoon?" (140). Mrs. Chesnut disliked the term "Nigger," now "in everybody's mouth, but I have never become accustomed to it" (*A Diary from Dixie,* 486).

came a happy thought. I mapped out a story of the war. Johnny is the hero, light dragoon and heavy swell. I will call it FF's, for it is the First Families both of South Carolina and Virginia. It is to be a war story, and the filling out of the skeleton was a pleasant way to put myself to sleep."[32]

"Johnny" was her husband's nephew, John Chesnut, just twenty-one at the War's outset, "fair and frail, tall and thin," with blond hair and a Roman nose. Mrs. Chesnut's hero bore some resemblance to the "leading men" of Southern romance: he was rich and reckless and rode "like an Arab"—but he did not quite fit the stereotype. His expressionless face concealed all thought and feeling; he spoke little, took notes, and was "a keen and merciless, caustic and cruel critic of men and manners." Some judged him effeminate because he owned dozens of monogrammed handkerchiefs purchased in Paris and wore ladies' gloves in size six and a half, but neither General Sherman nor Mrs. Chesnut misjudged the John Chesnuts of the Confederacy. Sherman called these young bloods brave to the point of rashness, bold riders, first-rate shots, "the most dangerous set of men that this war has turned loose upon the world."[33] And so the adoring aunt described her dare-devil nephew, "our cool captain," who rode with Stuart but never discussed the War, who knew nothing about politics and cared less, who fought not to protect slavery but to keep himself from becoming a permanent understrapper "for those nasty Yankees."[34]

She did not specify her heroine or list the main characters of her War story, but the *Diary* contains telltale clues. Far more enchanting and believable than any heroine in any Southern novel was Sally Buchanan Campbell Preston, known to all as "Buck," who numbered John Chesnut among her retinue of rejected suitors. Angelically beautiful, she "had a knack of being fallen in love with at sight, and of never being fallen out of love with. But there seemed to be a spell upon her lovers; so many were killed or died of the effects of wounds." The discriminating Mrs. Chesnut, an intimate of the Preston family, singled her out as the one person whom she would not want to see mentally, morally, or physically altered. She lovingly observed her as she rode with Johnny, blew hot and cold during General John Bell Hood's ardent courtship, recited poetry at social gatherings, and worked in the hospital, "her blue eyes swimming in tears all the time."[35]

A series of notable figures from the upper to the lower crust filled out the supporting cast.

James Chesnut, Sr.: the author's nonagenarian father-in-law and "Prince of Slaveholders," kindly "when not crossed, given to hospitality on a grand scale, jovial, genial, friendly, courtly in his politeness" but "as absolute a tyrant as the Czar of Russia, the Khan of Tartary, or the Sultan of Turkey." This half-patriarch, half *grand seigneur* refused to say grace and thanked God "for a good dinner" after he'd eaten. " 'My way,' " he explained, " 'is to be sure of a good thing before I return thanks for it.' " Once he had been a Unionist: " 'Without the aid and countenance of the whole United States, we could not have kept slavery.' " As he watched his great fortune melt away, he wrote to the Chesnuts in Richmond: "I despise your Confederate Government. It cheats."[36]

Mrs. James Chesnut, Sr.: resident of South Carolina for over sixty years, she still disliked "hominy for breakfast and rice for dinner, without a relish to give it some flavor." During her Philadelphia girlhood, she was a familiar in the Martha Washington ménage. She married in 1796. In 1860, she maintained a household of over sixty black servants, "two thirds of them too old or too young to be of any use." She was deaf but acutely sensitive to smells. Violets oppressed her; tea roses she banished from her room. She could only "tolerate a single kind of sweet rose." Yet she devoted hours every day to cutting clothes for Negro babies and doctoring the sick. She lanced gums skillfully, dressed wounds, and invented ways to keep her idle Negroes busy. Although the greediest of readers, her strict economy discouraged her from buying books and magazines, but unbookish friends and family inundated her with reading matter. Her daughter-in-law summed her up: "She likes everything and everybody better than they deserve, and praises them beyond what they merit."[37]

Judge Thomas J. Withers: a friend of the diarist's father, married to her aunt, kindly in his personal relations but an irascible fault-finder. He assumed the "meanness and dishonesty" of all men and abused his constituents of Kershaw District, South Carolina (who finally unseated him) as nincompoops. He had no faith in Jefferson Davis and said so. Colonel James Chesnut received anonymous letters advising him to arrest the Judge for sedition. He threw them into the fire.[38]

William Henry Trescot: lawyer, historian, diplomat. No references to his writing* or political career are mentioned in the *Diary*. Mrs. Chesnut placed him in the "brilliant circle" of men (including Judge Withers, Langdon Cheves, Louis Wigfall) who made life lively in Richmond. Like Mrs. Chesnut, he laughed at everything. James L. Petigru, the antisecessionist Charleston lawyer, summed

* Howells pronounced Trescot's memorials to Generals J. Johnson Pettigrew and Steven Elliot models of their kind, forbearing, sensible, and discriminating, that analyzed as much as eulogized their subjects. Though "an ardent lover of South Carolina," he pointed out that his state was "a small and not very important part of the civilized world" (*Atlantic Monthly*, XXVIII [July 1871], 125).

him up as "a man without indignation." Although she disapproved
of his views (Trescot was another opponent of the Davis government) she could not resist his conversation ("his brains bristle like
bayonets") and she preferred him to the "fools, suave, soft, politely
punctilious." He gave her "rough truths" to digest. The victory at
Manassas, he predicted, would ruin the South by lulling it "into a
fool's paradise of conceit at our superior valor" and awaken the
shamed manhood of the North.[39]

Louis Wigfall: secessionist Fire-Eater, former Senator from
Texas, and a stormy, blustering, destructive figure in Charleston
and Richmond. He fumed at Anderson's account of the defense of
Fort Sumter: "The only men of his killed, he killed himself, or they
killed themselves, firing a salute to their old striped rag." Wigfall lay
sacrilegious hands on George Washington ("This good slave owner
who set his Negroes free when he no longer needed them") as well
as Jefferson Davis. For all of his Texas crudities, he was kindly
toward his strident wife and handsome daughter, Louly, but he was
no favorite of the diarist.[40]

Confederate dignitaries and soldiers: Jefferson Davis, courteous, conscientious, thoughtful, the butt of persistent vilification
from the beginning of the War to the end. Mrs. Chesnut honored
and respected him and his wife; they liked and trusted her. She
described him addressing a group of returned prisoners, moving
gravely through drawing rooms. She reported at length on the death
of Davis's little son, crushed to death by a fall: "I see that funeral
procession as it wound among those tall monuments up that hill
side . . . and I see the dominant figure of that poor old grey-haired
man, standing bare-headed, straight as an arrow, clear against the
sky, beside the open grave of his son."[41]

Quick glimpses of General Lee bowing gracefully to Mrs.
Chesnut and her friends as he passed their open carriage astride his
beautiful mount; of Generals Stuart, Beauregard, Johnston,
Buckner, Breckenridge, Morgan; and a long sequence of shots of
General John Bell Hood in highly unmilitary settings laying siege to
perverse Buck Preston but never quite forcing her to capitulate.

Assorted black servants: each a person, each characterized, not
blended into the black supernumerary. Lawrence, her husband's
valet and man of all purposes, quiet, respectful, indifferent; a tailor,
an expert darner, indefatigable procurer of scarce items; occasionally drunk; abused by "mean whites" who resented his elegance;
freely entrusted with money and family valuables. Molly, Mrs.
Chesnut's maid and "bodyguard," violent-tempered and impolite but
withal, the diarist adds, "the best cook, the best dairy maid, the best
washerwoman, and the best chambermaid I know; and she will do
all that and more, for me. She has an idea people impose on my

good nature." Betsey, her sister Kate's maid: "She is a great stout, jolly, irresponsible, unreliable, pleasant-tempered, bad-behaved woman, with ever so many good points. Among others, she is so clever she can do anything, and she never loses her temper; but she has no moral sense whatever." The Walkers (William, Maria, John), sired by a Scots doctor and sold after he died by his white wife. Martha Adamson, the good-looking mulatto "sempstress" who married a coal-black barber. "How could she marry that horrid Negro?" she was asked. "She answered that she inherits the taste of her white father, that her mother was black."[42]

Mrs. Chesnut's Unfinished "Novel"

Mrs. Chesnut's novel never got written although history had prefabricated the plot and her *Diary* characters pulsated with life. Very likely her stiff and reticent husband—"High South Carolina," Mrs. Jefferson Davis called him[43]—would have frowned on his wife making a literary display of herself, and it is hard to imagine any novel as breezy, scandalous, and irreverent as the *Diary* being published during her lifetime. Yet the *Diary* is more genuinely literary than most Civil War fiction. It abounds with evocative description, turns of phrase, comic episodes, anecdotes, dramatic situations, conversational exchanges, trenchant comment, and down-to-earth realities conspicuously absent in the sappy fiction of her day and later, and it is filled with nostalgic sad, bitter, and funny Confederate scenes:

Several hundred sick soldiers, ghastly pale, lie sprawled across a railway platform: "one of the horrors of war we had not reckoned on."

Fierce matrons of the ladies' aid association make "their claws felt" as they debate whether or not to divide supplies equally between the Yankee and Confederate wounded and sick.

Mulberry, the Chesnut plantation, is depicted, in December 1861:

> My sleeping apartment is large and airy, with windows opening on the lawn east and south. In those deep window seats, idly looking out, I spend much time. A part of the yard which was once a deer park has the appearance of the primeval forest; the forest trees have been unmolested and are now of immense size. In the spring, the air is laden with perfumes, violets, jasmine, crabapple blossoms, roses. Araby the blest never was sweeter with perfume. And yet there hangs here as on every Southern landscape the saddest pall. There are browsing on the lawns, where Kentucky bluegrass flourishes,

Devon cows and sheep, horses, mares and colts. It helps to enliven it. Carriages are coming up to the door and driving away incessantly.

Dr. Fair advises a German woman who has been very ill "to try to speak English, because German was a very heavy language for one as weak as she was. . . . 'If not English [the Doctor says], then she had better try French, until she gains some strength.' " The woman meekly responds: " 'My own tongue is lighter for me.' "

Three men of the Foreign Legion, punished for an attempted garrotting, march to the tune of the "Rogues March" in "barrel shirts." Fellow soldiers who refuse to join in the hooting are struck by an officer with the flat of his sword.

The "highly painted dame" who keeps the railway hotel at Camden refuses the travel-worn Mrs. Chesnut and then apologizes for her mistake: " 'Well, you know you do look funny, with that bright Balmoral petticoat grinning through all them rips and tears. And you see we are obliged to be pertickler here, and respectable. . . . You know, lots come here and call themselves any name they think we know, and then slip away on a train and don't pay. We don't take in no impostors now. Nor no stray ladies with no servants and no protectors. But I made an awful mistake not to know you.' "

Mrs. Chesnut converses with an unknown dinner companion whom she later discovers to be the editor of a violently anti-Davis paper, but not before she denounces the same editor as a "black-hearted traitor" who deserves to be drawn and quartered.

Some "Sandhill" women sullenly traipse to the homes of the gentry and demand handouts. One Judy Bradley ("a one-eyed virago who also played the fiddle at all of the Sandhill dances") speaks out after being reproved for not earning her own bread: " 'And pray, who made you a Judge and the criterion of the world. Lord, Lord, if I had er knowed I had ter stand all this jaw, I wouldn't a took your old things.' "[44]

Mrs. Chesnut's humor darkened in the last months of the War, but it never deserted her. "No howling!" she writes in April 1865. "Our poverty is made a matter of laughing. We deride our own penury. Of the country, we try not to speak at all." She had always believed that gentlefolk bore suffering with more equanimity than *hoi polloi* did—property and possessions were not the foremost concerns of a true aristocrat—and she extracted as much value from bale as from bliss. Not mere whim made her wild about *Vanity Fair*, which she first read in a New York hotel a decade before the War. People complained of its slowness, that "dull, coarse, sneering" Thackeray "stript human nature bare and made it repulsive." They said the same of *Miss Ravenel's Conversion*, a novel similar in tone if not in point of view to her sardonic *Diary*. Humor is often a requisite of detachment. Because she saw life as a human comedy, she did not judge all Yankees as monsters,* jibe at Lincoln as a nasty baboon, or keen over the fallen South. Nor did her beloved South Carolina, the "gamecock" state, escape her ridicule. Those handsome men with their beautiful manners who took "fire and famine, nakedness, mud, snow, frost, gunpowder and all . . . as it comes" were also lazy and arrogant and adherents of a dubious ethic which ostracized a man for cheating at cards or cowardice but not for grosser immoralities. "If you have stout hearts—and good family connections—you can do pretty much as you please."[45]

Always, however, she ranged the venial South, burdened by its black curse, gallant, spirited, freedom-loving, against a powerful and organized host of Pharisees who fought for lucre—not for fun and principle as the South did. If she ever modified this simplistic view of the Yankees, the *Diary* contains no evidence of it, and she seems never to have suspected the motives that impelled the North's response to Lincoln's call.

What she did know were the human and social costs the War exacted from the South. The child of a nullifier, she belonged to the South Carolina seceders; awaiting the break with "nervous dread and horror," she accepted the inevitable remedy of bloodletting as the only cure for her state's intermittent fevers. As the horrors piled up, as funerals outstripped marriages, as the Southern economy slowly strangled, her Cassandra mood prevailed. Long before Appomattox, she knew in her heart that the South would lose. Having no religion to speak of ("This plan of thinking, or thanking God, fills me with utter despondency"), she could not fall back on its consolations. She had no need for religious books: "I am already provided with the Lamentations of Jeremiah, the Penitential Psalms of David, the denunciations of Isaiah, and above all the patient wail of Job. Job is my comforter now!" If God hated Yankees, as patriotic Southern ladies firmly believed, He proffered no miracles to the ravaged Confederacy.[46]

In July 1864, the beginning of the end, Mrs. Chesnut wrote in her *Diary*:

> When I remember all the true-hearted, the light-hearted, the gay and gallant boys who have come laughing and singing and dancing across my way in the three years past! I have

---

* Her disgust is evident in her report of "A terrible Confederate female of ardent patriotism and a very large damp mouth" who exclaimed on seeing a paroled United States surgeon, " 'How I would like to scalp that creature' " (*A Diary from Dixie*, 90). She sympathized with Northern wives and mothers living in the wartime South.

looked into their brave young eyes, and helped them as I could, and then seen them no more forever. They lie stark and cold, dead upon the battlefield or mouldering away in hospitals or prisons. I think if I dared consider the long array of those bright youths and loyal men who have gone to their death almost before my very eyes, my heart might break too. Is anything worth it? This fearful sacrifice, this awful penalty we pay for war?

A year later, feeling "the weight of the years" hanging on her leaden eyelids ("I am old, old, old"), she laid down her pen. "Enough! I will write no more!"[47]

Chapter 17

Sidney Lanier

I slew gross bodies of old ethnic Hates
That stirred long race-wars betwixt states and states;
I stood and scorned these foolish dead debates,
  Calmly, calmly, Nirvâna.

SIDNEY LANIER, 1869

The Great Wind

ON his release from a Federal prison in February 1865, after three years in the Confederate army and nearly four months of miserable incarceration, Sidney Lanier had seen enough war to provide him with material for a dozen chronicles. Yet he chose to leave the War virtually unsung and confined his military adventures to a brief section in a curiously uneven novel.

Like thousands of other American boys who went larking off to battle, Lanier yielded to the blatant and subtle coercions mentioned by Strother that compelled even reluctant secessionists to enlist. His father, a Macon lawyer and Yankeephobe, and his younger brother, Clifford, had already plumped for Southern independence before Lanier proclaimed himself "a full-blooded secessionist."[1] Having reasoned himself into that position by questionable logic,* he joined the Macon Volunteers as a private in July 1861.

Some inkling of Lanier's mood shortly after Fort Sumter can be gathered from a letter to the Macon *Daily Telegraph* reporting a

---

* "All fanaticism," he wrote to his father, "is a mixture of *pure* doctrine with bad: perhaps better, a *bad* application of pure doctrine." Crusaders and French revolutionists pursued good ends through improper means; Black Republicans perverted their "foundation principle"—the superiority of God's law over the laws of men—"by wicked application" (*The Centennial Edition of the Works of Sidney Lanier*, ed. C. R. Anderson [Baltimore, 1945], VII, 34–35).

flag ceremony at Oglethorpe University. He had returned as tutor
following his graduation the previous year, more enamored with
Jean-Paul Richter and flute-playing than with politics. Four months
later he marked in his letter the "sparkling eyes and flushing
cheeks" of the Oglethorpe "Guards" and approvingly reported their
determination to preserve their flag, emblem of liberty and the
sanctity of Southern womanhood, from the polluted foe.[2] Harper's
Ferry, Georgia's secession, and the prospects of Southern independence had heated his yeasty imagination.

Lanier was to look back to those days, when the great wind of
war blew over the South, with wonder and chagrin.

> Its sound mingled with the solemnity of the church-organs
> and arose with the earnest words of preachers praying for
> guidance in the matter. It sighed in the half-breathed words
> of sweethearts conditioning impatient lovers with war-
> services. It thundered splendidly in the impassioned appeals
> of orators to the people. It whistled through the streets, it
> stole in to the firesides, it clinked glasses in bar-rooms, it
> lifted the grey hairs of our wise men in conventions, it thrilled
> through the lectures in college halls, it rustled the thumbed
> book-leaves of the school-rooms.

"Who," he asked, could resist "the fair anticipations which the new
war-idea brought?" Certainly not Sidney Lanier, who believed one
Southerner could whip five Yankees and took his own invincibility
for granted, spare and underweight though he was. Only after the
War was over did he appreciate how completely Jefferson Davis and
his government expressed the will of the Southern majority, each of
whom found some reason to welcome it or were at least dazzled into
compliance:

> It challenged the patriotism of the sober citizen, while it in-
> flamed the dream of the statesman, ambitious for his country
> or for himself. It offered test to all allegiances and loyalties;
> of church, of state; of private loves, of public devotion; of
> personal consanguinity; of social ties. To obscurity it held out
> eminence; to poverty, wealth; to greed, a gorged maw; to
> speculation, legalized gambling; to patriotism, a country; to
> statesmanship, a government; to virtue, purity; and to love,
> what all love most desires—a field wherein to assert itself by
> action.[3]

Such reflections never crossed his mind in the summer of
1861, or, for that matter, throughout the War years. By all accounts
he was a brave and willing soldier, although his biographers can

only guess in what engagements he participated. His regiment fought in the "Seven Days" battles around Richmond and probably at Chancellorsville, but none of his letters refer to these events. Because of his studied reticence about the nasty details of soldiering, it is hard to tell whether he went through experiences comparable to those of De Forest or Bierce. Until his capture aboard a Confederate blockade runner in the fall of 1864, however, Lanier's War seems to have had its romantic interludes.

Transferred to the Signal Corps in July 1862, he exchanged the onerous life of the foot soldier for the less regimented but equally dangerous one of scouting the enemy and transmitting information to headquarters. His duties sometimes enabled him and his brother, Clifford, to break up the routine of the camp and to happily vary their regular diet of corn bread, bacon, and sassafras tea. Letters mention good dinners and musical evenings in the pleasant Virginia and North Carolina villages where the Lanier brothers were billeted at various times. In fact, Lanier looked back to the late summer days of 1864 with nostalgia:

> Our life during this period was full of romance as heart could desire. We had a flute and a guitar, good horses, a beautiful country, splendid residences inhabited by friends who loved us, and plenty of hair-breath 'scapes from the roving bands of Federals who were continually visiting the Debateable Land. I look back on that as the most delicious period of my life, in many respects: Cliff and I never cease to talk of the beautiful women, the serenades, the moonlight dashes on the beach of fair Burwell's Bay (just above Hampton Roads), and the spirited brushes of our little force with the enemy.[4]

Until his imprisonment, Lanier remained astonishingly optimistic about the outcome of the War. Early Confederate success pointed to a quick victory, and Lanier along with many Southerners expected Washington to capitulate after Pope's defeat at Manassas, in August 1862. The exploits of "our brave fellows" filled him with a "presentiment of great events" and encouraged "the wildest and most visionary prophecy." As late as 1864, hope still sustained him. Grant's tremendous losses during the early months of the Petersburg assault convinced him the Yankees once again were about to change commanders and abandon the campaign. Mounting peace sentiment in the North he took to be "an infallible indication of a wide-spreading belief in the ability of the South to *win* its independence *by force of arms*." The real leader of the peace party was General Lee, backed by a "ragged constituency" who voted by bullet.

As Lanier obstetrically expressed it: "The crisis is come—. The
Western Continent is in labor; the awe and agony of child-birth are
upon her—. But I believe by the New Year,/65, the gigantic throes
will cease, and it will be announced to the World-Family that
another son is born into it—."[5]

Lanier's dreams of glory ended in November when a Federal
cruiser captured the ship on which he served as signal officer.
Taken to Norfolk, he was first confined in Fort Monroe "along with
certain thieves and cut-throats, under custody of foolish negro
soldiers," and then removed after another stop to Point Lookout,
Maryland. Whether or not this prison rivaled Andersonville and
Libby in its ghastliness, as one of Lanier's biographers argues by
assertion, three months of skimpy rations, improper shelter, prison
filth, and exposure to disease almost finished him before his release
in February 1865. Lanier's hatred of war may very well date from
those shattering months in Point Lookout. "To go into a prison of
war," he wrote in *Tiger-Lilies*, "is in all respects to be born again.
For, of the men in all prisons of the late war, it might be said, as of
births in the ordinary world—they came in and went out naked." He
left prison in tatters, divested of all property save his precious flute.
Gone forever as well were his boyish illusions about Southern
omnipotence.[6]

Tiger-Lilies *and the Allegory of War*

The light the young Lanier had seen glimmering over the horizon,
in 1860, to paraphrase a post-War memorial, turned out to be shell-
fire, not the light of stars. It was also prelude to a four-year
explosion whose cost he totaled up as follows:

> To wit: some hundreds of thousands of men killed and hurt:
> some hundreds of thousands of widows and orphans: some
> billions of money destroyed by being created: some millions
> of characters male and female demoralized: some hundreds
> of thousands of boys doomed to ignorance by their inability
> to study on account of the noise of the shells: some billions
> of property burned by the intense heat: and a miscellaneous
> mass of poverty, starvation, disease and dirt precipitated
> upon the people: so suddenly that many were buried under-
> neath these vast fragments beyond hope of extrication, save
> by that Good Samaritan—Death, who may pull some out.

In a more high-flown response to the catastrophe (unhappily typical
of his epistolary style during this period), Lanier wrote to a woman
correspondent:

Himmel! Does the horrible bubble of the big war-waves still
roar in _your_ ears, as in mine? Does that tremendous sibilla-
tion of the wave-froth, which used to transform each surge
into the likeness of a Serpent whose hissing tongue was im-
measurable and whose malignity was unfathomable, still
curdle _your_ blood, as it does mine? Are your flowers all
flecked with blood which that sea of it dashed upon them?
And when this resurrected Tempest of the old war assails you
anew, is it your habit, (as mine) to stand on the shore and
uplift your hands over the bloody waters, and cry across them
to some friend that has power to speak the storm back to stillness?[7]

Regrettably, Lanier wrote _Tiger-Lilies_ (1867), his fullest
treatment of the War, when this mood of _Schwärmerei_ still enveloped him. His father had cautioned both of his soldier sons to play
down sentiment and to concentrate on facts. R. S. Lanier preferred
political and historial essays to poetry and romance, but if Sidney
and Clifford insisted on being poetical, let Spenser's "splendid al-
legories suggest a new mode of attacking the _demonology_ . . . of
the Purito-Blue-nose-Oh!-Radico-Abolitionism of North America.
. . . Oh! what a chance here for immortality." This War, he
predicted, would keep many writers employed for a century. But
Lanier, his brain still swimming in the mist of Germany, had no
thought of becoming the historian of the Confederate wars or of
writing anti-Yankee satires. Only one notion of his father is incorporated in the novel: _Tiger-Lilies_ is a kind of allegory which dramatizes the moral dichotomies of Head and Heart, Hate and Love,
idealism and materialism. Lanier's War is more symbolic than
sectional.[8]

Tiger-Lilies is not so irredeemably silly as some reviewers
found it,* but only the second half, based upon his experiences in

---

* "Conceive of a pleasant Southern gentleman who builds a country-seat in
a cove of the Tennessee River, and calls it Thalberg! Naturally there comes
to live near him, in great seclusion, among the mountains, Ottilie, a German
lady who has been betrayed by John Cranston, an American then visiting the
master of Thalberg. At the same time, Rubetsahl, formerly Ottilie's betrothed,
arrives. Surprises, discoveries, developments; a duel between Rubetsahl and
Cranston at a masked ball for love of Felix Sterling of Thalberg and for
revenge of Ottilie. The war of secession occurs at this period; and all our
friends go into the Southern army except wicked John Cranston, who becomes
a Federal major. The lord and lady of Thalberg are shot by a deserter from
the Southern army, and Felix and Rubetsahl are finally united at the capitol
gates in Richmond, after the Confederates have abandoned the city. It is
rather uncertain about Ottilie and Philip Sterling. Cranston goes vaguely to
the deuce" (_Atlantic Monthly,_ XXI [March 1868], 382).

the spring of 1864 and his subsequent imprisonment, is of much
interest. The real War is sometimes glimpsed behind the curtain of
rhetoric. He likes to juxtapose the macabre and the pastoral,
corpses in the Garden of Eden. He recalls the exhilaration of scouting and the blessed interludes when his autobiographical hero, John
Sterling, escapes the mud and the stench of wounds in music or in
transcendental discourse with fair ladies as bookish as himself.
Authentic speech of ordinary soldiers mingles with lofty talk of the
principals. Prisons are dank and verminous, and the blackly comic
messages prisoners pin on the bulletin board ("S Shankins had a
blanket 'which he would swop it fur a par of britches, pleese caul
at, &c' ") sound too realistic for invention.[9]

Yet Lanier's general picture of the War lacks the tough speci-
ficity of De Forest's or the suffocating actuality of Bierce's. He
tended to see it from a distance and to treat it emblematically so
that even the scenes of brute warfare are stuccoed with metaphor.
The Federals in the process of uprooting a railroad melt into "a
human machine with fifty thousand clamps moved by levers infinitely flexible." Countercharging Confederates are likened to a moving mass of rags or a pack of hounds scenting a quarry. The description of the celebrated "Rebel Yell" is vintage Lanier:

> From the right of the ragged line now comes up a single long
> cry, as from the leader of a pack of hounds who has found
> the game. This cry has in it the uncontrollable eagerness of
> the sleuth-hound, together with a dry harsh quality that con-
> veys an uncompromising hostility. It is the irresistible out-
> flow of some fierce soul immeasurably enraged, and it is
> tinged with a jubilant tone, as if in anticipation of a speedy
> triumph and a satisfying revenge. It is a howl, a hoarse battle-
> cry, a cheer, and a congratulation, all in one.
>   They take it up in the centre, they echo it on the left, it
> swells, it runs along the line as fire leaps along the rigging of
> a ship. It is as if some one pulled out in succession all the
> stops of the infernal battle-organ, but only struck one note
> which they all speak in different voices.

Sterling's comrade is shot through the mouth as he shouts a hurrah,
"and, with that eagerness to escape which argues the soul's great
contempt for the body, through this small aperture leaped out John
Briggs' ascending spirit." Novalis, Richter, Carlyle, Shakespeare,
and Tennyson pervade the entire narrative and prompt the moraliz-
ings of the all too literate author.[10]

During the infrequent moments in *Tiger-Lilies* where Lanier
trusted his eyes and ears, the fog lifted. These were likely to occur

when he dealt with lowly people, not the romantic stereotypes or concepts masquerading as characters. In Cain and Gorm Smallin, Lanier created two Tennessee mountaineers who behave and speak like recognizable people. One is a salty yeoman, true to his family honor and the Southern cause, the other a Snopesian renegade and bushwhacker. Lanier cannot resist interlarding the episodes in which they figure with melodramatic asides, but at least he makes believable the anguish of the villainous Gorm when he finds his house a pile of ashes and cries out against "the rich man's war an' a poor man's fight."[11]

Needless to say, this was not the message of the novel, but what then did Lanier have in mind when he wrote it? Slavery is not discussed. He is not concerned with the South's constitutional rights or the legitimacy of its independence. In *Tiger-Lilies,* he sided with neither section. Rather he seems to have used the War as a background for a moral fable, the overcoming of hate and disorder by harmonious love. Thus, in "The Tournament," a poem written in the same year as the novel, he allegorizes the War as a joust between Heart and Brain, with Brain the victor, but in the second joust Love banishes a hairy-fisted Hate into thin air. Lanier ranged the collective power and efficiency of the North against the intrepid, impetuous, and romantic South, but in 1867 he felt no rancor toward the Yankees.[12]

The test of his optimistic neutrality came in 1868 and thereafter, when to his "sorrowful surprise" the victors withheld the "vast generosities" he had expected and clamped upon the South a set of laws which "resulted in such a mass of crime and hatred and bitterness as even four terrible years of war had entirely failed to bring about." Reconstruction did not turn him into a Yankee-hater, but his disenchantment is detectible in the political poems he composed between 1867 and 1868, the "Raven Days of sorrow." Lanier wrote of "a lonesome, hungry land" and of tyrants who forgot "how fresh is the pall/ Over their dead and ours." "Wild mutineers" controlled the "Ship of Earth" and the "best sailors" lay dead on the bloody deck. Bitterly he arraigned the "coward hand/ Of the Northland,/ That after honorable war couldst smite/ Cheeks grimed in adverse battle."

> The stainers have decreed the stains shall stay.
> What clement hands might wash the stains away
> Are chained, to make us rue a mournful day.

In order to expose the "monstrous crime/ Of a sick time," Lanier began a political novel, *John Lockwood's Mill,* in January 1868. The

few pages he completed are of no consequence, save for the additional evidence they provide of Lanier's preoccupation with a theme
that was almost to obsess him: the iniquity of "Trade."[13]

He never defined the term any more precisely than Howells's
Colonel Woodburn. Presumably it meant to him everything inimical
to the canons of "Chivalry," another term resonant with private
overtones for Lanier. "Trade" connoted the sleazy and vulgar spirit
of commercialism, the religion of the huckster. He traced its origins
to the peasant's revolt in fourteenth-century France (the subject of
his unfinished narrative poem, "The Jacquerie," first planned in
1868), which cleared the way for the ultimate victory of the
Moneyed Lord over Chivalry. During the next four hundred years,
Trade came to dominate the life, thought, and morals of mankind
and imposed a tyranny "ten thousand times more grievous than the
worst tyrannies of the Feudal System ever were." The "chivalry" he
now called upon to overthrow it was not the traditional "Southron"
variety. Lanier had in mind the chivalry of "gentlemen," hostile to
the chicanery and meanness rampant in the Gilded Age and possessed to some degree by every man irrespective of birth. What
pleased him most about the poems of his friend Paul Hayne was the
total absence of the commercial in them. They had nothing to do
with *"Trade* in any of its forms," this same *"Trade* that hatched
John Brown, and broke the saintly heart of Robert E. Lee."[14]

Lanier's reference to John Brown and Lee suggests an unstated
interpretation of the War as a conflict between the machine-brain
and Nature-spirit, a view guardedly intimated in the writings of
Mark Twain. In three speeches delivered between 1869 and 1870,
Lanier obliquely identified the Southern cause with the vitalistic
principle. In one he celebrated the heroism and sacrifice of women
during "the war of Southern independence" who sent their men off
to war, chided cowards, and nursed the wounded. He bade his
female listeners emulate "those tall, lithe, graceful, redlipped,
brilliant-eyed, violet-breath'd, lissome-limbed queen-women, who
sometimes sate on the early thrones of Germany, France and
England." In another, he lauded the matchless and stainless Lee
("For, Sir, he is indeed greater than any antique deity"), and in the
third, a memorial to the Confederate dead, he reproved an age of
Trade that substituted adroitness for strength. The "stately grandeur" of Lee and Jackson shamed the noisy god of railroads and
factories "with his braggard pretensions, with his stertorous vaunt-
ing of himself and his wares."[15]

Lanier's diatribes against gross commercialism in no way indicated an aversion to progress. He distinguished between "the legitimate and illegitimate rush of commerce—between what is vile brag
and what is proper self-assertion in the merchant's advertisement."

After Reconstruction he became a qualified supporter of the New South and welcomed the corporation into the etherealized society hovering over the horizon. Sectional loyalty and reverence for the South's antique heroes never stilled his criticism of Southern parochialism;* and a few years before he died, aged thirty-nine, he complained to his brother about the backwardness of the South and offered an explanation for the Confederacy's defeat. The South was conquered by "the belief in the sacredness and greatness of the American Union among the millions of the North and of the great North-West." Its destruction followed swiftly after Lee invaded Pennsylvania:

> Our people have failed to perceive the deeper movements under-running the time; they lie wholly off, out of the stream of thought, and whirl their poor old dead leaves of recollections round and round, in a piteous eddy that has all the wear and tear of motion without any of the rewards of progress.[16]

Such sentiments did not sit too well with the latter-day Agrarians, who repudiated his alleged "New South" views and denied his talent, but Lanier never questioned Southern convictions on the race question and thereby escaped the obloquy heaped upon his contemporary, George Washington Cable, by an irate South.

---

* In his Furlow College Address, Lanier referred "in sorrowful fashion, to a certain insidious evil, which, especially since the war, has been the very bane and poison of all our humble artistic endeavor here in the South. I mean the habit of glossing over the intrinsic defects of artistic productions by appealing to the Southern sympathies of the artist's countrymen" (*Works*, V, 260).

Chapter 18

George Washington Cable

It [the right to secede] was exercised contrary to the belief and advice of hundreds of thousands of Southern men. That doubtful doctrine was not our cause; if the gentleman is a young man I pray him to leave the preaching of that delusion to the venerable ex-President of the Confederate States. It was the only ground upon which some of our Southern political advisers cast up the defenses behind which our actual cause lay fortified. Our real cause—the motive—was no intricate question. A president was elected lawfully by a party that believed simply what virtually the whole intelligence of the South now admits, viz., that African slavery—the existence of which was originally the fault of the whole nation—was an error in its every aspect, was cursing the whole land. And we chose the risks of war rather than in any manner to jeopardize an institution which we have since learned to execrate.

GEORGE WASHINGTON CABLE, 1884

The Un-Southern Confederate

To many of his Southern critics, George Washington Cable was no Southerner at all but a sort of crypto-Northerner accidentally born in the South who befouled his birthplace for Yankee gold. Paul Hamilton Hayne was not alone in stigmatizing Cable (whom he had never met and whose work he disdained to read) as a renegade and parvenu, a "mongrel cur."[1] As a twice-wounded Confederate veteran, Cable was presumably entitled to speak for his section— "we of the South," he insisted upon saying[2]—but his opponents never considered him a bona-fide Southern representative. Neither his father's birth in Winchester, Virginia, nor the presence of Cables in Virginia since before the Revolution could blot out the taint of his mother's Puritan heritage. It seemed logical enough to Henry W. Grady, editor of the Atlanta *Constitution*, that Cable

272

should end up in New England, for, Grady wrote in 1885, "he appears to have had little sympathy with his Southern environment."[3]

This same Cable in April 1862 watched Farragut's fleet "come slowly round Slaughterhouse Point into full view, silent, so grim, and terrible; black with men, heavy with deadly portent; the long-banished Stars and Stripes flying against the frowning sky."[4] Young Cable formed part of the mob who hurrahed for Jeff Davis and jeered at the two United States naval officers sent to negotiate the surrender of New Orleans. And when General Benjamin F. Butler began his notorious administration of the city in May of that year, the Cable family refused to take the oath of allegiance. In June of 1863, Cable's widowed mother, his two older sisters, and his younger brother were refugees in Confederate Mississippi. Four months later the diminutive eldest son, looking much younger and frailer than his eighteen years, joined Company J of the Fourth Mississippi cavalry.[5]

Unlike the deep-dyed, unreconstructed Rebels or the elegists of the "Lost Cause," Cable gave little thought to the Yankee invaders after he had been paroled as a prisoner of war and returned to New Orleans in the late spring of 1865. So closely, in fact, did his political de-conversion follow on the Confederate capitulation that spiteful antagonists like Hayne and Cable's most eloquent calumniator, the Creole historian Charles Gayarré, doubted whether Cable had ever been sincerely loyal to Dixie. Cable repeatedly testified to the bravery of Southern soldiers, but what rankled in the minds of his critics was his un-Southern appraisal of the War itself. No patriot to the Southern "nation" would dispose of Southern aims and claims in the spirit of a calculating pettifogger. Although not technically an alien, he was "alien" to them "in heart, soul, affection, & principle, while pretending to be 'to the manner born.' "[6]

Such allegations tell us more about the men who made them than about Cable himself, yet as his critics rightly inferred, he did not enlist in the Confederate army to defend Southern civilization against Yankee hordes. Several years of campaigning in Mississippi and Alabama neither seared his spirit nor changed his vision of life. He left the army the same pious, conscientious, and cheerful boy he was when he joined it. The few extant letters Cable wrote during the War years contain reassurances to his mother, admonitions to his brother, and very little about the War. He seems to have fretted about his and his brother's inglorious military record, "one," he reminded his brother, "brought out of a disgraceful skirmish with a slight flesh wound before the fight was done, the other hunted through the swamps, his horse and clothes captured, and himself escaping by precipitate flight."[7] The "slight flesh wound" (a bullet hole in the left armpit) produced no existential reverberations, and in the last months of his military service, when he clerked in the headquarters of General Nathan Bedford Forrest,* he found time to study mathematics, Latin grammar, and the Bible.

If his fiction is any test, the War affected Cable much less traumatically than it did De Forest or Bierce or Wendell Holmes, Jr. The few War episodes in his novels, written years after the events described, display some pictorial skill. At least three of them—*Dr. Sevier* (1884), *The Cavalier* (1901), and *Kincaid's Battery* (1908)—contain bits of realistic observation possibly based on personal experience, but they have less to do with the tragedy of war than with its dreariness and hardship, with "rains, bad food, ill-chosen camps, freshets, terrible roads, horses sick and raw-boned, chills, jaundice, emaciation, barely an occasional bang at the enemy on reconnoissances and picketings, and marches and counter-marches through blistering noons and skyless nights, with men, teams, and guns trying to see which could stagger the worst, along with columns of infantry mutinously weary of forever fortifying and never fighting."[8] This unglamorous catalogue probably sums up the War he actually knew, but Cable characteristically skirts military actions in his narratives almost as if they were unpleasant interludes to be suppressed rather than cherished.

Cable on the "Lost Cause"

Nothing Cable wrote during or after the War indicates he was ever an enthusiastic partisan of secession. He fought as a citizen-soldier because (as he told some of his army mates), he was "a citizen of this government, a soldier by its laws, sworn into service and ordered not to think, but to fight." Whatever his doubts about the wisdom of secession, at eighteen he did not question slavery as an institution and believed in a "White Man's Government." At the War's end, he felt "not one spark of loyalty to the United States Government."[9]

Two decades later Cable sketched the process by which he changed from a dutiful if lukewarm secessionist into a disbeliever of the Confederate cause and a civil libertarian. First doubts nagged him shortly after 1865 with the South apparently agreeing that the right of secession had been settled by the sword. He could under-

---

* Cable claimed to have made out the manumission forms for Forrest's Negro teamsters. How this experience may have influenced his views on slavery is a matter for speculation. See Arlin Turner, "George Washington Cable's Recollections of General Forrest," *The Journal of Southern History*, XXI (May 1955), 222–28.

stand why the *power* to secede had been so decided, but why the *right*? Had there ever been a right to secede? He turned to Justice Story's commentary on the Constitution for an answer and discovered no such provision:

> I rose at last from this study indignant against the propagators of that doctrine. I knew it had been believed by thousands of good men, but it seemed, and still seems, to me a perfidious doctrine. How, I queried, could good men—not boys, as I was—ever accept so shallow a piece of pettifogging literalism? What use or need had there been to set up such a doctrine and waste three hundred thousand young men's lives in its defense? There could be but one answer; it was to protect slaveholding.[10]

But granted secession arguments had been compounded of bad logic and bad history, rebellion and revolution were still defensible if slavery was right. This question opened up a new course of investigation for Cable, whose only brush with antislavery ideas had been a cursory reading of *Uncle Tom's Cabin* as a child and an acquaintance with a circumspect German abolitionist. He had no difficulty detecting the sophistry of the biblical sanction of slavery. A harder test was to look with understanding on "the Freedman in all his offensiveness; multitudinous, unclean, stupid, ugly, ignorant, and insolent." Gradually his concern over what white supremacists referred to as "our black peasantry" overcame his revulsion. Someone had to be brave or shameless enough to risk "a complete and ferocious ostracism," lest the old unjust order be preserved under a new name. "Politics" to Cable had come to mean something more than community service; it also required a man to serve his nation and the human race. The black man, he decided, by virtue of his nationality and humanity "must share and enjoy in common with the white race the whole scale of *public* rights and advantages provided under American government."[11]

So at least Cable wrote in 1888 after he had become notorious throughout the South as a renegade who had reaped "golden harvests by haranguing Northern audiences on the fascinating subject of the Southern sins."[12] It was an unjust aspersion. Cable had risked censure in New Orleans long before the North had ever heard of him. He had not deliberately set about offending the South. He wanted Southerners after "calm debate" to settle the "Southern problem" without outside intervention. The South, he thought, "would read from a Southern man patiently what it would only resent from a Northerner."[13]

Cable badly misjudged the audience, or at least underestimated the durability of time-tested Southern dogmas immune to logic and unaffected by even his brand of tactful argumentation. He seems to have anticipated the support of what he called the "Silent South," an inarticulate but substantial segment pleased to be disencumbered of slavery and ready to grant civil rights to Negroes. Speaking for them, he would challenge sincere but misguided "traditionalists" still bewitched by sectional and racial delusions. He would present himself as one who had found it hard to relinquish his antiquated beliefs, whose sympathies had "ranged upon the pro-Southern side of the issue" but whose convictions had been irresistibly drawn by coercive logic to the other side.[14]

Cable's essays and addresses, experiments in persuasion, are as fresh and trenchant today as they were when they first appeared. His tone is invariably conciliatory. He imputes the best of intentions to his adversaries, celebrates Lee and "his ragged grey veterans" in muted rhetoric, exhales love for the South ("I cannot here, yield to any one in pride in our struggle and in all the noble men and women who bore its burdens"),[15] deplores "the dreadful episode of Reconstruction," abjures the social intermingling of the races, insists on Northern complicity in the national tragedy. Nonetheless, these adroit and ingratiating lay-sermons are in essence a devastating arraignment of the Southern ethos, and they must have been all the more infuriating to the "adherents of the old regime" for their sweet reasonableness. Here is Cable's case in brief:

Slavery: Cable denounced it as nothing less than "a deplorable error . . . our crime and our curse." It prevented the emergence of a middle class (for Cable as for Howells the salt of the earth), throttled dissent, stifled culture, isolated the South from the outside world, concentrated and consumed the intellectual energy of the South in its defense, and left it "mired and stuffed with conservatism to the point of absolute rigidity."[16]

The War: Although the Union armies contained a good many abolitionists who enlisted to free the slaves, the majority of Northern soldiers fought for national unity, a cause which, as it turned out, required the destruction of slavery to win. Most Southern whites, on the other hand, would not have supported secession had there been any other way to preserve slavery. In short, the War came because the North and South espoused antipodal principles each held "to be absolutely essential to the safety, order, peace, fortune, and honor of society." The former declared the well-being of society to rest on "the free self-government of all under one common code of civil rights," the other that the highest social development required "the subjugation of the lower mass under the arbitrary protective supremacy of an untitled but hereditary privileged class, a civil caste." Out of the first came the schoolhouse, out

of the second the slaveyard. Had the North waived its conviction
and compromised with the advocates of caste, the blood of hundreds
of thousands might have been spared. It did not. "The freedom of the
Negro was bought at a higher price in white man's blood and
treasure, than any people ever paid, of their own blood and treasure
for their own liberty."[17] Legalized slavery was killed.

Aftermath: But "the ghost of that old heresy"—mass subjugation by a caste—survived. Public servitude replaced private bondage. "The ex-slave was not a free man; he was only a free Negro."
The same mentality that trusted to a geological time to solve
desperate problems, "the habit of letting error go uncontradicted
because it is ours," persisted in the post-War years. The tradition-
ists learned nothing from the past. They continued to preach black
inferiority while refusing to remove the crippling handicaps that
kept the Negro from sloughing off "the debasements of slavery and
semi-slavery." The reckoning could not be indefinitely postponed,
and necessary reform, if too long refused from the inside, would be
imposed by the outside.[18]

If these views were widely entertained in the South, then the
silent contingent must have held their tongues after the public
outcry provoked by Cable's published lectures and articles. Private
messages of appreciation and encouragement came from Southern
whites and blacks, but no sizable group dared openly to defend
him.

Cable's vindictive and scurrilous foes misrepresented his
motives and distorted his position on race. He did not, as they kept
repeating, preach social equality ("We may reach the moon some
day, not social equality"),[19] nor was he by any definition an amal-
gamationist. But they correctly pegged him as one who had drifted
so far from the Southern consensus that even his Confederate war
service did not entitle him to speak for the South. Any man who
openly expressed his preference for the civilized North, shook
hands with Frederick Douglass, numbered Garrison and Phillips
among "the great dead," blessed the birthday of Harriet Beecher
Stowe, and pronounced the Union cause just could hardly have
expected a sympathetic hearing from a people whose cherished
prejudices he flouted. "We are just as completely dedicated to God's
service," Cable wrote to his wife in 1885, "as though we were Chinese missionaries."[20] That was the year Cable cut his ties with his
benighted section and settled permanently in Northampton, Massachusetts—the final disqualification so far as the South was
concerned.

The men in charge of the New South wanted none of Cable's
evangelism. If he had been of old Southern stock and if he had been
more respectful of Southern traditions, they would not have found

his plea for social justice to the Negro any more palatable, but they
might have given it a more respectful hearing than it got. What
made him finally seem alien was his blend of missionary and realist
that Southerners had never relished. Cable's friends, Mark Twain
and Howells, shared his contempt for the brummagem of pseudo-
chivalry,[21] his conviction that sincere and brave men had nearly
wrecked the nation to preserve a shabby barbaric institution, but to
survivors of the War and Reconstruction, still spiritually unvanquished and revering the "Lost Cause," Cable's judgment of the War
was impious slander and particularly so coming from one reputedly
obsessed with Southern blemishes and blind to Northern ones.

The Grandissimes

A note of pessimism—sometimes close to cynicism—which Cable
usually excluded from his public utterances can be heard in his
autobiographical essay, "My Politics," written in 1888 as an introduction to a new collection of essays but posthumously published. It
was really, as Arlin Turner observed, an apologia, an answer to his
critics, and although pacific in tone, it suggests that Cable did not
pass through his ordeal unscathed. Experience had taught him
some sad truths. Nations fail to live up to their heroic ideas and at
best approximate them only after "painful and costly delays." The
public is likely to be wrong both as to facts and principles and the
"great mass of mankind unconsciously adjust their convictions to
the ends they have in view, often to the most short-sighted notions
of self-interest or the moment's emergency."[22]

These and other insights that informed his social writing he
incorporated into his one enduring work of fiction, *The Grandissimes* (1880), a romantic and often sentimental novel shot through
with darkness and terror. The time of the narrative is New Orleans
in 1803, the year in which Louisiana passed from France to the
United States. Given his state of mind in 1878 when he began his
novel for serial publication in *Scribner's Magazine*, it inevitably
became, as he said, "a study of the fierce struggle going on around
me, regarded in the light of that past history—those beginnings—
which had so differentiated the Louisiana civilization from the
American scheme of public society."[23]

Like Cable himself, the hero of *The Grandissimes*, Joseph
Frowenfeld, is an outsider alternately charmed and appalled by
Creole society. He is not unresponsive to those Creole traits—kindli-
ness, generosity, politeness, naïveté—Cable had already affection-
ately if sometimes satirically rendered in the local-color sketches of
New Orleans published a few years before his novel. Yet Frowen-

feld's Presbyterian morality cannot condone the Creoles' pleasure-seeking style of life or their grasshopperish irresponsibility. Nor can he abide the rigidity of their social distinctions and the cruel and impulsive acts of some Creole aristocrats. Above all, Cable's hero is sickened by the treatment of the Negro under Louisiana's *Code Noir* and by the tragic consequences of miscegenation.

Cable wrote his subversive novel to entertain as well as to instruct, but if he had settled for the role of agreeable storyteller he later assumed, an antiquarian delighting in quaint customs, odd forms of dialect, the romantic decor and varied types of exotic New Orleans, he would have remained at best a figure for anthologists, not the author of *The Grandissimes* who looked behind the social façade and described what he saw with a terrible veracity.

The subterfuge of placing the novel in New Orleans around the time of the Louisiana Purchase cannot disguise the obvious parallels between the South of Jefferson's day and the South of the 1870s and 1880s, or better, the South on the eve of secession and the South in Reconstruction. Cable's Creoles talk and think like the post-War die-hards. They hold the same notions of caste, evidence the same dislike and fear of democracy. A harangue by an anti-American Creole patriarch to his retainers might have come from some leader of the Ku Klux Klan or New Orleans White League, and the equivalent of his dying words predicting the recovery of "Old Louisiana's" trampled rights might have been heard in many quarters of Dixie after Appomattox.[24] Frowenfeld is tolerated only so long as he leaves community opinion unchallenged. When he fails, in the words of one Creole, to " 'teh-kyeh 'ow he stir the 'ot blood of Lousyanna!' " a mob wrecks his shop. General Claiborne, the new American Governor of the Territory, is regarded with the same intense hatred later generations in New Orleans reserved for "Beast" Butler and his minions. Cable was not writing allegory, of course, but he capitalized to the hilt on historical analogies and wrote, in effect, a contemporary exposé in the form of a historical romance.

The Grandissimes somewhat resembles *Uncle Tom's Cabin*, a book Cable claims to have read in his ninth year without explaining how it found its way into his family library. Both contain harrowing episodes of violence, play up the misery suffered by Southerners, white and black, as a result of miscegenation, and exploit the romantic (and sexual) associations clustering around the figure of the beautiful quadroon.[25] Repeating a device of Mrs. Stowe, Cable puts the most telling arguments against slavery in the mouth of a slaveowning aristocrat and singles out slavery as the root cause for everything bad that has befallen the South.

What distinguishes Cable's Negro characters from the black

cartoons of Mrs. Stowe is the variety and subtlety of his portraiture. The blacks in *The Grandissimes* range from the most
primitive servant to the educated f.m.c. (free man of color); collectively they cast "the shadow of the Ethiopian"[26] on a people too
enmeshed in the institution to see and judge it. Cable's Negroes
may be romantically touched up, but few Southern writers before or
later took a harder look at black/white relations. He blurted out
what the Silent South dared not say: that never for a minute did the
Negro accept the white man's cant about slaves faring better and
feeling happier than freed men. He never allowed his readers to
forget the murderous war constantly threatening to erupt between
the races or the hatred behind the obsequiousness and humor of the
servile class. His "bad niggers" have been forged in "fires that do not
refine, but that blunt and blast and blacken and char." Clemence,
the crafty old *marchande* of calas and ginger cakes, has none of
Uncle Tom's immaculacy. She is the heiress of

> starvation, gluttony, drunkenness, thirst, drowning, naked-
> ness, dirt, fetichism, debauchery, slaughter, pestilence and
> the rest . . . they left her the cinders of human feelings.
> She remembered her mother. They had been separated in her
> childhood, in Virginia when it was a province. She remem-
> bered, with pride, the price her mother had brought at auc-
> tion, and remarked, as an additional interesting item, that
> she had never seen or heard of her since. She had had
> children, assorted colors—had one with her now, the black
> boy that brought the basil to Joseph; the others were here
> and there, some in the Grandissime households or field-
> gangs, some elsewhere within occasional sight, some dead,
> some not accounted for. Husbands—like the Samaritan wo-
> man's. We know she was a constant singer and laugher.[27]

Throughout the novel, Cable shows how the white man's
"criminal benevolence" toward the Negro as well as his rage and
ferocity rest on fear. "It seems to be one of the self-punitive characteristics of tyranny," he observes, "whether the tyrant be a man, a
community, or a caste, to have a pusillanimous fear of its victim."[28]
The response of this community fear is "terrific cruelty," dramatized
in *The Grandissimes* by the half-mythic figure of a gigantic African
prince, Bras-Coupé, whose presence pervades the entire novel and
links all of the main characters. To some of them, he is merely a
"pestiferous darky," to others a source of enlightenment, a fearsome
portent, a symbol of black revenge. Slavery fails to diminish his
manhood and pride. He strikes down his master, ranges the swamps
as a fugitive, and is captured only after he leaves his sanctuary to
join his fellow slaves who are dancing in Congo Square. The whites

lash him, cut off his ears, and hamstring him according to the provisions of Louisiana's Black Code, but his death does not expunge their fears or allay their anxieties.

Cable's powerful statement about a mighty wrong is vitiated by his fits of sentimentality, his tendency to idealize his characters, his weakness for silly mystifications. He sandwiches sugary interludes between the grimmest scenes, perhaps to reassure the same feminine audience De Forest tried but failed to please. Cable succeeded better but at the cost of playing down his sociological bent. He soothed shocked sensibilities by ending his tale of miscegenation, mutilation, and murder with happy marriages. After the crazed black woman Clemence has been savaged by a steel trap and then shot in the back, and after an f.m.c., fathered by the sire of the white Honoré Grandissime, has stabbed a white man to death, Cable can still praise God for "love's young dream."

All the same, such concessions to his editors and to a squeamish public hardly weaken the force of this impressive novel, and not until Faulkner did American writers handle Cable's theme with comparable or greater power. While not specifically about the War, *The Grandissimes* is probably his most consummate statement about the men and ideas that made it come to pass. Implicitly it refuted the wishful thinking of an 1884 editorial in *Century Magazine* that "the passions and prejudices of the Civil War have nearly faded out of politics."[29] Despite the fraternizing of Confederate and Federal soldiers, Cable knew very well they remained.

Cable's experience in the Confederate army and, more important, his subsequent reflections on the War's causes and meaning had turned him into a strong critic of Southern racial prejudice. He sympathized with the woes of the South but not to the extent of pardoning or condoning what he took to be its sins. Had he been content merely to weave fictional tapestries with no hint of social criticism, he would have remained a favorite in the South as well as the North—doubly appreciated because of his trans-Southern reputation.* But the Presbyterian moralist drowned out or at least competed with the entertainer, and the South, angered by his allegations and proposals, drummed him out of Louisiana.

---

* In the interests of sectional harmony, Cable occasionally honored Confederate heroes. "The Gentler Side of Two Great Southerners" (*Century Magazine*, XLVII [Dec. 1893], 292–94), reports two anecdotes. In one, General Lee speaks kindly to an urchin who interrupts a conversation with President Davis; in the other, General Jackson worries about his colored Sunday School: "The noble gentleness of character that distinguished some of our Southern generals in the Civil War—I think the 'our' may rightly be offered in a national sense—will still, I venture to say, be a pleasant theme when the generation that fought that fight has passed away."

For more than a half-century thereafter, no literary renegade of comparable power arose to challenge the Confederate version of the War or Southern assumptions about black subordination. Insiders might be granted the privileges of irony and a degree of levity in treating the past, but sons and daughters of the South were generally more comfortable in the role of hierophants than subverters of Southern traditionalism. This attitude prevailed until the emergence of a new literary generation during or immediately after World War I.

That war, according to Allen Tate, marked the re-entry of the South into the modern world, but the consciousness of an earlier war, far from being obliterated by the newer one, was heightened by it: now his generation had "a double focus, a looking two ways, which gave a special dimension to the writings of our school." Between the two great wars of the twentieth century the long-barren South produced a dazzling literary crop. As before, the past remained an important ingredient in Southern literature, but a past intermingling with the present and stripped of much of its sentimentality and gentility. The Sacred Cause itself, a composite of fact and legend (felt if not mentioned or alluded to even in stories and poems about the contemporary South), smoldered in the Southern imagination.

The men and women writers of the "Renaissance" who returned to the "still visitable past"—the experiences of Southern people during the War and Reconstruction—rejected both the nostalgic fabrication of Thomas Nelson Page and the cheerful boosterism of the New South proponents. In their fiction and nonfiction, they made these years the testing ground of Southern character, manners, and political intelligence, and assessed the value of the Old South's legacy. They did not discount the flaws in the society smashed by the War, but they set the ideals and values of the defeated above those of the victors.

And over their writings the Ethiopian still cast his shadow.

Part Seven

RECONSTRUCTING THE SOUTHERN PAST

Chapter 19

The Neo-Confederates

Commercial activity and industrial development have their uses, no doubt, in any well-established society; but genius has been in even the most civilized periods a vagabond. And, with or without genius, the novel is more vital, and certainly more interesting, when it declines to become the servant either of sentimental tradition or of patriotic materialism.

ELLEN GLASGOW, 1943

I had previously been led to wonder, in travelling from Boston to New York, at what point Connecticut ceases to be a New England state and is transformed into a New York suburb; but to cross into Virginia is as definite an experience as to cross from England to Wales, almost as definite as to cross the English Channel. And the differences here, with no difference of language or race to support them, have had to survive the immense pressure towards monotony exerted by the industrial expansion of the latter part of the nineteenth and the first part of the twentieth century. The Civil War was certainly a disaster from which the country has never recovered and perhaps never will: we are always too ready to assume that the good effects of wars, if any, abide permanently while the ill effects are obliterated by time. Yet I think that the chances for the re-establishment of a native culture are perhaps better in the South than in New England. The Southerners are farther away from New York; they have been less industrialized and less invaded by foreign races; and they have a more opulent soil.

T. S. ELIOT, 1933

"A Holy Conviction Makes a Holy Cause"

EIGHT years old in 1861, Thomas Nelson Page had only a boy's-eye view of the War. Years later he recalled attending a militia muster with his father where men marched and wheeled in the dust of a stubblefield and where "a wild looking man with feathers

285

in his cap" hollered at the recruits as if they were cattle. After a subsequent muster his father and uncle (both opposed to secession) went off to fight the invaders. John Page enlisted as a private and much to his son's mortification marched instead of rode against the Yankees—an indignity the romantic author spared his fictional gentlemen-soldiers. The War swept across Hanover County, Virginia, without enveloping the small family plantation, but Page remembered it as "the most remarkable and vital thing in my childhood, or for that matter, in my entire life. It not only affected my growth of both body and mind, but after the actual conflict had passed, the consequences of it were such, in my part of the world, that they continued to impress themselves on us, which ever way we turned."[1]

Page wrote no War literature of any consequence (he had a slight talent at best), but he became very adept in the last two decades of the century as a purveyor of pathos and nostalgia. By then, as Tourgée predicted, the South had "won" the literary Civil War. Northern readers gobbled up fantasies about antebellum plantation life, especially when recollected by ancient ex-slaves still hankering for the days of blissful servitude and "keening in Negro dialect over the Confederacy's fallen glories."[2] Page specialized in delineating these devoted house servants stranded by a catastrophe that left them nothing save tinted memories of "Mars Chan" and "Meh Lady." He also contributed his share of "reconciliation" literature in which interchangeable Cavaliers and Yankees ended up with sympathetic mates from the opposite camp. Yet while promoting good will between the sections (his heroes are likely to be Unionists who reluctantly but honorably tag along with their neighbors), his underlying purpose was to glorify his forebears, "explain" the South to ignorant and prejudiced outsiders, and to correct popular errors about the Southern "race" and "Negro problem."

Page's hallowing of the South came at a time when the Yankeephobes, still breathing sacred hate against the Northern foe and his industrial civilization, were being challenged by the promoters of the New South, who condemned the "fatally vicious economic and agricultural theories" of the antebellum regime. But decidedly not, in Henry W. Grady's words, the "race of men and women whose virtues and whose attainments are worthy to be enshrined not only in every southern, but in every American heart." Grady and his fellow boosters carefully avoided outraging ancestral pieties. They publicized the New South as "simply the Old South under new conditions"[3] and in their promotional literature and speeches, touching references to mythical plantations blended happily with reports of real factories. Page may have disliked the phrase "New South,"[4] but his distilled version of the Southern past strengthened rather than contradicted the economic sales talk of the post-War progressives. It salved the emotional wounds of the unreconstructed nationalist while it revealed how and why the older generation should inspire, sustain, and guide the new. "I shall never forget," he said, "that it is to the Old South that the New South owes all that is best and noblest in its being."[5]

Why did Page, who could write realistically enough when he chose to, turn pre-War Virginia into a flower-land where all girls were beautiful and all men handsome and ardent and where the influence of what he called "race" explained every characteristic of the gentry—from their love of horses to their inborn capacity for command? Perhaps his desire to vindicate a defeated people exceeded even his desire to ingratiate himself with the victorious North. He spurned a reconciliation which would in any way tarnish the honor of his state and section, and in his zeal to refute anti-Southern slanders, he concocted a preposterous picture of the Old South that bordered closely on burlesque.[6]

The world, Page asserted with more heat than accuracy, looked upon Southerners as "an ignorant, illiterate, cruel, semi-barbarous section of the American people, sunk in brutality and vice," as a "race of slave-drivers" who "contributed nothing to the advancement of mankind" and who started a bloody war to protect their slave property. Such a view betrayed either folly or ignorance. Far from being sterile, the South established the nation "so firmly that not even it could overthrow it." Southerners "governed the country, maintained her credit, extended her limits, fought her battles, and established her fame" while "the North secured protection and under its influence waxed fat." They Christianized the Negro race and "gave it the only civilization it has ever possessed since the dawn of history." At the same time, the South upheld Caucasian supremacy: "It produced a people whose heroic fight against the forces of the world has enriched the annals of the human race—a people whose fortitude in defeat has been even more splendid than their valor in war. It made men noble, gentle, and brave, and women tender and pure and true."[7]

Politicians exploited the slavery issue to overthrow the South, thereby concealing the real cause—Northern lust for sectional supremacy. Abetted by the abolitionists, they poisoned national harmony until the South, unwisely but understandably, spent its tremendous energies in intemperate polemic. Finally it seceded, "with sublime scorn" for its foes. Secession may have been mistaken, but it was not ignoble; it was certainly not the fruit of conspiracy. Therefore, to hold Southern people in contempt, to deny them participation in the Union, was "a greater crime" than secession itself.[8]

Who would justify the South? Who would write the as yet unchronicled history of this unique civilization which perhaps fell short "in material development in its narrower sense" but which "abounded in spiritual development"? Modestly Page declined to propose himself. He spelled out, however, the specifications of the ideal champion:

> Such a one must have at once the instinct of the historian and the wisdom of the philosopher. He must possess the talisman that will discover truth amid all the heaps of false-hood . . . the sagacity to detect whatever of evil existed in the civilization he shall chronicle, though it be gleaming with the gilding of romance; he must have the fortitude to resist all temptation to deflect by so much as a hair's breadth from the absolute and the inexorable facts, even if an angel should attempt to beguile him. He must know and tell the truth, the whole truth, and nothing but the truth, so help him, God![9]

Unconsciously Page had described his opposite, for even his admirers conceded that in correcting the "provoking misconceptions" about the Old South, he magnified its virtues and painted over its blemishes.[10] In his eyes slavery was a benevolent institution.[11] Its abolition had turned the once-contented Negro into a "problem" complicated all the more by well-intended but fallacious arguments of men like Cable, whose literary gifts he esteemed but whose social views he considered "unsound and unsafe." Although Page refused to snipe at him in the style of Paul Hayne, he quietly seconded Cable's Southern critics who assailed his "grave errors . . . with that vehemence which has ever characterized the attacks made by the South, whether on the field of battle or in the arena of forensic discussion."[12] Page had in mind, of course, Cable's un-Southern interpretation of the Civil War as well as his charge that by preventing the Negro from choosing his own rulers, white Southerners denied him his "just rights." Page disagreed. The race issue for him boiled down to a simple question: should an inferior race govern a superior one or be governed by it?[13] Rejection of white supremacy not only threatened the New South; it also slurred the sacred past. Agreement with Cable, in Page's eyes, would have been tantamount to blackening the Confederacy, desecrating ancestral graves, and defaming "the purest, sweetest" civilization that ever existed.

He succeeded no better than most fiction writers of his time in presenting a credible picture of the South before, during, and after the War, but he managed to interpret what an acidulous contemporary critic called "the *spirit* of the South, that armored and helmeted spirit which survived the defeats of the Civil War, riding unconquered and unconquerable through bereavements, poverty, and the unimaginable humiliation of the Reconstruction period." The poetry Page extracted from the Southern experience had little basis in fact. It reassured the South, however, of "its invincible spirituality . . . more patriotic than religious (though not lacking in piety), and more personal than patriotic."[14] It also trivialized this experience, as Ellen Glasgow implied in her gentle denigration of Southern writers inhibited and insulated by their own gentlemanliness.

Ellen Glasgow did not write about the Civil War with vast success. She was even further removed from the days of the Confederacy than Page, and *The Battle-Ground* (1902), her one novel dealing directly with the background of the War, is an apprentice work rooted in family memories, but dependent as well on details garnered from old newspaper files and infused with "romantic idealism."[15] Later she acquired a deeper understanding, compassionate and ironic, of the War's significance. Sharing Page's affection if not idolatry for the old Virginia gentry, she nonetheless portrayed them and their black servants more objectively than he did. Her Negroes are individualized persons, not always childishly happy and contented, not blurred supernumeraries introduced to grace a Southern pageant. The following remarkable passage might serve as a comment on Page and post-War Southern literature in general:

> After the War, pursued by the dark furies of Reconstruction, the mind of the South was afflicted with a bitter nostalgia. From this homesickness for the past there flowered, as luxuriantly as fireweed in burned places, a mournful literature of commemoration. A prosperous and pleasure-loving race had been thrust back suddenly into the primitive struggle for life; and physical resistance had settled slowly into mental repression. Already those desperate political remedies which, according to the philosopher, begin in fear and end in folly, were welding the Southern States into a defense and a danger. From political expediency there emerged a moral superstition. What had begun as an emergency measure had matured into a sacred and infallible doctrine. And among these stagnant ideas the romantic memories of the South ripened, and mellowed, and at last began to decay. That benevolent hardness of heart, so necessary to the creative artist, dissolved, if it had ever existed, into the simple faith which makes novels even less successfully than it moves mountains. To defend the lost became the solitary purpose and the supreme obligation of the Southern novelist, while a living tradition decayed, with the passage of years, into a sentimental infirmity. Graceful, delicate, and tenderly reminiscent, the novels of this period possess that unusual merit,

the virtue of quality. Yet charming as they are in manner, they lack creative passion and the courage to offend which are the essential notes of great fiction. The emotions with which they deal are formal, trite, deficient in blood and irony, and true, not to experience, but to the attitude of evasive idealism. In the end, this writing failed to survive, because, though faithful to a moment in history, it was false to human behaviour.[16]

Ellen Glasgow's books link the period of mindless commemoration with a more irreverent and critical school of Southern writing that replaced her own rigorous and firmly wrought but genteel fashion of fiction writing. These writers made use of traditional stereotypes: Cavaliers, "Southern womanhood," "good" and "bad" Negroes. They also weighed a materialistic Northern civilization against a simpler and purer agrarian antebellum society. Where they differed from Page's school was their success, to use Ellen Glasgow's words, in blending "subjective vision" with "creative impulse," their refusal to confuse "emotions with ideas and mistaken tradition for truth,"[17] and their ability to subordinate feeling to imagination. Less provincial and more talented than most of their predecessors, they looked backward with a nostalgia tinged with irony. Before they reached the point where they could dignify the past, they had to pass through a period when they were excessively critical of the uncritical glorifiers of the Old South. Having begun by rejecting the sentimentalists, they ended by reseeing Southern fact and legend and adapting both to their social and private needs.

A Stand for Dixie

Sometime in the mid-1920s, a group of Southern writers began a serious and systematic examination of their heritage. Hitherto this coterie "of young poets and fresh minds," most of then affiliated with Vanderbilt University, had held themselves aloof from what they felt to be a fatally atavistic and sentimental literary tradition.* Their magazine, *The Fugitive* (1922–25), ground no political axes; if anything it repudiated both the vapidities of "professional Southernism" and the progressive gospel of the "New South." Nor were the "Fugitives," as they came to be called, attempting to escape from

---

* In 1926, Donald Davidson described the Southern writer as "an alien particle in the body politic" dependent on the outside for any artistic stimulation. "What wonder that his gaze flies beyond immediate surroundings to remote regions and that if he addresses himself to his locale at all, he often does so in ironic discontent" (*Saturday Review of Literature*, II [May 15, 1926], 782).

reality. Rather they fled from "poet-laureating, the cheapness and triviality of public taste, even among those supposed to be cultured," from "the high-caste Brahmins of the Old South," from a sterile culture indifferent to literature, art, and serious thought.[18]

Yet only a few years after the demise of *The Fugitive*, its most important contributors—John Crowe Ransom, Donald Davidson, Allen Tate, and Robert Penn Warren—felt compelled to defend their slandered region. By 1930, these four, together with eight other friends and supporters, had formed themselves into a belligerent and "conscious" Southern vanguard and taken a stand for Dixie.

The transformation of the Fugitives, ambivalent about the South and its culture, into Neo-Confederates—explainers and defenders of the Southern tradition—occurred in the mid-twenties. Angered by the cartoon vision of the South in the Northern press (touched off by the "Monkey Trial" in Dayton, Tennessee) and stung by the jibes of the Menckenians, they began to discern virtues in the Southern past undetected and undetectable by deracinated urban modernists. They had never really lost an affectionate regard for their region even as they marked the thinness and pretentiousness of its outmoded culture. Now they looked for and discovered the gold in the dross: the poetic truth lurking below the fundamentalist passion, the "moral seriousness" of narrow country folk, the antique courtesy missing in the cosmopolitan North, the "code" that for all its rigidity was preferable to the shapeless relativism and subjectivity of modern America. In short, without exactly condoning Southern backwardness, they underwent what Davidson described as "a spiritual 'Secession.'" And when Allen Tate exclaimed in 1927, "I've attacked the South for the last time," he spoke for his group as well as for himself. Their discontent with a disorderly present, their suspicion of "science," "industrialism," and alien panaceas, for "progress" itself, prompted their expedition in quest of a usable past.[19]

Each of the intrepid young explorers found what he was looking for. In some cases they distorted or at least exaggerated their findings, but an ingrained skepticism made them wary, and with the possible exception of Donald Davidson, they were less guilty of idealizing the culture and conduct of their ancestors than their critics alleged.* As literary men and remorseless critics, they had

* "What differentiated the Agrarians from other traditionalists was their disdain for the sentimental, overly romantic attitude which once helped to nurture this legend of the paradise which the evil North destroyed. However, their revolt against sentimentalism did not include revolt against the tradition itself" (Alexander Karanikas, *Tillers of a Myth: Southern Agrarians as Social Critics* [Madison, 1966], 60).

no taste for converting cultural brummagem into gold. To judge the Old South by its literature would distort its essential distinction, for, Ransom argued, "Southern artists . . . were frequently quite inferior to their Southern public in real aesthetic capacity." So if "the aesthetic of life" was the test of culture, then the Old South came out very well indeed.[20]

I'll Take My Stand (1930), a collective attack on the prevailing industrial order and its culture, met with a withering opposition North and South, not so much for its critique of industrial capitalism as for the vagueness and impracticability of its program. In essence, the contributors seemed to be calling for a return to subsistence farming and a withdrawal from the money system. Equally vulnerable to attack were some of their historical assumptions: the humanity of Negro slavery and its necessity as cement for the social order; the planter's disdain for commercial considerations; the Old South's hostility to industry and science, and the blissful life of the yeomanry. The Agrarians were by no means the first to discard the "befo' the Woh" plantation myths for a humbler but even more idyllic version of an antebellum Eden. A school of Southern historians had already described the Southern yeoman farmers "as the backbone of Southern society," and the slaveless small planter— democratic, proud, and independent—had appeared in Southern fiction by the turn of the century or earlier.[21] The Agrarians, who came roughly from the same area of the upper South (Tennessee and Kentucky), simply fleshed this conception.

State lines, as W. P. Trent once wrote, had greater importance in the South than elsewhere, and something of what he called the Tennessee ethos can be detected in the work of Donald Davidson and Andrew Lytle as well as Allen Tate and Robert Penn Warren, although Davidson would probably have spurned the notions of a "New South" renegade like Trent. The Tennessean, Trent observed,

can usually point to Scotch-Irish ancestors from whom he has inherited the love of independence and the sturdy democratic virtues that characterize the people of the mountain sections of the States on his eastern border, but he owes to these ancestors something that differentiates him from his kinspeople east of the Alleghenies. The latter have been somewhat abashed, somewhat kept in check, by their contact with the civilization of the tidewater, but he wears upon his forehead, whether he dwell on hill or plain, that "freedom of the mountaineer" of which Wordsworth sang. His fathers, whether they owned slaves or not, never ceased to be democrats.[22]

It is no accident that these Agrarians should feel closer to the yeomanry than to the planter aristocracy, to Stonewall Jackson and Forrest rather than to Lee, even though their political philosophy was closer to Calhoun's than to Jackson's.

Out of this philosophy laced with selective facts and ancestral legend came simplistic history, but out of simplistic history came fruitful myth. Tate, Warren, Davidson, Lytle, and Stark Young found material enough in Southern annals to fabricate their novels and poems. Whether the South they conjured up in prose and verse ever existed did not overly concern them. As one of Stark Young's characters remarks: "the point does not turn on whether some old fool of a colonel—or some scatter-brained old lady—is what we think he is—or she is. No, no. The point turns on what we believe in and desire, and want to find embodied somewhere, even in them."[23] It was sufficient that Southern history furnished them with stones for their literary sermons, with people, places, customs, attitudes, events out of which they could compose their dramatic variations on the collapse of the Old Order and the degeneration of the new.

Moving back from the Past-Ruined (the present) to the Past-Intact (the pre-War South), they disclosed a society possessing both a concrete and a metaphysical reality. The War destroyed it physically, releasing in the process forces that contaminated the nation. The ideal of the Old South—order, beauty, freedom—[24] remained to captivate the Agrarian imagination.

Uses of the Past

The "new history" might be more scientific than the old, Allen Tate remarked in 1929, but it did not refute "the dogma that the past should be magnified in order to keep the present in its place." The poet especially required "a perfectly ordered world which men have assimilated to their attitudes and convictions," and the closest if imperfect approximation of the world for a Southern American like Tate was the Old South. Over the skeleton of the historical ante-bellum Dixie, the Neo-Confederates draped their ingratiating fictions. They invented a buoyant and self-confident society stabilized by a gyroscopic code, its ceremonies functional, its humanism a check against human turbulence. However they differed in details and emphases,* their collective view of the Old South remained

---

* John Peale Bishop, for example, placed the apogee of "agrarian civiliza-tion" in the Federal period when "those marvelously talented Virginians who declared for independence and set the Republic on its foundations" were in

pretty close to Ransom's: "not so fine as some of the traditionalists like to believe," not showily elegant, but comfortable and leisurely. Its countrified "so-called aristocrats," a permeable caste, ably represented a kindly, realistic, and practical people:

> The arts of the section, such as they were, were not immensely passionate, creative, and romantic; they were eighteenth-century social arts of dress, conversation, manners, the table, the hunt, politics, oratory, the pulpit. These were the arts of living and not arts of escape; they were also community arts, in which every class of society could participate after its kind.[25]

This defense of the past was at once a private literary strategy, a *point d'appui* for the Southern traditionalist, and an attack on the contemporary industrial (Northern) order. Every virtue of the Old Order was balanced by a corresponding Northern vice: rural against urban, organic against disassociated society, concreteness against abstraction, rootedness against deracination. Whereas pre-War Southern culture was "based on gentle feeling, on a formal code of behavior, on a certain vainglory of polish and grandiloquence, and on the life of the affections,"[26] the North had already taken on the contours of the modern American state: a society that separated theory from conduct and competed without principles, a secretive legalistic society that debased the social sense. The War brought these two antagonistic civilizations into conflict with tragic results for both.

Whether they knew it or not, the Neo-Confederates' defense of their section and their arraignment of "high-powered modern industrialism and materialism" simply continued the partisan anti-Northern crusade less temperately conducted by their forebears before the War. The new crusaders also singled out nineteenth-century New England as the spawning ground for destructive "isms,"* and although they had no abolitionists or Black Republicans

---

the ascendant. Thereafter Southern thought declined in quality not because of slavery but because of the South's failure to construct means of communication commensurate with its size. The statesmen of Williamsburg and Alexandria—courageous, practical, critical—far surpassed the statesmen of the Confederacy (*The Collected Essays of John Peale Bishop*, ed. Edmund Wilson [New York, 1948], 12).

* According to Davidson, New England transcendentalism dissolved social and cultural as well as political and economic distinctions, thereby clearing the way for the centralized state: "When Emerson urged that we walk on our own feet and work with our own hands, the grandeur of his rhetoric obscured, for the moment, the insufficiency of the principle upon which he hoped to base the independence and unity of American letters. In that admirable peroration of 'The American Scholar' in which he deplored our divi-

to attack and no stake in slavery, they took on the ancestral duties of upholding Southern attitudes and parrying Northern slurs. Like the antebellum Yankeephobes, they slanted history in order to make the usable past more usable.* Yet they happened to be artists as well as self-appointed spokesmen for a "conscious minority" so they did not write their defiant or elegiac fables as agitprop or have to work up their locale or invent their characters. Steeped in a factual-fictional past, proficient in the mysteries of kinship, they found in family chronicles and in Southern history an ample supply of models for their emblematic characters. Hawthorne and Emily Dickinson maintained an equipoise between a pious and cynical view of the past more adroitly than they did, but on the whole their familiarity with Southern people and the Southern earth gave their best work "the potent magic of verisimilitude" so prized by Poe.

Biographical Narratives

But why was it, Davidson asked in 1936, that "heroic material" richly strewn through American history found no comparable expression in American literature?

> Whitman, who proposed to write national poems, celebrated Federal soldiers and nobly commemorated the fallen Lincoln; but he left the Confederate side alone. Benét's epical poem, *John Brown's Body,* although it deals generously with the Southern side, nevertheless by its very title, thesis, and conception makes the wrong approach to Southern feeling. . . . In our literature there is an astonishing scarcity of works of fiction, drama, or poetry that deal convincingly with Washington, Jefferson, Lee, and other great names.[27]

---

sion into a North and South, Emerson had no better principle of union to offer than the Yankee transcendentalism which, even at that moment, in another aspect than the literary, was about to attack and all but destroy the very foundations of Southern culture. His voice was not the voice of America, but of New England, and his plan of salvation was to result not in peaceful unification but in bloody disunion" ("Regionalism and Nationalism in American Literature," *American Review,* V [1935], 58). Before the War, Southern critics had attacked Emerson in much the same vein.

* As John L. Stewart rightly observes, the South since 1830 resented the contempt and hostility of Northern critics to all things Southern and replied to their aspersions by elaborating a political and cultural defense of the South as counterargument. Southern anger and bitterness were tinged with guilt, for the South knew the case against slavery had some basis. "Nothing so helps in the formulation of such a fantasy as the need to defy and defend when one knows at the heart that the facts and one's own sense of human justice are against one" (*The Burden of Time* [Princeton, 1965], 97).

The same question came up at a reunion of the Nashville Fugitive-cum-Agrarians at Vanderbilt University twenty years later. The reunioners agreed that the Neo-Confederates among them had not even tried to write a Confederate epic but disagreed as to why no such poem appeared. Society was too complex and riven for epic poetry which presupposed shared belief; in the Fugitive period the poets were interested in poetic experimentation, not politics; none of them was big or "God-like" enough to write it.[28]

Why then did the Neo-Confederates choose to "re-affirm old values" in prose when they did become aggressively political? And why did they tend to put into criticism, biography, and fiction what they could not say in verse? According to Ransom, "the epic arises as the expression of a nation which has gone through its strife. And it's the representation of the struggle to maintain its ideals and to express its religion and its culture and its heroism." In the 1930s, Ransom and his friends possessed the beliefs and the skills to attempt such a representation, but they lacked the will. As Davidson later explained the difficulty: "You can't find a hero that you can use, nor can you invent an adequate one at this time. Any hero you might take won't do for an epic, partly because he's been too well documented." He had attempted an "epical thing" on Nathan Bedford Forrest, but found himself competing with novelists and the biographical annotaters. The poet who chose Lee for his subject ran up against Freeman's monumental volumes. His only recourse was to write elegiac lyrics or poetic meditations, or to turn to other genres.[29]

If, as Tate and Warren declared, poetry hardened into "document" when dissolved in subject matter, then much of Neo-Confederate writing on the War could be so classified. Unlike the poet, the writer of "documents" knows where he is coming out. The true poem "discovers"; the "document" *communicates* to the already apprehending reader. Admittedly their novels tended to be more poetic, more exploratory than mere "documents," for they dipped into the legend of the Old South in search of objective correlatives— "a great variety of forms"—and used history "as the source or matrix of typical actions." In their biographical narratives of War figures, however, the Neo-Confederates "utilized" history to "communicate" a preconceived political and social message.[30]

By the late 1920s, it had almost become expected of the literary Agrarian to try his hand at some sort of historical writing, whether in the form of narrative poetry, reviews of monographs, or biography. Tate may have started the trend with his partisan and idiosyncratic *Stonewall Jackson, The Good Soldier* (1928), which he followed up with *Jefferson Davis, His Rise and Fall* (1929). In the same year, Warren published *John Brown, The Making of a*

Martyr, and in 1931 Lytle's *Bedford Forrest and His Critter Company* appeared.

Each of these books differed markedly in tone and style, if not in purpose. The authors were writing subjectively about a region, a people, and a culture. Although by no means uncritical apologists of all things Southern, there was no mistaking the adversary in their biographical narratives: the Universal Yankee Nation, or at least the ideas and values it fathered and fostered. Each author adhered to a theory of history writing in conflict with the ostensible academic aims of disinterestedness and objectivity. Tate probably spoke for other Agrarian biographers as well as for himself when he defined the ideal historian as one who read his values into the lives of his subjects. He possessed the "dramatic insight" of a novelist, kept his protagonist in the foreground "as a dramatic figure," reduced every idea and event to personal terms, cultivated an ironic tone, and subordinated "the scientific idea of truth-in-itself . . . to a cultural truth."* Above all he revealed an unmistakable political outlook.[31]

Read simply as history, these biographical narratives swell with tendentious generalizations and arbitrary pronouncements. The authors glorify, denigrate, extenuate at the drop of a hat. They seldom hesitate to editorialize about their major and minor characters, whose historical roles have already elevated or condemned them in the minds of their biographers.

The result is a series of psychologically simplistic portraits of rather complex personalities. Tate's Jackson is closer to Dick Taylor's and Strother's conception of the man than to Cooke's. He is quirky, ruthless, ambitious and yet unworldly, at once pious and gentle, proud and self-effacing. From anecdotal lore, Tate carefully fashions a type of rustic demigod. The studiedly laconic style of the biography does not quite succeed in masking the almost boyish idolator. Jefferson Davis, in contrast to his aggressive general, is the unbending constitutionalist, a man of honor and chilling rectitude but stubborn, tactless, and unimaginative. Tate saddles him with the chief responsibility for the defeat of the Confederacy. Warren's John Brown is resolute and brave; he is also a paranoid, a cheat, a

---

* Tate faulted both the War historians insufficiently concerned "with the significance of the War between the States, prior to that event or afterwards" and contemporary observers. As he put it: "Although the war generation wrote notable books, there was not possible to an eye-witness that peculiar union of passionate interest in details with detachment enough from their personal meaning, to permit much concern with literary form. We must have, of course, the eye-witness testimony; but the gift of the military biographer or historian should be the gift of the novelist Stephen Crane" (*Virginia Quarterly Review,* VII [Jan. 1931], 135–36).

liar, and a murderer. The Forrest of Andrew Lytle's virile biography is a fearless and ferocious soldier, a genius at tactics, and possibly the greatest of the Confederate generals.

Professional historians who patronized the authors of these books pointed out mistakes or omissions, and complained of their unwarranted interpretations, failed to comprehend the biographers' intentions and methods or to detect the design of a Southern "past" they were collectively weaving. The Agrarians did not consider the War primarily a national tragedy. They wrote as spiritual secessionists, spokesmen for a conquered people. Even Robert Penn Warren, the most inquiring and open-minded among them, was still several light years away from the Melville essayist and the author of *Wilderness* and *The Legacy of the Civil War*. Their search into the past was strictly a sectional matter. They had no interest in the North as such except as its abstracted soldiers and civilians inflicted suffering on an inoffensive people, the heirs of an older and more honorable culture. Underneath the brilliant and exciting surface of their narratives lay the Agrarian reading of the War.

In essence, it corroborated Seward's thesis of an "irrepressible conflict" although it defined the antagonists in somewhat different terms. The War was an episode in a much longer struggle between economic freedom and monopolistic tyranny; its origins went back as far as the breakdown of the feudal system. American independence freed the nation from the trammels of European consolidation—but only briefly. Gradually "the common enemy" reappeared, "destroying the Union and planting a central tyranny in its place." A few Southerners spotted the Hamiltonian conspiracy which aimed to supplant the sovereign states by a powerful central government, but even prescient Calhoun fatally erred in thinking the South could preserve its institutions and way of life inside a pseudo-Union.[32] Meanwhile, thirty years of abolitionist agitation had built up an accretion of Northern hate against the South which Black Republicans manipulated for political ends. After John Brown, "a horse-trader with homicidal cravings and a message from God crossed into Virginia to be a rallying point for a revolt of slaves that never came,"[33] the sections prepared for war.

Properly led, the South could have cast off the Northern yoke. Its yeomanry, the major part of the Confederate army, was invincible when commanded by competent generals. Unfortunately, the Davis administration did not know how to conduct the War and (according to Tate) "didn't want the South to win its own war." Davis "wanted it to act upon a noble and martyred defensive, so that Europe might be moved to intercede."[34] He refused the opportunities available to him and clung to his fetish of legality. By remaining constitutionalists (the virus of Unionism ran through their veins) Davis and his advisers perpetuated the follies they were ostensibly combating and neglected their tremendous advantages. *If* the Confederates had seized Washington after the first Manassas, *if* they had recognized the Western theater as the lynchpin of their defense, *if* they had elevated Forrest over Braxton Bragg, *if* they had not been politically outmaneuvered by the clever Lincoln (the "ifs" could be extended), they would have wrested their independence from the engulfing North.

So the North won—barely. Defeat punctured the hope of forestalling the Industrial Juggernaut and perhaps preserving the North itself from the tyranny it engendered. The War was thus the penultimate event, the last stand of the Old Order. After the War, even during it, the Southern code could no longer function as it once had. The War corrupted the honorable Southerner; its aftermath made his old way of life impossible. That was the real tragedy of the American *Iliad*.

Looking back at these events in which family and kin had figured, the Agrarians, "still rebels," could not pretend a detachment they did not feel. For one thing, as Stark Young explained, they had been born only three or four decades since the War and Reconstruction and grown up in a country "peopled with ghosts, warm, close, and human; the dead were often as present as the living." To have thrust aside the collective memories of burning houses and ruined cemeteries, the sadness and humiliations of "proud spirits whom history had slapped in the face" would have amounted to sectional treason as well as blunting the point of their thesis.[35]

The whole question of slavery was ancillary to the Neo-Confederates. If not a positive good, it was far less vicious than it had been painted and at the time an indispensable ingredient in preserving the best of the available social systems. Tate admitted that he and his friends were a bit vague on the race question, but offering his own views on the " 'oppression' (so-called)" of the blacks, he showed that at least one Agrarian held the same opinions of white supremacy as his antebellum forebears. When two races lived together, "not social justice but social order is the key to the situation," and "to maintain order" one race had to rule. Just as slave apologists once accused abolitionists of making the Negro a cat's-paw to gain ulterior ends, so Tate blamed Northern liberals for violence done to blacks in the South. Left alone, the South would guarantee them legal justice, except in the case of a black raping a white woman. On miscegenation ("The moral symbolism required that the source of life shall not be polluted") Tate hardly differed from Thomas Nelson Page.[36] Tate never expounded his ideas on black inferiority in print (he conveyed the above sentiments in a private letter), nor did the other Agrarians publicly address themselves to Negro-white relations. As for slavery, it is probably fair to say that they saw it as only one feature of the Southern way of life and agreed with Henry Adams's judgment: "the life of it—the vigor—the poetry—was its moral purpose of self."[37] This, they felt, was what the North could never understand.

Given the Neo-Confederate résumé of the War, their programmatic intention becomes clearer. Tate, Warren, Lytle, Young, and others aimed (as Lytle said of Tate) "to achieve the possession of experience in objective form."[38] That experience was Southern culture, the "setting" of the Old South and the forces that crushed it. The narrative as history, distinguished from historical narrative, strove to marry fable and fact, to make history emblematic. Agrarian history about the War (and the same could be said of Agrarian War fiction) is burdened with meanings, and the historical personalities who dominate the action serve an iconographic function. They are never walking abstractions, nonpeople; but they stand for certain ideals, principles, attitudes.

To some extent their actions are predictable, or at least partly determined, for they have been selected to represent characteristic aspects of their respective cultures. The Jefferson Davis familiar to professional historians becomes a symbol of the disassociated sensibility in whom logic and feeling are sundered. Half Mr. Facing-Both-Ways, half Hamlet—frail, aloof, indecisive—he is not really attuned to the civilization he had been elected to preserve. Neither his courage nor nobility in time of trial can compensate for his paralysis of will. He personifies the inherent weakness of the Confederacy. Lincoln, his Yankee counterpart, is less educated and intelligent. At best he is an unwitting tool of Black Republicanism, at worst a secretive, cold, and savagely humorous revolutionist who exemplifies the guile and ruthlessness of the Yankee nation. Yet by virtue of his instinct for leadership and sensitiveness to popular opinion, his monstrous political philosophy wins the day.[39]

Jackson and Forrest stand for the unadulterated yeoman South. Their performances are merely extensions of their beliefs; unselfconsciously they incarnate their culture, slavery and all, and are notably indifferent to the chivalric ethos. Sherman, the Union scourge, is just as ruthless, but he is much less all of a piece. Like Davis he is a tormented man unable to synchronize his public and private views, a victim of that old disassociation of sensibility whose personal and public codes never mesh. Disliking abolitionists and in no sense a champion of Negro liberties, he is a Unionist fighting for an abstraction. Where the Southern party "integrates, in terms of a harmonious life that blends substance and spirit, subject to God's will and the contingencies of nature," the Northern party (which

Sherman incarnates) "disintegrates and, using disintegration itself as a tool of power, presumes to mount beyond good and evil and to make human intelligence a quasi-God."[40]

Allen Tate and the Novel as History

Sherman became the prophet as well as the agent of doom in the Agrarian imagination. Denying his tactical genius, Andrew Lytle presented him as the mastermind of total war. "He knew at last who the enemy was: the women and children, the corn bins and smoke-houses; and he knew the weapons: fire and rapine." Stark Young detected in Sherman (who figures prominently in *So Red the Rose*) "a rough cleanness of soul" and an "impetuous integrity," yet saw him as one who paved the way for the post-War New Man "sustained by innocence, emptied by shallow choice, and run by steam."[41]

The displacement of a civilization grounded on "tradition, forefathers, and a system of living" by a noncivilization devoid of humane values is an implicit theme in Neo-Confederate fiction. Heretofore, most Southern writing on the War and Reconstruction had been the outgrowth of unreflective tribalism. Allen Tate charged the genteel literati who wrote and spoke for the South between 1865 and World War I with being bookish and shallow and of using "words like tradition and aristocracy with a disarming contempt for accuracy." Even antebellum writers, totally absorbed in defending their "special politico-economic order," were incapable of perceiving "that spontaneous self-examination . . . is the initial moral attitude which must preface the exacting business of beautiful letters." The same was true for their immediate forebears, deprived of the power and prerogatives of their sires. Until his own generation appeared, the Old and the New South had failed to produce a critical intelligence—some "historian of fine consciences" —who could apprise Southerners of their "cultural limitations."[42]

Tate set down these thoughts in 1925. A few years later he referred to his ancestors more appreciatively if no less critically. The task he outlined for himself and the talented corps of his contemporaries was to re-see the Southern experience as the Thomas Nelson Pages had singularly failed to do. Page's school had been handicapped for want of a culture of ideas. Later Tate ascribed the achievements of Faulkner, Porter, Gordon, Young, Warren, and Lytle to their sense "of a vanishing society about to be replaced by a new order the lineaments of which remain indistinct." The true character of the Old Order might be "disputable." The legend was

not. Every Southern writer held at least a part of it in his consciousness and, given sufficient genius, could objectify it in "a great
variety of forms."[43]

Tate and his friends distinguished between "historical novels"
and "novels as history." Gone With the Wind—panoramic yarn, a
piece of documented partisanship[44]—exemplified the former. For
all her storytelling skill, library research, and Dixie zeal, Margaret
Mitchell lacked a sense of the past that "mere documentary authenticity" can never alone evoke.[45] The "novel as history" derived from
the author's familiarity with "the cultural structure and beliefs of a
given society at a given moment." According to Tate, this "use of
history as the source or matrix of typical actions" was "not unlike
the 'history' floating in the background of Oedipus Rex and Oedipus
at Colonus. The action takes shape out of a vast and turbulent cloud
of events as the funnel of a tornado suddenly forms and descends."[46]
Whether the novelist succeeded or failed depended upon his
ability to filter historical events through "some striking personal
vision of life"* that would "give meaning to all the symbols of his
irresistible choice."[47] Judged by this criterion as well as by its purely
literary virtues, Tate's The Fathers (1938) is an impressive work. It
complements his historical narratives, but the novel is more poetic
and philosophical than his studies of Jackson and Davis. Tate, like
his narrator, Lacy Buchan, acknowledges the attraction or at least
the inevitability of what he dislikes and is irritated by the inade-
quacies of what he most admires.

In The Fathers, Tate describes—not exactly celebrates—a
defunct way of life ("dead as a herring") whose dissolution coin-
cides with and is hastened by the War. Lacy in his sixty-fifth year
probes the past of his boyhood. His mind travels back to 1860 when
he was sixteen. The Old Order, embodied for him in his father,
Major Lewis Buchan, and in the Virginia plantation society, is
already on the edge of extinction. In 1909 Lacy will not gloss over
the blemishes of "the fathers" civilization, its stiff insularity and
unintentional cruelties. Yet to Lacy, and presumably to Tate himself, it was superior in many ways to the bastard anarchic culture

---

* Tate found this "vision" lacking in Stephen Vincent Benét's popular
John Brown's Body (1928), still widely (and I think mistakenly) regarded as
the great Civil War epic. Conceding that Benét's poem was sound in its historical underpinnings and filled with striking passages and noting how skillfully the poet had stitched together fact and legend, Tate nonetheless pronounced it loose in structure and flawed by stretches of slack verse (The
Nation, CXXVII [Sept. 19, 1928], 274). The tragedy of the War, which Benét
sincerely felt, is frittered away in rhetoric, spectacle, and sentiment. I mean
no slur to either gifted man when I liken Benét's "cyclorama" to a hypothetical
edition of the Iliad illustrated by Norman Rockwell.

that supplanted it. If it produced no high art, it enabled the Southerner to live in harmony with his environment and to orchestrate his personal behavior. The "code" of the Old Order—mere flummery to the outsider—gave Southern society its integrity.

The boy Lacy, still imperfectly disciplined as the novel opens, shares his brother-in-law's impatience with the "code." George Posey physically personifies the Southern cavalier, but by nature he is precursor of the New American, subjective, isolated, disassociated. A man of rectitude, he is nonetheless a destructive force, because his logic and rationality operate beyond the guidelines of the Old Order. Posey does not fit into the enclosed and seamless world of the Buchans, whose rituals he ridicules or avoids. That world, Tate implies, was no less vulnerable to the stream of tendency than Major Buchan's plantation to Federal raiders. While it functioned, however, its institutions and traditions provided outlets for private anguish, kept birth, death, love, and marriage unfragmented, and worked against the separating of private and public life.

Although never so unreflectively a part of the Old Order as his father, Lacy Buchan comes to realize that his exposure to it permitted him "to survive the disasters that destroyed other and better men and to tell their story." He means the George Poseys who dispensed with institutional buffers and received all experiences through their "exacerbated nerves." The Poseys, Lacy decides, were more refined than the Buchans and less civilized. And then he reflects: "Excessively refined persons have a communion with the abyss; but is not civilization the agreement slowly arrived at, to let the abyss alone?" Ceremony, ritual, manners, the code form the indispensable enclosure. The older Lacy retrospectively considers himself at once a beneficiary and a casualty of the destroyed culture. He knows what was strong and good about his Virginia and what was unsatisfactory and unworkable in the ideas it stood for. Tate seems to be saying: "Let us appropriate what is beautiful and true about the Old Order without being beguiled by its self-deceptions."[48]

The War itself is of less importance in *The Fathers* than the conservative society it smashed and the New Order it prepared the way for. Tate's novel contains only a few battle scenes, and although it reproduces convincingly the apprehensions and excitement of Virginia Unionists and secessionists before Sumter and includes a few historical notables among the minor characters, it is not a "historical novel."* The sense of the past is unobtrusively

---

* The one "historical" incident in *The Fathers*—the killing of Colonel Elmer R. Ellsworth by James W. Jackson, proprietor of the Marshall House tavern in Alexandria, Virginia, May 24, 1861—does considerable violence to the facts. Lacy Buchan describes Jackson as "an excellent man" and his

registered in the setting of country and town, topographical fidelity, the formal and informal language of the speakers, the individualized portraits of slaves, maiden aunts, valetudinarian ladies, and members of the plantation squirearchy, old and young. With a few exceptions (who might have stepped out of a Hawthorne romance) the characters belong to the time.

The past is not so much recaptured in *The Fathers* as absorbed and reflected. Primarily a meditation on an era, it breathes none of the sectional truculence and bravado characteristic of Tate's biographical narratives. He salvaged something valuable from his backward excursion into the mid-century South—a vision of a style, a manner, an ideal which may never have existed in quite the finished form he pictured it but which provided him and his friends with a useful fiction.

The Meditations of Robert Penn Warren

Robert Penn Warren began his "meditations" on the War about the same time as Tate. From the start, however, he was less determinedly sectional than Agrarian friends like Donald Davidson, that self-appointed guardian of the Southern shrine.* The Nashville

---

father's friend. The real Jackson was a hotheaded hunter of abolitionists and Black Republicans, a kind of Confederate Horst Wessel. When Ellsworth, recently arrived at Alexandria with his regiment, personally removed a Confederate flag from the roof of the Marshall House, Jackson shot him as Ellsworth came down the stairs. Ellsworth's sergeant immediately shot down the assassin. Tate mistakenly makes Ellsworth an officer in a Massachusetts regiment. He correctly portrays Jackson as a superpatriot but plays down his ruffianlike propensities. According to a Confederate account of Jackson's "martyrdom," Jackson had been a belated participant in the Harper's Ferry incident. Arriving too late to help capture John Brown, "he brought back with him one of the celebrated pikes, and the ear of John Brown, Jr., and from Jackson's humor it is very probably [sic] that it was so. These he exhibited for a long time at his house, and would detail with lively interest his conversation with old Brown, and the way in which he obtained his trophies" (*Life of James W. Jackson, the Alexandria Hero, the Slayer of Ellsworth, the First Martyr in the Cause of Southern Independence, etc.* [Richmond, 1862], 22). Given the code of the Buchans, it is unlikely they would have had any truck with men of Jackson's reputation.

* The doughtiest and most un-Reconstructed of the Agrarian spokesmen, Davidson never hesitated to show his contempt for anyone, North or South, who did not instinctively divine what he meant by "Southern Culture." He was highly sensitive to real and fancied slurs against his region and continued to launch periodic forays against the North until his death. For a good example of Davidson's slashing style, see his "Mr. Cash and the Proto-Dorian South," *The Southern Review*, VII (1941–42), 1–20.

brethren agreed on no single program ("geography and poetry" and "mutual respect and common interests" held them together, Warren reminds us), and even his contribution to the Agrarian manifesto, *I'll Take My Stand*** (a title he abominated), betrayed a concern for moral issues transcending regional bias. Reflecting in later years on his article, written during an interlude at Oxford University, Warren remembered "the jangle and wrangle of writing the essay and some kind of discomfort in it, some sense of evasion." The explanation for this "discomfort" closely bears on Warren's attitude, then and subsequently, toward the War.[49]

He once explained it this way. After 1918 Southern intellectuals experienced a "cultural shock" comparable in intensity to the shock felt by their New England counterparts in the 1830s. Most of the writers associated with the Southern literary "renascence" lived or traveled outside of the South. Upon their return, they had to cope with tensions within themselves and their society, particularly the one growing out of race, and to resolve an internal debate. Two loyalties were in contention: the old "pieties" bound up with kinship, manners, regional pride, history, and what Warren called "a religious or moral sense," a phrase he did not define but which suggests values above and beyond loyalty to race and place. The conflict between them demanded a redefinition and re-examination of that fount of piety—the past.†

* "The Briar Patch" argued (1) that the War left the Negro peasant helpless in his "new-got freedom," abandoned by his former "friends," corrupted by Reconstructionists; (2) that education without economic self-sufficiency would not improve his condition; (3) that the dream of social equality was chimerical; (4) that the industrialization of the South might contribute to his well-being but only if Negroes and working-class whites in the South jointly resisted "an extravagant industrial expansion" which exploited racial antagonisms and capitalized on the competition for jobs; and (5) that agriculture constituted a slow but "probably the surest way" for the majority of Negroes "to establish themselves." Implicit throughout the essay was a sympathy for the black man's plight and an insistence upon the distinction between justice and social equality. In 1930, Warren considered the latter a millennial dream, but the white man, he said, who failed "to concede the negro equal protection" did "not properly respect himself as a man" (*I'll Take My Stand* [New York, 1962 edn.], 246–64).

† Robert Penn Warren, "The Art of Fiction," *Paris Review*, III (spring–summer 1957), 123. Perhaps all the Neo-Confederates previously mentioned oscillated between the pulls of these two magnetic poles. Some, like Davidson or Lytle, felt the pull of the "pieties" more powerfully than Warren and Tate. Writers longer exposed to the attitudes and modes of the trans-Southern world might be more relativistic and less wholeheartedly parochial in their attachments. Of course, the writer-as-propagandist or hot partisan usually plumped enthusiastically for one side, as Tate did in his biographical narratives. But in *The Fathers*, the two "pulls" tended to equalize each other. If "piety" finally prevailed, the contest was not so one-sided as it seemed to be in

With *John Brown, the Making of a Martyr* (1929), Warren took his first plunge into history. Substantively a swift and competent retelling of the story of that "ungodly godlike man," it is plain from the first pages that this is no ordinary biography. Warren is systematically demythologizing a myth, replacing the divinely inspired hero of the hagiographers with what Warren regards as the "historical" John Brown: the deceiving and self-deceived fanatic, shifty appropriator of other people's money, moral bully, cunning intriguer, and cold-blooded killer. Yet *John Brown* is far from being a debunking exercise. Warren is not untouched by Brown's courage or by his "different but haughty and self-reliant nature."[50] Conceived simply as phenomenon, a kind of human earthquake or tornado, Brown is an object of his wonder if not veneration. Warren's animus is not directed so much at Old Ossawattomie as at the society that hatched him and exploited his martyrdom.

Then and later Warren reserved a special scorn for a type he once described as "a certain breed of professional defender-of-the-good who makes a career of holding right thoughts and admiring his own moral navel."[51] New England abolitionists, he implied, were largely composed of that breed, and in *John Brown* Warren engaged in a considerable amount of Yankee nose-pulling.* In fact his effort to scrape off the crust of legend from the "real" John Brown might be likened to Henry Adams's impious assault against the legend of Pocahontas in 1863.† Like Adams, Warren aimed his arrows against the gods of his enemies. Brown's mental instability and his claim to be the Lord's lieutenant (sailing "with letter of marque from God," as Wendell Phillips put it) exposed the "Higher Law" men for what they were: believers in the doctrine that the

---

the work of Davidson, Lytle, Young, or Caroline Gordon. Warren seems to have started his literary career closer to the point of equilibrium, despite his partisan *John Brown*. We shall be better informed about these and related matters after Virginia Rock's forthcoming chronicle and critique of the Southern Agrarians.

* For example, his comment on Frank B. Sanborn, friend and backer of John Brown: "an earnest young man" who knew God's will and possessed "to a considerable degree that tight especial brand of New England romanticism which manifested itself in stealing Guinea niggers, making money, wrestling with conscience, hunting witches, building tea-clippers, talking about Transcendentalism, or being an Abolitionist" (226–27). Here Warren sounded like some editorial writer in the *Southern Literary Messenger* circa 1850–60.

† "It is in some sort a flank, or rather a rear attack on the Virginian aristocracy, who will be utterly gravelled by it if it is successful. I can imagine the shade of John Randolf [sic] turn green" (Henry Adams to J. G. Palfrey, March 20, 1862, quoted in E. N. Harbert, "Henry Adams; New England View: A Regional Angle of Vision?" *Tulane Studies in English*, XVI [1968], 111–12).

ends justify the means. Brown's chicanery, financial and otherwise, made all Yankee philanthropy suspect. His timorous allies may have stalemated the senatorial committee looking behind the agents of the Harper's Ferry episode for the alleged Yankee conspirators— but not his biographer. Warren more than fulfilled the Neo-Confederate task of exposing Yankeeism as a corrupt blend of materialism and abstract idealism.

In some respects *John Brown* was hardly less tendentious than the biographical narratives of Tate and Lytle. Warren simplified abolitionists and abolitionism to the point of distortion, played down the grimier and unpatriarchal side of slavery that aroused the Garrisons and Mrs. Stowes of the North, and took for granted the "Southern" view on Negro talent and character. The slave in *John Brown* never bothered his "kinky" head about the right or wrong of slavery. Of course "the system was subject to grave abuses,"[52] but generally speaking the blacks enjoyed tolerable conditions, if only for their cash value. Good-natured and irresolute, they harbored no hatred for their owners, as their unrancorous behavior during the War clearly proved. Warren neither condemned the North nor romanticized his own section, yet his biography invidiously contrasted two societies, one agitated by bloody-minded idealists, the other controlled by a pardonably impulsive but relatively stable gentry.

It also hinted of complexities and ironies unsuggested in the more frankly partisan "histories" of his friends. If Warren's New England humanitarians failed to "visualize the barbarous and pitiful consequences" of "divinely inspired" ends, neither did the great theoreticians, Calhoun and Webster, perceive how issues so clear to themselves would be translated into violent and savage action by wielders of bowie knives. Although Northern fanaticism kindled the great War, Southerners who mistook the passions of a handful for the will of an entire nation heaped on the coals. The South, Warren argued, rested its case on the rule of law; the North transposed the terms of disagreement into theology. "There is only one way to conclude a theological argument: bayonets and bullets."[53]

Warren weighed, qualified, revised, and expanded his thoughts on the War during the next twenty-five years, holding on to some of his youthful convictions while emancipating himself from parochial myths. The longer he studied it, the more dense, parodoxical, and ambiguous it seemed to him. Gradually he shifted a larger share for the responsibility of the War onto the shoulders of history without absolving the participants. "Contingency" now became a more revelatory word than "Blame."

Increasingly fascinated with the etiology of the War, Warren probed the American past and discovered the virus of the disease in the nation's origins. The United States, unlike other nations which were "accidents of geography or race,"[54] began as pure idea, a grand abstraction operating without benefit of deep-rooted traditions and institutional controls. Hence its susceptibility to epidemics of romanticism, of which transcendentalism and the cult of the Higher Law were characteristic samples. The Nashville Agrarians had saddled the North alone with the sin of Abstraction, the separation of life from thought. Warren in his mature view no longer exempted the South from its contagion. The Southern *mystique* of Legality was no less abstract. "It denied life also, and in a sense more viciously, in its refusal to allow, through the inductive scrutiny of fact, for change, for the working of the life process through history."[55]

So the War emerged in his eyes as a tragedy of unconscious complicity, as a fusion of nobility and beastliness, and the virtue and defects of its principal actors were inseparably intertwined. Without condoning the "personal absolutism" of the abolitionist mind, he now acknowledged abolitionism's just cause and conceded the darkness of the "anachronistic and inhuman" institution it sought to overthrow. A comparable sincerity and rigidity marked the defenders of slavery. "If in the North the critic had repudiated society, in the South society repudiated the critic; and the stage was set for trouble." At such moments in history the way is clear for terrible simplifiers like John Brown, who explode like dynamite and break up the moral log jam. Warren appreciated how the madness of martyrs can enthrall, but "who can fail to be disturbed and chastened," he asked, "by the picture of the joyful mustering of the darker forces of our nature in that just cause?"[56]

Only one figure loomed over the War's *personae*—Abraham Lincoln, whom Warren alone among the Neo-Confederates had honored in 1929: "humane, wise, and fallible," he called him, "but learning from his own failings."[57] Meditating on the War centennial, Warren found in Lincoln's principled practicality and serene common sense both a rebuke and an answer to the mad logic of extremism. Yet even that shrewd empiricist had no inkling of the "slick-faced fixers" who would take over in the post-War years or "the uncoiling powers of technology and finance capitalism, the new world of Big Organization."[58]

Writing as a Southerner and a moralist, Warren reflected on the peril of righteousness and totaled up the physical and psychological costs of "the great single event of our history": the immense drain of life and property, the rise of a new class of millionaire as brutal as any South Carolina Lord of the Lash, the eruption of industrial strife exceeding the terrors of slave insurrections, the spread of venality through public and private sectors of American life. Even one of the primary ends of the War—the abolishment of black servitude—was only partially realized, for the defeat of the Confederacy failed to liberate the liberated, and the Negro won at best "a shadowy freedom." North and South fell prey to their self-engendered illusions. To the North, the War signified sectional redemption, and thereafter it supplied the national "Treasury of Virtue" with an endless supply of fraudulent spiritual capital. It furnished the defeated with the "Great Alibi" by which the South could deny its culpability for social and racial iniquities and blame malign outside influences for every Southern ill.[59]

These were some of the unsavory consequences a smug America chose to ignore. But Warren was equally sensitive to the "nobility gleaming ironically, and redeemingly, through the murk." Men ungodlike in their weaknesses displayed in their best moments extraordinary independence, bravery, and self-control. The American *Iliad* had no shortage of heroes or marvels. It was almost too "massively symbolic" and "sibylline," however, for literary condensation as all truly incestuous civil wars are likely to be. Warren tried to unravel its mystery in his one novel with a War setting. He succeeded better in his centennial meditation. There he persuasively showed why the dimensions and ambivalences of our Homeric war have yet to be imaginatively encompassed.[60]

Chapter 20

William Faulkner

I think no one individual can look at truth. It blinds you. You look at it and you see one phase of it. Someone else looks at it and sees a slightly awry phase of it. But taken all together the truth is what they saw though nobody saw the truth intact.

WILLIAM FAULKNER, 1957

It suggests the transformation which begins to steal over all events from the moment of their occurrence, unless they are arrested and pinned down in writing by an alert and trained observer. Even then some selection cannot be avoided—a selection, moreover, determined by irrelevant psychological factors, by the accidents of interest and attention. Moment by moment the whole fabric of events dissolves in ruins and melts into the past; and all that survives of the thing done passes into the custody of a shifting, capricious, imperfect human memory. Nor is the mutilated fragment allowed to rest there, as on a shelf in a museum; imagination seizes on it and builds it with other fragments into some ideal construction, which may have a plan and outline laid out long before this fresh bit of material came to the craftsman's hand to be worked into it, as the drums of fallen columns are built into the rampart of an Acropolis. . . . The facts work loose; they are detached from their roots in time and space and shaped into a story. The story is moulded and remoulded by imagination, by passion and prejudice, by religious preconception or aesthetic instinct, by the delight of the marvellous, by the itch for the moral, by the love of a good story; and the thing becomes a legend. A few irreducible facts will remain; no more perhaps, than the name of persons and places . . .

F. M. CORNFORD, 1907

Faulkner and the Agrarians

ONLY after the flurry of Agrarianism petered out did the Neo-Confederates come to a proper appreciation of William Faulkner. Some of them knew him, of course, in the 1930s as one of the talented representatives of the Southern literary "renascence,"* but a decade passed before they canonized him belatedly as "the most powerful and original novelist in the United States and one of the best in the modern world,"[1] and inadvertently made his achievement ancillary to their own social and aesthetic dicta. The exegeses of Warren and especially of Cleanth Brooks influenced Faulkner scholarship so profoundly, in fact, that the differences between him and the Nashville group have become obscured. Yet Faulkner remained outside the Agrarian orbit. He had no taste for sectional polemic, and if he commemorated the values of the Old Order in the Agrarian vein, he explored more profoundly than Tate or Warren the complexities and paradoxes of his section. "Loving all of it," he wrote of himself in 1954, "while he had to hate some of it because he knows now that you don't love because: you love despite; not for the virtues, but despite the faults."†

The War did not interest him much—only its aftereffects; but thanks to luck and genius, he was able to make literary capital out of it: first because he was a Southerner, a legatee of defeat, imaginatively close enough to the War to inhale its essence yet detached enough to see it critically; and second, because he had the wit to read the War's meaning not in its heroes and battles but in the consciousness of a people.

---

* In 1963, Allen Tate declared that "since the early Thirties" he had considered Faulkner "the greatest American novelist after Henry James" although he disliked him personally. I have been unable to discover anything in Tate's critical writings during that decade which anticipates this comment. Nor is Faulkner's "great theme" adequately conveyed in Tate's summary: "The destruction of the Old South released native forces of disorder and corruption which were accelerated by the brutal exploitation of the carpetbaggers and an army of occupation; thus the old order of dignity and principle were replaced by upstarts and cynical materialists. Federal interference in the South brought this about" ("William Faulkner, 1897–1962," *Sewanee Review*, 71 [Jan.–March 1963], 160–64). Tate, it seems to me, oversimplifies Faulkner's intention and converts him into a spokesman of Warren's "Great Alibi."

† Quoted in James B. Meriwether, "Faulkner's 'Mississippi,'" *Mississippi Quarterly*, XXV (spring 1972, Supplement), 21.

Licensed Chronicler

Northern writers failed to do justice to the War, Faulkner told
Malcolm Cowley, because "the Northerner had nothing to write
about regarding it. The only clean thing about war is losing it."[2] He
was not the first to notice the literary advantages accruing to the
losers. As early as 1884, Albion Tourgée denounced an apostate
North for abandoning the ideals of its conquering armies. Remorseful Yankees, he complained, erased the names of victories from
their battle standards, removed commemorative inscriptions from
captured Rebel cannon, extolled Southern heroism at the expense of
Northern. "The South surrendered at Appomattox, and the North
has been surrendering ever since. It has followed up its four years
of war with twenty years of apology." Northern self-abasement,
Tourgée concluded, enabled the South to snatch literary victory
from military defeat. As evidence he could have pointed to the
plethora of romantic fiction featured in Northern books and periodicals which re-enforced idyllic plantation myths and to the predominantly female readership inordinately fond of twaddle about gallant
Confederate cavaliers and solicitous slaves.

But long memories and a reverence for the past were no
guarantee for quality. The South could only be said to be winning
the literary war if the criterion was the popularity of "magnolia and
moonlight." Most Southern fiction was pretty dismal stuff, and
Southern poetry, with a few notable exceptions, even worse. Something of the grandiloquent Southern tone is suggested in Paul
Hamilton Hayne's oration to the Ladies of the Memorial Association
of Alabama in 1872: his theme, the Southern war of independence.

> Many are the tongues that have essayed to narrate its history,
> but not for us, not in *our* generation, can the *Iliad* of the
> Southern war be "said or sung"!
>
> About us still lingers too densely the smoke of battle,
> and the bloody haze of a slaughter and of sacrifice.
>
> A century hence, however, (if we but garner up the
> great body of our historical facts, and keep them untarnished
> and unperverted in their splendid integrity), some earnest
> genius, who combines the large sympathetic imagination of
> the Poet, with the penetrating insight of the philosopher, will
> delineate this epoch with the terse vigor of Tacitus, and the
> picturesque generalization of Thucydides. And well I know
> that whatever else so consummate an artistic thinker may
> say, he cannot fail to point out the fact that here in this ma-
> terial 19th century, an age after Burke had declared "the days

of chivalry were passed"—among a people branded by uni-versal Christendom as upholders of a brutal, arrogant slaveoc-racy—a drama presented itself, which in the course of a solitary *lustrum*, re-illustrated act by act, and scene by scene, *all* the rarest virtue of knighthood—the gallantries of an antique time, with its single-hearted devotion, and uncalcu-lating self-sacrifice—its purity, honor, courage, heroism, and majestic patience.[3]

It took less than a century for the South to produce Hayne's "earnest genius" with the poet's imagination and the philosopher's "insight" to "delineate this epoch," but in literary terms, an immense distance separates the pomposities of his "lost-cause" version of the War from Faulkner's compassionate but at the same time ironic and deflationary one. Given on occasion to flourishes, Faulkner was persuasively commonsensical. He did not glorify his ancestors in the spirit of Hayne's address to the Alabama ladies; he summoned them to justice.

There is nothing reverential in his following reflection on the Old Order:

> Re. literature (songs too) in the South 1861–65. It was prob-ably produced but not recorded. The South was too busy, but the main reason was probably a lack of tradition for invent-ing or recording. The gentle folk hardly would. For all their equipment for leisure (slavery, unearned wealth) their lives were curiously completely physical, violent, despite their physical laziness. When they were not doing anything—not hunting or superintending farming or riding 10 and 20 miles to visit, they really did nothing: they slept or talked. They talked too much, I think. Oratory was the first art; Con-federate generals would hold up attacks while they made speeches to their troops. Apart from that, "art" was really no manly business. It was a polite painting of china by gentle-women. When they entered its domain through the doors of their libraries, it was to read somebody else's speeches, or politics, or the classics of the faintly school, and even these were men who, if they had been writing men, would have written still more orations. The Negroes invented the songs and their songs were not topical nor even dated in the sense we mean.*

---

* Malcolm Cowley, *The Faulkner–Cowley File: Letters and Memories, 1944–1962* (New York, 1966), 79. Cf. Tourgée: "Slavery has unquestionably left a negroid stamp upon Southern thought and sentiment, just as it broadened our vowels, strengthened our labials and modified almost every form of our speech. It was a game of give and take—the white man taking purposely the slave's liberty—his unrequited toil—and giving unconsciously

The attitude expressed here is decidedly modern. Although gently ironic asides on Southern pieties could occasionally be heard in the nineteenth century from Confederate veterans (George C. Eggleston saw the War in retrospect as "a very ridiculous affair" and concluded the South had ruined itself for an abstraction),[4] few Southern writers made assaults on cherished legends until the 1920s—and then only for a short period.

William Faulkner belonged to no literary party and remained uncaptivated by stylish myths. He was steeped in the Southern past, of course, but he contemplated it without benefit of ideology and contrived a special language (in which mockery and piety, blasphemy and belief curiously commingled) to evoke it. This style, he told Malcolm Cowley,[5] who had found it "full of over-blown words," was "further complicated by an inherited regional or geographical (Hawthorne would say, racial) curse. You might say, studbook style: 'by Southern Rhetoric out of Solitude' or 'Oratory out of Solitude.' "* Whatever its kinship with old-style oratory, Faulkner's

---

year by year something of his own manhood to transform the African into an American. The master was undoubtedly compelled by the irony of fate to bear something of his slave's burden and take on his tongue and brain the stamp of his generic attributes. Out of these facts it arose that the song to which the footsteps of your soldiers echoed on their unresisting march to victory, was but the creaking of the gallows-tree at Charlestown, made comprehensible by words irrelevant and quaint enough to suit themselves to the life the maniac-martyr had lived and the unlawful but beneficent purpose for which he had died. At the same time, the South took from the negro's lips the song which it did not only make its real national anthem, but with strange inconsistency constituted also the battle-cry of a conflict waged for the perpetuation of slavery" (*The Veteran and His Pipe* [Chicago and New York, 1886], 230–31).

* Allen Tate may have exaggerated in saying Faulkner presented himself as emerging "full-grown, out of the unlettered soil of his native state," but his essay "A Southern Mode of the Imagination" presents a plausible explanation of Faulkner's stylistic inheritance. According to Tate, "Confederate prose" was a "mode of discourse," Ciceronian and rhetorical if not always florid, common in the South down to World War I. The "rhetorical expression" of a social group still living (mentally at least) in a preindustrial America, it presupposed that "somebody at the other end is listening." But it did not allow for conversational exchange or dialectic. A society in which mental and physical activities were inseparable and which cultivated no "divisions of intellectual labor" was unlikely to produce an artistic flowering. As the South began to acquire the self-examining habits so necessary to the art of literature, the new Southern writers (heirs of the rhetorical form of discourse and the tradition of Southern storytelling—including the "tall tale") fell quite naturally into the old habit of public recitation. What differentiated their writing from their precursors' was the addition of an internal dialogue, a conflict within the self, that accompanied the public rhetoric. For the first time, Southern writers discovered the truth of Yeats's words: "Out of the quarrel with others we make rhetoric; out of the quarrel with ourselves,

"mode of discourse" admirably conveyed his mixed and complex feelings toward a still palpitating past—a past he simultaneously honored and deflated. It enabled him to punctuate his own grandiosity. Imaginatively drawn to what he could not rationally subscribe to, his own language sometimes swelled with the afflatus he ridiculed in his ancestors. He felt the pull of what he disbelieved, but the prevailing tone of his "discourse" was unrapturous, sardonic, tragicomic. He may not have treated the War as tragicomedy, but while acknowledging the nobility or bravery of those who knew or did not know what they were fighting for, he recorded its ludicrous and unheroic features.

Faulkner's War is multidimensional. He sees it as historical event, as a mirror reflecting personal and sectional character, and finally, and most important, as a buried experience that must be unearthed before it can be understood. Yet it defies exhumation because the reality is inseparable from the myth. Never a shrill partisan, he acts as the chronicler of a clan, not the historian looking for causes or the moralist dispensing praise and blame. He stands aside and comments, pours into his story vast amounts of random misinformation and legend, enters sympathetically into the minds of the self-deluded and deceived—the unconscious mythmakers. No one character speaks for him, and it is never unmistakably clear whether the authorial voice or community opinion is being heard. Perhaps the author is best described as a one-man chorus, challenging, raising questions, identifying himself with the myth-makers at some points (for he, too, is filled with Southern ghosts), yet withdrawing at other times and refusing to side with the emotionalists. As a privileged insider, he is entitled by virtue of his origins and his bardic role to say things no outsider would be permitted to say.

In the South, Mark Twain had noted, the War remained the principal topic of conversation; it was "what A.D. is elsewhere; they date from it."* According to Tourgée, the Southerner denied "the

---

poetry." When they realized "the Yankees were not to blame for everything," they began to substitute "the dialectic of tragedy" for the rhetoric of melodrama (Tate, *Collected Essays* [Denver, 1959], 554–68). Faulkner, it would follow from Tate's argument, is the supreme example of the modern consciousness interacting with the past.

* "All day long you hear things 'placed' as having happened since the waw; or du'in' the waw; or befo' the waw; or right aftah the waw; or 'bout two yeahs or five yeahs or ten yeahs befo' the waw or aftah the waw. It shows how intimately every individual was visited, in his own person, by that tremendous episode. It gives the inexperienced stranger a better idea of what a vast and comprehensive calamity invasion is than he can ever get by reading books at the fireside" (Mark Twain, *Life on the Mississippi* [New York, 1961], 257–58).

past died with yesterday." To him "Yesterday, Today, and Tomorrow" were "indivisible yet distinctly tripartite" and "the good and evil of Today . . . but the fruit of yesterday's seeding." Faulkner also saw history as a seamless web, past, present, and future inextricably one. So did every Southern boy for whom the War was an intimate memory, a part of family history, a measurement for dating. Young Quentin Compson carried the War in his bones. Faulkner likened his body to "an empty hall echoing with sonorous defeated names" and to "an empty barracks filled with stubborn back-looking ghosts." Even in bleak Massachusetts he remained "not a being, an entity" but a whole "commonwealth" of familial associations, unable to escape his "entailed birthright" or to drown out the plaints of outraged ancestral spirits still cursing General Sherman. It is not only the Compsons who possess or who are possessed by this heritage. Sartorises, De Spains, and other country gentry figuratively if not literally derive from "a long line of colonels" who died at Pickett's charge.[6]

The "slender white pencil of the Confederate monument" standing in the center of Jefferson is a community ikon. All roads of the County converge upon or radiate from "the marble soldier." Jefferson's jail, a promontory around which the tides of war have swirled, is also a point of historical measurement. It "watches" Mississippi "plunge off its precipice" in 1861 and takes "cognizance" of John Sartoris's untried and ignorant regiment being sworn in on the Courthouse Square. Until sixty-four the jail only hears the War "as from a great and incredible dreamy distance, like far summer thunder," but then it boils up briefly as a main Confederate body passes through the town followed by a "rear-guard action of the cavalry," a "rush and scurry of horsemen." They dash past the jail led by a lieutenant who in the process of "firing a pistol backward at a Yankee army" catches a glimpse of "a frail and useless girl musing in the blonde mist of her hair beside the window-pane." Pursuing Yankees occupy Jefferson and cauterize it with fire—but the jail escapes. In June 1865 the paroled lieutenant (who in the meantime has exchanged his horse for a mule) returns to the Jefferson jail after a trek "across the ruined land" between the seaboard and Mississippi. He stops only long enough to persuade the jailkeeper and his wife to let him marry their useless daughter—and then heads for Alabama.[7]

Such ephemeral and unrecorded incidents keep the War alive in Yoknapatawpha County; frequent retellings so transform them that in a few generations no one can disentangle fact from fancy. Every antebellum plantation has "its legend of the money and plate buried in the flower garden from Yankee raiders."[8] Black retainers lovingly minister to their masters in the field or keep faithful attendance at home. Unfrightened matrons run the plantations while their men are off fighting.

Faulkner does not treat these half-legends as total fiction. He sees the truth in the cliché (to write realistically about the War, the historian or novelist dare not play down its "romantic" ingredients), but he takes a long and unbedazzled look at what lies behind the frozen tableaux of camp and hearth. It is as if a historical-minded member of a family—somewhat skeptical of the legends about kinfolk dinned into his ears since childhood—tries to piece together bits and fragments of information gathered from a variety of sources in order to discover what really did happen to a fabulous grandfather or a notorious aunt. Gradually the skeletons in the closet begin to rattle, a telltale piece of repressed or forgotten evidence comes to light, and a favorite tale (once so glamorous and flattering to family pride) turns into something else. After the sympathetic yet skeptical chronicler has completed his examination, Family History is disclosed as a thick shell of legend and lie and exaggeration encasing a kernel of fact.

Legend-Makers (Men)

Since Faulkner's ex-veterans are largely incommunicative about their War experiences—for like most veterans they want to forget what they have seen and done—the custodians of the Museum of Recollection are largely the stay-at-homes, the women and children. Bayard Sartoris, left behind with the women and black servants, revels in dreams of glory and conjures up a highly unreal and romantic picture of war until he is inundated by the real thing. He and his black playmate gradually discover the obverse of the myth: the War is not subsumed in the plumes of Jeb Stuart's hat; it also includes "the very shabby and unavoidable" realities. When he sees his father and the other soldiers "return home, afoot like tramps or on bait horses, in faded and patched (and at times obviously stolen) clothing, preceded by no flags nor drums and followed not even by two men to keep step with one another," he comes to see the War as a "sorry business." Only "the will to endure" sustains it, "a sardonic and even humorous declining of self-delusion which is not even kin to that optimism which believes that which is about to happen to us can possibly be the worst which we can suffer."[9]

This recognition enables Bayard in the final section of *The Unvanquished* to transcend or reinterpret if not to reject the Southern code as an adjunct to the myth of the War, but Faulkner's young patricians in succeeding generations are less fortunate than

Bayard. They must rely on hearsay. Quentin Compson's version of the Civil War after he comes of age is really no more romantic than Bayard's; but he is the beneficiary of several generations of myth-making. He can neither accept the legend nor break cleanly with it. Assured by his heritage of the Old South's blameless nobility, reason (reinforced after investigation and speculation) tells him that this same Old South had to be destroyed. That is why Faulkner can divide him into "the two separate Quentins now talking to one another in the long silence of not people, in not language."[10]

Gail Hightower, the minister in *Light in August,* is even more enmeshed in the Civil War legend. Part of him derives from his father, clergyman turned physician, a man of "Spartan sobriety" and an abolitionist to boot; and the other part from his swash-buckling soldierly grandfather, a lusty humorous adherent to the Southern Code whose exploits are known to him through the hyper-bolical yarns of an old black woman. His ambivalent feelings toward his father and grandfather tinge his mixed religio-military fantasies called sermons in which "absolution" is orchestrated by "choirs of martial seraphim," and "galloping cavalry" with "defeat and glory." The madcap episode of his grandfather, killed while robbing a henhouse during a Confederate raid on Jefferson—at that moment occupied by Federals and stocked with military stores—becomes the usurping event of his consciousness. The heroic "prank" carried out by "boys riding the sheer tremendous tidal wave of living" blots out reality. From the time he first hears of the exploit from Cinthy, the Negro cook, he is haunted by his own lurid imaginings of the glori-ously inglorious venture. He says to his wife:

> "You can see it, hear it: the shouts, the shots, the shouting of triumph and terror, the drumming hooves, the trees uprear-ing against that red glare as though fixed too in terror, the sharp gables of houses like the jagged edge of the exploding and ultimate earth. Now it is a close place: you can feel, hear in the darkness horses pulled short up, plunging; clashes of arms; whispers overloud, hard breathing, the voices still triumphant; behind them the rest of the troops galloping past toward the rallying bugles. That you must hear, feel: then you see. You see before the crash, in the abrupt red glare the horses with wide eyes and nostrils in tossing heads, sweat-stained; the gleam of metal, the white gaunt faces of living scarecrows who have not eaten all they wanted at one time since they could remember; perhaps some of them had al-ready dismounted, perhaps one or two had already entered the henhouse. All this you see before the crash of the shotgun comes: then blackness again. It was just one shot. 'And of course he would be right in de way of hit,' Cinthy said.

'Stealin' chickens. A man growed, wid a married son, gone to a war whar his business was killin' Yankees, killed in somebody else's henhouse wid a han' ful of feathers.' Stealing chickens."

This obsession with a clownishly martyred grandfather, slayer of hundreds, drives him to seek a pulpit in Jefferson and turns him into a crucifier of his wife and a betrayer of his congregation— "figure antic as a showman, a little wild: a charlatan preaching worse than heresy, in utter disregard of that whose very stage he preempted, offering instead of the crucified shape of pity and love, a swaggering and unchastened bravo killed with a shotgun in a peaceful henhouse, in a temporary hiatus of his own avocation of killing."[11]

Similar expressions of admiring disapproval can be found in most of Faulkner's references to Confederate demigods. The dutiful son of the South retells the already romantically garbled tales of the War; the chronicler suspects and perhaps burlesques the sectional rhetoric and music he is so adept at rendering.

In *Sartoris*, at once a romantic and sardonic glimpse of the War, the author seems to favor the legend-makers. His straight-backed, hawk-faced aristocrats riding with Stuart or fighting later under Forrest resemble uncomfortably their fictive cousins in the extravaganzas of John Esten Cooke. The War is a game to them. They bear no hostility to the North. Larking Bayard Sartoris I and Jeb Stuart, his commander, welcome battle as a godsend and stand "like two flaming stars garlanded with Fame's burgeoning laurel and the myrtle and roses of Death." Bayard, shot off his horse as he plunges through General Pope's camp in search of anchovies, perfectly embodies the jocund and hair-brained recklessness popularly attributed to gentleman officers. General Stuart treats a captured Federal major with "exquisite courtesy" at the conclusion of an escapade that began when Stuart and his "military family" talked themselves into "a state of savage nostalgia" and, thirsty for Federal coffee, made a sunrise raid on Pope's camp. Stuart is concerned about the comfort of the horseless Yankee. Would a "cavalry leader and General Lee's eyes" risk the safety of his men to procure a horse for a single prisoner? the Major asks. "Not for the prisoner, sir," Stuart replies haughtily, "but for the officer suffering the fortune of war. No gentleman would do less." "No gentleman has any business in this war," the Major retorts. "There is no place for him here. He is an anachronism, like anchovies."[12]

Faulkner speaks here for both officers, but the skeptical note in *Sartoris* is submerged. Henceforth he undercut the legend by presenting it through the conflicting observations and disagreements of its keepers. The War was "romantic" to the extent that it came down to us through the romantic responses of its commentators; the romantic response was one of the War's realities.

Legend-Makers (Women)

Bayard Sartoris II of *The Unvanquished*, Quentin Compson of *Absalom! Absalom!* and Gail Hightower of *Light in August* achieve some insight into the past; they know enough at least to puzzle over its meanings, to savor its insidious charm, or to question details of the legend. Not so Faulkner's women. They are the priestesses guarding it from doubters and detractors; they are the true "unvanquished," the "indomitable" ones.

He presents these keepers of the flame with a degree of irony, but the irony is diluted with pity. Virginia Du Pre, the "Aunt Jenny" whose version of the anchovies fiasco the narrator is transmitting, has told the story so many times that the tale grows "richer and richer, taking on a mellow splendour like wine."[13] Images from the past distorted by nostalgia and fantasy sustain her, as they do her Confederate sisters. Their ritualistic evocations of the cavalier ideal, Honor, the Holy Cause, may be at odds with unromantic actualities, but the ladies who cling devotedly to them are compensating for the deprivations of their loveless lives. The perpetuation of ghosts helps them to endure their enforced spinsterhood. Even so his Yoknapatawpha ladies are almost invariably unsexed, corrupted, or embittered by the War and its consequent humiliations.

Drusilla Hawk is one of Faulkner's most poignant female casualties. After her husband-to-be is killed at Shiloh, she internalizes the disorder and destruction of her society by the act of shedding her skirts and riding with Colonel John Sartoris's cavalry troop. Faulkner puts into her mouth one of his most bitter denouncements of war:

> "Who wants to sleep now, with so much happening, so much to see? Living used to be dull, you see. Stupid. You lived in the same house your father was born in, and your father's sons and daughters had the sons and daughters of the same Negro slaves to nurse and coddle; and then you grew up and you fell in love with your acceptable young man, and in time you would marry him, in your mother's wedding gown, perhaps, and with the same silver for presents she had received; and then you settled down forevermore while you got children to feed and bathe and dress until they grew up, too; and then you and your husband died quietly and were buried together maybe on a summer afternoon just before supper-

time. Stupid, you see. But now you can see for yourself how fine it is; it's fine now, you don't have to worry now about the house and the silver, because they get burned up and carried away; and you don't have to worry about the Negroes, because they tramp the roads all night waiting for a chance to drown in homemade Jordan; and you don't have to worry about getting children to bathe and feed and change, because the young men can ride away and get killed in the fine battles; and you don't even have to sleep at all; and so, all you have to do is show the stick to the dog now and then and say, 'Thank God for nothing.' "

Having abnegated her womanhood by wearing trousers, cropping her hair, and fighting, she is too badly seared by her experience even to attempt a readjustment after the War is over. Public pressure and her mother's insistence require her to marry Colonel Sartoris (hadn't she ridden with his troop for half a year and bivouacked "at night surrounded by sleeping men"?). When her husband, tired of killing, allows himself to be assassinated by a rival in 1876, she fills her spiritual emptiness by trying to seduce her stepson into murderous reprisal. The "code" demands of a son that he uphold the family honor by avenging his father's death. But the War has so completely deranged Drusilla's values that she can no longer distinguish between the life- and death-dealing forces or between valid or empty ritual. For her, the pistols she thrusts upon Bayard are as "slender, invincible, and fatal as the physical shape of love."[14]

Poor broken Drusilla may have misused her sex. Faulkner clearly prefers her, nonetheless, to her mother, one of those respectable pillars whose ladylike propriety not even a bloody war can shake. Mrs. Hawk (Aunt Louisa) preserves her conception of the South "as a heritage of courageous men and spotless women." In her eyes the death of her daughter's lover "reserved for Drusilla the highest destiny of a Southern woman—to be the bride-widow of a lost cause." Hence Drusilla's unnatural behavior strikes her not only as "a shame to her father's memory" but also as a form of sacrilege.[15]

None of this contingent of unvanquished women, neither those who refuse to admit the War is lost and the Old South is dead nor those who unresistingly endure, pass through the War years and Reconstruction unscathed. They merely suffer in different ways and in different degrees. Miss Rosa Millard's moral corruption in *The Unvanquished* is a by-product of her compulsion to protect her family and dependents. Why shouldn't she cheat the hated blue-coated invaders? Faulkner complicates the ethical problem by presenting her swindled enemy as a most unvillainous sort and by showing that her habit of lying for a good cause gradually goes

beyond the call of necessity, despite her disclaimers and rationali-
zations. He links her untragic death to an inward flaw. Once again
the dislocations produced by the War have their complement in
moral aberration.

All the women in *Absalom! Absalom!* are victims. Miss Rosa
Coldfield, the demon-obsessed sister-in-law of Thomas Sutpen, is
doomed to spinsterhood because, as she says, "The young men
whom I would have known ordinarily were dead on lost battlefields." Faulkner likens her to a "crucified child," and she is full of
"impotent and static rage." In her stranded state, her outlet is to
write bad verse about the heroic dead, her slaughtered would-be
husbands. Ellen Sutpen, Rosa's sister and demon Sutpen's wife, is
an early casualty. Too weak to adjust herself to a collapsing civilization and without a shred of the toughness and resiliency of her
daughter, Judith, she simply wastes away. Even Judith, tempered
and enlightened by disaster, is manacled to the past. "Years ago,"
Jason Compson says, "we in the South made our women into ladies.
Then the war came and made the ladies into ghosts."[16]

Judith Sutpen is one of the living ghosts, and so, in her way, is
Miss Virginia Du Pre (Miss Jenny), who appears briefly in *The
Unvanquished* and is more fully treated in *Sartoris*. A widow
(her husband had been killed early in the War "by a shell from a
Federal frigate at Fort Moultrie"), she seeks out her brother, Colonel John Sartoris, in Mississippi and thereafter functions as one of
Faulkner's clan priestesses. She is more womanly than Drusilla. She
sees through the "code"—designed, she says, "for small boys or fool
young women"—while honoring the Sartoris men who live by it,
and not in spite but because of their allegiance to it. Just how
closely she is gripped by the past and by Sartoris vainglory is made
clear when she unintendingly hastens her grandnephew to his
death by invidiously contrasting him to his glamorous namesake,
the martyr to anchovies. "At least he got himself decently killed," she
says.[17]

The Truths of Fantasy

What is to be made of Faulkner's undercutting of family legends?
Why do the stories of gallantry and heroism that swell the hearts of
the pious turn out to be, on closer examination, ludicrous antics of
quixotic boys memorialized, as Aunt Jenny puts it, by "strutting and
swaggering" tombstones? Faulkner was certainly no Mississippi
Cervantes, a writer he much admired, even though his recounting
of henhouse raids as chivalric exploits arouses a sort of bleak mirth.
If the War and the Southern response to it can sometimes border

close to the mock-heroic or the comic in his fiction,* it is more usually a black comedy akin to tragedy. The illusions that flourished happily in antebellum Yoknapatawpha County contribute to the social chaos and suffering after 1861. Faulkner's humor, so often based (like Mark Twain's) upon the disproportion between illusion and reality, is shot through with pain.

Since the characters who allude directly or indirectly to the War, who meditate on it or attempt to interpret it, are not authorized by the author to speak for him, the ultimate "Truth" of Faulkner's War amounts to a residue of hundreds of partial and conflicting truths entertained by a diverse company of biased observers. For Saucier Weddel, en route from Virginia to Mississippi after four excruciating years of death and deprivation, the War underscores the emptiness of words like "victory" or "defeat" and the solidity of words like "peace" and "home." For the Tennessee mountaineer and erstwhile Unionist who bushwhacks him, it signifies the arrogance of a planter aristocracy who would conscript him and his kind to protect their "nigger" property.† Brother Fortinbride, ex-Confederate private turned Methodist preacher, tells his flock that victory without God is "mockery and delusion," that "defeat with God is not defeat." Defeat can be interpreted by some as a necessary step in God's plan for Southern redemption, by others as a bloody testament of God's disfavor toward a cursed people.[18]

Two of Faulkner's alleged surrogates take the former view: the opinionated and garrulous lawyer, Gavin Stevens, and Isaac McCaslin—of all the Yoknapatawpha inhabitants the one most obsessed

---

* As, for example, in his story "My Grandmother Millard and General Bedford Forrest and the Battle of Harrykin Creek" (*Collected Stories of William Faulkner* [New York, 1950], 667–99). Or the episode told by Will Falls in *Sartoris* and in *The Unvanquished* of how Colonel John Sartoris captured an entire Yankee company singlehanded.

† "Mountain Victory" (*Collected Stories*, 745–77). In *A Fable*, Faulkner describes these Negro-hating folk living "where the corners of Georgia and Tennessee and Carolina meet." When the War threatened their privacy, they "quitted their misty unmapped eyries to go for miles and even weeks on foot to engage in a war in which they had no stake and, if they had only stayed at home, no contact, in order to defend their land from Negroes; not content merely to oppose and repudiate their own geopolitical kind and their common economic deprivation, they must confederate with its embattled enemies, stealing, creeping (once at a crossroads tavern a party of them fought something resembling a pitched battle with a Confederate recruiting party) by night through Confederate lines to find and join a Federal army, to fight not against slavery but against Negroes, to abolish the Negro by freeing him from them who might bring Negroes among them exactly as they would have taken their rifles down from the pegs or deer antlers above the hearth and doorway to repel, say, a commercial company talking about bringing the Indians back" (190).

with the question of why and where the South went wrong. Both give the "people named Sambo" a key role in the Southern drama of damnation and salvation and offer different strategies for circumventing the curse. Stevens invites—almost commands—the "homogeneous" Southern Negro to spurn the "paper alliance of theorists and fanatics and private and personal avengers" from the mongrelized North and to affiliate with the better elements of the "homogeneous" South. The South will be saved only if it obliterates its self-engendered evil without alien intervention: "That's what we really are defending: the privilege of getting him free ourselves; which we shall have to do for the reason that nobody else can since going on a century ago now the North tried it and have been admitting for seventy-five years now that they failed. So it will have to be us."[19] McCaslin personally assumes sectional guilt. By renouncing his birthright, by putting himself under instruction to a forest deity and learning and cultivating the Hunterly Virtues, he hopes to expiate the South's crimes against man and nature that set off the train of disasters.

Neither strategy was necessarily Faulkner's. The editorializings of Gavin Stevens and the protestations of the "criminally benevolent" (to borrow Cable's phrase) are mocked by Faulkner's Negroes. And Faulkner allows for the possibility that Ike McCaslin removed himself from a flawed community to escape rather than to confront his responsibilities. He faces the same test as an earlier prototype—Hawthorne's Young Goodman Brown—who also goes into the forest to meet *his* tutelary genius and who also (having been "instructed") fails to meet the test of maturity. To both Hawthorne and Faulkner, "maturity" signifies the acceptance of a corrupted humanity with its sin-flecked history, not an insulation from it.

Faulkner seems to be suggesting, although one can never be sure, that the Southern mind has never abandoned its providential view of the War. Although the issue over which it was fought, slavery, has been settled, the fever produced by this issue is still a symptom of the South's moral malaria. Never conceding defeat, the South still refuses to examine its history candidly and hugs its illusion-ridden past. Or to put it another way, it has been unable to exorcise its demon and continues, metaphorically speaking, to save its Confederate money.* The "demon" that haunts even the most

---

* "It's all over *now* you see. Yesterday wont be over until tomorrow and tomorrow began ten thousand years ago. For every Southern boy fourteen years old, not once, but whenever he wants it, there is the instant when it's still not yet two oclock on that July afternoon in 1863, the brigades are in position behind the rail fence, the guns are laid and ready in the woods and the furled flags are already loosened to break out and Pickett himself with his long

honorable and high-souled of the Confederates and their descendants, including those who detest slavery, is the conscious or unconscious dehumanization of the black race, whether in acts of solicitude or cruelty. Not all of Faulkner's Negro characters are favorably presented, especially those whom he infected with the Snopesian virus, but he never treated them as nonpeople, never denied their individual integrities or blurred or demeaned them.

Faulkner's speculations and meditations on the sins of Yoknapatawpha County in no way imply the North was less deluded or any more understanding about the War's import. The North was too busy and too enamored with the future to brood over the meaning of four terrible years: it by-passed the past. But the technical power unleashed against the South proved in the end to be the enslaver of its ostensible masters and to create a civilization entirely without charm or nobility. The Puritan strain in Northern abolitionism, admirable or at least impressive in some of its human incarnations, simply compounded the wrongs John Brown and his followers had set out to eradicate.

The distrust Faulkner felt for the Puritan mind in both its Northern and Southern manifestations was mitigated by a covert respect for it. Miss Rosa Millard was a Puritan, and so was John Brown, a masked figure who lurks in the background of Faulkner's chronicle. He is the arch-misleader, the duper and the duped who would dissolve organic evil by moral fiat. He is also the "one" in *Go Down, Moses* "simple enough to believe that horror and outrage were first and last simply horror and outrage and was crude enough to act upon that." God and Brown agree that they are against the same Great Injustice. *"Then where are you going with that gun?"* God demands,

> and the other told him in one sentence one word and He: amazed: Who knew neither hope nor pride nor grief *But your Association, your Committee, your Officers. Where are your Minutes, your Motions, your Parliamentary Procedures?*

---

oiled ringlets and his hat in one hand probably and his sword in the other looking up the hill waiting for Longstreet to give the word and it's all in the balance, but it hasn't happened yet, it hasn't even begun yet, it not only hasn't begun yet but there is still time for it not to begin against that position and those circumstances which made more than Garnett and Kemper and Armstead and Wilcox look grave yet it's going to begin, we all know that, we have come too far with too much at stake and that moment doesn't need even a fourteen-year-old boy to think *This time. Maybe this time* with all this much to lose and all this much to gain: Pennsylvania, Maryland, the world, the golden dome of Washington itself to crown with desperate and unbelievable victory the desperate gamble, the cast made two years ago" (*Intruder in the Dust* [Modern Library College edn., New York, 1948], 194–95).

> and the other *I ain't against them. They are all right I reckon
> for them that have the time. I am just against the weak be-
> cause they are niggers being held in bondage by the strong
> just because they are white.*[20]

Faulkner never declares explicitly whether Brown was an agent of
light or darkness; yet for all of their courage and self-sacrifice and
felt religion, the Browns and the Miss Rosas (as Cleanth Brooks
says) are "noticeably lacking in awe and reverence and humility"[21]
—too impatient with the dilatoriness of their too patient and serpentine Commander.*

He spoke for them and through them, just as he did for those
who buried the War in clouds of nostalgia and for others who were
at least partially educated by events. No matter for whom he spoke,
however, the authorial voice when referring to the Civil War was
usually elegiac or ironic, or a blend of both. You can hear it in Mr.
Compson's imaginative re-creation of the Oxford, Mississippi, muster in 1861 when families from farther away than Jefferson came to
watch their sons and brothers participate in what was "probably the
most moving mass-sight of all human experience, far more so than
the spectacle of so many virgins going to be sacrificed to some
heathen Principle, some Priapus—the sight of young men, the light
quick bones, the bright gallant deluded blood and flesh dressed in a
martial glitter of brass and plumes, marching away to a battle." Or
again in Charles Bon's letter to Judith Sutpen in which the once
brave company of youth is reduced to a pack of starving scarecrows.
Four years of war taught Charles the mystery of laughter: "that it
really requires an empty stomach to laugh with, that only when you
are hungry and frightened do you extract some ultimate essence out
of laughing just as the empty stomach extracts the ultimate essence
out of alcohol."[22]

The "ultimate essence" of the Civil War Faulkner extracted
from a welter of fact and fantasy and myth about a ruined land, a
brave but fallible people, and an outraged race. Like Mark Twain,
another sardonic and compassionate observer, he made no partisan
pronouncements. Neither side won Faulkner's War. A great wrong
was extirpated in a clumsy, bloody, and perhaps necessary way.
Then a new set of chains tightened about the race John Brown
elected to redeem. The War, like the portent of Brown himself,
remained a mystery susceptible to any man's interpretation after
quickly crumbling into myth.

* "And don't yawl worry about Granny," Ringo says. "She 'cide what she
want and then she kneel down about ten seconds and tell God what she aim
to do, and then she git up and do hit. And them that don't like hit can git
outen the way or get trompled" (*The Unvanquished* [New York, 1938],
105–6). His words would have applied equally well to John Brown.

Conclusion

"Such Was the War"

I apprehend that no people ever built up the skeleton of a warlike history so rapidly as we are doing. What a fine theme for a poet!

HAWTHORNE, 1861

The lesson that our war ought most of all to teach us is the lesson that evils must be checked in time, before they grow so great. The Almighty cannot love such long-postponed accounts, or such tremendous settlements. And surely He hates all settlements that do such quantities of incidental devils' work. Our present situation, with its rancors and delusions, what is it but the direct outcome of the added powers of government, the corruptions and inflations of the war? Every war leaves such miserable legacies, fatal seeds of future war and revolution, unless the civic virtues of the people save the State in time.

WILLIAM JAMES, 1897

*Two months after marching through Boston,
half the regiment was dead;
at the dedication,
William James could almost hear the bronze Negroes breathe.*

*The monument sticks like a fishbone
in the city's throat.*

ROBERT LOWELL, 1961

i

When Walt Whitman predicted the "real war will never get in the books," he was saying in effect, H. A. Beers explained, that "no dignified, formal history dealing with things in their *ensemble*, will ever give a notion of the details of private suffering, individual

327

sacrifice, personal heroism, which are known only to eyewitnesses and participants."[1] The important words in Beers's comment are "dignified" and "formal." Whitman really thought he *had* got the "real" War into his verse and prose. So did others before and after him who contributed to the panoramic melange of fact and legend.

But the long-anticipated "epic" remained unwritten, and no philosophical poet, including Whitman, emerged to provide a comprehensive inspection of the War or to piece out an intelligent design from its myriad disconnected fragments. Melville saw a pattern obscurely. Hawthorne, Whitman, Mark Twain, Tourgée, De Forest, Cable, and Faulkner glimpsed its shadowy outlines. Some writers were not sufficiently haunted by the War, or outraged enough, or imaginatively teased by it enough, to look; others must have found it too vast and too shocking to take in, and the profound misgivings it aroused about America in particular and human nature in general were probably not confined to Herman Melville.

The War was not so much unfelt as unfaced. Northern writers found it easier and more reassuring to portray it as an exalted example of national redemption than as a grisly historical moment when the political system broke down and the nation took a "moral holiday." Falling back on God, History, "Manifest Destiny"* enabled them to avert their eyes from its meaner aspects and to present it as a struggle between antipodal civilizations or as an episode in a people's progress toward political, economic, and cultural coalescence. America in their eyes emerged from its bloodbath cleansed of the Great Sin. Eventually their vindictiveness against a traitorous foe yielded to sympathy and pleas for reconciliation. After the North and South agreed both sides were "right" as well as sincere and gallant and neither wholly to blame, the War became a reason for national gratulation rather than a subject for reflective soul-searching. By this time Whitman's "real" War lay buried underneath reams of special pleading and irrelevant minutiae.

ii

In recent years, historians and biographers have more often come closer to "the real sense" of the War than fiction writers, poets, and literary critics, although illuminating flashes appear in the pages

---

* "Is it a good thing to 'extend the area of freedom' by pillaging some feeble Mexico? and does the phrase become a bad one only when it means the peaceful progress of constitutional liberty without our own borders? The phrases which oppression teaches become the watchwords of freedom at last, and the triumph of Civilization over Barbarism is the only Manifest Destiny of America" (T. W. Higginson, *Atlantic Monthly*, VII [Jan. 1861], 61).

of Robert Frost, F. Scott Fitzgerald, Ernest Hemingway,* and Robert Lowell and in the overviews of Allen Tate, Robert Penn Warren, and Edmund Wilson. The most important and sustained of these is Wilson's.

Wilson's *Patriotic Gore* (1962), a commentary on thirty-odd writers who lived through the 1860s and on the intellectual and cultural agencies that shaped them, has been criticized for its dubious analogies, factual errors, and wilful pontifications. Yet it is hard to think of any recent writer who has brought to the subject such a blend of intelligence and passion or indicated more explicitly the controversies and issues seldom transmuted into literature. What ideas and conditions supplied the fuel for the apocalyptic fires that flared in both sections? What were the origins of the mystique that imbued thousands of civilians and soldiers? Why the "marked fascination of each of the two camps with each other, the intimate essence of a conflict which, though fratricidal, was also incestuous?" These are not the questions customarily raised in petticoat romances and painterly histories. *Patriotic Gore*, a Tolstoyan meditation on the power of myth, is also an informative book and, like much of Wilson's other writings, a speculative, perverse, and didactic one—the work of a prickly Northerner with Southern connections who responded to American history as if it were a family chronicle and for whom the past and present flowed in a single stream.

---

* For example, Frost's idiosyncratic comments on Lee and Grant in reference to Evelyn Scott's Civil War novel, *The Wave* (1929)—"American history shouldn't be written by women novelists with English sympathies for the arrogant old slave-holding days." He dismissed as nonsense the interpretation of the War as a victory of Northern industry over Southern agriculture (the South was "licked" by the agricultural Middle West), and he thought Grant superior to Lee. Frost's Lee was "the tragic figure of the fighter who never saw anything beyond winning battles. His vision wasn't large enough for a whole war or even campaign. His dispositions for battle were beautiful. His two great divisions under Longstreet and Jackson were like pistols in his two hands." But Lee was parochial, "not large enough to see the United States." Frost was touched by Lee, "so noble in character, so brilliant and punishing a smiter in the field," but Lee fell far behind Grant in statesmanship and strategy. "You may not like generals in general, but you have to concede him rank with the greatest our race has had" (*Selected Letters of Robert Frost*, ed. Lawrence Thompson [New York, 1964], 410–11). For Fitzgerald's imaginative use of the War in *Tender Is the Night* (1934), see Robert Sklar, *The Last Tycoon* (New York, 1967), 272–79. For Hemingway (whose mind was flooded with thoughts about the American Civil War while he reported the Spanish Civil War and wrote *For Whom the Bell Tolls*), see Robert O. Stephens, *Hemingway's Non-Fiction. The Public Voice* (Chapel Hill, N.C., 1968), 99, 135, 142, 283, 297–99.

Wilson wrote from the point of view of one at once appalled and fascinated by what he interpreted as a national mania, the consequence of repulsive enthusiasms, and his gothic drama (couched in the form of literary history) sustains the lurid title of his book. It abounds with men and women who are impelled by manias, languish in prisons, see ghosts and are exposed to all manner of terrors and violence. The principal actors, each telling his own version of the same story, are deeper and more complex than most characters in War fiction. Coincidence and mistaken identities occur in the family war, but they are the coincidences of fact. Familiar names keep cropping up in diaries and memoirs; the hero of one account is the villain of another.

Patriotic Gore also examines the War's impact on the literary survivors. Antebellum America had promised something better, Wilson recalls, than mass butchery and a long and painful convalescence. The architecture of Jefferson, "the marvelous plates of John James Audubon" which captured the openness and opulence of the primitive wilderness, Poe's tales "crystallized like precious gems," the "bright spontaneity in the poems and notebooks of Emerson," the "liquid translucencies and densities of *Walden*," Melville's voyages—all presaged a golden day that never came. For the writers who succeeded them the War was an unmitigated disaster, and among its casualties must be included those who technically survived it as well as those who died or who were physically maimed on the battlefields.

Forgotten in the War's aftermath was the truth Melville and Lincoln saw with their instructed eyes: America could not escape history. More discernible and congenial to the living were the myth of a South that may have existed long before the War (or never existed) and the presence of a stern and righteous North, swollen with the conceit of its mission. Wilson contrasts "the North's Armageddon-like vision" of the "holy crusade" with the hallowed and hollow "ideal of gallantry, aristocratic freedom, fine manners, and luxurious living" which the South counterposed to "the materialism and vulgarity of mercantile Northern society." The romanticism so intoxicating to many Southerners before the War persisted in the Reconstruction period and later befuddled Northern as well as Southern novelists. Whether or not Sir Walter Scott induced the disease of "jejune romanticism" in the receptive South, as Mark Twain angrily charged, Southern writers continued to suffer from it after 1865.

How discouraging these years were is borne out in Wilson's discussions of writers like De Forest, Bierce, Tourgée, and Cable, whose experiences had purged them of shallow sectional pieties and whose double vision separated them from myopic contemporaries. He writes of the "slow strangulation" of gifted and truthful writers by prudish culture-guardians in the North and by the post-War Southern patriots who could neither forgive nor forget. "Nobody North or South," he observes, "wanted by that time to be shown the realities," especially those related to history, the Negro, and sex. The War speeded up the feminizing of American culture under way before 1860. If Henry Adams was right to equate the demasculinizing of the American male with the increase of mechanic power, then this War, fought, in Melville's words, "by crane/ Pivot, and screw," may have helped to rivet the manacles of propriety around the wrists of the genteel American muse. After the War, a group of men who had been literally mired in mud and blood were expected to make their experiences palatable to the predominantly female readership by prettifying or mythologizing what they had seen and thought and done. But the War, and temperament perhaps, made them realists and kept them, in spite of their own efforts, from writing the salable thing.

By constricting the literary imagination, Wilson argues, Calvinism limited the area of conflict to the good and the bad, the acceptable and the unacceptable, courage and cowardice. It produced tough soldiers and thinkers, conditioned the soul to temporal discomforts, inculcated the lessons of adversity, but it hardly encouraged largeness of sympathy, tolerance for weaknesses of the flesh, a qualified relativism in matters of human behavior.

Patriotic Gore, besides being a remarkable literary synthesis, is also a dramatic monologue and a homily, weakest when it merely asserts, strongest when it describes and demonstrates. Throughout it reflects the author's bias against myth-makers and pietists. For Wilson, Negro slavery and the Union were merely "rabble-rousing" or "pseudo-moral issues" introduced to rationalize an aggressive power drive, so that he seems to reduce the War to an organized form of animal bellicosity comparable to battles waged by army ants, baboons, and birds. Fortunately his prejudices flavor without shaping his undulating story of courage, delusion, and ferocity, and the partisan author keeps disappearing into the "Bible-drugged" idealists, plain-spoken generals, regional patriots, inspired or rueful women, who figure in his chapters. Unlike all but a few interpreters of the War, he recognizes a part of himself in both of the contesting sections, "an unreconstructed Southerner who will not accept domination" and "a benevolent despot who wants to mould others for their own good."

But Wilson's overview, remarkable as it often is, leaves too many questions unanswered, blurs or omits too much, and his zoological reduction of history is too sweeping and too simplistic to serve as a valid theoretical underpinning for his rich and complex narrative.

iii

A striking feature of the literature I have mentioned in this book is its comparative inattention to what many once believed and still believe to be the central issue of the War—the Negro. Slavery, the presence of which contradicted democratic claims, provoked curiously inconsistent responses: abolitionist jeremiads, demonstrations of Negro inferiority, idyllic descriptions of the "peculiar institution," expressions of anger against the South for dramatizing an evil better left in the shadows, and futile schemes for the amelioration of blacks. Only a few writers before and after 1865 appreciated the Negro's literal and symbolic role in the War.

All but a small minority assumed his inferiority if they did not utterly despise him—not only the vulgarly prejudiced but also educated people who subscribed to the most up-to-date scientific opinion. Most Northern writers, excepting an occasional Whittier, shared the prevailing liberal sentiment on slavery. That is to say, they considered it a social evil (more detrimental, some would argue, "in its effects upon the whites who live in immediate contact with it than upon the blacks")[2] and an embarrassing anachronism that exposed the United States to European slurs.[3] Not implanted slavery so much as Southern efforts to extend it hardened their resistance to the oligarchs, and their antislavery polemics often weighed more heavily on the iniquities of the master than on the plight of his bondsman. They tended, in short, to justify the War not as a crusade to free the slave (although this was seen to be an inevitable consequence of repressing rebellion), but as the long-suffering North's reply to Southern bullies; or as an ordeal devised by God to purge the Americans of their materialism; or as a struggle to make the Union what the South had prevented it from becoming—a nation in the European sense of the word, a country to be proud of.* Emancipation did not signal a national change of heart; it was a tolerated tactical war measure to discourage the enemy at home and win approval abroad.

Unlike the franker Confederate publicists and politicians who asserted privately and sometimes publicly the South's intention to preserve slavery, Southern writers usually soft-pedaled this morally

---

* It is worth noting that one of the most popular War stories, Edward Everett Hale's "The Man Without a Country" (1863), does not condemn the rebels for slaveholding—only for their impious desecration of the Union.

ambiguous issue and wrote no sequels to William Grayson's pastoral on black servitude, *The Hireling and the Slave* (1854). They glossed over the exploitation of human flesh (which most of them had no relish for anyway) with such euphemisms as "Southern Rights" or "Southern Independence" or the "Southern Way of Life," and like their Northern counterparts allowed the Negro no more than a supernumerary part in what they chose to see as a white man's war.

Blacks had formed an unassimilable foreign body: a dangerous necessity in slave territory, an unwholesome and unwelcome excrescence elsewhere. The War modified without essentially changing the popular image of the Negro as a docile child or putative rapist.[4] Frederick Law Olmsted, a member of the United States Sanitary Commission, pronounced the Negro "little better than a cunning idiot, and a cowed savage." To Bret Harte in 1874, the "nigger" was "the innocent, miserable, wretched, degraded, foreordained by race and instinct and climate to be forever helpless and a useless part of the nation. This 'curse' lolls in the sunlights, slouches in the shadow, evades his responsibilities, is truant to his duty, to his future, to the North, to the South—and is miserably free and wretchedly happy." Mark Twain, as Justin Kaplan has shown, suppressed without concealing his disgust of miscegenation and predicted Negro supremacy—"whites under feet"—by 1985. In 1886, Maurice Thompson, Confederate veteran, novelist, and poet, composed his polemic against miscegenation, "A Voodoo Prophecy." This poem, Thompson wrote to the editor of the *Century Magazine*, reflected "the awful fate of the white soul that feels the infusion of negro blood! and the despair of the negro that feels the white curse in its essence!" It is tempting to read into the fury of the intersectional war a redirected or displaced aggression against blacks—outcasts before, during, and after the War.[5]

The defeat of the Confederacy, however, removed an embarrassing stigma for old antislavery men. The filthy institution now expunged and the Negro legally free, writers in good conscience could trivialize him in pseudo-epics featuring the "Blue and Gray," or in plantation romances in which black menials expatiated on a spurious past. Although black slavery was the root cause of the War, it is hard to name one War novel containing a fully realized Negro character. Given black invisibility and the almost total ignorance of the Negro's inner and outer history, it is not surprising that few writers of any literary stature dealt with him at all. The notable exceptions—Melville, Mark Twain, Cable, and Faulkner—were haunted by racial nightmares in which Negroes necessarily figured. Even for them the Negro served primarily a symbolic function and seldom appeared from behind his various masks.

iv

The Negro is not the only important theme slighted in the literature of the War, a body of writing as remarkable for what it leaves out as for what it includes. The noble and shoddy story of those "convulsive" days still lies buried in newspapers, magazines, diaries, memoirs, and official records. American writers have not overlooked its vainglorious features, but none has managed to comprehend a society enmeshed in contradictions and smouldering in sectional, class, and racial hatreds. Nor has literary justice been done to the companies of men, North and South, who purchased their immunity from military service.* A bare handful of fictional works have explored with any power or insight the loyal and disloyal opposition in both camps or even suggested the misery of warfare conveyed in the letters of ordinary soldiers. Yet all this too is part of the unwritten War.

Ordinarily, the common soldier provided no "striking object" for the educated eye. Collectively he served as the background for the poetry of gentlemanly action, and no major literary figure explored and explained him. He sometimes got his due in books like Joseph Kirkland's *The Captain of Company K* (1891), a wooden novel about a body of Illinois volunteers, but only a few writers placed on record, either in verse or "in the sober dignity of prose" (my authority is Charles Graham Halpine, journalist, soldier and poet),

> the splendid devotion, the unsparing sacrifices and the superb spirit of the unnamed Demigods of the rank and file.
>   The men who had the dustiest place in the column on the line of march; who had the thinnest blankets and the narrowest shelter-tents to sleep under; the most exhausting and dangerous duties to perform; and the poorest and hardest fare to support their unappreciated lives.

---

* "The real difficulty in obtaining recruits consists in the superior attractions of commercial gain over the blandishments of the romance attaching to patriotism. Thus it is that you will see columns of the New York *Herald* and papers of similar stamp swarming with temptations, to men to go as substitutes of gentlemen who have been drafted. You will judge of the enormous profits of trade by the fact that as much as $800 being given to a man who will join the army as the representative of some enterprising manufacturer" (*Yankeeland in Her Trouble. An Englishman's Correspondence During the War*, Letters written by Mr. Siddons, Oct. 1864, to John Bright's newspaper, the *Star*, Huntington Lib.). The sordid, squalid, and unchivalric side of the War is suggested by Rebecca Harding Davis in her *Bits of Gossip*, (Boston and New York, 1904), 122–24.

> In a word, the men who were killed and wounded in every engagement and battle from the first Bull Run to the Five Forks; and who had their names wrongly spelled in the gazettes—if they were named at all—as the only reward a grateful country could give their gallantry.[6]

Halpine was referring to men like Private William Hill, whose barely literate correspondence to his wife has no analogue in War literature. Hill's letters to "Dear Wife" describe the "poor man's fight" without heroics. He assures her he has no intention of re-enlisting to eat maggoty crackers: "You have nothing to do but just whistle and the[y] will come marching up from the cook house." To details of casualties and complaints of the high cost of chewing tobacco ("we have to pay $.50 Per Plug") he adds: "Dear Mary you would be astonished to see us, we hardly ever wash Eat in mud and Live in mud altogether." In June 1863, he records a thirty-six-hour march without food and only swamp water ("it had dead horses in it") to drink. He found it "verry hard" to charge Rebel batteries when shot and shell made him think "the air was all on fire." It was also "hard" to see the Rebel rifle pits piled high with dead, to rise at three in the morning with nothing to eat or drink and to fight and march the whole day through. "Dear Wife," he wrote, "I am verry sorry we don't get paid so that I could send you some money for I now you are in wants of it."*

No literary contemporary of Private Hill, it seems, was sufficiently acquainted with the underlying population to recreate his thoughts and feelings or to comprehend his bewilderment. A gifted philosopher-soldier who had survived a few campaigns, who felt easy with farm boys, laborers, mechanics, tradesmen, and who possessed insight and honesty as well as literary power might have done justice to the "Marching Soldier." But none came forth with the ability or even the curiosity to write a satisfactory imaginative work about the citizen army.

Our classical writers simply did not know the land and people they spoke to and spoke for. Emerson, who observed and interpreted the trans-Concordian world, seldom dropped his portmanteau of

---

* On October 25, 1864, J. R. McCalister, Delegate of the Christian Commission, notified Mary Hill that for the past week he had been attending the sick and wounded at City Point Hospital, Virginia. It was his painful duty to inform her that her husband had not survived the amputation of his leg and she must resign herself to God's will. A few weeks later she heard from an officer in her husband's company that, in his opinion, diarrhea killed her husband, that she was eligible for $300 and a pension, and that six dollars found in her husband's pocket would be forwarded to her (Eldridge Papers, Huntington Lib.).

New England assumptions. Whitman, with a more intimate knowledge of the average foot soldier than any of his writer-contemporaries possessed, constantly searched for quintessential democratic types; his Americans at times seem almost as emblematic as Hawthorne's. Melville buttressed his fictions on concrete experience, but by 1861 he had insulated himself from his countrymen. These and other writers mentioned heretofore pondered the fate of democracy and the Union. Not many of them besides Whitman made any effort to immerse themselves in the democratic tub. Rather, they distinguished themselves from the People. The People were "They"—the Farmer, the Mechanic—Brave Fellows in their noble incarnations, Scum and Riffraff in their depraved ones. The Country or Nation evoked by literary patriots was still an abstraction. By the time American writers had shrugged off genteel restraints and learned to write uninhibitedly about the lower orders, the War was virtually uncapturable. The scores of War novels published during the past half-century, some of them well-made, competently written stories full of naturalistic detail and conscientiously unglamorous, are often more remote from the truths and spirit of 1861–65 than the romances of John Esten Cooke.

A bare handful of writers who lived through these years remained detached enough even to record and appraise the War's course from its jaunty beginnings until the death of Lincoln. Retrospectively we can see why this should have been so. The thrill of fear after the first exultation and the abrupt change from haphazard engagements to massive and machine-made slaughter stunned the imagination. For most Americans, the War had begun almost fortuitously. Its exfoliation coincided with technological advances which neither side could intellectually or emotionally comprehend. Americans were still largely a rural people. It took time for them to adjust to the enormous scale of the War and to tally its material and human cost. Traditional notions of heroism had to be modified when instruments of precision killed by remote control. "Like a witches' prayer—a saintly orison read backwards," wrote the English observer G. A. Sala, in an anti-Emersonian reflection, "the phenomena of modern warfare present a horrible parody of the doctrine of compensation. More men can be killed, and they can hold out before they *are* killed. Soldiers are fain to become earthclads, as, on the ocean, sailors trust in iron-clads. Analogically, the difference is very slight between plating the sides of your ship and burrowing in the earth like a mole."[7] Chivalry had been eclipsed, as Hawthorne and Melville noted, by impersonal and brutal mechanization. Wood yielded to iron, gold to brass, innocence to experience. The War signalized to men of their generation the collapse of old republican institutions as much as it did the birth of a powerful state.[8]

One way to blot out the uncongenial truth was to celebrate the War, if not declare it an unmitigated good. A sensitive foreigner like John Ruskin, much attached to the United States before 1861, considered such an attitude, he wrote to Charles Eliot Norton, the equivalent of "washing your hands in blood and whistling."[9] Ruskin may have oversimplified the American dilemma, as did a good many other Englishmen, but his revulsion from the War had nothing in common with venomous anti-Americanism that flourished in certain British circles. It sprang rather from his detestation of *"modern war—scientific war—chemical and mechanic war, worse even than the savage's poisoned arrow."* Whatever its causes and goals and however justified, war to Ruskin (and to many like-minded people on both sides of the ocean) was a vicious problem-solver:

> If you have to take away masses of men from all industrial employment,—to feed them by the labor of others,—to move them and provide them with destructive machines, varied daily in national rivalship of inventive cost; if you have to ravage the country which you attack,—to destroy for a score of future years, its roads, its woods, its cities, and its harbours;—and if, finally, having brought masses of men, counted by hundreds of thousands, face to face, you tear those masses to pieces with jagged shots, and leave the fragments of living creatures countlessly beyond all help of surgery, to starve and parch, through days of torture, down into clots of clay—what book of accounts shall record the cost of your work;—What book of judgement sentence the guilt of it?[10]

Ruskin's question was easily answered. No "book of judgement" would sentence the Engineers of Destruction who had only carried out Heaven's mandate. Few Northern and virtually no Southern writers totaled up the costs of the War by Ruskin's reckoning or inveighed in his language against its abominations. Southerners burned incense to their armies, victorious in defeat, and deified their generals. Not war in general but Yankee depredations obsessed them. Northerners turned their eyes from the carnage and looked beyond to the encouraging future.

v

"We are accustomed to say," Thomas Wentworth Higginson wrote in 1870, "that the war and its results have made us a nation, subordinated local distinctions, cleared us of our chief shame, and given us the pride of a common career. This being the case, we may afford to treat ourselves to a little modest self-confidence."[11] At the same time he and others appreciated the problems of consolidation brought about by the War and the need to blend antebellum idealism with the new conditions of the post-War era.[12] Henceforth writers and intellectuals would have to think and to act *nationally* and to rationalize their mental resources with the same skill and purposefulness with which corporations were rationalizing the material resources of the country.* The War discouraged amateurism. Higginson compared the preacher turned novelist, the editor turned historian, the writers who kept shifting hats, to street musicians playing instruments simultaneously. "There is nothing in American life," he warned, "that can make concentration cease to be a virtue. Let a man choose his pursuit, and make all else count for recreation only."[13]

New conditions also required a new style of writing, one commensurate with the practical requirements of the nation. The War "chastened" literary style, for in "those angry days" words and phrases had grown "hot, clear, pure, and plain."[14] Writers in post-War America were now urged to cultivate a soldierly or businesslike style to

> tax their ingenuity and their powers of compression to the end that they may be more in sympathy with the peculiar spirit and situation of the community in which we live. Word paintings, graceful paraphrases, sparkling antitheses, ambiguous involutions, and subleties of diction are very fine things in their way, but surely the most important things to aim at now are ideas—ideas in contradistinction to words. We require point, simplicity, directness; in brief, more matter and less art than we have been accustomed to. If we are in Rome, we must do as the Romans do.[15]

---

* One literary promoter called "for an institution that shall give to every writer in the land a fair market for the disposition of his works—the valuation to be made by a disinterested board." He recommended an authors' "Exchange" housed in rooms close to the publishing firms where buyer and seller could meet. Its main object would be to provide careful criticism for new writers. Competent critics hired by the Exchange would judge the value of the literary wares and recommend marketing procedures. Both writers and publishers would be protected, the former from gouging editors, the latter from annoying attentions of writers. The Exchange would house files of periodicals, provide a bureau of general information for writers all over the country, arrange for lyceums and lecture tours, and thereby obviate an enormous amount of correspondence (*The Round Table*, 111 [July 14, 1866], 440–41).

All such talk about a new age of centralization ushered in by the War and the "direct, straightforward expression" which alone could reflect its character did not, as John W. De Forest discovered to his chagrin, revolutionize popular taste. Busy men did not read novels; their wives preferred "word paintings" and "graceful paraphrases" to realistic transcriptions of life. Nor did the War inspire a spate of literature continental in scope and national in spirit. On the contrary, post-War writers exploited the characterological and linguistic "local color" of their chosen regions rather than attempting to write "the great American novel" or a great Civil War epic. An ever-expanding audience of readers, no sticklers for quality, simply stimulated the production of perishable literary "shoddy" in "the slop-shops of letters."[16] Far from affecting American literature for the good and creating a climate for masterpieces, the War seemed to one disenchanted critic "a great intellectual disturbance, fatal to the arts during its progress, and in the period of reconstruction. At its close, genius vanished."[17] Literary genius did not vanish, but the War cannot be said to have inspired very much of it. Certainly "genius" glowed feebly and fitfully in the fictional works with a War background published between 1880 and 1929.[18]

v i

In the preface to his book on Pindar, Basil Gildersleeve defended the Theban poet's adherence to his state during the Persian wars. It was "no discredit to Pindar," he argued, "that he went honestly with his state in the struggle. . . . The Greece that came out of the Persian war was a very different thing from the cantons that ranged themselves on this side and that of a quarrel which, we may be sure, bore another aspect to those who stood aloof from it than it wears in the eyes of moderns, who have learned to be Hellenic patriots." Here Gildersleeve hinted, I suspect, at a cousinship between the Theban and the Southern patriot whose love of country was not a "poor abstraction" but rooted in a particular piece of earth.[19]

The strength and interest of Southern writing from Simms to Faulkner lie in its rootedness, its sense of place—its weakness in the absence of "historic vision" which, we have been assured, the experience of defeat invariably provides. But historical-mindedness is not the same as historical insight, and "the blood-knowledge of what life can be in a defeated country on the bare bones of privation"* (the inheritance of every authentic Southern child) cannot by itself unriddle the past. Historical-mindedness often leads to

* See C. Vann Woodward, *The Burden of Southern History* (New York [Vintage edn.], 1960), 53. Woodward is quoting Katharine Anne Porter.

hagiolatry. Southern writers, embosomed in history, could not or would not subject the Good Old Cause to critical examination. Although Southern War fiction and poetry occasionally rose above the parochial, it remained for the most part a literature of small distinction until the advent of the "Renascence." There is no basis for James G. Randall's claim that "in song and story" the South "won the decision at Appomattox."[20] The military metaphor he employed to express his erroneous judgment merely indicates that writing about the War was for him still a partisan act. Surely the clues to its meaning are less likely to be found in pietistic exercises or in historical novels like *Gone With the Wind* (that blend of solid journalism, dogged research, and personal fantasizing)[21] than in Faulkner's novels or in Robert Penn Warren's passionate yet disinterested reflections.

Who *won* the literary War is of no importance. Of more consequence is the fact that for over a century the War as a subject has not powerfully attracted many of the finer talents, even though constant allusions to it indicate its continued hold on the literary imagination. To Sherwood Anderson, growing up in a Middle West peopled by old veterans endlessly retelling their military experiences, the War remained a vivid but ungraspable story:

> For four years the men of American cities, villages and farms walked across the smoking embers of a burning land, advancing and receding as the flame of that universal, passionate, death-spitting thing swept down upon them or receded toward the smoking sky-line. Is it so strange that they could not come home and begin again peacefully painting houses or mending broken shoes? A something in them cried out. It sent them to bluster and boast upon the street corners. When people passing continued to think only of their brick laying and of their shovelling of corn into cars, when the sons of these war gods walking home at evening and hearing the vain boastings of the fathers began to doubt even the facts of the great struggle, a something snapped in their brains and they fell to chattering and shouting their vain boastings to all as they looked hungrily about for believing eyes.

Anderson was not the first or last to conclude: "No real sense of it has yet crept into the pages of a printed book."[22]

Our untidy and unkempt War still confounds interpreters.

SUPPLEMENTS

Supplement 1

The War Prefigured

IN the 1860s, passages from Milton's poem and allusions to the heavenly struggle he recorded came readily to the minds of clergymen, orators, versifiers, and novelists—especially in the North. Jefferson Davis may have lacked Satan's gloomy magnificence, but the rebellion he led, as Edward Everett declared at Gettysburg, was barely less blasphemous than that related by Milton:

> for while rebellion against tyranny—a rebellion designed, after prostrating arbitrary power, to establish free government on the basis of justice and truth—is an enterprise on which good men and angels may look with complacency, an unprovoked rebellion of ambitious men against a beneficent government for the purpose—the avowed purpose—of establishing, extending and perpetuating any form of injustice and wrong, is an imitation on earth of that first foul revolt of "the Infernal Serpent," against which the Supreme Majesty sent forth the armed myriads of his angels and clothed the right arm of his Son with the three-bolted thunders of omnipotence.[1]

James Russell Lowell connected "the first great secessionist" with his paler pupil more directly and sardonically. Satan, he said, "would doubtless have preferred to divide heaven peaceably, would have been willing to send commissioners, must have thought Michael's proceedings injudicious, and could probably even now demonstrate the illegality of hell-fire to any five-year-old imp of average education and intelligence."[2]

For any American who viewed secession as a "foul conspiracy" against a God-ordained Union, Milton was the ideal War-laureate. His militancy, religious fervor, and rhetoric, and his Manichean imagery* explained and illuminated the Secession War. Like their

* "And yet posterity will perhaps with truth assert that 'Paradise Lost' has wrought more intellectual evil than even its base contemporaries, since it has

343

supernal counterparts, the firebrands of the South revolted against the most just and benign government on earth, tried to set up a rival power equal or superior to the Union, employed a specious logic to justify their rebellion, and challenged the decree of Heaven,

> since by strength
> They measure all, of other excellence
> Not emulous nor care who them excells. (VI, 818 ff.)

When Gabriel cried to Satan,

> "Was this your discipline and faith ingag'd,
> Your military obedience, to dissolve
> Allegiance to th' acknowledg'd Power supreme?" (IV, 954 ff.)

he rebuked Confederate West Pointers. Against them raged God's avenging angels, Grant, Sherman, Thomas, and Sheridan, their swords guided by the spirit of Washington whose "mighty shade hovered over the miserable Lord of Misrule, the leader of the insurgents," Jefferson Davis:

> Author of evil, unknown till thy revolt,
> Unnam'd in Heav'n, now plenteous, as thou seest
> These Acts of hateful strife, hateful to all,
> Though heaviest by just measure on thyself
> And thy adherents: how hast they disturb'd
> Heav'n's blessed peace, and into Nature brought
> Misery, uncreated till the crime
> Of thy Rebellion? how hast thou instill'd
> Thy malice into thousands, once upright
> And faithful, now prov'd false. But think not here
> To trouble Holy Rest; Heav'n casts thee out
> From all her confines. . . .
> Hence then, and evil go with thee along
> Thy offspring, to the place of evil, Hell,
> Thou and thy wicked crew. (VI, 262 ff.)

So a Northern Michael might have addressed "the Confederate Lucifer" banished to "the hell of baffled ambition."*

---

familiarized educated minds with images which, though in one sense sublime, in another are most unworthy, and has taught the public a dreadful materialization of the great and invisible God. A Manichean composition in reality, it was mistaken for a Christian poem" (J. W. Draper, *History of the Intellectual Development of Europe* [New York, 1876], II, 245).

* Samuel Osgood quotes this passage and draws the parallel in "The Second Life of Washington" (*Harper's Magazine*, XXXII [March 1866], 466–67). Many other disquisitions on Southern wickedness written shortly before the end of the War allude to Milton. Two characteristic examples are A. J. H.

It was natural for the descendants of the Puritans, bred on the poetry of Milton, to claim him "as the grand exponent of our morality." His political philosophy had sustained their revolutionary forebears in the eighteenth century; now it bolstered their resistance to the Southern Cavaliers in the nineteenth. But Americans from both sections seem to have regarded their own war as a sequel to the English civil wars and to have relished the similarities.

Southern magazines featured articles contrasting invidiously planter "Cavaliers" and Yankee "Roundheads," much to the disgust of Northern publicists who sneered at the genealogical megalomania of Southern gentry. ("If nothing else should come of the war," one of them observed in 1861, "it would have effected enough to my mind in this, that a vast amount of sickening folly and disgusting mock romance, like this precious Norman-blood fancy, will have been ridiculed out of sight.")* According to the Norman-Saxon thesis advanced in some Southern quarters, the Yankees, descended from the wild Britons, had been conquered if not entirely subdued by the Roman and Saxon invaders. Caesar's description of these people resembled their Yankee posterity: "wild, savage, bold, fond of freedom, and greatly given to religious rights, exercises and beliefs, and quite as greatly under the influence of the Druid priests and *sacred women*." Cromwell's revolution was a reassertion of this aboriginal temper, Puritanism, but such was the excess of Puritan zeal and anarchy (misnamed "religious liberty") that the English people recalled their king, and the Puritans migrated to New En-

---

Duganne, *Camps and Prisons. Twenty Months in the Department of the Gulf* (New York, 1865), 15, and C. C. Coffin, "Late Scenes in Richmond," *Atlantic Monthly*, XV (June 1865), 755, which compare the conquered South to Milton's Hell and liken Southern leaders who once occupied the Union heaven to the fallen angels gnashing their teeth in Pandemonium.

George Templeton Strong records the following in his diary: "Story of Senator Dixon calling on the President and suggesting a parallel between secession and the first rebellion of which Milton sang. Very funny interview. Abe Lincoln didn't know much about *Paradise Lost* and sent out for a copy, looked through its first books under the Senator's guidance, and was struck by the coincidences between the utterances of Satan and those of Jefferson Davis, whom by-the-by he generally designates as 'that t'other fellow.' Dixon mentioned the old joke about the Scotch professor who was asked what his views were about the fall of the Angels and replied, 'Aweel, there's much to be said on both sides.' 'Yes,' said Uncle Abraham, 'I always thought the Devil was *some* to blame!'" (*The Diary of George Templeton Strong*, ed. Allan Nevins and M. H. Thomas [New York, 1952], III, 308).

* *The Knickerbocker Magazine*, LVIII (Sept. 1861), 267. Not all the Southern writers took this romantic tack. Despite the constant antitheses made between Puritan and Cavalier, a South Carolinian wrote in 1859, "there was very little of the Cavalier element in the settlement of this State" (*Russell's Magazine*, II [July 1859], 289–307).

gland. There they ruled themselves "and continued to exhibit those severe traits of religious fanaticism which had ever marked their history . . . squabbling, fighting, singing psalms, burning witches, and talking about liberty." Clearly such people needed the guiding hand of a master race, "fierce and fearless in a contest, yet just, generous and gentle in command" and possessing "every quality necessary to rule the Northern people."[3]

The Northern brand of ancestral piety did not rely quite so heavily on spurious history, but some Yankee chauvinists also looked back to the time of the Stuarts and accepted, although with different interpretations, the stereotypes of "Roundhead" and "Cavalier." Roundheads might be zealots, and "very hard to deal with when once inflamed,"[4] yet they defended civil liberty against "kingly and priestly"[5] despotism and served mankind, as George Bancroft rightly said, better than a chivalry given over to show, pleasure, and pride.[6] Cromwell's revolution only postponed the restoration of the Stuarts, but it ultimately strengthened English liberty and helped create the rationale for American independence. Just as the Puritans sapped the kingly prerogative and humbled the arrogant Cavaliers, so their descendants smashed the legatees of royalism in the Southern states. Each civil war produced its popular leader who, pushed on by the common sense of the people, "found out how to lead." Clarendon's summary of Cromwell applied equally well to Lincoln, whose prudence and caution and whose steadiness of purpose when once resolved resembled the Protector's.* Both leaders prepared the way for a single and united country; both subverted the institution of chivalry with the weapon of industry.

The temporary setbacks of the Parliamentary forces also furnished face-saving analogies for the North after Bull Run, a debacle that touched off sarcastic aspersions on Yankee cowardice in the Southern and English press. Searching for examples of panicking armies in Old World annals, a writer in the *Atlantic Monthly* reminded his readers how raw Roundheads had panicked at Edgehill and how both sides had caught the panic infection at Marston Moor and Naseby. These instances proved "the Englishman's aptitude for running" and showed "that if we have skill in the use of our heels, we have inherited it." Even the bravest peoples were not

---

* "When he appeared first in the Parliament, he seemed to have a person in no way gracious, no ornament of discourse, none of these talents which use to reconcile the affections of the stander by: yet as he grew into place and authority, his parts seemed to be raised, as if he had had concealed faculties, till he had occasion to use them; and when he was to act the part of a great man, he did it without any indecency, notwithstanding his want of custom" (G. D. Boyle, *Characters and Episodes of the Great Rebellion* [Oxford, 1889], 277–78).

immune from "panic terror." The point to remember was the ultimate triumph of the Cromwellians over the "conquering chivalry of
Normandy." Their American successors, he predicted, would subdue
the chivalry of the South.[7]

Initial victories of the Highland Scots over the English troops
during the Jacobite Rebellion of 1745–46 suggested to Northern
apologists in 1861 another comforting historical analogy to their
own civil war.* Indeed, bookish Yankee essayists found history
bursting with pertinent parallels and lessons. To Dr. Oliver Wendell
Holmes, the American Civil War called to mind the uprisings of the
gladiators under Spartacus and the Punic Wars. (In time Crassus
learned how to handle "the fierce gladiators with their classical
bowie-knives" and Fabius the military style of "the hot Southern
invaders.")†

---

* Hazewell referred to the English defeat at Gladsmuir in 1745, but the
most extended parallel between the two wars was drawn by Walter Mitchell
in the *Atlantic*. Mitchell likened the Highlanders to Southern "Fire-Eaters,"
as different from their English neighbors as Indian tribes from the first
settlers. Patriarchal, attached to their chiefs, agricultural, bred to arms,
fiercely national, the Scots hated the Hanoverians more bitterly than Charleston did Boston. "Scotsman" to the English was "a comprehensive name for a
greedy, beggarly adventurer, knavish and money-loving to the last degree, full
of absurd pride of pedigree, clannish and cold-blooded, vindictive as a Corsi-
can, and treacherous as a modern Greek." The Highlander regarded the
Englishman as "a bullying, arrogant coward,—purse-proud, yet cringing to
rank,—without loyalty and without sentiment,—given over to mere material
interests, not comprehending the idea of honor, and believing, as the fortieth
of his religious articles, that any injury, even to a blow, could be compensated
by money." After the Highlanders routed the English troops, many "croakers"
wanted to appease Scotland. The Government was filled with traitors and
submissionists, but time, "the ablest of generals and wisest of statesmen,"
favored the English. The Jacobites expected to hold out in their fastnesses,
but they failed through inner dissensions, want of sufficient aid from France,
and the sentiment for Union prevailing in the hearts of the Scottish majority.
The Southern rebellion would fail like its Jacobite equivalent. Both were
arbitrary, contrary to law and principle; both were combats "so often begun
in the world, yet so inevitably ending always in the same way, between misguided enthusiasm and the great public conviction of the value of order,
security, and peace" ("What We Are Coming To," *Atlantic Monthly*, VIII
[Oct. 1861], 487–89).

† A peaceful people, Holmes observed, was not prepared to cope with sudden war. Hence a republic must expect to lose at first to "any concentrated
power of nearly equal strength." Holmes also saw a parallel of the War in the
Anglo-Spanish conflict of the sixteenth century. The Indies were the "King
Cotton" of that day. Then, as well, peace-mongers spread false rumors and
treachery operated in high places, but in the end England's raw and badly
equipped troops proved more reliable than the gallants and ruffians "from the
disreputable haunts of London" and ended the threat of Spanish tyranny
("The Wormwood Cordial of History. With a Fable," *Atlantic Monthly*, VIII
[Oct. 1861], 507–12).

Another *Atlantic* contributor found food for thought in the Peloponnesian War that arrayed "two opposite types of civilization . . . in mortal combat": Sparta, a land power, "thoroughly brutalized," producing not "a single master-piece of intellect," exploiting a permanently enslaved Helot class, glorifying military prowess while living virtually under martial law; and Athens, a sea power, advocate of "pure democracy," hospitable to the arts, liberal toward slaves and captives and permitting emancipation. For this writer, Lincoln was Pericles "modern *redivivus*," bedeviled as Pericles was by sympathizers with the enemy and baffled by generals who intrigued politically like Alcibiades and had no faith in the cause. Athens suffered defeat because it never understood what it was contending for. To escape Athens's fate, the Union would have to recognize that the "avenue to future glory lies through the blood-red path of war, of desperate unrelenting war." Only effective military enterprise could turn back the barbarous system that "dares to array its brutal features against the sunlight of this nineteenth century."[8]

Supplement 2

Lincoln and the Writers

Aᴏᴛᴇʀ the death of Lincoln, it dawned upon many American writers that a great man had been living among them. A few, penetrating the disguise of the uncouth Western lawyer during the last two years of the War, had marked his strength and capacity, but the encomiums on "kindly," "good," and "sagacious" Abraham were more often than not tinged with condescension. Praising Lincoln became another way of flattering democracy. Was he any more, really, than the ordinary citizen heightened by history, the genius of the commonplace incarnate, the embodiment of "our continental idiosyncrasies"?[1]

Most of the eminent writers and men of letters in the United States knew of Lincoln only by hearsay, if at all, when the Chicago convention nominated him for the presidency. The majority of them lived in the Northeast and like the Republican consensus of that section would have preferred the gentlemanly William H. Seward to represent the party of freedom instead of the stump-speaker from Illinois. The radical intelligentsia considered him insufficiently zealous on behalf of the holy cause; the conservatives mistakenly suspected him of abolitionism. But both welcomed the displacement of the lame-duck incumbent to whose weakness and treachery anti-Southern Northerners attributed the sickness of the state.

Lincoln's ugliness and awkwardness seem at first to have embarrassed his well-wishers as well as to have delighted Confederate and Copperhead propagandists who referred to (or drew) him as "gorilla," "ape," "baboon," "clod-hopper," and "peasant." Presidents are supposed to look statesmanlike and to behave like gentlemen, but in contrast to courtly Jefferson Davis, Lincoln looked the railsplitter fresh from a frontier husting. His well-publicized casualness in dress and manner enforced the impression of the amiable buffoon singularly unequipped for high office.*

---

* "Lamentations were heard on every side over his want of education, as if it was not just as good, as far as mere schooling went, as that of George

First impressions of the President did not alter the stereotype, although Herman Melville—one of the crowd attending the inaugural levee in March 1861—found Lincoln younger and better looking than he had expected. "He shook hands like a good fellow," Melville wrote to his wife, "working hard at it like a man sawing wood."[2] The popular historian, John Lothrop Motley (soon to go to Austria as Ambassador), was also agreeably surprised when he met Lincoln a few months later and became one of his firm defenders. From then on, like so many other writers and scholars, Motley depicted Lincoln as an ingenuous and unsophisticated chap, modest, conciliatory, ready to concede his ignorance in state and foreign affairs, and occasionally exhibiting in his public papers what Motley called "considerable untaught grace and power."[3]

That opinion was to prevail among the literary establishment, especially in New England, where the Brahmins, in lieu of a grander leader, were content that a man "of very considerable native sagacity" and "simplicity of character" should pilot the nation in the storm of civil war. "We must accept the results of universal suffrage," Emerson adjured himself, "and not try to make appear that we can elect fine gentlemen. We shall have coarse men, with a fair chance of worth and manly ability, but not polite men to please the English or the French." Lincoln would "not walk dignifiedly through the traditional part of the President of America." Lucky for the country that it had an uncouth clown for a ruler, good-natured, honest, and faithful, instead of "an elegant *roué* and malignant self-seeker."[4] Indeed, the sympathy Lincoln gradually inspired among the literary men may have in part derived from the widely held supposition that he had not succumbed to his damning defects.[5] Weak, indecisive, ignorant, vacillating (so many regarded him as late as 1864), he somehow managed to sustain the War through sheer tenacity of purpose.[6]

A small number recognized quite early Lincoln's "hard distinc-

---

Washington, and a good deal better than that of Andrew Jackson. Many people were greatly distressed when they found out that Southerners in England were contrasting his deportment with that of Jefferson Davis. They wished they had not elected him, and declared they never would have voted for him if they had known he was to represent the nation through such a crisis as was then impending" (*Life and Letters of Edwin Lawrence Godkin*, ed. Rollo Ogden [New York, 1907], I, 269). On hearing the news of Lincoln's election, a Yankee literary lady responded: "—Oh, and Mr. Seward isn't nominated. I suppose you have heard before now, and Mr. Lincoln *is*. I don't feel the least enthusiasm myself. . . . They talk of 'honest Abe' (a hideous nickname) and his 'splitting rails and mauling Democrats,' but that isn't the very best recommendation a man can have for such an office" (H. A. Dodge, ed., *Gail Hamilton's Life in Letters* [Boston, 1901], I, 289–90).

tion."[7] One of them was John Hay, his private secretary, later to win some renown as poet and novelist and more as a diplomat. Hay revered his "backwoods Jupiter," wielding the "bolts of war" and the "machinery of government" with a steady hand and "better than all the trained logicians at snaking a sophism out of its hole."[8] And so, belatedly, did George Templeton Strong. He had sized up the President after meeting him in 1861 as "Decidedly plebeian," "superficially ugly," and "clear-headed and sound-hearted, though his laugh is the laugh of a yahoo, with a wrinkling of the nose that suggests affinity with the tapir and other pachyderms, and his grammar is weak." From time to time Strong complained of the President's zigzagging policies and want of dignity, but he never disavowed the "lank and hard-featured man"—"despised and rejected by a third of the community, and only tolerated by the other two-thirds." Strong foresaw that Lincoln "would be ranked high as the Great Emancipator twenty years hence," but he "did not suppose his death would instantly reveal—even to Copperhead newspaper editors—the nobleness and the glory of his part in this great contest."[9]

The majority of Lincoln's friends and enemies never detected the complicated self behind the melancholy and genial masks of Uncle Abe. And American writers, with a few notable exceptions like Whitman, showed hardly more acumen than the rest of the population in gauging Lincoln, although they added considerably to the mythology of the "Martyred Chief" after John Wilkes Booth murdered him.

The outpouring of literary lamentation in the form of sermons, elegies, and orations evoked by Lincoln's death registered the national grief and shock. Coming as it did at the end of a long civil war fought by a people alert to portents, it also blurred the image of Lincoln, the man. Not surprisingly, a religious people read all manner of meanings into the astonishing coincidences associated with the War and its origins that betrayed "to even the inattentive student the presence of a High Controlling Power more plainly perhaps than any war that ever preceded it."

Some of them have already been mentioned. It is enough to say here that to his countrymen, Lincoln's death climaxed a concatenation of God-directed events. As one Boston writer put it in 1865:

> With a kind of awe the imagination lays hold on such facts as these: The North, which had already poured out such rivers of blood in expiation of its guilty acquiescence in wrong, cannot be released till it has made one crowning offering more—its first-born child and chosen leader. The man whose election was the occasion of the war, becomes its victim. The President who had dealt so tenderly with Northern traitors, had

forgiven them, had treated with them, had almost cherished them, is stung to death at last by the serpent he would insist on taking to his bosom. Destiny would not let the war close till it had clearly demonstrated that the worst foe was at home.

So the last hour of the War was Lincoln's last:

> Such a rigid time-keeper is Destiny. And how closely Nemesis pursues the murderer! The spirit he sought to slay arrests him and brings him down. The genius of America uses her symbols to ensnare him. The national flag catches his heel, breaks his leg, and makes his escape impossible. The ball that ends his wretched life is fired by a man named Boston. The assassin breathes his last at the same hour of the morning to a minute which the clock marked when his illustrious victim died.[10]

Given the mood of the times, the analogy of Lincoln and Christ proved irresistibly apt. Poets played upon the association of the "cruelest month" with the Jewish Passover, the crucifixion day and Resurrection. Lincoln's blood was "freedom's eucharist," his death at the moment of "victory and gratulation" a "picture on the largest human scale, of the eternal and divine contrast between the triumph of Palm Sunday—and the wretchedness and glory of the crucifixion." America's homely Christ, guileless, toil-weary, merciful, "led his people with a tender hand." Clearly such a saint was unsuited for the harsh tasks of Reconstruction, and many of his eulogists consoled themselves with the thought that God had seen fit to remove His compassionate servant, Abraham (disqualified by his tender nature from administering retribution), before a reaction against him could set in. His career properly ended when "its dramatic unity was complete."[11]

Supplement 3

A Further Note
on the "Collegians"

MELVILLE'S sympathetic and ironic reflections on gentlemen-collegians complement the lives of young soldiers like Theodore Winthrop whose gallantry, arrogance, and temerity (like Melville's doomed Colonel in "The Scout Toward Aldie") brought him glory and death at Great Bethel in 1861 before the grimness and terror of war had become commonplace to the American public. He belonged to the company of martyrs described by Mrs. Jessie B. Frémont to Elizabeth Peabody, "whose home training and social influences found their fittest expression in their beautiful heroism in battle." Contemplating these young men, "so young & so surrounded with all the appliances for a life of happiness and ease," she felt for them "the same sort of tender regret that one does for a woman's life ended by violence."[1]

Winthrop also embodied the cocksureness of the young who answered Lincoln's call. "I find the men best informed about the South," he wrote to G. W. Curtis, "do not anticipate much severe fighting. Scott's Fabian policy will demoralize their armies. . . . The Virginians are not Spaniards or Swiss, they are not united, and they have their slaves always in the rear. . . . A few burned villages, a dozen guerrillas hung, one scouring [?] or battle will pacify a whole state."[2] But Winthrop was not at all characteristic of Yale, where comparatively few shared his Unionist convictions. More typical was another poet's response to the War—Edward Rowland Sill, who never gave a thought to enlisting and whose view of the War is caught in his Yale Commencement Poem:

> What is the grandeur of serving a state
> Whose tail is stinging its head to death like a scorpion?
> To simper over a counter, to lie for a piece of coin,
> To be shrewd and cunning, to cheat and steal

Business-like and mercantile,—
An army of rats and foxes—who will join?[3]

Elsewhere in the East the collegians exhibited a comparable
apathy. In Philadelphia, S. Weir Mitchell wrote to his sister, in
August 1861: "If I were nig I should go in for it all, but being white,
I decline."[4] (Mitchell eventually took a position as a "contract surgeon" which permitted him to remain at home, but he saw the War
at its grimmest in the hospitals.) After the first flurry of enthusiasm,
a graduate of Dartmouth later recalled, his classmates experienced
little of the "incentives and excitements" that attend foreign wars.[5]

The *Harvard Memorial Biographies* notwithstanding, by no
means all of the New England patriciate, including the Harvard
officer fraternity, were idealistic crusaders. Harvard's record in the
War was much better than Yale's, where "the majority, either lukewarm or indifferent, remained merely spectators through the entire
conflict,"[6] but many of Oliver Wendell Holmes's brothers-in-arms
took a neutral stand on the War issues and some were Copperheads.
They emulated the professional officers, despised abolitionists,
hated Governor Andrew, and supported McClellan. Although
Holmes had come from an abolitionist household, the War chilled
his humanitarian zeal: "His greatest loyalty and his greatest admiration were given to those associates who made gallantry their ideal
and who cared little for the constitutional and moral cause for
which they fought."[7] Forty per cent of the class of 1861 did not
enlist. Only a single member of the faculty, a German, joined the
Federal army.[8]

Supplement 4

Emily Dickinson's "Private Campaign"

THE War burst upon Emily Dickinson's pleached world. Far from drawing her from her seclusion, it drove her further into herself. Yet isolation did not signify indifference. The War inflamed her imagination, illuminated old enigmas, touched her deeper sympathies. Since the national conflict coincided with her private anguish, martial analogies and imagery naturally entered into her depictions of the wars of the Heart and Mind. Rival armies clashed in faraway places (some of the Amherst collegians swallowed up by the War were dear friends) as Emily Dickinson conducted "that Campaign inscrutable/ Of the interior."[1]

She fought her War without benefit of public bulletins ("The only News I know/ Is Bulletins all day/ From Immortality"), and entrenched behind her poetic redoubt, she dueled with an Antagonist skilled in the arts of deception. This "Bodiless Campaign" she declared of greater moment than all the "prevalent" battles even though invisible and unrecorded. Usually she found herself on the losing side ("My Portion is Defeat—today—/ A paler luck than Victory—") uncelebrated by paeans, bells, and drums. But she also reported the compensations of failure:

> If any sink, assure that this, now standing—
> Failed like Themselves—and conscious that it rose—
> Grew by the Fact, and not the Understanding
> How weakness passed—Force—arose—
>
> Tell that the Worst, is easy in a Moment—
> Dread, but the Whizzing, before the Ball—
> When the Ball enters, enters Silence—
> Dying—annuls the power to kill.[2]

Although the public War raging outside her private one "scarcely touched Emily Dickinson as an artist," its pomp and

355

horror, the loss of friends, the burials of collegiate "crusaders" like Lieutenant Frazer Stearns (son of the President of Amherst College) aggravated doubts and terrors and forced her to confront "a face of Steel/ That suddenly looks into Ours/ With a Metallic Grin;/ The Cordiality of Death/ Who Drills his welcome—in—." The personal and public War blended in her chilling summary of desolation after the military drills and drilling bullets: " 'Tis populous with Bone and Stain—/ And Men too straight to stoop again,/ And Piles of solid Moan—/ And Chips of Blank—in Boyish Eyes—/ And scraps of Prayer—/ And Death's surprise,/ Stamped visible —in Stone—." All of her strategies to ritualize Death—to cloak it in Latin tags, study it obsessively, accustom herself to its "fit"—could not obliterate the thought that War was "Murder," and she dared to wonder whether the "Alive" deserved "Liberty" if lives had to be piled up "like Dollars" to obtain it.[3]

So she speculated as young men "dropped like Flakes," anonymous in "the Seamless Grass." Her prevailing tone was elegiac. The soldiers who lay in "the Distinguished Dust" formed a "Present Divinity," but in 1872 she observed: "Could Prospect taste of Retrospect/ The tyrannies of Men/ Were Tenderer—diviner/ The Transitive toward./ A Bayonet's contrition/ Is nothing to the Dead."[4]

Although the War intensified ideas and emotions in Emily Dickinson which had already surfaced in her poems, the years between 1861 and 1865 proved to be her most intensely creative ones.[5] Writing in wartime she compared to singing "off charnel steps," yet "the anguish of others" seemed to medicine her own, and the omnipresence of death made her feel all the more keenly the might and stupendousness of everyday life.[6]

NOTES

Notes

A KEY TO ABBREVIATIONS FREQUENTLY CITED

AM	The Atlantic Monthly
C	Century Magazine
H	Harper's New Monthly Magazine
JSH	The Journal of Southern History
N	The Nation
NAR	The North American Review
RT	The Round Table
S	Scribner's Magazine
SR	The Southern Review
SLM	The Southern Literary Messenger
VQR	Virginia Quarterly Review

Introduction

1. *Putnam's Magazine,* I (Jan. 1868), 120–21.
2. John Weiss, "War and Literature," *AM,* IX (June 1862), 674–84.
3. *Ibid.*
4. *AM,* XX (July 1867), 121.
5. *S,* XXXV (Jan.–June 1904), 764.
6. Quoted in R. W. Smith, *The Civil War and Its Aftermath in American Fiction* (Chicago, Ill., 1937), 50.
7. John Macy, *The Spirit of American Literature* (New York, N.Y., 1911), 12–13.
8. *RT,* III (May 19, 1866), 306.
9. Thomas Beer, *Stephen Crane* (New York, N.Y., 1927), 45.
10. *Henry James. The American Essays,* ed. Leon Edel (New York, N.Y., 1956), 221.
11. Oscar Handlin, "The Civil War as Symbol and as Actuality," *The Massachusetts Review,* III (autumn 1961), 133–43.
12. Bernard DeVoto, *Mark Twain's America* (Boston, Mass., 1932), 112.

Chapter 1
WRITERS AND POLITICS

1. Edward C. Wagenknecht, *John Greenleaf Whittier* (New York, N.Y., 1967), 21.

2. Kay House, *Cooper's Americans* (Columbus, O., 1965), 82–83. See also *The Letters and Journals of James Fenimore Cooper*, ed. J. F. Beard (Cambridge, Mass., 1968), VI, 207–209, 245.

3. J. K. Paulding, writer and statesman, a leading figure in the Knickerbocker circle and intimate of Andrew Jackson, defended slavery and Southern rights. From 1851 until his death in 1860, he was the darling of the Southern ultraists. See *The Letters of James Kirke Paulding*, ed. R. M. Aderman (Madison, Wis., 1962).

4. H. R. Floan, *The South in Northern Eyes* (Austin, Tex., 1958), 185.

5. Charles Eliot Norton, *Considerations on Some Recent Social Theories* (Boston, Mass., 1853), 149.

6. *Journals of Ralph Waldo Emerson*, ed. E. W. and W. E. Emerson (Boston, Mass., and New York, N.Y., 1909), I, 16–17; III, 565, 308–309.

7. *Ibid.*, VI, 341–43, 91–92.

8. *Ibid.*, VIII, 180 ff.

9. *Ibid.*, 198.

10. *Life of Henry Wadsworth Longfellow*, ed. Samuel Longfellow (Boston, Mass., 1886), II, 347. Samuel Gridley Howe had invited Longfellow to meet Brown: "You like to see *originals,* & you may have a chance to see a great one by calling at my office on Friday or Saturday between 9. & 12. The great *practical* abolitionist, the one who *never talks,* will be there" (Howe to Longfellow, Nov. 26, n.d. [Longfellow Papers, Houghton Lib.]).

11. *The Life of John A. Andrew*, ed. H. G. Pearson (Boston, Mass., and New York, N.Y., 1904), I, 100–101.

12. James S. Pike, *First Blows of the Civil War. The Ten Years of Preliminary Conflict in the United States. From 1850 to 1860* (New York, N.Y., 1879), 449–50.

13. *Vanity Fair*, I (March 7, 1860), 183.

14. John Wise, *The End of an Era* (Boston, Mass., and New York, N.Y., 1900), 136.

Chapter 2
The "Wholesome Calamity"

1. Bronson Alcott, *Notebooks*, Jan. 2, 1861 (Houghton Lib.).

2. C. E. Norton, "Emancipation and the Constitution" (unpublished essay, Sept. 1861, C. E. Norton Papers, Houghton Lib.).

3. *SLM*, XXX (Jan. 1860), 72–73.

4. *SLM*, XXVI (Feb. 1858), 155.

5. *SLM*, XXXI (Dec. 1860), 470.

6. *The Letters of William Gilmore Simms*, ed. M. S. S. Oliphant, A. T. Odell, and T. C. D. Eaves (Columbia, S.C., 1955), IV, 290, 295.

7. *Ibid.*, 301.

8. William Taylor, *Cavalier and Yankee* (New York, N.Y., 1961), is a searching examination of this theme.

9. *Vanity Fair*, III (Apr. 27, 1861), 209.

10. *Ibid.* (May 18, 1961), 238.

11. J. J. Delchamps, *Love's Ambuscade: or the Surgeon's Stratagem. A War Drama in Three Acts* (Mobile, Ala., 1863).

12. *SLM*, XXXI (Nov. 1860), 343–44; and (Dec. 1860), 469.

13. W. H. Holcombe, "The Alternative: A Separate Nationality, or the Africanization of the South," *SLM*, XXXII (Feb. 1861), 86.

14. *Ibid.* (Jan. 1861), 74.

15. "The Massachusetts' Regiments," *ibid.* (June 1861), 442.
16. *SLM*, XXXIII (Oct. 1861), 316.
17. *SLM*, XXXVI (Sept.–Oct. 1862), 585.
18. *SLM*, XXXII (Feb. 1861), 83–85.
19. *Ibid.* (March 1861), 344.
20. *The Diary of George Templeton Strong*, ed. Allan Nevins and M. H. Thomas (New York, N.Y., 1952), III, 119.
21. *Ibid.*, I, 217.
22. *Ibid.*, II, 287.
23. *Ibid.*, 304–305.
24. *Ibid.*, 36, 274–75.
25. *Ibid.*, II, 474; III, 42.
26. Edward Dicey, *Six Months in the Federal States* (London, Eng., and Cambridge, Eng., 1863), II, 237.
27. Rufus Choate, *Addresses and Orations of Rufus Choate* (Boston, Mass., 1883), 504.
28. Horace Bushnell, *Reverses Needed. A Discourse Delivered on the Sunday After the Disaster of Bull Run, in the North Church, Hartford* (Hartford, Conn., 1861), 25.
29. Lowell wrote in 1858: "To be an American, in Europe, is to be the accomplice of filibusters and slave-traders" ("Mr. Buchanan's Administration," *AM*, I [Apr. 1858], 758).
30. *Letters of Charles Eliot Norton*, ed. Sara Norton and M. A. DeWolfe Howe (Boston, Mass., and New York, N.Y., 1913), I, 199, 201.
31. *Ibid.*, 213–16.
32. Oliver Wendell Holmes, *Pages from an Old Volume of Life. A Collection of Essays, 1857–1881*, in *The Complete Writings of Oliver Wendell Holmes* (Boston, Mass., and New York, N.Y., 1892), VIII, 95.
33. *Ibid.*, 87, 106.
34. *Ibid.*, 83, 85, 87–88.
35. *Ibid.*, 117, 116, 101.
36. *Ibid.*, 58, 61, 17, 32.
37. *Ibid.*, 9, 36–37.
38. *Ibid.*, 42, 82.
39. *The Anti-Slavery Papers of James Russell Lowell* (Boston, Mass., and New York, N.Y., 1902), I, 4; II, 83, 44, 21–22, 19.
40. *Ibid.*, II, 14, 25–26.
41. *Ibid.*, I, 166–75, 17, 205, 22.
42. For fuller accounts of Lowell's retrogression, see H. E. Scudder, *James Russell Lowell. A Biography* (Boston, Mass., and New York, N.Y., 1901), 2 vols., and Martin Duberman, *James Russell Lowell* (Boston, Mass., 1966).
43. *Letters of James Russell Lowell*, ed. C. E. Norton (New York, N.Y., 1894), I, 298.
44. James Russell Lowell, *Political Essays* (Boston, Mass., and New York, N.Y., 1899), 56, 50.
45. *Ibid.*, 41, 132.
46. *AM*, VIII (Dec. 1861), 767.
47. Lowell, *Political Essays*, 74.
48. *AM*, VIII, 767.
49. Lowell, *Political Essays*, 66.
50. The most trenchant and illuminating study of this theocratic dream is G. M. Frederickson, *The Inner Civil War* (New York, N.Y., 1965).
51. Lowell, *Political Essays*, 212.
52. Lowell, *Letters*, I, 344.

53. *Ibid.*, II, 10.

54. *The Writings of James Russell Lowell* (Boston, Mass., and New York, N.Y. [Riverside edn.], 1892), VIII, 156.

55. Ralph Waldo Emerson, "American Civilization," *AM*, IX (Apr. 1862), 504.

56. *Ibid.*, 506, 511.

57. *The Letters of Ralph Waldo Emerson*, ed. R. L. Rusk (New York, N.Y., 1939), V, 253.

58. *Journals of Ralph Waldo Emerson*, ed. E. W. and W. E. Emerson (Boston, Mass., and New York, N.Y., 1909), IX, 464–65.

59. *Ibid.*, 493, 552.

60. "The lesson learned here is of the greatest political importance [i.e., the rescue of Frank Sanborn from his persecutors in Concord, April 1860]— resistance the most vigilant and determined to the tendency toward centralization. Let us hate and dread it. As Paris has become the mistress of France, so Washington aspires to become the centre of America and all the power of the nation tends toward the national government. Let the States resist the government and the cities the States, and the villages the cities. That is the greatest protection of the law and the government—that the people are jealous of their rights and ready to resist the slightest encroachment under any circumstances." (This reference to Emerson's speech at the reception of Sanborn in Concord, April 5, 1860, is clipped and included in Bronson Alcott's *Notebooks*, volume for 1860, 123.)

61. Emerson, *Journals*, X, 79.

62. Emerson, "American Civilization," 508.

63. Emerson, *Journals*, IX, 512–13.

64. *Ibid.*, IX, 362, 484–85, 462–64; X, 93–94.

65. W. A. Huggard, "Emerson and the Problem of War," *University of Iowa Humanistic Studies*, V (1938), 9.

66. Emerson, *Journals*, X, 231.

67. *Ibid.*, 308.

68. *Ibid.*, X, 308; IX, 493–94, 461–62.

69. Quoted in Huggard, "Emerson and the Problem of War," 67.

70. Emerson, *Journals*, IX, 330; J. E. Cabot, *A Memoir of Ralph Waldo Emerson* (Boston, Mass., and New York, N.Y., 1893), II, 601; *The Complete Works of Ralph Waldo Emerson*, ed. E. W. Emerson (Boston, Mass., 1903), II, 237.

Chapter 3
HAWTHORNE: LONELY DISSENTER

1. Later published as *Autograph Leaves of Our Country's Authors*, ed. John Pendleton Kennedy (Baltimore, Md., 1864).

2. William Dean Howells, "The Personality of Hawthorne," *NAR*, CLCCVII (Dec. 1903), 881–82.

3. James T. Fields, *Yesterdays with Authors* (Boston, Mass., 1882), 107.

4. M. D. Conway, *Life of Nathaniel Hawthorne* (New York, N.Y., 1890), 205–6.

5. G. W. Curtis, "Nathaniel Hawthorne," in *Essays from the North American Review*, ed. A. T. Rice (New York, N.Y., 1879), 351–52.

6. For Hawthorne's complicated and shifting view of the War that so disturbed Curtis, see Randall Stewart, "Hawthorne and the Civil War," *Studies in Philology*, XXXIV (Jan. 1937), 91–106; L. S. Hall, *Hawthorne, Critic of Society* (New Haven, Conn., 1944); H. F. Floan, *The South in Northern Eyes, 1831–1861* (Austin, Tex., 1958).

7. Hall, *Hawthorne, Critic of Society*, 155.

8. Quoted in Julian Hawthorne, *Nathaniel Hawthorne and His Wife* (Boston, Mass., 1885), II, 273. Elsewhere he wrote: "The war continues to interrupt my literary industry, and I am afraid it will be long before Romances are in request again, even if I could write one." Hawthorne to W. D. Ticknor, Feb. 4, 1861. See also letter to Francis Bennoch, Oct. 12, 1862. I am greatly indebted to Professor Norman H. Pearson of Yale University for granting me permission to consult his file of Hawthorne letters before his edition of them appears. Unless otherwise indicated, all the Hawthorne letters cited are in the Pearson file.

9. George P. Lathrop, *A Study of Hawthorne* (Boston, Mass., and New York, N.Y., 1893), 319.

10. Stewart, "Hawthorne and the Civil War," 106.

11. George Fredrickson, *The Inner Civil War* (New York, N.Y., 1965), 1–4.

12. Nathaniel Hawthorne, "Miscellanies," in *The Complete Writings of Nathaniel Hawthorne* (Boston, Mass., and New York, N.Y., 1900), XVII, 75.

13. Hawthorne to Elizabeth Peabody, Aug. 13, 1857.

14. *Ibid.*, Oct. 8, 1857.

15. J. Hawthorne, *Hawthorne and His Wife*, II, 269.

16. Hawthorne to Henry Bright, Dec. 17, 1860.

17. Hawthorne to Ticknor, May 26, 1861.

18. Edward Dicey, "Nathaniel Hawthorne," *Macmillan's Magazine*, X (July 1864), 245; Hawthorne to Elizabeth Peabody, July 20, 1863.

19. Hawthorne to Henry Bright, Nov. 14, 1861.

20. Hawthorne to Horatio Bridge, Oct. 12, 1861.

21. Hawthorne to Francis Bennoch, July ?, 1861.

22. Hawthorne to Francis Bennoch, Oct. 12, 1862.

23. Quoted in M. D. Conway, *Emerson at Home and Abroad* (Boston, Mass., 1882), 273.

24. Dicey, "Nathaniel Hawthorne," 245.

25. Hawthorne to Henry Bright, Nov. 14, 1861.

26. Hawthorne to Henry Bright, March 8, 1863.

27. Quoted in Conway, *Emerson*, 274. In the same vein: "Then, too, a bullet offers such a brief and easy way, such a pretty little orifice, through which the weary spirit might seize the opportunity to be exhaled!" (Hawthorne, *Complete Writings*, XVII, 405).

28. Hawthorne to Henry Bright, March 8, 1863.

29. *Journals of Ralph Waldo Emerson*, ed. E. W. and W. E. Emerson (Boston, Mass., and New York, N.Y., 1909), X, 41.

30. Hawthorne was the guest of his old friend (then chief of the Naval Bureau of Provisions) Horatio Bridge. His publisher, William Ticknor, accompanied him. During his stay, Hawthorne visited Harper's Ferry and Fort Monroe, inspected the *Monitor*, sat for his portrait, and reflected on "War matters." The trip is described in Caroline Ticknor, *Hawthorne and His Publisher* (Boston, Mass., and New York, N.Y., 1913), 258–82.

31. Conway, *Life of Nathaniel Hawthorne*, 2, 3, 4.

32. Hawthorne, *Complete Writings*, XVII, 361, 364.

33. J. Hawthorne, *Hawthorne and His Wife*, II, 311–12.

34. Hawthorne, *Complete Writings*, XVII, 361 and *passim*.

35. *Ibid.*, 366–67.

36. *Ibid.*, 388–89.

37. G. W. Curtis to Charles Eliot Norton, June 26, 1862 (Houghton Lib.).

38. Dicey, "Nathaniel Hawthorne," 244.

39. Quoted in J. C. Austin, *Fields of the Atlantic Monthly* (San Marino, Cal., 1953), 218–19.

40. *Ibid.*, 219; Hawthorne to W. D. Ticknor, May 7, 1862.

41. Hawthorne, *Complete Writings*, XVII, 376–78.

42. Fields, *Yesterdays*, 105.

43. Hawthorne to Elizabeth Peabody, July 20, 1863.

44. Hawthorne to Horatio Bridge, Feb. 13, 1862.

45. Hawthorne, *Complete Writings*, XVII, 397.

46. Hawthorne to Horatio Woodman, June 22, 1862.

47. Horatio Bridge, *Personal Recollections of Nathaniel Hawthorne* (New York, N.Y., 1893), 169.

48. Hawthorne to Henry Bright, Nov. 14, 1861.

49. J. Hawthorne, *Hawthorne and His Wife*, II, 271.

50. Hawthorne, *Complete Writings*, XVII, 407–409.

51. Hawthorne to Horatio Bridge, July 21, 1863.

52. J. Hawthorne, *Hawthorne and His Wife*, II, 273.

53. Hawthorne to Francis Bennoch, Oct. 12, 1862.

54. *SR*, XIV (Apr. 1870), 332–33.

Chapter 4
WHITMAN: THE "PARTURITION YEARS"

1. *The Collected Writings of Walt Whitman*, ed. G. W. Allen and Sculley Bradley (New York, N.Y., 1963–64), VIII, 724.

2. *Ibid.*, 731.

3. Included in Clifton J. Furness, *Walt Whitman's Workshop* (Cambridge, Mass., 1937), 85–113.

4. *Ibid.*, 105 and *passim*.

5. *Ibid.*, 113.

6. First published in *Galaxy* in two parts: "Democracy" (1867) and "Personalism" (1868).

7. Furness, *Whitman's Workshop*, 101.

8. Clara Barrus, *Whitman and Burroughs, Comrades* (Boston, Mass., and New York, N.Y., 1931), 335.

9. Whitman, *Collected Writings*, I, 115.

10. L. M. Clark, *Walt Whitman's Concept of the Common Man* (New York, N.Y., 1955), 67.

11. Furness, *Whitman's Workshop*, 74.

12. Quoted in Edward Carpenter, *Days with Walt Whitman* (London, Eng., 1906), 26.

13. Walt Whitman, *The Gathering of the Forces*, ed. Cleveland Rodgers and John Black (New York, N.Y., 1920), I, 193.

14. *Ibid.*, 60.

15. Walt Whitman, *I Sit and Look Out. Editorials from the Brooklyn Daily Times*, ed. Emory Holloway and Vernolian Schwarz (New York, N.Y., 1932), 46; Whitman, *Gathering of the Forces*, I, 195.

16. Whitman, *Gathering of the Forces*, I, 202, 238–39.

17. Whitman, *Collected Writings*, VII, 67.

18. *Walt Whitman's Civil War*, ed. Walter Lowenfels (New York, N.Y., 1960), 286.

19. Horace Traubel, *With Walt Whitman in Camden* (New York, N.Y., 1915), II, 46–47.

20. C. I. Glicksberg, *Walt Whitman and the Civil War* (Philadelphia, Pa., 1933), 166.

21. Whitman, *Collected Writings*, I, 69.

22. *Ibid.*, 69, 171, 172.

23. *Ibid.*, 166, 75, 157.

24. *Ibid.*, 112.

25. *Ibid.*, 89, 159, 83.

26. Whitman, *Whitman's Civil War*, 15.

27. Whitman, *Collected Writings*, I, 142, 112, 122.

28. *Ibid.*, 80. Undoubtedly some of his War "experiences" came secondhand from his brother George Washington Whitman, who served in the Federal army from April 1861 to July 1865. He rose from private to major and fought in many of the bloodiest campaigns of the War. Captured in September 1864, he suffered in Libby and other prisons until his parole in February 1865. His factual and down-to-earth letters to his mother are full of what Whitman called "the real article." See Clarence Gohdes and R. G. Silver, *Faint Clews & Indirections, Manuscripts of Walt Whitman and His Family* (Durham, N.C., 1949), 143–82.

29. Whitman, *Collected Writings*, VII, 62.

30. Glicksberg, *Whitman and the Civil War*, 164.

31. Whitman, *Collected Writings*, I, 82.

32. Whitman, *Whitman's Civil War*, 10.

33. Whitman, *Collected Writings*, I, 246–47.

34. William Dean Howells in *RT*, II (Nov. 11, 1865), 147.

35. Henry James, "Mr. Walt Whitman," *N*, I (Nov. 16, 1865), 625–26.

36. T. W. Higginson, "Unmanly Manhood," *The Woman's Journal*, XII (Feb. 4, 1882), 33.

37. Barrus, *Whitman and Burroughs*, 339.

38. Furness, *Whitman's Workshop*, 93.

39. Traubel, *With Walt Whitman*, II, 452.

40. *RT*, II (Sept. 23, 1865), 36.

41. Whitman, *Collected Writings*, I, 82–83.

42. Quoted in W. E. Barton, *Abraham Lincoln and Walt Whitman* (Indianapolis, Ind., 1928), 170; Glicksberg, *Whitman and the Civil War*, 174.

43. Traubel, *With Walt Whitman*, III, 78.

44. Whitman, *Collected Writings*, I, 215, 113.

45. *Ibid.*, VIII, 508.

46. *Ibid.*, 603–604.

47. James Russell Lowell, "Abraham Lincoln," *Political Essays* (Boston, Mass., and New York, N.Y., 1899), 192.

48. E. P. Whipple, *American Literature and Other Papers* (Boston, Mass., 1887), 111.

49. Traubel, *With Walt Whitman*, I, 115.

50. Whitman, *Collected Writings*, VIII, 707.

51. *Ibid.*, 377.

52. *Ibid.*, 756.

53. *Ibid.*, 43.

54. *Ibid.*, VII, 81.

55. *Ibid.*, 100, 114.

56. *Ibid.*, 113, 117.

57. Quoted in Glicksberg, *Whitman and the Civil War*, 134.

58. Whitman, *Collected Writings*, VIII, 582.

59. Traubel, *With Walt Whitman*, III, 582.

60. Whitman, *Collected Writings*, I, 100.

Chapter 5
MELVILLE: THE CONFLICT OF CONVICTIONS

1. *The Collected Writings of Walt Whitman*, ed. G. W. Allen and Sculley Bradley (New York, N.Y., 1963–64), VII, 324.

2. *Ibid.*, 427.

3. G. W. Allen, *The Solitary Singer* (New York, N.Y., 1955), 127–28.

4. Jay Leyda quotes tributes from James Thomson and Robert Buchanan (*The Melville Log. A Documentary Life of Herman Melville, 1819–1891* [New York, N.Y., 1951], II, 740, 792) and a portion of Buchanan's poem, "Socrates in Camden, with a Look Round." The last, a tribute to Whitman, contains twenty-one lines praising Melville, the "sea-compelling man" and "my sea-magician" who "shall still endure, or I'm no prophet!" Buchanan looked for Melville in New York City but found no one, he claimed, "who seemed to know anything of the one great imaginative writer fit to stand shoulder to shoulder with Whitman on that continent" (*The Academy*, XXVIII [Aug. 15, 1885], 103). See also J. W. Barrs to Melville, Jan. 13, 1890, quoted in Leyda, *Melville Log*, II, 821.

5. Whitman, *Collected Writings*, VII, 310.

6. Hennig Cohen, Introduction to *The Battle-Pieces of Herman Melville*, ed. Hennig Cohen (New York, N.Y., 1963), 12.

7. Melville, *Battle-Pieces*, 33.

8. Francis Grierson, *The Valley of the Shadows* (London, Eng., and New York, N.Y., 1913), 2.

9. Melville, *Battle-Pieces*, 260–61.

10. *Ibid.*, 196–202.

11. Herman Melville, *Clarel, A Poem and a Pilgrimage to the Holy Land*, ed. W. E. Bezanson (New York, N.Y., 1960), xxxiii.

12. Melville, *Battle-Pieces*, 195.

13. Melville, *Clarel*, 422–23, 475, 482–84.

14. *Ibid.*, 484.

Chapter 6
HENRY ADAMS

1. Quoted in Ernest Samuels, *Henry Adams, The Major Phase* (Cambridge, Mass., 1964), 313.

2. *A Cycle of Adams Letters, 1861–1865*, ed. W. C. Ford (Boston, Mass., and New York, N.Y., 1920), I, 102.

3. *Letters of Henry Adams (1858–1891)*, ed. W. C. Ford (Boston, Mass., and New York, N.Y., 1930–38), I, 53.

4. Henry Adams, *The Education of Henry Adams* (Boston, Mass., and New York, N.Y., 1918), 98.

5. *The Great Secession Winter of 1860–61 and Other Essays by Henry Adams*, ed. George Hochfield (New York, N.Y., 1958), 30.

6. Adams, *Letters*, 76–77.

7. *Ibid.*, 78–79, 58, 82.

8. *Charles Francis Adams, 1835–1915. An Autobiography* (Boston, Mass., and New York, N.Y., 1916), 107.

9. Charles Francis Adams, Sr., to Henry Adams, Dec. 15, 1859 (Massachusetts Historical Society).

10. Adams, *A Cycle*, I, 10.

11. Charles Francis Adams, Sr., *Diary*, Jan. 1, 1862 (Massachusetts Historical Society).

12. Charles Francis Adams, Sr., to Henry Adams, Nov. 18, 1859 (Massachusetts Historical Society).

13. Adams, *Education*, 111–12, 128.

14. Adams, *A Cycle*, II, 48–49.

15. Adams, *Education*, 208.

16. Adams, *A Cycle*, I, 23, 24–25, 30.

17. *Ibid.*, 30, 40, 46, 163, 136, 151.

18. *Ibid.*, 183.

19. Adams, *Education*, 114–15.

20. Harriet Martineau to C. G. Loring, Jan. 2, 1863 (Loring Papers, Houghton Lib.).

21. *The Works of John Lothrop Motley* (New York, N.Y., and London, Eng., Netherlands edn., 1900), XVI, 287.

22. Adams, *A Cycle*, I, 244.

23. *Ibid.*, I, 120; II, 46–47; I, 22.

24. Adams, *Education*, 100.

25. Adams, *A Cycle*, I, 182–83.

26. *Ibid.*, 243.

27. *Ibid.*, II, 20; I, 118, 128, 133.

28. *Ibid.*, I, 149.

29. *Ibid.*, II, 215–20.

30. *Ibid.*, 47.

31. Motley, *Works*, XVI, 313.

32. Adams, *A Cycle*, II, 47; I, 196.

33. *Letters of Francis Parkman*, ed. W. R. Jacobs (Norman, Okla., 1960), I, 145–46, 160–61.

34. Geoffrey Blodgett, "Reform Thought and the Genteel Tradition," in *The Gilded Age*, rev. and enl. edn., ed. H. Wayne Morgan (Syracuse, N.Y., 1970), 55–76.

35. *The Selected Letters of Henry Adams*, ed. Newton Arvin (New York, N.Y., 1957), 266.

36. Adams, *Letters* (ed. Ford), I, 166–67.

37. Henry Adams, *Democracy* (New York, N.Y. [Farrar, Straus and Young], 1952), 235, 231.

38. Parkman, *Letters*, I, 165.

39. Adams, *Democracy*, 131.

40. *Ibid.*, 53.

41. Herman Melville, *Clarel, A Poem and a Pilgrimage to the Holy Land*, ed. W. E. Bezanson (New York, N.Y., 1960), 475.

42. Adams, *Democracy*, 145, 148.

43. Adams, *A Cycle*, I, 135.

Chapter 7
HENRY JAMES

1. Henry James, *Notes of a Son and Brother* (New York, N.Y., 1914), 311.

2. *Ibid.*, 243.

3. *Ibid.*, 243–44.

4. *Ibid.*, 296–97.

5. Leon Edel, *Henry James. The Untried Years* (Philadelphia, Pa., and New York, N.Y., 1953), 173–81.

6. James, *Notes*, 296–97, 317–18. For a highly suggestive psychoanalytic study of Henry James's "obscure hurt" and the Civil War, see Saul Rosenzweig's pioneer essay, "The Ghost of Henry James," *Partisan Review* (Feb. 1944), 436–55.

7. G. W. Allen, *William James. A Biography* (New York, N.Y., 1967), 64.

8. Quoted in Edel, *James. The Untried Years*, 171–72.

9. Henry James, Sr., *The Social Significance of Our Institutions* (Boston, Mass., 1861), 37.

10. Henry James, Sr., to Elizabeth Peabody, July 22, 1863 (Horace Mann Papers, Massachusetts Historical Society).

11. James, *Notes*, 379–80, 395.

12. *Ibid.*, 310–15.

13. *Ibid.*, 244–45, 373–74.

14. *Ibid.*, 245.

15. Henry James, Sr., to Elizabeth Peabody, Aug. 8, 1863 (Horace Mann Papers, Massachusetts Historical Society). For a full account of the Fort Wagner incident, see Luis F. Emilio, *A Brave Black Regiment. History of the Fifty-Fourth Regiment of Massachusetts Volunteer Infantry, 1863–1865* (Boston, Mass., 1894), 67–104.

16. Quoted in Freeman Bishop, "Henry James Criticizes *The Tory Lover*," *American Literature*, XXVII (1955–56), 263.

17. Leon Edel, *Henry James. The Treacherous Years: 1895–1901* (Philadelphia, Pa., and New York, N.Y., 1969), 210.

18. *The Complete Tales of Henry James*, ed. Leon Edel (Philadelphia, Pa., and New York, N.Y., 1962), I, 67, 91.

19. *Ibid.*, 241.

20. James, *Notes*, 428.

21. *Ibid.*, 407–12.

22. *Ibid.*, 406.

23. *Ibid.*, 407, 430.

24. *Ibid.*, 431.

25. Edel, *James. The Treacherous Years*, 121.

26. Henry James, *The American Scene* (New York, N.Y., and London, Eng., 1907), 355, 357.

27. *Ibid.*, 402, 358, 393–94.

28. *Ibid.*, 364.

29. *Ibid.*, 379, 360.

30. *Ibid.*, 360.

31. *Ibid.*, 371, 360.

32. *Ibid.*, 371–72.

33. *Ibid.*, 373, 389.

34. *Ibid.*, 397–98.

35. *Ibid.*, 293.

36. *Ibid.*, 362.

37. *Ibid.*, 402–3.

Chapter 8
WILLIAM DEAN HOWELLS

1. Edward C. Wagenknecht, *William Dean Howells. The Friendly Eye* (New York, N.Y., 1969), 206; E. H. Cady, *The Road to Realism: The Early Years, 1837–1885, of William Dean Howells* (Syracuse, N.Y., 1956), 89; Kenneth S. Lynn, *William Dean Howells: An American Life* (New York, N.Y., 1971),

107–109, 112–13. When it looked for a time as if Howells's brother, Joe, might be drafted, the Consul tried to salve his conscience by pleading with his father to help purchase a substitute.

2. *N*, I (Dec. 28, 1865), 804–805.

3. Wagenknecht, *Howells*, 212.

4. William Dean Howells, *A Fearful Responsibility and Other Stories* (Boston, Mass., 1881), 3.

5. William Dean Howells, *My Literary Passions* (New York, N.Y., 1895), 195.

6. *Life in Letters of William Dean Howells,* ed. Mildred Howells (New York, N.Y., 1928), I, 34, 26, 33. See also Lynn, *Howells*, 107; C. W. Fryckstedt, *In Quest of America: A Study of Howells' Early Development as a Novelist* (Uppsala, Sweden, 1928), 31.

7. "Better fifty years of Boston than a cycle of New York, if one may so delapidate 'Lockesley Hall.' The truth is, there is no place quite so good as Boston—God help it! and I look forward to living there some day—being possibly the linchpin in the hub." Howells to J. T. Fields, Aug. 22, 1860 (Howells Papers, Houghton Lib.).

8. "If the salary of this consulate has not been permanently increased, and is only fixed at $1500 during the war, I'll resign directly the war is over; for it won't pay to stay here for $750." Howells to Victoria Howells, Apr. 26, 1862, in *Life in Letters*, I, 57–58, 85, 90.

9. *Ibid.*, 60–61; Howells to Charles Hale, Jan. 31, 1863 (Hale Papers, Smith).

10. *Life in Letters*, I, 60–61, 79; J. M. Comly to Howells, Jan. 4, 1863 (Howells Papers, Houghton Lib.).

11. J. L. Windress, Jr., *Howells in Italy* (Durham, N.C., 1952), 169–70; Howells, *A Fearful Responsibility*, 4, 5, 26.

12. *AM*, XVIII (Oct. 1866), 520; *N*, II (Feb. 1, 1866), 133; *AM*, XXIII (Apr. 1869), 517; XIX (June 1867), 721–22.

13. *AM*, XXIII (Feb. 1869), 261; XIX (Jan. 1867), 126; *H*, LXXX (May 1890), 968; *AM*, XXVIII (July 1871), 124–26.

14. The first installment of the series, Howells wrote to the author, "had brought a hornet's nest about his ears," but by the time the second appeared the hornets had "begun to sing psalms in his ears." Quoted in G. C. Eggleston, *A Rebel's Recollections*, Introduction by David Donald (Bloomington, Ind., 1959), 22.

15. *AM*, XXXV (Feb. 1875), 238; *H*, LXXV (Aug. 1887), 478; William Dean Howells, *Years of My Youth* (New York, N.Y., 1916), 226.

16. Howells, *Years of My Youth*, 190, 188–89.

17. *Ibid.*, 122, 234, 169–70, 231, 233, 226.

18. *N*, II (Feb. 22, 1866), 229; *AM*, XXIV (Nov. 1869), 644; XXXIII (Feb. 1874), 234. See Kermit Vanderbilt, *The Achievement of William Dean Howells* (Princeton, N.J., 1968), 107–108.

19. *NAR*, CLXXIII (Aug. 1901), 280–88.

20. Howells, *Years of My Youth*, 226–27; *NAR*, CXCIII (Jan. 1911), 33.

21. *H*, LXXXII (Jan. 1891), 317–18.

22. Howells, *Years of My Youth*, 233–34.

23. *Ibid.*, 159–60, 234.

24. William Dean Howells, "A Difficult Case," in *A Pair of Patient Lovers* (New York, N.Y., and London, Eng., 1891), 160, 174.

25. *NAR*, CLVIII (Jan. 1894), 193.

26. William Dean Howells, *A Hazard of New Fortunes* (New York, N.Y., 1952), 194, 190, 381, 373, 209.

27. William Dean Howells, *Criticism and Fiction and Other Essays*, ed. C. M. and R. Kirk (New York, N.Y. 1959), 373; *H*, CXL (Jan. 1920), 279.

28. *H*, LXXII (March 1886), 649–50.

29. *Ibid.*

30. *AM*, XVII (May 1866), 647; Howells, *Years of My Youth*, 202–203; *H*, LXXXII (Feb. 1891), 478–83; CXXXVIII (Dec. 1918), 134–36; LXXVI (May 1888), 967; *AM*, XLVIII (Nov. 1881), 707.

31. *H*, LXXXII (Feb. 1891), 480–81.

Chapter 9
MARK TWAIN

1. *Mark Twain's Speeches*, Introduction by William Dean Howells (New York, N.Y., and London, Eng., 1910), 295–97.

2. William Dean Howells, *My Mark Twain* (New York, N.Y., 1911), 36.

3. Arlin Turner, "Mark Twain and the South: An Affair of Love and Anger," *SR*, IV, n.s. (spring 1968), 497.

4. Mark Twain, *Life on the Mississippi* (New York, N.Y. [New American Library], 1961), 277.

5. Paul Fatout, *Mark Twain in Virginia City* (Bloomington, Ind., 1964), 196.

6. The most detailed study of this episode is John Gerber, "Mark Twain's 'Private Campaign,'" *Civil War History*, I (March 1955), 37–60. Gerber includes the text of "The Campaign" in his discussion. All my subsequent citations of it are to his edited version.

7. Mark Twain, *Life on the Mississippi*, 93.

8. Gerber, "'Private Campaign,'" 53.

9. *Ibid.*, 48, 54–55.

10. *Ibid.*, 57–58.

11. Justin Kaplan, *Mr. Clemens and Mark Twain* (New York, N.Y., 1966), 225–27.

12. For a summary of Mark Twain's social and political ideas, see L. J. Budd, *Mark Twain's Social Philosophy* (Bloomington, Ind., 1964).

13. Quoted in H. N. Smith, *Mark Twain's Fable of Progress: Political and Economic Ideas in "A Connecticut Yankee"* (New Brunswick, N.J., 1964), 93.

14. *Ibid.*, 46.

15. Mark Twain, *Life on the Mississippi*, 16.

16. *Ibid.*, 185.

17. *Ibid.*, 237.

18. *Ibid.*, 238. What Mark Twain called the "Sir Walter disease" is discussed at length in S. J. Krause, *Mark Twain as Critic* (Baltimore, Md., 1967), 148–89.

19. Krause, *Mark Twain as Critic*, 173–74.

20. Smith, *Mark Twain's Fable*, 68.

21. *Ibid.*, 93–94.

Chapter 10
GENTLEMEN OF PEACE AND WAR

1. E. C. Stedman, *The Battle of Bull Run* (New York, N.Y., 1861).

2. *Life and Letters of Bayard Taylor*, ed. M. Hansen-Taylor and Horace Scudder (Boston, Mass., 1895), I, 381.

3. Charles G. Leland, *Sunshine in Thought* (1862), facsimile reproduction ed. B. Y. Spencer (Gainesville, Fla., 1959).

4. C. E. Norton to F. L. Olmsted, Sept. 16, 1866 (Olmsted Papers, Library of Congress).

5. Charles G. Leland, *Memoirs* (London, Eng., 1893), II, 22.

6. William Winter, *In Memory of Edmund Clarence Stedman* (New York, N.Y., 1909), 7–8.

7. *Life and Letters of Edmund Clarence Stedman*, ed. Laura Stedman and G. M. Gould (New York, N.Y., 1910), I, 241–43.

8. *Ibid.*, 309–10.

9. George Henry Boker, *Poems of War* (Boston, Mass., 1864), 133.

10. *Ibid.*, 134.

11. Stedman, *Life and Letters*, I, 352.

12. Olmsted Papers, Library of Congress.

13. Oliver Wendell Holmes, "Our Battle Laureate," AM, XV (May 1865), 589–91.

14. Henry Howard Brownell, *Lines of Battle and Other Poems*, ed. M. A. DeWolfe Howe (Boston, Mass., and New York, N.Y., 1912), 59.

15. *Ibid.*, 41.

16. *Official Records of the Union and Confederate Navies in the War of the Rebellion*, Series I, XXI, 415, 420.

17. Brownell, *Lines of Battle*, 29–52.

18. *Ibid.*, 105.

19. Henry Howard Brownell, *Lyrics of a Day; or, Newspaper-Poetry* (Hartford, Conn., 1863), iii–v.

20. RT, III (Jan. 20, 1866), 35.

21. N, LXXXIV (Jan. 10, 1907), 34.

22. N. S. Shaler, "The Border State Men of the Civil War," AM, LXIX (Feb. 1892), 256.

23. *The Autobiography of Nathaniel Southgate Shaler* (Boston, Mass., and New York, N.Y., 1909), 173, 216.

24. *Ibid.*, 196, 195, 211.

25. N, LXXXIV (Jan. 10, 1907), 34–35.

26. N. S. Shaler, *From Old Fields. Poems of the Civil War* (Boston, Mass., and New York, N.Y., 1906), viii.

27. *Ibid.*, 1, 201, 8.

28. *Ibid.*, 3–4.

29. *Ibid.*, 5–8.

30. N. S. Shaler, "The Halted Battle," "The Way with Mutineers," "Those Mules," "The Smugglers," *ibid.*, 9–11, 20–26, 29–38, 86–89.

31. *Ibid.*, 180.

32. Henry James, *The Bostonians* (New York, N.Y. [Modern Library], 1956), 248.

33. T. W. Higginson, "Letter to a Young Contributor," AM, IX (Apr. 1862), 409–10.

34. T. W. Higginson, ed., *Harvard Memorial Biographies* (Cambridge, Mass., 1866), I, v.

35. *Ibid.*, II, 464.

36. *Ibid.*, I, 139.

37. William James, *Memories and Studies* (New York, N.Y., 1911), 57.

38. *Speeches of Oliver Wendell Holmes* (Boston, Mass., 1934), 14, 13.

39. O. W. Holmes, Jr., to C. E. Norton, Apr. 17, 1864 (Houghton Lib.).

40. Quoted in Mark DeWolfe Howe, *Justice Oliver Wendell Holmes. The Shaping Years, 1841–1870* (Cambridge, Mass., 1957), 71.

41. O. W. Holmes, Jr., to C. E. Norton, Apr. 17, 1864 (Houghton Lib.).

42. Howe, *Holmes. The Shaping Years*, 109–10.

43. *Ibid.*, 104, 118, 174, and Holmes, *Speeches*, 4, 11.

44. Holmes, *Speeches*, 3, 59.

45. *The Life and Poems of Theodore Winthrop*, ed. by his sister (New York, N.Y., 1884), 2.

46. Ellsworth Elliot, Jr., *Yale and the Civil War* (New Haven, Conn., 1932), 24–25.

47. John Macy, *The Spirit of American Literature* (New York, N.Y., 1913), 13.

48. *A Cycle of Adams Letters, 1861–1865*, ed. W. C. Ford (Boston, Mass., and New York, N.Y., 1920), II, 32.

49. Higginson, *Harvard Memorial Biographies*, I, 112.

50. *AM*, XIX (Jan. 1867), 125–26.

Chapter 11
JOHN W. DE FOREST

1. John W. De Forest, *A Volunteer's Adventures* (New Haven, Conn., 1946), xvii.

2. John W. De Forest, *European Acquaintance: Being Sketches of People in Europe* (New York, N.Y., 1858), 5.

3. James Light, *John William De Forest* (New York, N.Y., 1965), 15.

4. De Forest to Mrs. George F. De Forest, Dec. 16, 1855 (De Forest Papers, Yale).

5. John W. De Forest, "Charleston Under Arms," *AM*, VII (Apr. 1861), 490.

6. De Forest to Mrs. George F. De Forest, Dec. 16, 1855 (De Forest Papers, Yale).

7. De Forest, "Charleston Under Arms," 490, 489, 496.

8. *Ibid.*, 490.

9. *Ibid.*, 494, 495.

10. John W. De Forest, *Oriental Acquaintance; or, Letters from Syria* (New York, N.Y., 1856), 4–5.

11. De Forest to Andrew De Forest, Nov. 9, 1855 (De Forest Papers, Yale).

12. De Forest to Andrew De Forest, Nov. 14, 1855 (De Forest Papers, Yale).

13. De Forest to Mrs. George F. De Forest, Dec. 16, 1855 (De Forest Papers, Yale).

14. For example, "The Colored Member," *The Galaxy*, XIV (March 1872), 293–94.

15. De Forest, *A Volunteer's Adventures*, 9, 141.

16. *Ibid.*, 108.

17. De Forest to Andrew De Forest, July 17, 1863 (De Forest Papers, Yale).

18. *Ibid.*, Nov. 27, 1863.

19. *Ibid.*, Aug. 17, 1863.

20. De Forest, *A Volunteer's Adventures*, 66, 123, 190.

21. John W. De Forest, *Miss Ravenel's Conversion from Secession to Loyalty* (New York, N.Y., 1955), 460, 453.

22. Edmund Wilson, *Patriotic Gore. Studies in the Literature of the American Civil War* (New York, N.Y., 1962), 690.

23. De Forest, *Miss Ravenel's Conversion*, 461.

24. *Ibid.*, 319.

25. *AM*, XLIV (Nov. 1879), 569.

26. *Ibid.*, 572.

27. *Ibid.*, 573.

28. *Ibid.* (Sept. 1879), 287.

29. *Ibid.*, 288.

30. *Ibid.*

31. *Personal Memoirs of U. S. Grant* (New York, N.Y., 1885), I, 139.

32. *Ibid.*, 96, 92–93.

33. *Ibid.*, 223–24.

34. *Ibid.*, 170.

Chapter 12
AMBROSE BIERCE

1. Paul Fatout, *Ambrose Bierce. The Devil's Lexicographer* (Norman, Okla., 1951), 48–49.

2. Carey McWilliams, *Ambrose Bierce,* with a new Introduction by the author (New York, N.Y., 1967), 55.

3. *The Collected Works of Ambrose Bierce* (New York, N.Y., 1966), IV, 132.

4. Walter Neale, *Life of Ambrose Bierce* (New York, N.Y., 1929), 158.

5. Fatout, *Bierce,* 36.

6. McWilliams, *Bierce,* 29.

7. Fatout, *Bierce,* 159.

8. McWilliams, *Bierce,* 311.

9. Bierce, *Collected Works,* I, 270.

10. *Ibid.*, II, 76.

11. *Ibid.*, I, 225–33.

12. Fatout, *Bierce,* 52.

13. Bierce, *Collected Works,* I, 236, 256, 267, 269, 254–55.

14. *Ibid.*, III, 108–109.

15. *Ibid.*, I, 262.

16. *Ibid.*, 258, 259, 265.

17. *Ibid.*, 290, 284, 291.

18. *Ibid.*, 324, 269.

19. *Ibid.*, II, 63.

20. *Ibid.*, 158, 164.

21. Fatout, *Bierce,* 149.

22. McWilliams, *Bierce,* 67–68.

23. Bierce, *Collected Works,* IV, 118.

24. *Ibid.*, I, 341.

25. *Ibid.*, XI, 398.

26. *Ibid.*, IV, 336.

27. *Ibid.*, V, 64.

28. *Ibid.*, III, 361.

29. *Ibid.*, IV, 116–18.

30. McWilliams, *Bierce,* 319–20.

31. S. C. Woodruff, *The Short Stories of Ambrose Bierce. A Study in Polarity* (Pittsburgh, Pa., 1964), 115.

Chapter 13
ALBION W. TOURGÉE

1. O. H. Olsen, *Carpetbagger's Crusade: The Life of Albion Winegar Tour-gée* (Baltimore, Md., 1965), and T. L. Gross, *Albion W. Tourgée* (New York, N.Y., 1963).

2. Albion W. Tourgée, *Figs and Thistles* (New York, N.Y., 1879), 277.

3. Albion W. Tourgée, *The Story of a Thousand. Being a History of the 105th Ohio Volunteer Infantry, in the War for the Union from August 21, 1862, to June 6, 1865* (Buffalo, N.Y., 1896), 1–2.

4. *Ibid.*, 32, 154.

5. Quoted in Olsen, *Carpetbagger's Crusade*, 24–25.

6. Tourgée, *Figs and Thistles*, 188.

7. Albion W. Tourgée, *An Appeal to Caesar* (New York, N.Y., 1884), 44.

8. *Ibid.*, 56.

9. Gross, *Tourgée*, 31.

10. *The Continent*, IV, No. 23 (1883), 731.

11. Albion W. Tourgée, *Hot Plowshares* (New York, N.Y., 1883), Preface.

12. *The Continent*, IV, No. 23 (1883), 731–32.

13. Tourgée, *An Appeal to Caesar*, 22, 23, 26.

14. Tourgée, *Hot Plowshares*, Preface.

15. Tourgée, *The Story of a Thousand*, 18, 13.

16. Tourgée, *An Appeal to Caesar*, 31.

17. Albion W. Tourgée, *A Royal Gentleman* (New York, N.Y., 1881), iii–iv.

18. Albion W. Tourgée, *Bricks Without Straw* (New York, N.Y., 1886), 176, 253.

19. *Ibid.*, 254.

20. Tourgée, *A Royal Gentleman*, 253–54.

21. Tourgée, *Hot Plowshares*, 66–67, 69, 70.

22. *Ibid.*, 72, 298, 294–95, 295–96.

23. Albion W. Tourgée, *The Veteran and His Pipe* (Chicago, Ill., and New York, N.Y., 1886), 238, 241, 236, 26.

24. *Ibid.*, 232, 229, 230–31.

25. *Ibid.*, 143.

26. Tourgée, *An Appeal to Caesar*, 58, 61, 40, 66.

27. *Ibid.*, 91, 112.

28. Tourgée, *The Veteran and His Pipe*, 157.

29. Tourgée, *An Appeal to Caesar*, 104.

30. Tourgée, *Hot Plowshares*, 149.

31. Tourgée, *An Appeal to Caesar*, 283.

32. Quoted in Gross, *Tourgée*, 143.

Chapter 14
STEPHEN CRANE AND HAROLD FREDERIC

1. *Stephen Crane: An Omnibus*, ed. R. W. Stallman (New York, N.Y., 1952), 211.

2. A vast literature has accumulated on the alleged influencers of Crane, among them Zola, Tolstoy, Kipling, and Bierce. Scholars have detected possible parallels in several books by Jonathan T. Crane (the author's father), and the popular *Corporal Si Klegg, and His "Pard"* (1887), by Wilbur F. Hinman. The latter furnished Crane with essential themes and incidents. *Stephen Crane. The Red Badge of Courage*, ed. Sculley Bradley, R. C. Beatty, and E. Hudson Long (New York, N.Y. [Norton Critical Edns.], 1962), 132–86, summarizes Crane's use of sources. An indispensable source of Craneana is R. M. Stallman, *Stephen Crane. A Biography* (New York, N.Y., 1968).

3. George F. Williams, "Lights and Shadows of Army Life," C, XXVIII (Oct. 1884), 803–19.

4. Ira S. Dodd, *The Song of the Rappahannock* (New York, N.Y., 1898), 3.

5. *Ibid.*, 43.

6. *Ibid.*, 47.

7. *Ibid.*, 61.

8. *Ibid.*, 98.

9. Quoted in *Stephen Crane: Letters*, ed. R. W. Stallman and Lillian Gilkes (New York, N.Y., 1960), 139.

10. Edward Garnett, "Stephen Crane: An Appreciation," *London Academy*, Dec. 17, 1898. Reprinted in *Stephen Crane. The Red Badge of Courage*, 201.

11. Stephen Crane, *The Red Badge of Courage. An Episode in the American Civil War*, ed. F. C. Crews (Indianapolis, Ind. [The Library of Literature, Bobbs-Merrill], 1964), 4.

12. Crane, *The Red Badge*, 37.

13. *Ibid.*, 50, 53.

14. *Ibid.*, 56, 57–59, 60–61, 82, 87.

15. *Ibid.*, 124, 132.

16. *Ibid.*, 128.

17. *The Works of Stephen Crane*, ed. Wilson Follett (New York, N.Y., 1925), II, 30, 39.

18. *Ibid.*, 44–45, 39.

19. *Ibid.*, 46, 49, 47.

20. Quoted in Stallman, *Stephen Crane*, 186.

21. *Ibid.*

22. Stephen Crane, "Harold Frederic," *The Chap-Book*, VIII (March 15, 1898), 358–59.

23. "Dedication" to Stephen Crane, *The Copperhead and Other Stories of the North During the American War* (London, Eng., 1894).

24. "Marsena," in *Harold Frederic's Stories of York State*, ed. T. F. O'Donnell (Syracuse, N.Y., 1966), 198–99.

25. *Ibid.*, 201, 208.

26. Frederic, "The Copperhead," in *ibid.*, 212–13.

27. *Ibid.*, 276, 290, 121, 330.

28. *Ibid.*, 3, 4, 6.

29. *Ibid.*, 7.

30. *Ibid.*, 38, 106.

31. T. F. O'Donnell and H. C. Franchere, *Harold Frederic* (New York, N.Y., 1961), 23, 27.

32. *The Diary of George Templeton Strong*, ed. Allan Nevins and M. H. Thomas (New York, N.Y., 1952), III, 389, 390, 455, 536.

33. O'Donnell and Franchere, *Harold Frederic*, 41.

34. Stewart Mitchell, *Horatio Seymour of New York* (Cambridge, Mass., 1939), 240. For further accounts of New York State's political scene during the War, see R. J. Rayback, "New York State in the Civil War," *New York History*, XLII (Jan. 1961), 56–70, and J. A. Frost, "The Home Front in New York During the Civil War," in *ibid.* (July 1961), 273–97.

35. Frederic, *Stories of York State*, 62.

36. *Ibid.*, 217, 216, 286–87.

37. *Ibid.*, 165.

38. Crane, "Harold Frederic," 359.

39. Frederic, *Stories of York State*, xv, 234.

40. David G. Croly, *Seymour and Blair. Their Lives and Services* (New York, N.Y., 1868), 84.

Chapter 15
WRITERS IN THE CONFEDERACY

1. *The Letters of William Gilmore Simms,* ed. M. S. S. Oliphant, A. T. Odell, and T. C. D. Eaves (Columbia, S.C., 1955), IV, 346; III, 548–49.

2. *Ibid.,* III, 465–66, 469.

3. See J. R. Welsh, "William Gilmore Simms, Critic of the South," *JSH,* XXVI (May 1960), 201–14, and J. V. Ridgly, *William Gilmore Simms* (New York, N.Y., 1962), 124, 130.

4. Simms, *Letters,* IV, 266, 356.

5. *Southern Field and Fireside,* II (Apr. 1860), 28; *The Index,* IV (1864), 474–75; Simms, *Letters,* I, cxxv.

6. Quoted in J. B. Hubbell, "Literary Nationalism in the Old South," in *American Studies in Honor of William Kenneth Boyd,* ed. D. K. Jackson (Durham, N.C., 1940), 207–208; *SLM,* XXXIII (Sept. 1861), 237.

7. *The Southern Monthly,* I (Sept. 1861), 4.

8. *SLM,* XXXIV (May 1862), 313; XXXIII (Oct. 1861), 316–17; XXXII (Apr. 1861), 310; XXXIV (May 1862), 313; XXXVII (Oct. 1863), 621–24; *The Confederate.* By a South Carolinian (Mobile, Ala., 1863), 54.

9. *SLM,* XXXIV (May 1862), 314; *Southern Field and Fireside,* III (Sept. 1861), 21, 140; *SLM,* XXXVII (Oct. 1863), 624; *Southern Field and Fireside,* IV (1862), 15.

10. *The Index,* III (1863), 347–48; *SLM,* XXXVIII (May 1864), 314; *Southern Field and Fireside,* III (Nov. 1861), 24, 188; III (Feb. 1862), 38, 255.

11. Joseph L. King, *Dr. George William Bagby. A Study of Virginia Literature, 1850–1880* (New York, N.Y., 1927), 105.

12. *Ibid.* See George C. Eggleston, ed., *American War Ballads and Lyrics* (New York, N.Y., and London, Eng., 1888), I, 7; G. A. Sala, *My Diary in America* (London, Eng., 1865), I, 394.

13. C. G. Leland, "War Songs and Their Influence on History," *The United States Service Magazine,* I (Jan. 1864), 48; Brander Matthews, "The Songs of the Civil War," in *Pen and Ink. Papers on Subjects of More or Less Importance* (New York, N.Y., 1902), 185; Richard G. White, ed., *Poetry, Lyrical, Narrative, and Satirical, of the Civil War* (New York, N.Y., 1866), iii–iv.

14. *The Essays of Henry Timrod,* ed. E. W. Parks (Athens, Ga., 1942), 160–61; J. B. Hubbell, *The Last Years of Henry Timrod, 1864–1867* (Durham, N.C., 1941), 156; W. P. Trent, *William Gilmore Simms* (New York, N.Y., 1892), 297.

15. Sidney Lanier to P. H. Hayne, March 5, 1870 (copy in Hayne Papers, Duke); Hayne to J. R. Lowell, Dec. 28, 1859 (Houghton Lib.); Hayne to Horatio Woodman, Aug. 19, 1860 (Massachusetts Historical Society); Hayne to ?, n.d. (summer 1866, copy Hayne Papers, Duke); Hubbell, *Last Years,* 103.

16. P. H. Hayne to R. H. Stoddard, July 23, 1855 (Hayne Papers, Duke); William Fidler, "Unpublished Letters of Henry Timrod," *SLM,* II (Nov. 1940), 605.

17. Timrod, *Essays,* 86–87.

18. *Ibid.,* 88, 97, 100.

19. Fidler, "Unpublished Letters," *SLM,* II (Dec. 1940), 650.

20. *Ibid.* (Nov. 1940), 608; *The Collected Poems of Henry Timrod,* ed. E. W. Parks and A. W. Parks (Athens, Ga., 1965), 93, 95.

21. Timrod, *Collected Poems,* 96, 98, 135, 100; Hubbell, *Last Years,* 141.

22. Fidler, "Unpublished Letters," *SLM*, II (Nov. 1940), 609; Hubbell, *Last Years*, 141, 143.

23. Timrod, *Collected Poems*, 115–16.

24. E. W. Parks, *Henry Timrod* (New York, N.Y., 1964), 38.

25. Timrod, *Collected Poems*, 127, 117, 124, 126.

26. *Ibid.*, 118; Hubbell, *Last Years*, 144–45, 142.

27. Hubbell, *Last Years*, 136, 134, 147; Sarah B. Elliott, "Some Data, a Sketch," in *From Dixie* (Richmond, Va., 1893), 160.

28. *Crescent Monthly*, I (Apr. 1866), 67; "Is the South Sunk in Barbarism?" *The Land We Love*, I (Aug. 1866), 286.

29. *Crescent Monthly*, I (Apr. 1866), 67; (May 1866), 156–58; *The Land We Love*, II (March 1867), 332; V (Aug. 1868), 370–71; W. H. Browne to P. H. Hayne, July 30, 1870 (Hayne Papers, Duke).

30. W. H. Browne to P. H. Hayne, July 30, 1870 (Hayne Papers, Duke).

31. *The Southern Review*, XI (July 1872), 42.

Chapter 16
THE UNWRITTEN NOVEL

1. Diary of Paul Hamilton Hayne, Dec. 19, 1870 (Hayne Papers, Duke).

2. John W. De Forest, "Chivalrous and Semi-Chivalrous Southerners," *H*, XXXVIII (Jan.–Feb. 1869), 347.

3. Quoted in Kenneth Lynn, *Mark Twain and Southwestern Humor* (Boston, Mass., 1959), 231.

4. De Forest, "Chivalrous and Semi-Chivalrous Southerners," 347.

5. J. B. Hubbell, *The South in American Literature* (Durham, N.C., 1954), 520.

6. Quoted in John Esten Cooke, *Outlines from the Outpost*, ed. Richard Harwell (Chicago, Ill., 1961), xviii.

7. *Ibid.*, 61.

8. Quoted in J. O. Beaty, *John Esten Cooke, Virginian* (Port Washington, N.Y., 1965), 109.

9. J. E. Cooke, *Surrey of Eagle's Nest* (New York, N.Y., 1866), 10.

10. J. E. Cooke, *Mohun or, The Last Days of Lee and His Paladins* (New York, N.Y., 1869), 3, 9–10.

11. Edmund Wilson, *Patriotic Gore. Studies in the Literature of the American Civil War* (New York, N.Y., 1962), 690.

12. Richard Taylor, *Destruction and Reconstruction: Personal Experiences of the Late War*, ed. R. B. Harwell (New York, N.Y., 1955), 110.

13. Cooke, *Outlines*, 49–50, 52.

14. Taylor, *Destruction*, 89, 91.

15. *Ibid.*, 111–12, 81, 87; Cooke, *Surrey of Eagle's Nest*, 221–23.

16. Cecil D. Eby, Jr., *"Porte Crayon": The Life of David Hunter Strother* (Chapel Hill, N.C., 1960), 100, 106.

17. David Hunter Strother, "Personal Recollections of the War," *H*, XXXIII (June 1866), 7.

18. Eby, *"Porte Crayon,"* 117.

19. *A Virginia Yankee in the Civil War. The Diaries of David Hunter Strother*, ed. Cecil D. Eby, Jr. (Chapel Hill, N.C., 1961), xvi–xix.

20. *Ibid.*, 150, 120, 22.

21. *Ibid.*, 67, 121–22, 191.

22. *Ibid.*, 67, 140; Eby, *"Porte Crayon,"* 154–55.

23. *H*, XXXIV (Jan. 1867), 181; Strother, *Diaries*, 208.

24. Mary Boykin Chesnut, *A Diary from Dixie* (Boston, Mass., 1949), 196, 118, 463, 89.

25. *Ibid.*, 331.

26. *Ibid.*, 255, 219.

27. *Ibid.*, 213, 430, 433.

28. *Ibid.*, 489.

29. *Ibid.*, 20, 168.

30. *Ibid.*, 21–22, 122.

31. *Ibid.*, 165, 163, 169.

32. *Ibid.*, 346.

33. Quoted in Wilson, *Patriotic Gore*, 195.

34. Chesnut, *A Diary from Dixie*, 319, 374, 461, 218.

35. *Ibid.*, 280, 281, 449.

36. *Ibid.*, 169, 172, 534, 510, 161, 390.

37. *Ibid.*, 229, 64, 142, 172.

38. *Ibid.*, 156, 159.

39. *Ibid.*, 212, 91.

40. *Ibid.*, 46, 347.

41. *Ibid.*, 411.

42. *Ibid.*, 468, 162.

43. *Ibid.*, 382.

44. *Ibid.*, 82, 115, 166, 239, 461, 408, 543.

45. *Ibid.*, 11, 521, 363, 345, 247.

46. *Ibid.*, 131, 488, 38.

47. *Ibid.*, 545, 547.

Chapter 17
SIDNEY LANIER

1. C. R. Anderson, ed., *The Centennial Edition of the Works of Sidney Lanier* (Baltimore, Md., 1945), VII, 34.

2. *Ibid.*, V, 198.

3. *Ibid.*, 96–97.

4. *Ibid.*, VII, 226–27.

5. *Ibid.*, 61, 163.

6. *Ibid.*, VIII, 35; A. H. Starke, *Sidney Lanier: A Biographical and Critical Study* (Chapel Hill, N.C., 1933), 65; Lanier, *Works*, V, 154.

7. Lanier, *Works*, V, 204; VII, 304.

8. *Ibid.*, VI, 92, 97–98, 230.

9. *Ibid.*, V, 159.

10. *Ibid.*, 134, 135.

11. *Ibid.*, 166.

12. *Ibid.*, I, 6–8.

13. *Ibid.*, xi, 303, 4, 15, 167.

14. *Ibid.*, IX, 121–22; VIII, 223–24.

15. *Ibid.*, V, 249, 263, 275, 266.

16. *Ibid.*, V, 266; X, 122–23.

Chapter 18
GEORGE WASHINGTON CABLE

1. C. R. Anderson, "Charles Gayarré and Paul Hayne: The Last Literary Cavaliers," in *American Studies in Honor of William Kenneth Boyd*, ed. D. K. Jackson (Durham, N.C., 1940), 247.

2. George Washington Cable, "We of the South," *C*, XXIX (Nov. 1884), 152.

3. Henry W. Grady, "In Plain Black and White. A Reply to Mr. Cable," *C*, XXIX (Apr. 1885), 917.

4. George Washington Cable, "New Orleans Before the Capture," *C*, XXIX (Apr. 1885), 922.

5. Arlin Turner, *George W. Cable. A Biography* (Durham, N.C., 1956), 24–26.

6. Anderson, "Gayarré and Hayne," 226. See also Charles Duffy, "A Southern Genteelist: Letters of Paul Hamilton Hayne to Julia C. R. Dorr," *The South Carolina Historical and Genealogical Society*, LCIII (Jan. 1952), 22.

7. Quoted in Kjell Ekstrom, *George Washington Cable. A Study of His Early Life and Work* (Uppsala, Sweden, and Cambridge, Mass., 1950), 27.

8. George Washington Cable, *Kincaid's Battery* (New York, N.Y., 1908), 163.

9. George Washington Cable, *The Negro Question. A Selection of Writings on Civil Rights*, ed. Arlin Turner (New York, N.Y., 1958), 4.

10. *Ibid.*, 5.

11. *Ibid.*, 6–9.

12. *Ibid.*, 21.

13. *Ibid.*, 15.

14. *Ibid.*, 81.

15. Cable, "We of the South," 151.

16. Cable, *The Negro Question*, 39, 41.

17. *Ibid.*, 134, 135, 155.

18. *Ibid.*, 139, 116, 63.

19. *Ibid.*, 71.

20. For the reference to Douglass, see Guy A. Cardwell, *Twins of Genius* (Lansing, Mich., 1953), 22. The tribute to Garrison and Phillips is quoted in Arlin Turner, *Mark Twain and George W. Cable. The Record of a Literary Friendship* (Lansing, Mich., 1960), 85. Turner's *George W. Cable*, 22, 206, is my source for the birthday letter to Mrs. Stowe and Mrs. Cable.

21. "But I believe the time is not very far away," he told a graduating class at the University of Mississippi in 1882, "when anyone who rises before you and addresses you as 'Southrons' shall be stared at as the veriest Rip Van Winkle that the time can show" (Cable, *The Negro Question*, 44).

22. *Ibid.*, 2–5.

23. *Ibid.*, 14.

24. George Washington Cable, *The Grandissimes*, ed. Newton Arvin (New York, N.Y. [American Century Series], 1957), 282–84, 326–27.

25. Lafcadio Hearn, an admirer of *The Grandissimes*, argued that abolitionists would never have won over the racist-minded to their position without the presence of the "colored race," his name for the people of mixed blood: "In the first place, they formed as a body the great living testimony to slavery's worst sin; and that testimony . . . more than any other, brought in the courts of human conscience, and in the courts of governments, the conviction and condemnation of the sin itself. Their very existence tended above all else to kindle the world's shame of slavery as a vice; while the force, beauty, and intelligence of the race conquered the sympathy of humanity. There are many evidences in the pages of anti-slavery literature to show that the writer was thinking of the man of color while pleading for the negro, whose nature he never clearly understood." Albert Mordell, ed., *An American Miscellany* (New York, N.Y., 1924), 225–26. In another comment applicable to Cable's novel, Hearn suggested that the denial of race quality on the part of whites forced "men of color" into an alliance with Negroes. The latter were used to slavery

and had known it in Africa. But the mixed-blooded Negro taught the blacks the injustice of their bondage and inculcated into them the moral power to rebel.

26. Cable, *The Grandissimes*, 197.

27. *Ibid.*, 251.

28. *Ibid.*, 315.

29. *C*, XXVIII (Oct. 1884), 943.

Chapter 19
THE NEO-CONFEDERATES

1. Thomas Nelson Page, "Personal Recollections of the Opening of the Civil War" (copy, Dec. 10, 1912, in Thomas Nelson Page Papers, Duke).

2. James Branch Cabell, *Let Me Lie* (New York, N.Y., 1947), 241, quoted in J. B. Hubbell, *The South in American Literature* (Durham, N.C., 1954), 803.

3. Quoted in P. M. Gaston, *The New South Creed. A Study in Southern Mythmaking* (New York, N.Y., 1970), 56, 174, 167, 173.

4. Hubbell, *The South in American Literature*, 801.

5. *The Novels, Stories, Sketches and Poems of Thomas Nelson Page* (New York, N.Y., 1906–12), XII, 363. Henceforth referred to as Page, *Works*.

6. J. B. Cabell successfully parodied Page in *The Rivet in Grandfather's Neck* (New York, N.Y., 1915). Here is a sample: " 'Why, jes arter dat, suh, a hut Yankee cap'en, whar some uv our folks done shoot in de laig, wuz lef on de road fer daid'—a quite notorious custom on the part of all Northern armies—'un Young Miss had him fotch up ter de gret house, un nuss im same's he one uv de fambly, un dem two jes fit un argufy scanlous un never spicion huccom dey's in love wid each othuh till de War's ovuh' " (1920 edn., 159).

7. Page, *Works*, XII, 346, 359, 221.

8. *Ibid.*, 360, 368.

9. *Ibid.*, 221, 369.

10. Edwin Mims, "Thomas Nelson Page," *AM*, C (July 1907), 115.

11. Page's insistence on White Supremacy (which at times came close to Thomas Dixon's in virulence) is fully discussed in Harriet R. Holman, *The Literary Career of Thomas Nelson Page* (doctoral diss., Duke, 1947), in Edmund Wilson, *Patriotic Gore. Studies in the Literature of the American Civil War* (New York, N.Y., 1962), 604–11, and in T. L. Gross, *Thomas Nelson Page* (New York, N.Y., 1967), 105–12.

12. Thomas Nelson Page, "Literature in the South Since the War," *Lippincott's Monthly Magazine*, XLVIII (Dec. 1891), 748.

13. Thomas Nelson Page, *The Negro: The Southerner's Problem* (New York, N.Y., 1904), 240.

14. Corra Harris, "The Waning Influence of Thomas Nelson Page," reprinted in *Current Opinion*, XLIII (Aug. 1907), 171.

15. Ellen Glasgow, *A Certain Measure, An Interpretation of Prose Fiction* (New York, N.Y., 1943), 21.

16. *Ibid.*, 138–39.

17. *Ibid.*, 140, 143.

18. Louise Cowan, *The Fugitive Group: A Literary History* (Baton Rouge, La., 1959), 245, 116, 44; Frederick Hoffman *et al.*, *The Little Magazine: A History and Bibliography* (Princeton, N.J., 1946), 121.

19. Cowan, *Fugitive Group*, 241, 244.

20. Cowan, *Fugitive Group*, 247; John L. Stewart, *The Burden of Time. The Fugitives and Agrarians* (Princeton, N.J., 1965), 118.

21. R. A. Lively, *Fiction Fights the Civil War* (Chapel Hill, N.C., 1957), 63, 187.

22. W. P. Trent, "Dominant Forces in Southern Life," *AM*, LXXIX (Jan. 1897), 46.

23. Alexander Karanikas, *Tillers of a Myth: Southern Agrarians as Social Critics* (Madison, Wis., 1966), 59–74; Stark Young, *So Red the Rose* (New York, N.Y., 1934), 384.

24. "He [Calhoun] had argued justly that only in a society of fixed classes can men be free." Allen Tate, *Stonewall Jackson, The Good Soldier* (New York, N.Y., 1928), 39.

25. *New Republic*, LIX (July 10, 1929), 212; XLIX (Feb. 9, 1927), 329; John Crowe Ransom, "Reconstructed but Unregenerate," in *I'll Take My Stand*, by Twelve Southerners (New York, N.Y. [Harper Torchbooks], 1962), 13, 12.

26. Stark Young, *The Pavilion. Of People and Times Remembered, Of Stories and Places* (New York, N.Y., 1951), 28.

27. Donald Davidson, "A Note on American Heroes," *SR*, I (winter 1936), 447.

28. R. R. Purdy, ed., *The Fugitives' Reunion: Conversations at Vanderbilt* (Nashville, Tenn., 1959), 49.

29. *Ibid.*, 34, 62.

30. *Ibid.*, 149–50, 161; Allen Tate, Foreword to Andrew Lytle, *The Hero with the Private Parts* (Baton Rouge, La., 1966), xvi.

31. Allen Tate, quoted in Leonard Greenbaum, *The Hound & Horn. The History of a Literary Quarterly* (London, Eng., The Hague, Neth., Paris, Fr., 1966), 131; *New Republic*, LXVI (Feb. 18, 1931), 24–25.

32. Andrew Lytle, in *Hound & Horn*, V (July–Sept. 1932), 688–90.

33. Andrew Lytle, *Bedford Forrest and His Critter Company* (New York, N.Y., 1931), 27.

34. Allen Tate, *Jefferson Davis, His Rise and Fall* (New York, N.Y., 1929), 69.

35. Young, *The Pavilion*, 60–61.

36. Allen Tate to Lincoln Kirstein, May 10, 1933, quoted in Greenbaum, *Hound & Horn*, 145–48.

37. Allen Tate, in *New Republic*, LIX (June 10, 1929), 211; R. P. Warren, "The Second American Revolution," *VQR*, VII (Apr. 1931), 288.

38. Quoted in George Core, "A Mirror for Fiction: The Criticism of Andrew Lytle," *Georgia Review*, XXII (summer 1968), 211.

39. R. K. Meiners, *The Last Alternatives. A Study of the Works of Allen Tate* (Denver, Colo., 1963), 28; *The Collected Essays of John Peale Bishop*, ed. and with an Introduction by Edmund Wilson (New York, N.Y., 1948), 54. Andrew Lytle, "The Lincoln Myth," *VQR*, VII (Oct. 1931), 620–26.

40. Donald Davidson, Introduction to Young, *So Red the Rose*, xxxi.

41. Lytle, *Hero with the Private Parts*, 460; Young, *So Red the Rose*, 305, 316, 385.

42. Young, *So Red the Rose*, 395; Allen Tate, "Last Days of the Charming Lady," *N*, CXXI (Oct. 28, 1925), 485.

43. Allen Tate, Foreword to Lytle, *Hero with the Private Parts*, xvi.

44. J. C. Ransom, in *SR*, II (1936–7), 403.

45. Davidson, Introduction to Young, *So Red the Rose*, xxx.

46. Tate, Foreword to Lytle, *Hero with the Private Parts*, xiv.

47. Allen Tate, in *N*, CXXVII (Sept. 19, 1928), 274.

48. Allen Tate, *The Fathers* (New York, N.Y., 1938), 101, 185, 179, 185–86.

49. Robert Penn Warren, "The Art of Fiction," *Paris Review*, IV (spring–summer 1957), 122, 124; Irving Howe, in *The New York Review of Books*, Aug. 8, 1965, 26.

50. Robert Penn Warren, *John Brown, The Making of a Martyr* (New York, N.Y., 1929), 332.

51. Warren, "The Art of Fiction," 125.

52. Warren, *John Brown*, 332.

53. *Ibid.*, 318, 136, 391, 314.

54. Warren, "The Art of Fiction," 119.

55. Robert Penn Warren, *The Legacy of the Civil War* (New York, N.Y., 1961), 34.

56. *Ibid.*, 36, 23.

57. Warren, *John Brown*, 317.

58. Robert Penn Warren, "Edmund Wilson's Civil War," *Commentary*, XXXIV (Aug. 1962), 153.

59. Warren, *Legacy of the Civil War*, 3, 68.

60. *Ibid.*, 103, 80.

Chapter 20
WILLIAM FAULKNER

1. Allen Tate, *Collected Essays* (Denver, Colo., 1959), 292.

2. Malcolm Cowley, *The Faulkner–Cowley File: Letters and Memories, 1944–1962* (New York, N.Y., 1966), 79.

3. *The Address of Col. Paul H. Hayne of South Carolina, Before the Ladies of the Memorial Association of Alabama* (Montgomery, Ala., 1872), 8.

4. Cowley, *Faulkner–Cowley File*, 78–79; G. C. Eggleston, *A Rebel's Recollections*, Introduction by David Donald (Bloomington, Ind., 1959), 57.

5. Cowley, *Faulkner–Cowley File*, 78.

6. Albion W. Tourgée, *The Veteran and His Pipe* (Chicago, Ill., and New York, N.Y., 1886), 235–36; William Faulkner, *Absalom! Absalom!* (New York, N.Y., 1951), 12; William Faulkner, *Intruder in the Dust* (New York, N.Y. [Modern Library], 1948), 194–95.

7. William Faulkner, *Requiem for a Nun* (New York, N.Y., 1950), 229–37.

8. William Faulkner, *The Town* (New York, N.Y. [Vintage Books], 1959), 7.

9. William Faulkner, *The Unvanquished* (New York, N.Y. [New American Library], 1959), 107–109.

10. Faulkner, *Absalom! Absalom!*, 9.

11. William Faulkner, *Light in August* (New York, N.Y. [Modern Library], 1959), 447, 57, 458–59, 462.

12. William Faulkner, *Sartoris* (New York, N.Y., 1929), 10, 16.

13. *Ibid.*, 9.

14. Faulkner, *The Unvanquished*, 114–15, 220, 273.

15. *Ibid.*, 29.

16. Faulkner, *Absalom! Absalom!*, 9, 12.

17. Faulkner, *Sartoris*, 230.

18. Faulkner, *The Unvanquished*, 155.

19. Faulkner, *Intruder in the Dust*, 215–16.

20. William Faulkner, *Go Down, Moses* (New York, N.Y., 1942), 284–85.

21. Cleanth Brooks, *William Faulkner. The Yoknapatawpha Country* (New Haven, Conn., and London, Eng., 1963), 94.

22. Faulkner, *Absalom! Absalom!*, 122, 130.

Conclusion
"Such Was the War"

1. H. A. Beers, *Points at Issue* (New York, N.Y., and London, Eng., 1904), 69.

2. W. H. Gardiner to C. G. Loring, March 9, 1863 (Loring Papers, Houghton Lib.).

3. Count Agéner de Gasparin, *The Uprising of a Great People. The United States in 1861* (New York, N.Y., 1861), 10–11.

4. J. S. Haller, Jr., *Outcasts from Evolution: Scientific Attitudes of Racial Inferiority, 1859–1900* (Urbana, Ill., 1971).

5. Olmsted to C. E. Norton, March 3, 1862 (Olmsted Papers, Library of Congress); *The Letters of Bret Harte,* ed. G. B. Harte (Boston, Mass., and New York, N.Y., 1926), 41; Notebook #18, Oct. 1884–Apr. 1885 (Mark Twain Papers, University of California, Berkeley); Maurice Thompson to R. W. Gilder, Aug. 30, 1889 (Century Collection, New York Public Lib.).

6. Charles G. Halpine, "The Marching Soldier. His Joys and Sorrows" (unpublished lecture, *c.* 1865, Halpine Papers, Huntington Lib.).

7. G. A. Sala, *My Diary in America* (London, Eng., 1865), I, 391.

8. Oscar Handlin, "The Civil War as Symbol and as Actuality," *The Massachusetts Review,* III (1961), 143.

9. *Letters of John Ruskin to Charles Eliot Norton* (Boston, Mass., and New York, N.Y., 1905), I, 146.

10. John Ruskin, *The Crown of Wild Olives* (Philadelphia, Pa., 1895), 112–13.

11. T. W. Higginson, "Americanism in Literature," in *Atlantic Essays* (Boston, Mass., 1871), 53.

12. Robert Falk, *The Victorian Mode in American Fiction, 1865–1885* (Lansing, Mich., 1965), 20.

13. Higginson, "Americanism in Literature," 56.

14. *The Complete Works of Theodore Tilton* (London, Eng., 1897), xxxix–xl.

15. *RT,* IV (Apr. 11, 1866), 24.

16. E. K. Whipple, *Success and Its Conditions* (Boston, Mass., 1871), 299.

17. W. B. Harte, "Why American Novels Are Flabby," *The Anti-Philistine,* No. IV (Sept. 15, 1897), 275.

18. More than three hundred, according to R. A. Lively, *Fiction Fights the Civil War* (Chapel Hill, N.C., 1957), 22.

19. Basil Gildersleeve, ed., *Pindar. The Olympian and Pythian Odes* (New York, N.Y., 1885), viii–xii.

20. James G. Randall, *Lincoln the President: Springfield to Gettysburg* (New York, N.Y., 1945), I, 93.

21. For a shrewd comment on *Gone With the Wind,* see David Donald's review of Finis Farr, *Margaret Mitchell of Atlanta,* in *Book Week,* Jan. 23, 1966, 5.

22. Sherwood Anderson, *Windy McPherson's Son* (New York, N.Y., 1916), 21–22.

Supplement 1

1. Quoted in W. E. Barton, *Lincoln at Gettysburg* (Indianapolis, Ind., 1930), 239.

2. James Russell Lowell, *Political Essays* (Boston, Mass., and New York, N.Y., 1899), 53.

3. "The Difference of Race Between the Northern and the Southern People," *SLM*, XXX (June 1860), 401–409.

4. *H*, XXIV (Feb. 1862), 406.

5. *Ibid.*, XXV (Oct. 1862), 628.

6. *Ibid.*, 633.

7. C. C. Hazewell, "Panic Terror," *AM*, VIII (Oct. 1861), 497–98.

8. H. M. Alden, "Pericles and President Lincoln," *AM*, XI (March 1863), 390–91.

Supplement 2

1. Charles G. Halpine, *Baked Meats of the Funeral, Collection of Essays, Poems, Speeches, Histories, and Banquets* (New York, N.Y., 1866), 91–92.

2. *The Letters of Herman Melville*, ed. M. R. Davis and W. H. Gilman (New York, N.Y., 1960), 209–10.

3. *The Correspondence of John Lothrop Motley*, ed. G. W. Curtis (New York, N.Y., and London, Eng., 1900), in *Works*, XVI, 143, 158, 262; XVII, 556–57.

4. *Journals of Ralph Waldo Emerson*, ed. E. W. and W. E. Emerson (Boston, Mass., and New York, N.Y., 1909), IX, 556–57.

5. For characteristic denigrations of Lincoln by the bookish class, see estimates of Charles Francis Adams, in *The Journal of Benjamin Moran*, ed. S. A. Wallace and F. E. Gillespie (Chicago, Ill., 1948), II, 1092; Orestes Brownson, in the *Boston Quarterly Review*, I (Apr. 1864), 210–35; and *Letters of Francis Parkman*, ed. W. R. Jacobs (Norman, Okla., 1960), I, 153.

6. *A Virginia Yankee in the Civil War. The Diaries of David Hunter Strother*, ed. C. D. Eby, Jr. (Chapel Hill, N.C., 1961), 191.

7. The phrase is Edmund Wilson's. See *Patriotic Gore. Studies in the Literature of the American Civil War* (New York, N.Y., 1962), 117.

8. *Lincoln and the Civil War in the Diaries and Letters of John Hay*, ed. Tyler Dennett (New York, N.Y., 1939), 91.

9. *The Diary of George Templeton Strong*, ed. Allan Nevins and M. H. Thomas (New York, N.Y., 1952), III, 188, 587.

10. O. B. Frothingham, "The Murdered President," *The Friend of Progress*, I (June 1865), 235–36.

11. See John Weiss, "April 19, 1865," *The Friend of Progress*, I (June 1865), 225–26; Adam Gurowski, *Diary: 1863–'64–'65* (Washington, D.C., 1866), 398–99; Edward Everett Hale, Jr., *The Life and Letters of Edward Everett Hale* (Boston, Mass., 1917), I, 382; G. H. Boker, *Our Heroic Themes* (Boston, Mass., 1865), 4–20; M. A. DeWolfe Howe, *Memories of a Hostess* (Boston, Mass., 1922), 28; Garth Wilkinson James to his parents, Apr. 27, 1865 (Massachusetts Historical Society); *The Life of John A. Andrew*, ed. H. G. Pearson (Boston, Mass., and New York, N.Y., 1904), II, 245.

Supplement 3

1. Mrs. Jessie B. Frémont to Elizabeth Peabody, Jan. 27, 1864 (Horace Mann Papers, Massachusetts Historical Society).

2. Theodore Winthrop to G. W. Curtis, May 15–19, 1861 (George Washington Curtis Papers, Houghton Lib.).

3. Quoted in A. R. Ferguson, *Edward Rowland Sill* (The Hague, Neth., 1955), 47.

4. Quoted in E. P. Earnest, *S. Weir Mitchell, Novelist and Physician* (Philadelphia, Pa., 1950), 46.

5. W. J. Tucker, *My Generation. An Autobiographical Interpretation* (Boston, Mass., and New York, N.Y., 1919), 51–52.

6. Ellsworth Elliot, *Yale in the Civil War* (New York, N.Y., 1932), 8.

7. Mark DeWolfe Howe, *Justice Oliver Wendell Holmes. The Shaping Years, 1841–1870* (Cambridge, Mass., 1957), 84.

8. F. DeWolfe Miller, Introduction to *Drum-Taps and Sequel to Drum-Taps (1865–6)*, a facsimile reproduction (Gainesville, Fla., 1959), xv; and Howe, *Holmes. The Shaping Years,* 72–73.

Supplement 4

1. *The Poems of Emily Dickinson,* ed. Thomas H. Johnson (Cambridge, Mass., 1955), III, 830.

2. Emily Dickinson to T. W. Higginson, quoted in Jay Leyda, *The Years and Hours of Emily Dickinson* (New Haven, Conn., 1960), II, 90; Dickinson, *Poems,* II, 456, 491; I, 285–86.

3. David Higgins, *Portrait of Emily Dickinson. The Poet and Her Prose* (New Brunswick, N.J., 1967), 109; Dickinson, *Poems,* I, 205; II, 491; I, 330, 343.

4. Dickinson, *Poems,* I, 318; III, 826 ("Step lightly on this narrow spot—"), I, 343; III, 854.

5. Thomas W. Ford, "Emily Dickinson and the Civil War," *The University Review–Kansas City,* XXXI (spring 1965), 199.

6. *The Letters of Emily Dickinson,* ed. Thomas H. Johnson (Cambridge, Mass., 1958), II, 397.

Acknowledgments

A NUMBER OF FRIENDS and colleagues were good enough to read parts of this book in manuscript and to offer useful criticisms. Among them were Marcus Cunliffe, David Cavitch, Stanley Elkins, Dean Flower, Arnold Goldman, Sidney Kaplan, R. W. B. Lewis, Kenneth S. Lynn, Norman MacKenzie, James Meriwether, Frank Murphy, Virginia Rock, Sylvan Schendler, and Arlin Turner.

I am especially indebted to Elizabeth Duvall, former archivist of the Sophia Smith Collection at Smith College, and to Richard Harwell, Kay S. House, Harold M. Hyman, Justin Kaplan, and Allen Weinstein for their extensive criticisms and suggestions. Norman Holmes Pearson generously made his collection of Hawthorne letters available to me.

My thanks and gratitude go to the staffs and directors of the Huntington Library, the New York Public Library, the Library of Congress, the Massachusetts Historical Society, the Duke University Library, the University of North Carolina Library, the Harvard University Library, the Yale University Library, the Library of the Boston Athenaeum, and the Smith College Library.

Professor Allan Nevins, the inspirer and former General Editor of this series, died before he was able to edit my manuscript. His death deprived me of his learned counsel, and the book undoubtedly suffers as a consequence. I take this occasion, however, to honor his memory and to offer posthumous thanks for his kindness and encouragement.

INDEX

Index

Numbers in italics are those of the chapter or section devoted to the author in question.

A NOTE ABOUT THE AUTHOR

Daniel Aaron is professor of English at Harvard University. Born in Chicago, he received his A.B. from the University of Michigan, and his Ph.D. from Harvard in 1943. For over twenty years he taught English at Smith College, before returning to Harvard in 1971. He has also taught at the University of Warsaw and at Sussex University in Great Britain. He was a Guggenheim Fellow in 1947 and a Fellow at the Center for Advanced Study in the Behavioral Sciences, 1958–59. Professor Aaron is the author of *Men of Good Hope: A Story of American Progressives* (1950) and of *Writers on the Left: Episodes in American Literary Communism* (1961), of which Irving Howe wrote: "Admirable, indispensable, a testimonial to what is best in American liberal scholarship"; and is co-author, with Richard Hofstadter and William Miller, of *The United States: The History of the Republic* (1957), editor of *America in Crisis* (1952), and co-author, with Alfred Kazin, of *Emerson: A Modern Anthology* (1959). He contributes widely to literary and public affairs journals.

A NOTE ON THE TYPE

The text of this book was set on the Linotype in a new face called PRIMER, designed by Rudolph Ruzicka, earlier responsible for the design of Fairfield and Fairfield Medium, Linotype faces whose virtues have for some time now been accorded wide recognition.

The complete range of sizes of Primer was first made available in 1954, although the pilot size of 12 point was ready as early as 1951. The design of the face makes general reference to Linotype Century (long a serviceable type, totally lacking in manner of frills of any kind) but brilliantly corrects the characterless quality of that face.

Composed, printed, and bound by
American Book–Stratford Press, Inc.

Typography and binding based on designs by

WARREN ⚭ CHAPPELL